Toward a Pentecostal Theology of the Lord's Supper

of the Lord's Supper

Foretasting the Kingdom

TOWARD A PENTECOSTAL THEOLOGY OF THE LORD'S SUPPER

FORETASTING THE KINGDOM

Chris E.W. Green

CPT Press
Cleveland, Tennessee

Toward a Pentecostal Theology of the Lord's Supper
Foretasting the Kingdom

Published by CPT Press
900 Walker ST NE
Cleveland, TN 37311
USA
email: cptpress@pentecostaltheology.org
website: www.cptpress.com
    www.pentecostaltheology.org

Library of Congress Control Number: 2012943424

ISBN-10: 193593130X
ISBN-13: 9781935931300

DEDICATION

To Nan and Paz, for all your incredible generosity and support

TABLE OF CONTENTS

PREFACE

It seems most fitting to begin a book dedicated to the Eucharist by giving thanks to those who have made it possible. So, first, I want to thank my *Doktorvater*, John Christopher Thomas, who has provided skillful and wise direction at every stage in the process of developing and completing this work. To my grandparents, Nan and Paz; my mom and dad, Robert and LaCrisa Green; my parents-in-law, Chuck and Irene Niemyer; and everyone at Divine Life Church, I want to say that I am beyond grateful for your tremendous generosity and constant support. A special thanks is due to a host of other friends as well, including my fellow PhD students and a number of colleagues at Oral Roberts University, Southwestern Christian University, and – as of this summer – Pentecostal Theological Seminary. I need to mention, in particular, Jeff Lamp and Don Vance. How many times I held them captive in heavy conversation for hours on end and they never failed to provide valuable affirmation and critique. Obviously, my greatest debt is to my wife, Julie, and to my kids, Zoë and Clive. Over the past few years, they have reordered their lives to make room for me to devote myself to this work, and somehow they did it joyfully, always believing in me and cheering me on along the way.

The idea for this book began to germinate years ago during undergraduate conversations with my good friend, Dr Doug Beacham, and grew to form over time in worship at Divine Life Church, where we celebrated weekly Communion and devoted many times together to teaching and to prayerful study and reflection on the meaning of the Eucharist-event for us as a community. Without that experience, and the many mysterious effects it worked on my heart and mind, I simply would not have had the power to imagine the shape of this work and the energy necessary to complete it.

My work, whatever its faults, is rooted and grounded in the Pentecostal tradition; and though some of the roots no doubt run under the wall, it is intended first and foremost as a conversation starter for the Pentecostal communities. Nothing would please me more than for the book, in spite of its weaknesses and limitations, in some way to contribute to a renewal of Pentecostal sacramental thought and practice. Of course, I also hope the branches reach over the wall so that Christians of other traditions find good fruit as well.

I am honored to publish this work with CPT Press, to have it listed in the company of landmark works like John Christopher Thomas' *The Devil, Disease and Deliverance*, Steven Land's *Pentecostal Spirituality*, Roger Stronstad's *The Prophethood of All Believers*, Larry McQueen's *Joel and the Spirit*, and Ken Archer's *A Pentecostal Hermeneutic*. I hope my own work is received as companion to works like these.

ABBREVIATIONS

Early Pentecostal Periodicals

AF	*The Apostolic Faith*
CE	*The Christian Evangel*
COGE	*The Church of God Evangel*
LRE	*The Latter Rain Evangel*
PE	*The Pentecostal Evangel*
PHA	*The Pentecostal Holiness Advocate*
PT	*Pentecostal Testimony*
TBM	*The Bridegroom's Messenger*
TP	*The Pentecost*
WE	*Weekly Evangel*
WW	*Word and Witness*

Other

AJPS	*Asian Journal of Pentecostal Studies*
ANF	*A Select Library of Ante-Nicene Fathers*
ATR	*Anglican Theology Review*
BEM	*Baptism, Eucharist and Ministry*, Faith and Order Paper No. 111 (Geneva: World Council of Churches, 1982).
BNTC	Black's New Testament Commentary Series
BTC	Brazos Theological Commentary Series
CPT	Centre for Pentecostal Theology
DPCM	Burgess, S.M. *et al.* (eds.), *Dictionary of Pentecostal and Charismatic Movements* (Grand Rapids: Zondervan, 1988).
IJST	*International Journal of Systematic Theology*
IVP	InterVarsity Press
JBL	*Journal of Biblical Literature*
JEPTA	*Journal of European Pentecostal Theology Association*
JETS	*Journal of the Evangelical Theological Society*

JPT	*Journal of Pentecostal Theology*
JPTSup	Journal of Pentecostal Theology Supplement Series
JSNTS	Journal for the Study of New Testament Supplement Series
NIDPCM	Burgess, S.M. and E.M. van der Maas (eds.), *The New International Dictionary of Pentecostal and Charismatic Movements* (Grand Rapids: Zondervan, 2003).
NPNF	*A Select Library of Nicene and Post-Nicene Fathers*
NTT	New Testament Theology Commentary Series
OUP	Oxford University Press
Pneuma	*Pneuma: The Journal of the Society for Pentecostal Studies*
SBL	Society of Biblical Literature
SNTSMS	Studiorum Novi Testamenti Societas Monograph Series
SVS	St Vladimir's Seminary Press
SVTQ	*St Vladimir's Theological Quarterly*
TPNTC	Pillar New Testament Commentary Series
WJKP	Westminster John Knox Press

1

INTRODUCTION

Purpose and Focus of the Study

The purpose of this study is to develop a distinctly Pentecostal theology of the Lord's Supper that contributes to the larger project of 'revisioning' Pentecostal theology.[1] Owing to the fact (or at least perception) that Pentecostals have devoted comparatively little attention to the sacraments, this study is needed.[2] Several presuppositions undergird the structure and flow of the argument.

First, as a 'living tradition', Pentecostalism can and should be revisioned constantly without betraying itself or losing its character.[3]

Second, in the effort to revision itself faithfully, Pentecostal theology should be informed by a critical conversation with the earliest years of the movement; for, as Walter Hollenweger first argued, the spirituality of early Pentecostalism represents the heart and not the infancy of the movement.[4]

Third, it is necessary for a self-consciously Pentecostal theology to be as concerned with *method* as it is with content. For, as Terry

---

[1] Steven J. Land, *Pentecostal Spirituality: A Passion for the Kingdom* (JPTSup 1; Sheffield: Sheffield Academic Press, 1993), p. 7.

[2] This has been clear in much of the secondary literature, as well as in ecumenical conversations. For example, the document *Lutherans and Pentecostals in Dialogue* ([Strasbourg: Institute for Ecumenical Research, 2010], p. 15) acknowledges that 'Pentecostal sacramental theology continues to develop'.

[3] Alasdair C. McIntyre, *After Virtue: A Study in Moral Theology* (2nd ed.; Notre Dame, IN: Notre Dame University Press, 1984), p. 222.

[4] Walter J. Hollenweger, *The Pentecostals* (Peabody, MA: Hendrickson, 1988), p. 551.

Cross and others have contended, Pentecostal experience makes possible and so calls for the articulation of a unique theological methodology.[5]

Fourth, owing to the role of Scripture in the tradition, Pentecostal theology should be deeply *biblical*, rooted in and directed by the reading of the canonical scriptures. However, this affirmation alone is not enough. A Pentecostal approach to Scripture requires a hermeneutical strategy that remains at all points in keeping with the core convictions of the movement's spiritual and theological tradition. Such a hermeneutic would include *inter alia* narrative sensitivity, a concern for canonical context, and even go so far as to take seriously the texts' effective history, including but not limited to the witness of early Pentecostal interpretations.

Fifth, Pentecostal theology necessarily concerns itself with *praxis*, with what the proposed claims mean for the church's life in mission and worship.[6] Put differently, Pentecostal theology in order to be true to itself, must carry through 'theory' and systemization to engagement with 'real life' issues and the specific concretions of the church's critical and reflective thought in the life of adoration, witness, and discipleship. In other words, attempts at articulating orthodox theologoumena must always already concern themselves with ortho*praxy* as well.

Sixth, Pentecostal theology should be conversant with the theological tradition(s) of the church catholic, so that the finished product is not only distinctly Pentecostal but also recognizably *Christian*. Although this study is not intended first and foremost as a contribution to the ecumenical conversation, it assumes that ecumenical resonance is one of the final tests for the viability of any proposed theologoumena. Also, as Simon Chan and others have insisted, I

---

[5] Among Pentecostals, Terry Cross has helped to lead the way in making this point. See Terry L. Cross, 'The Rich Feast of Theology: Can Pentecostals Bring the Main Course or Only the Relish?' *JPT* 16 (Apr 2000), pp. 27-47; Terry L. Cross, 'The Divine-Human Encounter: Towards a Pentecostal Theology of Experience', *Pneuma* 31.1 (2009), pp. 3-34. Cross has engaged the theological methodologies of contemporary Evangelicalism as well; see Terry L. Cross, 'A Proposal to Break the Ice: What Can Pentecostal Theology Offer Evangelical Theology', *JPT* 10.2 (Apr 2002), pp. 44-73.

[6] This is, seemingly, a theological *habitus* that has remained largely unchanged throughout the history of the Pentecostal movement(s), and no doubt has deep roots in the Wesleyan and Holiness movements out of which Pentecostalism arose.

assume that Pentecostals have much to learn from as well as to teach their ecumenical partners.[7]

Structure and Flow of the Argument

Given the assumptions that guide this study, the argument begins (Chapter 2) with a survey of the scholarly literature, documenting what Pentecostal scholars have said and are saying about the sacraments in general and the Lord's Supper in particular.

Chapter 3 includes a careful reading of the early Pentecostal periodical materials, following the model Kimberly Ervin Alexander used in her work on early Pentecostal soteriologies and healing practices.[8] A wide range of material is covered, both in terms of chronology (from 1906-1931) and in terms of the various denominations and movements (e.g. the Wesleyan-Holiness and Finished Work 'streams') within early Pentecostalism. This reading seeks to search out and to sketch the contours of early Pentecostal sacramentality on its own terms. Chapter 3 ends with a summation of the sacramental convictions and habits that characterized the earliest days of the movement.

Chapter 4 makes two discrete contributions: it opens with the development of a proposed Pentecostal interpretive strategy in conversation with an emerging Pentecostal hermeneutical paradigm, and informed by this engagement with early Pentecostal sacramentality turns next to sustained narrative-theological readings of three New Testament Eucharistic texts. In these readings, I draw heavily on the texts' 'effective history', allowing what the texts have meant to other Christian readers, pre-modern and contemporary, to influence the shape of my own reading.

Chapter 5 is devoted to a constructive Pentecostal theology of the Eucharist, addressing in detail those issues that are judged to be especially important to Pentecostals. This includes questions of how God works in and through the church's celebration of the Communion rite and how Christ and the Spirit are personally present and active in the eating and drinking of the Eucharistic bread

---

[7] Simon Chan, *Pentecostal Theology and the Christian Spiritual Tradition* (JPTSup 21; Sheffield: Sheffield Academic Press, 2000), pp. 37-38, 107-08.

[8] Kimberly E. Alexander, *Pentecostal Healing: Models in Theology and Practice* (JPTSup 29; Blandford Forum, Dorset, UK: Deo Publishing, 2006).

and the wine. Considerable attention is devoted to issues of praxis, including an exploration of how it is that frequent, regular participation in the Eucharist might be done without betraying Pentecostal distinctives.

The study concludes (Chapter 6) with a description of major contributions and an invitation to further research.

2

THE SACRAMENTS IN PENTECOSTAL PERSPECTIVE(S): A BIBLIOGRAPHIC REVIEW

Introduction

It is widely believed – both within and without the movement – that Pentecostals[1] have given comparatively little attention to sacramental thinking and practice, and the facts are that Pentecostals often have spoken about the sacraments in predominantly negative terms, articulating what they do *not* believe regarding the sacraments rather than positively stating their beliefs. This is far from the whole of the story, however. Recently, Pentecostal scholars have been devoting increased attention to the sacraments, sometimes with a view to developing a self-consciously Pentecostal theology of the sacraments. With those developments in mind, this chapter examines the state of Pentecostal theological reflection with regard to the sacraments, generally, and the Eucharist, specifically. For the most part, this chapter restricts itself to engagement with *scholarly* Pentecostal works, and while it does not claim to be exhaustive, it does aim to engage the key influential works of leading Pentecostals from various corners of the tradition. These works are engaged in chronolog-

---

[1] Throughout this study I am using 'Pentecostal' to refer specifically to classical Pentecostalism in its various forms, as distinct from the broader charismatic movement. I am aware that such a distinction is in some cases impossible to maintain, given the cross-pollination that has taken place over the years. I will engage some scholars who speak from and to both Pentecostal and charismatic contexts, but for the most part I will focus on the work of those who self-identify as Pentecostals and who belong to classical Pentecostal churches and/or work in Pentecostal educational institutions.

ical order, ranging from 1932 to present day. This chapter, then, is set aside exclusively for engagement with Pentecostal theological scholarship, but a separate chapter is devoted to the literature of the first generation of Pentecostals (from 1906-1931), and the constructive part of the thesis (Chapter 5) engages key ecumenical voices and non-Pentecostal assessments of Pentecostal sacramentality.

Reading Pentecostals on the Sacraments

Myer Pearlman
In a 1934 *Pentecostal Evangel* article, Myer Pearlman, who published the first systematic treatment of doctrine from a Pentecostal perspective, orders his thoughts on the Lord's Supper as an exposition of Paul's instructions to the Corinthians (1 Cor. 11.23-26). He designates the Supper as 'the distinctive rite of Christian worship' and the church's 'most sacred rite'.[2] The meal, Pearlman explains,

> consists of the religious partaking of bread and wine, which, after having been presented to God the Father in memorial of Christ's inexhaustible sacrifice, becomes a means of grace whereby we are inspired to an increased faith and faithfulness to Him who loved us and redeemed us.[3]

The celebration of the Lord's Supper, he believes, is a 'means of grace' because it communicates a triad of values to the church. First, it 'sets forth symbolically the two fundamental doctrines of the gospel: the Incarnation and the Atonement'.[4] Second, it serves as 'the most impressive means for continually presenting before our minds and hearts the central fact of His life'; it manages to do this because it 'enlists the services of three senses, sight, taste, and touch' to remind us of Christ's work on our behalf. This is exactly what Christ intended in instituting the Supper, because he 'foresaw our need of being regularly reminded of what He means to us'. Third, the Lord's Supper has inspirational value. It 'stirs our souls'[5] and provokes God-ward adoration and worship and passion for mission and evangelism.

---

[2] *PE* 1077 (Dec 8, 1934), p. 9.
[3] *PE* 1077 (Dec 8, 1934), p. 9.
[4] *PE* 1077 (Dec 8, 1934), p. 9.
[5] *PE* 1077 (Dec 8, 1934), p. 9.

Pearlman finds an immensity of meaning in the symbols of bread and wine. As he sees it, the bread of the Table teaches us that Christ is 'the food of the soul' that we must consume; the wine, that we can be partakers of the divine life and nature. Somewhat bizarrely, Pearlman compares the eating and drinking of the Communion elements to the 'savage' custom of eating a victim's heart in order to 'partake of his spirit'.[6] Affection is critically important to proper receiving of the Lord's Supper. When Paul warns against partaking 'unworthily', Pearlman understands this as a caution against partaking 'irreverently'. That occurs, he believes, 'when a person approaches the Lord's table, intoxicated so to speak, by a wrong emotion that blinds him for the time being to the true significance and appreciation of the sacred ordinance'.[7]

Nearly a decade later, Pearlman addresses the issue again. He continues to hold that baptism and the Supper, known by the church as sacraments because 'they are ceremonies by which we show outwardly our devotion to the Lord Jesus Christ',[8] are 'means of grace' – along with prayer, church attendance, and Bible reading – by which we may grow spiritually', provided we partake 'intelligently'.[9] By this Pearlman means a discernment of the spiritual realities 'beyond' the bread and wine.

> Let us also remember that as we partake of the emblems we are to look beyond them, and beyond the server, and see the Lord Jesus Christ Himself, who said, 'I am the Bread of Life'. Beyond the wine we must see His shed blood, which is His divine life poured out for us. The Head of the church will Himself administer the Sacrament, as we receive Him by faith.[10]

In conclusion, Pearlman reminds his readers to prepare carefully for the celebration of Holy Communion, for 'in the communion service we signify the fact that we are having fellowship with the Son of God Himself'.[11]

---

[6] *PE* 1077 (Dec 8, 1934), p. 9.
[7] *PE* 1077 (Dec 8, 1934), p. 9.
[8] *PE* 1479 (Sept 12, 1942), pp. 2-3 (2).
[9] Pearlman, 'The Bread and Blood Covenant', p. 2.
[10] Pearlman, 'The Bread and Blood Covenant', p. 3.
[11] Pearlman, 'The Bread and Blood Covenant', p. 3.

Ernest Swing Williams

In the third installment of his three-volume systematics, Assembly of God theologian and church officer E.S. Williams devotes a chapter to the 'ordinances of the church'. He lists two: water baptism and the Lord's Supper; no mention is made of footwashing.[12] The Christian rite of water baptism, according to Williams, 'signifies our identification with Christ'. He is careful to insist that the water rite is not a 'saving ordinance', but merely 'follows, or *accompanies* repentance and salvation'.[13] Infant baptism – a practice he repudiates, devoting considerable space to arguments against it – is both flatly 'unscriptural' and in the final analysis unnecessary, in Williams' opinion, because 'baptism makes no change' in the infants' relation to God for they are already 'saved through the redemption which is in Christ Jesus' so long as they die 'before accountability'. It would seem that the question of the appropriateness of infant baptism was a critical issue in debates of the time, because Williams acknowledges that if it were not for the fact that some consider infant baptism a saving ordinance, he would not object to the use of water in the dedication of children, for Jesus himself 'put His approval on the use of different material elements in association with faith in Him'.[14] As it is that many abuse the practice, however, he must stand against it in no uncertain terms.

Comparatively speaking, Williams devotes little space to the Lord's Supper, slightly more than a paragraph, in fact. After observing that many refer to the Lord's Supper as the Eucharist 'because of [the] thanks offered before the Sacrament',[15] he quotes from an unnamed theological dictionary that defines a sacrament as 'an outward ceremony of the Church, ordained as a visible sign of an inward and spiritual grace … a sign of the union of the soul with God'.[16] Williams does not distance himself from this definition, leaving the quotation to stand without comment, which would seem to indicate some form of basic agreement. He concludes his

---

[12] Ernest Swing Williams, *Systematic Theology* (3 vols.; Springfield, MO: Gospel Publishing House, 1953), III, p. 149.

[13] Emphasis added.

[14] Williams, *Systematic Theology*, III, p. 153. It is not clear at this point if these supporters of paedobaptism Williams criticizes stand within or without the Pentecostal movement.

[15] Williams, *Systematic Theology*, III, p. 154.

[16] Williams, *Systematic Theology*, III, p. 154.

brief treatment of the Lord's Supper with four one-sentence summary statements: (1) the Lord's Supper has 'taken the place of the Passover', (2) the Supper 'shows forth the death of Christ, with promise of His return', (3) the Supper 'is to be partaken of in a worthy manner', and (4) the Supper 'signifies our union with Christ and with one another'.[17] After each statement, he parenthetically cites Scripture references as support for his assertions.

C.E. Bowen

In the mid-1950's, C.E. Bowen, a licensed minister in the Church of God (Cleveland, TN), published a book-length treatment of footwashing and the Lord's Supper.[18] In keeping with the *ethos* of the Pentecostal movement, Bowen emphasized the importance of *obeying* Jesus in observing the instituted ordinances, and of *imitating* him in the enacting of the rites.[19] And he is careful to connect the institution of the rites of Communion and footwashing also to Israel's history: nearly half the book is devoted to an exploration of the myriad connections between Israel's rituals and experiences of God and the church's observance of the dominically-instituted sacraments. As Bowen sees it, the Lord's Supper has replaced the Passover;[20] the Passover pointed forward to Christ's death, whereas Communion points forward to Christ's 'second coming'; the Resurrection made Passover obsolete.[21]

Like many of his Pentecostal brothers and sisters of the time, Bowen was convinced that the Supper was a means of healing for those who received the meal in faith. The Supper, when properly observed and received in faith, is not only a 'symbol' of Christ's

---

[17] Williams, *Systematic Theology*, III, p. 154.

[18] C.E. Bowen, *The Lord's Supper and Footwashing* (Cleveland, TN: Church of God Publications, 1955). In the book's forward, Charles Conn, then the editor-in-chief of Church of God publication ministries, remarks that Bowen's study – which he characterizes as 'beneficial and thorough ... adequate and stimulating ... vigorous and studious' – is a piece of a larger movement of 'increased attention to these ordinances', a resurgence Conn believes is 'largely due to the upsurge of holiness and Pentecostal belief'. In typical restorationist idiom, Conn laments the loss of the 'pristine simplicity' of the ordinances in the abuses of the post-apostolic church and its non-biblical traditions, and he celebrates Bowen's contribution to the renaissance of appreciation for the ordinances in all of their original simplicity and meaningfulness.

[19] A recurring theme throughout the book, but see especially Bowen, *The Lord's Supper and Footwashing*, pp. 108-109.

[20] Bowen, *The Lord's Supper and Footwashing*, pp. 18-19.

[21] Bowen, *The Lord's Supper and Footwashing*, p. 93.

atoning death but also a 'spiritual feast of good things'.[22] At the Table, he says, 'we are taking into our beings life and power to heal our bodies …'[23] He is confident:

> … if we come together in faith to commemorate the death of Jesus Christ and in the proper order, we will not be weak and sickly as was the Corinthian Church. For if we are sick when we meet, we can be healed while we eat the bread – a symbol of his body – if our heart is right in the sight of God, and we discern the Lord's body and it broken for us. Seeing the purpose and believing with all of our heart and accepting the provision made for us in the atonement, we can go away from this supper with strong bodies, possibly live a much longer life and a more useful life in the service of God.[24]

Bowen is troubled that so few churches observe the Supper and footwashing frequently and that fewer still do so with genuine appreciation for the rites' power and beauty. Those who come to the Table only once a quarter 'do not know what they are missing'. He believes that churches should celebrate Communion at least once a month,[25] and that this can be done without descent into mere ritualism. If Roman Catholics err, it is *not* from observing the Supper too often.[26]

M.A. Tomlinson

In 1961, while he served as the general overseer of the Church of God of Prophecy, M.A. Tomlinson, the son of A.J. Tomlinson and brother of Homer Tomlinson, published a collection of his radio sermons under the title *Basic Bible Beliefs*. In the book, he dedicates several sermons to the three ordinances: water baptism, Holy Communion, and footwashing. He acknowledges that almost every Christian denomination and movement recognizes some ordinance which 'makes use of the bread and the fruit of the vine', whether they refer to this rite as the Lord's Supper, Holy Communion, or

---

[22] Bowen, *The Lord's Supper and Footwashing*, p. 81.
[23] Bowen, *The Lord's Supper and Footwashing*, p. 19. He parenthetically cites Isa. 53.5-7 as support of this claim. Throughout, Bowen's reflections are guided for the most part by his readings of John 6 and 1 Corinthians 11.
[24] Bowen, *The Lord's Supper and Footwashing*, p. 87.
[25] Bowen, *The Lord's Supper and Footwashing*, p. 97.
[26] Bowen, *The Lord's Supper and Footwashing*, pp. 100-101.

the Sacrament.[27] Regardless of superficial differences, he stands convinced that the reasons for its observance are the same for all Christians. It would seem, then, 'hardly necessary' to speak at length or in any detail of the meaning and purpose of the Lord's Supper. Inexplicably, however, some individuals fail to realize 'the importance of observing the Lord's Supper and the great spiritual blessings that can be obtained from it'.[28] Tomlinson admits that he cannot countenance the arrogance of those who refuse to take the Lord's Supper or observe it only rarely, and he draws on a biblical analogy to reprove them:

> If such terrible vengeance were pronounced upon those who failed in the observance of the Passover, how much more do we displease God if we fail to commemorate the death of His Son who was wounded for our transgressions ...[29]

To him, the issue is as straightforward as it can be: given the command of Jesus and the promise of God, the believer should be 'eager to partake of the Supper at every opportunity',[30] a claim that perhaps reveals his indebtedness to the Wesleyan sacramental heritage.

James L. Slay

In the early 1960's, missionary James L. Slay authored and published *This We Believe*, a text that served as an official training course for the Church of God (Cleveland, TN). He opens the chapter dedicated to the doctrine of the church's ordinances with a caveat: Church of God worship is spontaneous and simple, in keeping with the 'primitive Christian church'; therefore, only three ordinances are observed, and these are accepted only because they have clear biblical and apostolic approval.[31] In his judgment, so long as worshippers are 'really led of the Spirit', then no 'prescribed liturgical form' is necessary, for the Spirit 'will govern our activity'.[32]

---

[27] M.A. Tomlinson, *Basic Bible Beliefs* (Cleveland, TN: White Wing Publishing, 1961), p. 54.
[28] Tomlinson, *Basic Bible Beliefs*, p. 54.
[29] Tomlinson, *Basic Bible Beliefs*, p. 56.
[30] Tomlinson, *Basic Bible Beliefs*, p. 58.
[31] James L. Slay, *This We Believe* (Cleveland, TN: Pathway Press, 1963), p. 98.
[32] Slay, *This We Believe*, p. 98.

Slay takes up the ordinance of water baptism first. In keeping with the prevailing opinion in the Pentecostal movement at the time, Slay insists on so-called 'believer's baptism'. The waters of baptism do not save, he says, so only those who have already been regenerated may properly be baptized. Put another way, baptism is nothing less or more than 'the profession of a spiritual change already wrought' prior to and entirely apart from the rite of washing. Baptism, then, is not for the sake of the convert but for the sake of the convert's friends, family, and fellow believers. 'People are baptized, not in order to be saved, but to show others that they are really saved.'[33] Infants are not to be baptized, for the Church of God 'has found no Scriptures which would implicitly or explicitly warrant a belief in infant baptism'.[34] Although he does not provide any historical support for the claim, Slay states that paedobaptism was not an apostolic teaching but 'came about as a result of the influence of sacramentalism in the early days of Christianity'.[35]

A certain disdain for 'sacramentalism' permeates Slay's work. In his view, the rite of the Lord's Supper has been 'grossly perverted' by the church and 'so misinterpreted and abused as to subvert many and cause dissension' among believers is unsurprising.[36] Slay finds it appalling that the erroneous view of the Catholics persists in spite of the plain witness of Scripture; although he does not believe it should be necessary, he nonetheless takes space to address the notions of transubstantiation and consubstantiation, the latter of which he finds as nothing less than a 'Lutheran compromise' with the former mistaken, unbiblical position.[37] These doctrines, he maintains, are 'falsely based' on Jesus' statements: 'This is my body' and 'This is my blood'. It is 'certain', Slay believes, that Jesus could not have been speaking 'literally'; his words were intended metaphorically. 'The bread, crumbled in His hands, was not His flesh, but a *symbol* of His broken body.'[38] The wine, similarly, was '*only a symbol* of His efficacious outpouring'.[39] Slay admits that 'our Lord undoubtedly used the fermented juice of the grape', but he does not

---

[33] Slay, *This We Believe*, p. 101.
[34] Slay, *This We Believe*, p. 103.
[35] Slay, *This We Believe*, p. 106.
[36] Slay, *This We Believe*, p. 106.
[37] Slay, *This We Believe*, p. 110.
[38] Slay, *This We Believe*, p. 110. Emphasis added.
[39] Slay, *This We Believe*, p. 110. Emphasis added.

find the Church of God's use of unfermented grape juice an unwarranted departure.[40] Unlike Roman Catholics, who forbid the cup to
communicants, Slay insists that everyone should partake of both
elements.

Given his distaste for the high sacramentalism of the Catholic
and Lutheran traditions, it might be found surprising that Slay believes the Lord's Supper belongs at the heart of the Pentecostal life.
In his judgment, the 'believing and victorious Christian' partakes of
the Communion meal 'as often as possible', for in so doing the believer responds to 'a divinely appointed ordinance', commemorates
'the death and victory of Christ for himself', and obtains 'inspiration and assurance for the current Christian conflict'.[41] In keeping
with his Pietistic leanings, Slay insists on the importance of the participants' affections. The Supper should be celebrated with 'joyful
reverence', never 'casually nor with a spirit of frivolity or irrever-
ence', and should be observed often enough 'to keep Calvary fresh'
in the minds of the participants, but 'not too often to cheapen its
value or minimize its significance'.[42]

Walter Hollenweger

Walter Hollenweger's pathbreaking work on Pentecostalism, first
published in German in 1969 by R. Brockhaus (Wuppertal) as *En-
thusiastisches Christentium: die Pfingstbewegung in Geschichte und Gegen-
wart*, devotes considerable attention to early Pentecostal understanding of the sacraments. He begins with the observation that so
far no 'fully developed Eucharistic doctrine in the Pentecostal
movement' has emerged.[43] According to him, Pentecostals, at least
typically, exhibit in their explicit theological statements – insofar as
such statements are made at all – what is best identified as a version
of the Zwinglian understanding of the Lord's Supper. He finds that
a tension between liturgical rubrics and the dynamic, charismatic
work of the Spirit remains ever-present, especially among the older,
classical Pentecostal denominations. In his view, however, the dis-
trust of liturgical rites and the relative lack of theological sophistication do not efface the vibrancy of Pentecostal liturgical *practice*, even
though it exists under another name. In fact, as he sees it, Pentecos-

---

[40] Slay, *This We Believe*, p. 107.
[41] Slay, *This We Believe*, p. 110.
[42] Slay, *This We Believe*, p. 107.
[43] Hollenweger, *The Pentecostals*, p. 385.

tals evidence 'a clear and well-developed pattern of Eucharistic devotion and practice'.[44] He readily admits that this seems surprising,
given that Pentecostals belong to the free-church tradition and emphasize the believer's immediate experience of the Spirit. Nonetheless, his study of various Pentecostal movements convinces him
that the celebration of the Eucharist rite is the 'central point of Pentecostal worship', a veritable 'holy of holies' of the worship service.
To underscore the point, he cites the Italian Assemblee di Dio's
statement that speaks of the Lord's Supper symbolizing Jesus' sacrificial death and the doctrinal declaration by the Congregacao Crista
that the Eucharist is a means of 'intimate communion' with Christ.

In Hollenweger's judgment, in spite of the fact that Pentecostals
come to the Table out of a sense of obligation – the chapter in his
book is entitled: '"To Them that Obey Him": The Sacraments' –
Pentecostals nonetheless 'expect from this communion with the
Son of God the strengthening of their inner being, strength in everyday temptations, and the healing of sickness'.[45] This is due to
what he believes is the distinctive character of Pentecostal sacramentality:

> … a combination of the 'love of Jesus', that is love for the faith-
> ful friend who is called Jesus, 'blood and wounds mysticism', an
> absorption in the suffering and death of Jesus, and a looking
> forward to the coming marriage feast with Jesus, in the experi-
> ence of the sacrament.[46]

He also finds in certain aspects of Pentecostal Eucharistic devotion – especially their understanding of the meal as a community
event, not restricted to a priestly caste or even to the pastor and
deacons – a prophetic critique of the church catholic and its sacer-
dotal practices.[47]

Raymond Pruitt

In 1981, Raymond Pruitt, an ordained minister in the Church of
God of Prophecy, published his *Fundamentals of the Faith*. The
foreword, written by General Overseer M.A. Tomlinson, describes
the book as 'a rather comprehensive work' and an 'introduction to

---

44 Hollenweger, *The Pentecostals*, p. 385. Emphasis original.
45 Hollenweger, *The Pentecostals*, p. 386.
46 Hollenweger, *The Pentecostals*, p. 387.
47 Hollenweger, *The Pentecostals*, p. 389.

doctrinal studies', although he does not give the book official sanction and admits that some of the contents may not meet with universal approval on all points. Pruitt addresses himself to the ordinances (as usual: water baptism, the Lord's Supper, and footwashing) in the chapter dedicated to the 'membership, function, and destiny of the church'.[48]

He prefaces his remarks about the ordinances with a brief word about the inexpressible depth of human communication. 'Words are inadequate to express the deeper meanings even of human relationships, to say nothing of those transcendent, indescribable experiences with God.' No words, regardless of how expertly written or spoken, can express love as well as 'the touch of a hand, the affectionate kiss, the light of the eyes, or the radiance of the face'. He finds it undeniable, then, that these non-verbal 'signs and symbols' sometimes serve as *better*, more effective communiqués of certain dimensions of meaning than do words. 'A single tear coursing down the cheek expresses sorrow better than ten thousand words.' It follows, then, that 'the experiences of the soul and spirit are best expressed in the universal language of signs and symbols'. Given this, it should come as a surprise to no one that Christ has given his Church such 'means of expression in the ordinances, or sacraments, which He has instituted'.[49] This does not mean, however, that the signs and symbols themselves actually impart 'spiritual grace'. They are not sacraments in *that* sense, Pruitt says, for they are only '*expressions* of what has been imparted through our relationship with Christ' immediately by the Spirit.[50] For instance, he holds that the Lord's Supper commemorates Jesus' death; that is to say, it *portrays* the realities of redemption, and *symbolizes* both the believer's 'participation in the crucified Christ' and believers' union with one another.[51] In the same way that water baptism substituted for circumcision, the Lord's Supper substitutes for the Old Testament rite of Passover, for Christ fulfilled all the symbolism and foreshadowing of the Mosaic Law.[52] The sacrament of the Lord's Supper 'points back' to Jesus' death exactly as the Passover meal 'pointed forward'

---

[48] Raymond M. Pruitt, *Fundamentals of the Faith* (Cleveland, TN: White Wing Publishing, 1981), pp. 361-71.
[49] Pruitt, *Fundamentals of the Faith*, p. 365.
[50] Pruitt, *Fundamentals of the Faith*, p. 365. Emphasis added.
[51] Pruitt, *Fundamentals of the Faith*, p. 366. Emphasis added.
[52] Pruitt, *Fundamentals of the Faith*, p. 367.

to it, and the bread of Communion is his body in the same way that the bread of the Passover was his body – *symbolically*.[53]

In Pruitt's judgment, however, it is not enough to say that communicants merely reflect on the symbols, as if Communion effects a merely cognitive experience. Instead, celebrants actually 'feed upon' the symbols – as well as the 'emblems', and figuratively eat Jesus' flesh and blood. And in this way, they demonstrate that they have indeed 'appropriated the benefits of His sacrificial death' to themselves.[54]

Pruitt acknowledges the long and heated controversy regarding Jesus' words of institution (Mt. 26.26; Mk 14.22; Lk. 22.19; 1 Cor. 11.24). The Roman Catholics, he explains, take a 'very literal view' in their doctrine of transubstantiation, which teaches that when the elements are blessed they 'become the very body and blood of Christ' so that communicants actually receive the 'saving and sanctifying grace from God'. As one might expect, Pruitt rejects this position outright:

> Of course, this view must be rejected for valid reasons: (1) If Jesus had meant the elements to be taken literally, there would have been two bodies of Christ present at the last supper – the Person offering the elements would have been one body, and the elements themselves would have been the other. (2) If the elements are the actual body of Christ, partaking of them smacks of cannibalism and is repugnant. (3) Such a notion also denies that Christ's offering of Himself on the cross was a once-for-all sacrifice for sin.[55]

Strong as the rejection is, Pruitt offers no comparable alternative, presumably because he believed it unnecessary.

Regarding the administration of the Supper, Pruitt indicates that churches of his denomination observe the ordinance at least once a quarter, even though the Scriptures do not set a specific number of times the rite should be observed per year. Also, he holds that only 'licensed or ordained male ministers' should officiate the Communion rite, in keeping with the 'high and holy nature' of the event, and given the fact that the New Testament provides no examples of

---

[53] Pruitt, *Fundamentals of the Faith*, pp. 367-68.
[54] Pruitt, *Fundamentals of the Faith*, p. 366.
[55] Pruitt, *Fundamentals of the Faith*, p. 367.

'women or of lay members either baptizing candidates or administering the Lord's Supper'.[56] Further, small children should almost certainly not be allowed to partake of the meal, because they 'normally do not have the maturity to participate worthily' because they 'cannot discern their relationship to Christ, and cannot recognize the difference between the bread and wine as symbols of the body and blood of Christ, and ordinary bread and grape juice'. If this is so, then 'they are not ready to participate'.[57]

Guy Duffield and N.M. Van Cleave

In the early 1980's, Foursquare theologians Guy Duffield and N.M. Van Cleave, instructors at L.I.F.E. Bible College, produced a kind of systematic theology for Pentecostals.[58] In the book's preface, the authors evince their Evangelical convictions regarding theological method: 'The Pentecostal movement is not just based on an inspirational experience. It is grounded upon the entire Bible as the Word of God. We are a Bible-believing people. We subscribe to "all the counsel of God" (Acts 20:27)'. Pentecostal theology, then, is systematic insofar as it is a faithful compilation and re-presentation of 'the Scriptural teachings'. Theology, in the final analysis, is nothing more or less than the synthesizing of the whole range of scriptural teaching, the full Gospel. For obvious reasons, this biblicist methodology shapes Duffield's and Van Cleave's theology of the ordinances. They define the ordinances as 'outward rites or symbolic observances commanded by Jesus, which set forth essential Christian truths'.[59] In their judgment, only two ordinances – baptism and the Lord's Supper – are 'clearly and unmistakably commanded' by Scripture. They do not comment on any other Christian tradition, although they do specify the Roman Catholic observation of seven sacraments an unfortunate medieval accretion without in fact anathematizing it altogether.

---

[56] Pruitt, *Fundamentals of the Faith*, p. 369.
[57] Pruitt, *Fundamentals of the Faith*, p. 369.
[58] Guy P. Duffield and Nathaniel M. Van Cleave, *Foundations of Pentecostal Theology* (San Dimas, CA: L.I.F.E. Bible College, 1983), pp. 437-38.
[59] Duffield and Van Cleave, *Foundations of Pentecostal Theology*, p. 435.

After giving only cursory attention to water baptism,[60] the authors address the rite of the Lord's Supper, which they contend was instituted by Jesus at his 'last Passover' as a 'memorial of His Atoning Death'.[61] The clearest evidence for the sacramental nature of the Lord's Supper, according to the authors, is found in 1 Corinthians 11, where Paul warns that those who partake 'unworthily' eat and drink condemnation to themselves so that many become sick, even to death. They sketch four of the views on offer regarding the nature of the Eucharistic elements. They dismiss the Catholic doctrine of transubstantiation on the grounds that it is 'contradicted by experience' and by logic, and the Lutheran doctrine of consubstantiation because it is unsupported by Scripture and encourages superstition by overemphasizing the physical dimension of the Supper, losing sight of its spiritual blessing. They also reject the teaching that the Supper is 'merely a memorial act that mediates no blessing', which they characterize as the other extreme from the Catholic and Lutheran position. They conclude that the 'more scriptural view' is the Reformed view, i.e. of 'Calvin and the majority of reformers': 'The elements, when received by faith, mediate to the believer the spiritual benefits of Christ's Death'.[62] The bread and wine, in themselves, are 'only tokens'. Still, 'real communion with the Lord is experienced' when believers receive them in faith.[63] The section concludes with the Foursquare declaration of faith regarding the Lord's Supper:

> We believe in the commemoration and observing of the Lord's supper by the sacred use of the broken bread, a precious type of the Bread of Life even Jesus Christ, whose body was broken for us; and by the juice of the vine, a blessed type which should ever remind the participant of the shed blood of the Savior who is the True Vine of which His children are the branches; that this

---

[60] Interestingly, Duffield and Van Cleave devote 20 pages to their treatment of the 'baptism with the Holy Spirit' (pp. 304-25), but less than one full page to water baptism (p. 436). They do briefly refer to water baptism in two other instances (pp. 230, 313).

[61] Duffield and Van Cleave, *Foundations of Pentecostal Theology*, p. 436.

[62] Duffield and Van Cleave, *Foundations of Pentecostal Theology*, p. 437.

[63] Duffield and Van Cleave, *Foundations of Pentecostal Theology*, p. 437.

ordinance is a glorious rainbow that spans the gulf of the years between Calvary and the coming of the Lord ...[64]

John Bond

In 1989, John Bond, a South African Assemblies of God pastor, in a chapter-length contribution to a book co-edited by University of South Africa professors Henry Lederle and M.S. Clark, championed what he deemed to be the distinctive features of classical Pentecostal theology.[65] Bond argues that, generally speaking, Pentecostals adhere to Evangelical convictions, which means that Pentecostal theological reflection tends to be, in his words, 'conservative and usually fundamentalist'. In his judgment, Pentecostals do not so much differ from Evangelicals in *what* they believe – with the exception of their beliefs regarding the baptism in the Spirit – as in *how* they believe it, that is, with 'unique intensity'.[66] Their basic affinities with Evangelical theology notwithstanding, Pentecostals do work from a distinctive epistemology characterized by the privileging of the immediate experience of God's presence. According to Bond, the authentic Pentecostal always 'eschews the thought of truth merely as conceptualised [*sic*] in a theory or an abstraction', instead holding that truth must be *experienced*, and that otherwise it is not valid – 'a mere form of religion without power'. Therefore, Pentecostal thinking resists formalization and structure. In some ways, this distinctive epistemology emerged as a defense against the fury of the mainline Protestant resistance to the Pentecostal revival. In Bond's opinion, '[f]ormal theology failed in the beginning of the revival when it sat in judgment' against the charismatic manifestations and '[s]tructured religion' anathematized those seeking the Pentecostal experience.[67]

Given all of this, one cannot be surprised to find that Bond strongly resists sacramentalism in any form. For example, while water baptism retains in his view an important place in Pentecostal missional practice, it does so *only* as a 'step of obedience', an act that for all its importance is never to be regarded as 'necessary for

---

[64] Duffield and Van Cleave, *Foundations of Pentecostal Theology*, p. 438.

[65] John Bond, 'What is Distinctive about Pentecostal Theology', in M.S. Clark and H.I. Lederle (eds.) *What is Distinctive about Pentecostal Theology* (Pretoria: University of South Africa, 1989), pp. 133-42.

[66] Bond, 'What is Distinctive about Pentecostal Theology', p. 139.

[67] Bond, 'What is Distinctive about Pentecostal Theology', p. 135.

salvation or as being a means to regeneration'. Regarding the Lord's Supper specifically, Bond admits that he is deeply concerned that the popular attitude among Pentecostals regarding the bread and wine 'betrays a doctrinal shallowness and even savours [*sic*] of superstition'. More than that, he believes that many Pentecostals hold a quasi-magical view of the elements, in spite of the fact that such a view is fundamentally out of sorts with traditional Pentecostal theology, as he understands it. Somehow, the sacerdotalism that accompanies the traditional sacramental practices of the 'high church' traditions, Catholic and Protestant, also has worked its way insidiously into Pentecostal worship, he says. So much so that 'one feels that sometimes the Communion table in a subtle unconscious way is treated as an altar, and the officiating pastor very often acts somewhat as a priest'.[68] Committed as he is to the distinctives of classical Pentecostal spirituality, Bond worries that the thought and practice of the burgeoning charismatic movement, especially of the 'sacramental school', threatens to efface the genuinely Pentecostal experience.[69] For instance, the liturgical changes effected by the charismatic renewal, such as singing and dancing in the Spirit, in his estimation have negatively altered the shape of the Pentecostal worship service so that less time remains in the service for 'individual response of worship or praying', a change that he finds 'damaging and pernicious to the experience of Holy Ghost moving which Pentecostal theology extols'.[70]

William Menzies, Stanley Horton, and Michael Dusing

In the early 90's, Assemblies of God systematic theologian Stanley Horton edited, and with William Menzies – a fellow AG theologian – expanded Menzies' *Understanding Our Doctrine*, previously published (1971) treatment of Assemblies of God beliefs, republishing the book under the new title *Bible Doctrines*. The introduction identifies the book's agenda as providing a treatment of 'fundamental truths' from a 'Pentecostal perspective', and the chapter on the ordinances opens with a direct, fundamentalist assertion: 'Biblical

---

[68] Bond, 'What is Distinctive about Pentecostal Theology', p. 140. Insofar as Bond's estimation of Pentecostal practice is accurate, it seems that many Pentecostal churches – at least in Bond's context – held at least a quasi-sacramental view of the Lord's Supper.

[69] Bond, 'What is Distinctive about Pentecostal Theology', p. 141.

[70] Bond, 'What is Distinctive about Pentecostal Theology', p. 141.

Christianity is not ritualistic or sacramental'.[71] The authors claim that no 'special merit' or 'saving power' derive from the 'mechanical performance' of water baptism or the Lord's Supper, or even from the obedient observation of them. What matters is personal relationship with God, so that whatever blessing one may receive from the ordinance is strictly 'a matter of the heart'.[72] Water baptism, then, is merely ceremonial, symbolizing the 'beginning of the spiritual life' by publicly identifying the believer with Jesus. Therefore, they hold that the rite of 'water baptism is for believers only', exactly as the New Testament teaches.[73] As Horton and Menzies understand it, no ground – biblical or theological – can be found to support the practice of infant baptism; those who argue that water baptism is a new-covenant substitute for the ancient rite of circumcision are simply misreading the biblical texts.

Similarly, according to Horton's and Menzies' view, the Lord's Supper is merely 'commemorative, instructive, and inspirational', rather than sacramental. Like Duffield and Van Cleave, the authors of *Bible Doctrines* believe that Jesus' claims regarding the bread and wine are metaphorical, for Jesus was indisputably 'actually present with the disciples when He said this'.[74] Like those who defend infant baptism by appeals to Israel's circumcision rite, those who hold to transubstantiation or consubstantiation are mishandling the Scripture. To be sure, believers are required to partake of the Supper as Christ directed, although Scripture does not prescribe either a rubric for the observance of the Lord's Supper or impose a rule for how often the church should celebrate it. And Communion is indeed a 'solemn time for remembering the focal point of Christ's work'; it may at times become a moment for 'great spiritual blessing', but only insofar as participants come to the Lord's Table in the 'proper frame of mind'.[75] Therefore, communicants must take seriously Paul's warning (1 Cor. 11.27-30) and examine themselves for unconfessed sins and 'unworthiness of attitude and behavior'; otherwise sickness or even death may fall on them.[76]

---

[71] William W. Menzies and Stanley M. Horton, *Bible Doctrines: A Pentecostal Perspective* (Springfield, MO: Logion Press, 1993), p. 111.

[72] Menzies and Horton, *Bible Doctrines*, p. 113.

[73] Menzies and Horton, *Bible Doctrines*, p. 113.

[74] Menzies and Horton, *Bible Doctrines*, p. 116.

[75] Menzies and Horton, *Bible Doctrines*, p. 119.

[76] Menzies and Horton, *Bible Doctrines*, p. 119.

The official Assemblies of God *Systematic Theology*, edited by Stanley Horton and published in 1994, more or less reiterates the positions of Menzies and Horton outlined in their *Bible Doctrines*, although at certain points it engages those positions in more detail. Michael Dusing, then professor of theology and philosophy at Southeastern College of the Assemblies of God, is author of the chapter in the systematics that treats the doctrine and practice of ordinances.[77] Pentecostals, Dusing explains, prefer the term 'ordinance' to 'sacrament' in order to avoid magical connotations, and in so doing they agree with the Reformers, who also intended to effect a departure from the Catholic sacramental tradition. According to Dusing, most Pentecostals and Evangelicals do not perceive the ordinances as 'producing a spiritual change by themselves'; instead, they regard them as 'symbols or forms of proclamation of what Christ has already spiritually effected in the believer's life'.[78] Water baptism 'symbolizes a great spiritual reality', to be sure; but 'the symbol itself should never be elevated to the level of that higher reality' that comes by the immediate work of the Spirit apart from the rite of washing. Most Christians agree that Christ is present in some sense at His table, but this reality is understood in many different ways, four of which Dusing briefly considers. Most Pentecostals, he finds, hold to a position that combines and modifies the Zwinglian and Calvinist positions. Beyond this brief description of typical Pentecostal thought and practice, he offers no substantial comment or prescription.

Horton himself, perhaps owing to his strong Pietistic leanings, was deeply suspicious of sacramentalism, practices he associated with the rise of the (in his judgment, apostate) Roman Catholic Church. In his *Into All Truth*, written for layman and published in the mid 1950's, Horton provides a brief but pointedly critical reading of the church's history, laying out the case of the need for a 'restoration' of the 'full gospel'. His restorationism is complete and unadulterated. 'Take a look back through church history', he says, 'and it will be apparent that we today are far more fortunate and the truth is now far more widely accepted than at any time since the

---

[77] Michael Dusing, 'The New Testament Church', in Stanley Horton (ed.) *Systematic Theology* (rev. ed.; Springfield, MO: Logion Press, 1998), pp. 525-66.

[78] Dusing, 'The New Testament Church', p. 558.

first century'.[79] On his reading, Christians began to lose touch with the Spirit and with the truth of the gospel as they engaged in philosophical debates with unbelievers, taking up the categories and concerns of pagan philosophy in the course of these debates. He cites Justin Martyr and Origen as telltale examples of this error that led Christian doctrine to become 'more and more a matter of the mind rather than of the heart' and the perfectly clear teachings of Scripture were obscured by the allegorical readings used to satisfy the curiosities of the philosophers. At the same time, as the church grew in numbers and cultural power, the persecution died away; the church became 'fashionable', and soon enough the degeneration was full-blown: ungodly men rose to power in ecclesial office, the doctrine of Christ's 'second coming' was spiritualized, miracles and charismatic manifestations became rare, and – perhaps most egregiously – the biblical teaching of salvation by grace alone was perverted, as the churches began to teach that God worked salvation through the sacraments. The rite of baptism was believed to bring about salvation, rather than faith alone, and 'under the influence of Stoic philosophy which made matter and spirit an essential unity, magical effects were ascribed to the water' of the initiating rite. Given his view of the sacrament of water baptism, Horton's rejection of the early Christians' view of the Lord's Supper is unsurprisingly forceful:

> Another perversion was the gradual change of the communion of the Lord's Supper into the mass where the bread and wine were treated as a sin-offering magically changed into the real and actual body of Jesus, so that Jesus was crucified all over again in each mass.[80]

As a strong restorationist, Horton believed that throughout the church's history the Spirit has continually worked to restore the faith and holiness of the first Christians. Here and there, Spirit movements, such as Montanism, emerged as a beginning of the full restoration of the true church, although these movements were always quickly suppressed by the hierarchical, ecclesial powers. In the late middle ages, the Reformers recovered the authority of Scripture

---

[79] Stanley Horton, *Into all Truth: A Survey of the Course and Content of Divine Revelation* (Springfield, MO: Gospel Publishing House, 1955), p. 135.
[80] Horton, *Into All Truth*, p. 141.

and the doctrine of salvation by grace alone, and the Anabaptists recovered the biblical practice of full immersion for adult believers. In the early 19th century, J.N. Darby and the Plymouth Brethren rediscovered the plain teaching of Scripture on the pre-millennial coming of Christ, and later in the same century the doctrine of healing in the atonement and the promise of divine healing was restored to the church. Horton believed that the Pentecostal movement – and especially its distinctive experience of and teaching on Spirit baptism – was the last in this series of recoveries that constituted the restoration of the true faith. With the coming of the Holy Spirit in the Pentecostal experience, 'the full restoration of the whole gospel' was accomplished.[81] 'With the Pentecostal revival, not just a part, but ALL the gospel has been preached.'[82]

John Christopher Thomas

In his monograph on footwashing,[83] first published in 1991, the Church of God (Cleveland, TN) New Testament scholar and biblical theologian John Christopher Thomas surveys traditional churchly and critical readings of John 13.1-20,[84] a text that has invited a dizzying variety of interpretations including some that are mutually exclusive.[85] Based largely on his own close reading of the text, Thomas proposes that footwashing was for the Johannine community a discrete religious rite that 'signified the forgiveness of post-conversion sin'.[86] In fact, as he sees it, footwashing was at least for that community the 'model sacrament', alongside if not over against the Eucharist or water baptism.[87] In conversation with the luminaries of Johannine scholarship, Thomas insists that although the Gospel of John is not outright *anti*-sacramental, it nonetheless *is* critical of the sacramental views and practices of other communities, or perhaps of some within the Johannine community itself. He suggests that the Fourth Gospel may offer a corrective to an emerging 'quasi-magical view of the sacraments', perhaps on the order of

---

[81] Horton, *Into All Truth*, p. 143.

[82] Horton, *Into All Truth*, p. 144.

[83] John Christopher Thomas, *Footwashing in John 13 and the Johannine Community* (JSNTS 61; Sheffield: JSOT Press, 1991).

[84] This is the only canonical account of Jesus washing the disciples' feet.

[85] Thomas, *Footwashing in John 13*, p. 17.

[86] Thomas, *Footwashing in John 13*, p. 172.

[87] Thomas, *Footwashing in John 13*, p. 183.

that later expounded by Ignatius of Antioch and others like him.[88] Seen in the light of John's Gospel, then, the traditional Pentecostal practice of footwashing, as well as the observance of the rites of water baptism and the Lord's Supper, are truly sacramental, but are not in any sense 'magical rites'. This means, essentially, that they do not 'stand alone' but must be 'accompanied by faith'.[89]

Thomas reiterates this warning against hyper-sacramentalism in his *The Devil, Disease, and Deliverance*, a monograph on sickness, divine healing, and the will of God. In that work, Thomas engages at length 1 Cor. 11.27-34, a *textus classicus* of sacramental theology. He suspects that the Corinthian Christians – much like those to whom the Fourth Gospel is addressed – might have held an extremely high, even 'quasi-magical', view of the sacraments; a view which Paul felt compelled to confront, apostolically and pastorally.[90] When Paul warns the Corinthians that their 'unworthy' participation in the Eucharist has brought about sickness and even death, Thomas acknowledges that it is *possible* that the text means 'sickness and death are related to the Eucharistic elements in a causal way'. Nonetheless, he holds that one need not conclude that, for 'while the Corinthians may have had a somewhat magical view of the sacraments, there is no indication that Paul did'.[91]

Notwithstanding his repeated warnings against forms of 'quasi-magical' sacramentalism, Thomas insists that the sacraments do have a rightful and even central place in the Pentecostal life. In his 1998 Society for Pentecostal Studies presidential address, he calls for a re-appropriation of the sacraments along the lines of the traditional five-fold gospel.[92] He considers it unfortunate that Pentecostals have not thought deeply enough about ecclesiology or about sacraments, and calls for the development of a genuinely Pentecostal account of the church and the sacraments.[93] In particular, he invites the emerging generation of Pentecostal scholars to address

---

[88] Thomas, *Footwashing in John 13*, p. 183.

[89] Thomas, *Footwashing in John 13*, p. 183.

[90] John Christopher Thomas, *The Devil, Disease, and Deliverance: Origins of Illness in New Testament Thought* (JPTSup 13; Sheffield: Sheffield Academic Press, 1998), pp. 43, 49.

[91] Thomas, *The Devil, Disease, and Deliverance*, p. 50.

[92] John Christopher Thomas, 'Pentecostal Theology in the Twenty-First Century', *Pneuma* 20.1 (Spring 1998), pp. 3-19.

[93] Thomas, 'Pentecostal Theology in the Twenty-First Century', p. 17.

these issues – and other issues like them – by constructing authentically Pentecostal theological paradigms that both express an earnest gratitude for their Pentecostal forbearers and at the same time prove 'faithful to the ethos and worldview of the tradition' even while they revision it.[94] More specifically, Pentecostal theology should be fired by a 'passion for the theological heart of Pentecostalism',[95] which Thomas, in conversation with Donald Dayton and Steven Land, believes is the five-fold gospel. In his own words, 'when a Pentecostal theology is written from the ground up, it will be structured around these central tenets of Pentecostal faith and preaching'.[96] Hence, his own proposal – he calls it a 'trial balloon' – suggests a sacramental practice corresponding to each one of the tenets of the five-fold: water baptism for salvation, footwashing for sanctification, glossolalia for Spirit baptism, anointing with oil for healing, and the Eucharist for the second coming.

J. Rodman Williams

J. Rodman Williams, a charismatic Presbyterian and a leading theologian of the charismatic renewal movement, published the first volume of his three-volume systematics in 1988. Although he does not disparage the sacramental traditions, he is careful to point out that the preaching of the Word and the administration of the sacraments in and of themselves do not bring about any real encounter with God. 'Often, even the gospel is preached, the Bible fully accepted as the Word of God, and the sacraments regularly shared in, there is little spiritual vitality.'[97] This changes only by the outpouring of the Spirit on the worshipping community. Williams wants to focus attention on Christ's mandate, and so prefers the term 'ordinance' to 'sacrament' for naming the rites of baptism and Eucharist. Whatever formula one may use in baptizing converts, Christ personally is the 'central reality' of the rite of baptism, a rite that Williams regards as 'a sign, a seal, and a means of grace'.[98] In the hope of avoiding extremes, he stops short of defending the traditional teaching of baptismal regeneration, but nonetheless maintains that

---

[94] Thomas, 'Pentecostal Theology in the Twenty-First Century', p. 6.
[95] Thomas, 'Pentecostal Theology in the Twenty-First Century', p. 6.
[96] Thomas, 'Pentecostal Theology in the Twenty-First Century', p. 17.
[97] J. Rodman Williams, *Renewal Theology* (3 vols.; Grand Rapids: Zondervan, 1988-96), I, p. 309.
[98] Williams, *Renewal Theology*, III, p. 223.

the rite of washing may be the 'channel' through which regeneration and the forgiveness of sins come.[99] The Lord's Supper, which Williams believes is 'the vivid symbol and continuing reminder of that new covenant, which Christ's death made possible' is also an 'occasion of remembrance' a graceful means of 'present personal communion' with Christ.[100] Williams decides against the idea that Christ is bodily present in the bread and wine of the Communion rite; instead, drawing on a standard reading of the bread of life discourse in John 6, he argues for the Reformed idea of *spiritual communion* with Christ.[101] After having raised the Catholic transubstantiationist and Lutheran consubstantiationist positions, Williams cites Calvin's description of 'partaking' of Christ's 'substance' (*Institutes* 4.17.11) but concludes that even this is stated too strongly; it is 'better', he believes, 'not to speak of partaking of Christ's substance but of communing with Christ spiritually through partaking of the elements of bread and wine'.[102] Although believers enjoy this communion even apart from the Supper, there is a special 'enhancement' of communion in sharing at the Lord's Table.[103]

French Arrington

French Arrington, a Church of God (Cleveland, TN) biblical theologian, devotes a section of the third volume of his three-volume *Christian Doctrine: A Pentecostal Perspective* to the ordinances. He includes in this section five practices characteristic of Pentecostal worship, only three of which are properly designated ordinances.[104] Unlike Duffield and Van Cleave, Arrington does not reference the sacramental views of other Christian traditions. He makes no use of the term 'sacrament', but nonetheless does propose an expansive definition of 'ordinance'. 'The ordinances of the church are visible signs of the saving work of Jesus.' Although they are strictly 'outward representations', they nonetheless, for believers, are 'not mere

---

[99] Williams, *Renewal Theology*, III, p. 221.

[100] Williams, *Renewal Theology*, III, pp. 246-47.

[101] Williams, *Renewal Theology*, III, pp. 248-49.

[102] Williams, *Renewal Theology*, III, p. 249.

[103] Williams, *Renewal Theology*, III, pp. 249-50.

[104] Arrington indicates that his own Church of God (Cleveland, TN), the Church of God of Prophecy, and the Pentecostal Apostolic Church of God of Romania regard footwashing as an ordinance, in addition to water baptism and the Lord's Supper, which other Pentecostals recognize as ordinances.

ceremony' but in fact prove to be 'a means of real communion with God and of strengthening grace'.[105]

Arrington advances a series of propositions on the Lord's Supper, as previously he had done with baptism. He insists that the Supper is 'a remembrance of the Lord',[106] and a proclamation of Christ's death in the time before the *parousia*.[107] Arrington holds that the Supper, like water baptism, 'requires faith for proper participation'.[108] However, he also offers that the church's experience at the Table of the Lord's Supper is genuine communion (*koinonia*), by which there is a 'partaking of the blood of Christ – His saving benefits – *in a spiritual way*'.[109] Believers are 'spiritually nourished by Christ', who is 'the host of the Supper'. In fact, as believers engage in Communion, 'Christ is present to give us the spiritual blessings signified by the bread and cup'.[110] In what might strike some as a surprising move given typical Protestant distaste for thinking of Communion in sacrificial terms, Arrington speaks of Eucharistic participants appearing 'in the presence of God with our sacrifices of praise and thanksgiving for the Sacrifice of Calvary'.[111]

In the final analysis, Arrington seems to hold at least a quasi-sacramental view of the Supper. Certainly, there are sacramental overtones to his position. Much of what he says fits the profile of mere memorialization, to be sure; but others of his statements betray the conviction that there is an effective dimension to the Communion celebration. For instance, even when speaking of the Supper as a 'remembrance' (*anamnesis*), Arrington argues that 'this word is so powerful it signifies that the death of Christ is *made effective now* and brings blessings into the present'.[112] He reports that sometimes people receive healing or are baptized in the Spirit when participating in the Communion meal.[113] Pentecostals, he says, 'have

---

[105] French L. Arrington, *Christian Doctrine: a Pentecostal Perspective* (3 vols., Cleveland, TN: Pathway, 1994), III, p. 208.

[106] Arrington, *Christian Doctrine*, III, p. 212.

[107] Arrington, *Christian Doctrine*, III, p. 213.

[108] Arrington, *Christian Doctrine*, III, p. 214.

[109] Arrington, *Christian Doctrine*, III, p. 213. Emphasis added.

[110] Arrington, *Christian Doctrine*, III, p. 213.

[111] Arrington, *Christian Doctrine*, III, p. 212.

[112] Arrington, *Christian Doctrine*, III, p. 212. Emphasis added.

[113] Arrington, *Christian Doctrine*, III, p. 214.

a sense of the profound presence of Christ and His blessing at the Supper'.[114]

Harold Hunter

In his response to *Baptism, Eucharist and Ministry* – the so-called Lima document[115] published by the World Council of Churches in 1982 – theologian and ecumenist Harold Hunter indicates that Pentecostals, as well as Christians of other traditions, welcome the 'renewed excitement about ground gained and hope for more converging paths' accomplished by the emerging ecumenical consensus.[116] Speaking for classical Pentecostals, Hunter appreciates the document's 'healthy respect for scripture',[117] which he predicts will go a long way toward allaying many of the fears of Pentecostals regarding the agenda of the ecumenical movement. Nonetheless, he insists that Pentecostal spirituality remains categorically different from that of Evangelicals who defend the 'primacy of the spoken word as a means of grace' on the one hand, and '"high-church" traditionalists' who emphasize 'sacramental acts' on the other hand. Pentecostals 'look to multiple manifestations of deity', instead.[118]

Of the water baptism rite in particular, Hunter declares that 'Pentecostals at large will not own a view of sacramental efficacy … independent of the participants' faith'[119] – as evidenced he believes by Pentecostals' reluctance to use the term 'sacrament'; but he remains confident that Pentecostals can find ways to take seriously other traditions' views of baptism. In spite of the fact that most Pentecostals[120] decry paedobaptism and regularly practice rebaptism,[121] Hunter finds 'hopeful signs' developing among Pentecostals that indicate a possible acceptance of the basic understanding of baptism laid out in *BEM*, although he does not quite call for Pentecostals to accept it. As for Communion, Hunter deems it extremely

---

[114] Arrington, *Christian Doctrine*, III, p. 214.

[115] *Baptism, Eucharist, and Ministry*, Faith and Order Paper 111 (Geneva: World Council of Churches, 1982).

[116] Harold D. Hunter, 'Reflections by a Pentecostalist on Aspects of *BEM*', *Journal of Ecumenical Studies* 29.3-4 (Summer-Fall 1992), pp. 317-45 (345).

[117] Hunter, 'Reflections by a Pentecostalist', p. 323.

[118] Hunter, 'Reflections by a Pentecostalist', p. 331.

[119] Hunter, 'Reflections by a Pentecostalist', p. 329.

[120] The Pentecostal Holiness Church officially endorsed infant baptism, at least in the beginning. It has never officially repudiated this position.

[121] Hunter approvingly cites Thomas' work on footwashing as an alternative to rebaptism.

'unlikely that Pentecostals *en masse* would be given to accept the eucharist as "the central act of the Church's worship"',[122] and he cites the fact that 'no major pentecostal denomination in the U.S.A. is moving toward a weekly observance of the eucharist' as evidence of this fact. He suspects that 'Pentecostal defaming of the anglo-catholic view of the sacraments may owe something to evangelical influence',[123] an influence that also shows itself in the Pentecostal privileging of the Bible in worship and theology.[124] Pentecostals, in keeping with most in the Protestant tradition, have not developed the concept of the Lord's Supper as a sacrifice for fear that it might 'compromise the uniqueness of the death of Christ on the cross'; and they discern Christ's presence 'not in the elements but among the devotees', in line with the Zwinglian tradition. In spite of all this, Hunter does believe Pentecostals 'may reverently concede' that Christ's presence in the Eucharist is 'unique'[125] and may accept the 'conjoining of *anamnesis* and *epiklesis*' if 'magical connotations relative to the elements' do not come into play.

Hunter's concerns seem to be largely descriptive and analytical, rather than prescriptive or constructive. In most of his writing, at least, he attempts to provide a faithful account of what it is that Pentecostals do believe and what they are likely to find acceptable or unacceptable in the ecumenical conversations. He admits that traditional Pentecostalism was and is 'far from uniform', even in some of the most basic doctrines and practices.[126] On his reading, the early Pentecostals generally regarded water baptism and Holy Communion as 'external rites directed by Scripture and observed by the gathered people of God', whether they used the term 'ordinance', most commonly, or 'sacrament', which they did only rarely, concerned to avoid the implications of 'self-contained efficacy'. Even now, Pentecostals typically do not find in the Eucharist a source of forgiveness for sins. Unlike Roman Catholics, Pentecostals virtually from the beginning of the movement have insisted that communicants partake in 'both kinds', that is, of both the loaf and

---

[122] Hunter, 'Reflections by a Pentecostalist', p. 337.
[123] Hunter, 'Reflections by a Pentecostalist', p. 340.
[124] Hunter, 'Reflections by a Pentecostalist', p. 338.
[125] Hunter, 'Reflections by a Pentecostalist', p. 337.
[126] See Harold D. Hunter, 'Ordinances, Pentecostal', in Stanley M. Burgess and Eduard M. van der Maas (eds.), *NIDPCM* (Grand Rapids: Zondervan, 2002), pp. 947-49.

the cup. Pentecostals, also unlike the high-church traditions, do not restrict the administration of the sacraments to the ordained clergy. As Hunter has it, they find this practice 'biblically allowable but not mandatory'. Western Pentecostals, [127] particularly, seem unconcerned with certain dimensions of traditional Eucharistic practice, such as the use of an altar or the posturing of the minister's body. Further, classical Pentecostals, at least an overwhelming majority of them, refuse the use of fermented wine in the Eucharistic celebration. [128] Intercommunion is seldom if ever an issue, as Pentecostal churches practice open communion.

Steven J. Land

According to Steven Land's seminal work, *Pentecostal Spirituality*, published in early 1990's, the first Pentecostals' celebration of the ordinances [129] witnessed their deeply-held conviction that 'bodily dedication was necessary', that the spiritual and the corporeal were not opposed but existed as complimentary dimensions of God's reality. [130] The ordinances themselves they regarded as 'signs': baptism was 'the sign of starting out in service to the Lord or the way to the kingdom' and the Lord's Supper was 'the sign of ongoing nurture and fellowship'. [131] Because the Spirit was immediately present to the worshipping community, the ordinances belonged to the larger order of God's intervening work in and for the believers. Christ could and did work through a range of activities, including but not restricted to testimonies, songs, prayers, offerings, manifestations of gifts, preaching, and teaching. [132] All of these – and not merely baptism and the Lord's Supper – were 'means of grace', and the whole congregation engaged in these activities, not only the

---

[127] Hunter finds Pentecostals in countries dominated by Greek Orthodox traditions do concern themselves with these matters, at least to a greater degree than do Pentecostals in the West.

[128] Hunter, 'Ordinances, Pentecostal', p. 948.

[129] Land notes that these included, for most Pentecostals, baptism and the Lord's Supper. Other groups, such as the Church of God (Cleveland, TN), also considered footwashing an ordinance. Usually, they practiced footwashing in conjunction with the taking of Communion, often – but not only – during the traditional 'watch-night service', in which the church gathered on the evening of December 31st to usher in the new year.

[130] Land, *Pentecostal Spirituality*, p. 114.

[131] Land, *Pentecostal Spirituality*, p. 115.

[132] Land, *Pentecostal Spirituality*, p. 140.

clergy.[133] Evidently, this democratic and egalitarian impulse marks the Pentecostal spiritual tradition, now as well as then.

The early Pentecostals, Land says, did not often use the term 'sacrament' because they saw it as a 'non-biblical word of Roman Catholic derivation which was associated with mechanical ritual'.[134] They differed from the classical Christian tradition in numerous ways: they did not consider baptism or the Lord's Supper as 'converting' ordinances;[135] they rarely baptized infants,[136] regularly practiced re-baptism in keeping with the Anabaptist tradition, and they celebrated the Lord's Supper only occasionally.[137] Nonetheless, Pentecostal baptisms and celebrations of Communion were not mere memorializations, for there remained a 'richness of the actual practice' that always exceeded the theological explanations on offer, which were few and inchoate, if they appeared at all. Still, whether they could make theological sense of it or not, first-generation Pentecostals believed 'Christ was made effectively present by virtue of the Holy Spirit'.[138] 'To eat, drink, baptize and wash feet was to do it unto the Lord; and he was present in, with, under and through these acts.'[139] Jesus, through the Spirit, acted on the believers during the celebration of the Lord's Supper. 'Persons could be converted, healed, sanctified and filled with the Spirit *in conjunction with* the Lord's Supper.'[140] In other words, the saving and healing power of the Spirit was not mediated directly through the eating and drinking of the Communion elements, but was made effective indirectly – *alongside* the meal, so to speak.

Land refers to the ordinances as 'means of grace', as has been mentioned already. However, he also insists in another place that

---

[133] Land, *Pentecostal Spirituality*, p. 75.

[134] Land, *Pentecostal Spirituality*, p. 115.

[135] Land, *Pentecostal Spirituality*, p. 115.

[136] Instead, they performed 'baby dedications', a ceremony in which the parents pledge their child to God before the gathered community. The pastor charges the parents and the congregation with their responsibility to the family and to the child, and typically, the pastor closes the ceremony by blessing the child, often anointing the child with oil. For further explanation, see Thomas F. Best, *Baptism Today: Understanding, Practice, Ecumenical Implications* (Collegeville, MN: Liturgical Press, 2008), pp. 161-62.

[137] Land notes that only the Elim Pentecostal churches of Great Britain celebrate the Lord's Supper weekly.

[138] Land, *Pentecostal Spirituality*, p. 115.

[139] Land, *Pentecostal Spirituality*, p. 117.

[140] Emphasis added.

Pentecostal theology resists the use of this language as unnecessarily impersonal and abstract. In fact, he goes so far as to criticize the 'domestication of the Holy Spirit'[141] effected by doctrines that speak of receiving 'grace' rather than God the Holy Spirit. On his view, the Lord's Supper is genuinely a 'means of grace' in the sense that the Holy Spirit uses it to nurture the life of Christ in the believer and in the believing community. The 'moral integration' that emerges from the Spirit's transformative work happens through 'an ongoing, daily gift of grace' received through 'all the means of grace', including but not limited to the Eucharist. He provides no definitive list, but cites confession and footwashing as among the several means that belong to the same order as Holy Communion.[142] For Land, then, the means of grace are best understood as (trans)formative *practices*, practices that by dint of habit-forming repetition discipline the heart, mind, and body for life in the Spirit. Living in the presence of God, Land believes, is the essence of Pentecostal spirituality, but such a life does not always entail 'constant sensations'; instead, a certain praxis involving 'private and corporate prayer, living in the Scriptures, walking in fellowship, the Lord's Supper, fasting' make possible this life in God's presence, training one to 'attend to the Spirit in following Christ' even in the non-sensational moments of life in Christ.[143]

Peter Hocken

Father Peter Hocken, a charismatic Catholic theologian and a historian of the charismatic movement, believes his Pentecostal experience of Spirit baptism has fundamentally altered his view of the *parousia* and its implications for the church's life. Before his Spirit baptism, Christ's 'second coming' was, he admits, merely an 'external' reality that in no way affected his own 'inner life'.[144] After the renovation of his faith experienced in the charismatic renewal, Hocken found himself awakened to a deep and vibrant hope for the second coming of Jesus, an awakening he came to desire for others. For, 'as we welcome the gift of the Spirit in this life, we ex-

---

[141] Land, *Pentecostal Spirituality*, p. 39.
[142] Land, *Pentecostal Spirituality*, p. 204.
[143] Land, *Pentecostal Spirituality*, p. 177.
[144] Peter Hocken, 'The Holy Spirit Makes the Church More Eschatological', in William K. Kay and Anne E. Dyer, *Pentecostal and Charismatic Studies: A Reader* (London: SCM Press, 2004), pp. 43-46 (43).

perience a desire for the fullness of the gift of the Spirit in the resurrection'.[145] Hocken quickly recognized that this realization would
bear fruit for a theology of the sacraments. In the Catholic cate-
chism, he found the Eucharist spoken of as the 'pledge' of the
world to come, an 'anticipation of the heavenly glory'.[146] Further,
history shows that the church has from the beginning aimed her
liturgy toward the '*Marana tha!*', and understood the second petition
of the Lord's Prayer – 'Thy Kingdom come' – within the context of
the Eucharistic celebration, facts that point unmistakably to the
church's hope in Christ's return and the eschatological meaning of
the sacrament.[147] If 'the Holy Spirit makes the church more eschatological', the sacraments, and in particular the Eucharist, embody
this truth most completely. Through the Spirit, the sacraments and
especially the Lord's Supper become a way of God's directing the
community's life to the hope of 'total salvation' and

> the deliverance of all creation from its bondage to decay, the es-
> tablishment of the new heavens and the new earth, our resurrec-
> tion in glorified spiritual bodies, in which there will be total
> communion with all the saints and angels in the perfect harmony
> and eternal life of the Most Holy Trinity.[148]

In sum, then, Hocken's account of the sacraments is radically eschatologized, so that, for example, the *signum/res* relation in the
Sacrament is body of Christ/joys of the Eschaton.

Frank Macchia

Few Pentecostals or charismatics have made more creative contributions to sacramental theology than Frank Macchia, a Basel-
trained systematician and professor of theology at Vanguard University, an Assemblies of God institution. In his 1993 essay
'Tongues as Sign', Macchia argues that in spite of the shape of Pentecostal practice at the grass roots level, Pentecostal spirituality
'does not advocate an unmediated encounter with God, nor a subjectivist emotionalism unrelated to an objective means of grace',[149]

---

[145] Hocken, 'The Holy Spirit Makes the Church More Eschatological', p. 44.
[146] Hocken, 'The Holy Spirit Makes the Church More Eschatological', p. 44.
[147] Hocken, 'The Holy Spirit Makes the Church More Eschatological', p. 45.
[148] Hocken, 'The Holy Spirit Makes the Church More Eschatological', p. 46.
[149] Frank D. Macchia, 'Tongues as a Sign: Towards a Sacramental Understanding of Pentecostal Experience', *Pneuma* 15.1 (Spring 1993), pp. 61-76 (75).

as a close inspection of the Pentecostal emphasis on visible/audible signs such as glossolalia and healing makes clear. In spite of the fact that many if not most Pentecostals are uncomfortable with the term 'sacrament' because of its associations with institutionalism, formalism, clericalism, and the like, and their fear that 'sacramental efficacy' might be understood as 'necessitated by a causative dynamic intrinsic in the elements',[150] Macchia maintains that Pentecostal spirituality can rightly be designated 'sacramental' – *if* the term is carefully defined.[151] Further, he believes that even if many Pentecostals claim a Zwinglian view of the Eucharist, 'their actual Eucharistic devotion is more complex'.[152] Despite the non- or weakly-sacramental theological descriptions of their experiences, Pentecostals nonetheless experience baptism and the Lord's Supper as 'occasions for God's redemptive presence through the power of the Spirit'.[153] He considers it fortunate that Pentecostal sacramental *practice* surpasses the theology of the sacraments so far advanced by Pentecostal theologians. He believes the time has come for Pentecostal sacramental theology to attempt to 'catch up' to the community's experience.

Still, Macchia does not want to dismiss too quickly the characteristic Pentecostal 'uneasiness' with the liturgical formalities of the high-church traditions.[154] It is not without reason that Pentecostals have an 'allergic response' to the sacramentalism of these traditions: on the one hand, it shows the healthy fear of the dead ritualism that has dogged many liturgical traditions, and on the other hand, it points up the Pentecostal commitment to the 'spontaneity and freedom of the Spirit'. Glossolalia, then, is a different kind of sacrament, one that befits characteristic Pentecostal spirituality. For, as

---

He takes his lead from Simon Tugwell's observation that Pentecostal speaking in tongues functions as a sacrament, and argues that that is indeed what glossolalia is and does.

[150] Macchia, 'Tongues as a Sign', p. 61.

[151] Macchia's sacramental understanding is shaped to a great degree by the works of Paul Tillich and Karl Rahner. Macchia believes Rahner and Tillich have managed to emphasize the objectivity of the sacraments without restricting divine freedom because they conceive it primarily in personalistic and not metaphysical terms.

[152] Frank D. Macchia, 'Eucharist: Pentecostal' in Paul F. Bradshaw (ed.), *The New Westminster Dictionary of Liturgy and Worship* (Louisville: WJKP, 2002), pp. 189-90 (190).

[153] Macchia, 'Is Footwashing the Neglected Sacrament?', p. 241.

[154] Macchia, 'Tongues as a Sign', p. 63.

he says, speaking in tongues 'accents the free, dramatic, and unpredictable move of the Spirit of God, while the liturgical traditions stress an ordered and predictable encounter with the Spirit'.[155] He concludes that Pentecostals possess a 'chaotic' or 'protest' sacramentality that emerged from the 'protest to any attempt at a formalization or objectification of the Spirit in liturgical rites'.[156] In Macchia's judgment, this distinctively Pentecostal sacramentality arises from a theology that is 'more "theophanic" than incarnational'. This is due to the fact that Pentecostal spirituality – which understands itself in light of the 'dramatic descent of the Spirit on the Day of Pentecost' – has developed as a way of life characterized by 'a fervent expectation for the signs and wonders of God's Spirit'.[157]

Throughout his work, Macchia writes with ecumenical concerns, which for obvious reasons affect the whence and whether of his project. He engages Roman Catholic theology at many points in his *oeuvre*, and although he assumes that in the final analysis Pentecostals will maintain theological and practical commitments that are unacceptable for those in the Catholic tradition, he nonetheless believes Pentecostals have much to gain from Catholicism, especially given the changes initiated by Vatican II. Drawing on Karl Rahner's discussion of 'charismatic manifestations' and 'ecclesial sacraments', he finds that the theological accents of Pentecostals and Catholics are 'more complementary than contradictory' and that a renewed and deeper appreciation for the sacraments among Pentecostals can help Pentecostals 'bridge' their charismatic spirituality and efforts for social justice and peace-making.[158] He is quick to add that Pentecostals have much to teach Catholics, as well. The Pentecostal 'protest' or 'inchoate' sacramentality serves to remind Catholics that 'both worship and social renewal require spontaneous and unpredictable turns toward liberation and healing' and the Spirit's freedom is always already 'calling for the need to question and renew our programs and institutional structures'.[159]

In the last few years, Macchia has begun to work out in increasing detail a fully-orbed theology of the sacraments in conversation

---

[155] Macchia, 'Tongues as a Sign', p. 63.
[156] Macchia, 'Tongues as a Sign', p. 64.
[157] Macchia, 'Tongues as a Sign', p. 73.
[158] Macchia, 'Tongues as a Sign', p. 75. See also Macchia, 'Eucharist: Pentecostal', p. 189.
[159] Macchia, 'Tongues as a Sign', p. 75.

with the witness of early Pentecostals, contemporary Pentecostals scholarship (especially the work of John Christopher Thomas, Simon Chan, and Amos Yong), and a coterie of dialogue partners from around the ecumene. For Macchia, the sacraments signify the 'reality of the coming Kingdom', and the Lord's Supper, in particular, 'anticipates the messianic feast and the renewal of the earth'. Moreover, he is concerned not only with the eschatological dimensions of the sacred meal, but also its missional character. In his vision, the communion with Christ that the church's celebration of the Lord's Supper facilitates is 'a communion in the love of God for the world'. Hence, at the Eucharistic table believers both 'commune with Christ crucified and risen for the world' and 'renew [their] dedication to participate in his act of reconciling the world to God'.[160] He is committed to the view that the Lord's Supper belongs at the heart of Pentecostal worship, along with preaching and the *charismata*.[161]

But Macchia is also deeply concerned with intra-Pentecostal conversations, and often brings his knowledge of ecumenical sources to bear in his engagement with Pentecostal concerns and issues. For example, in his review of Thomas' monograph on footwashing, Macchia praises Thomas for helping him 'rethink how [Pentecostals] view baptism and the eucharist', exploring ways in which they might approach these principle sacraments.[162] This is particularly needed, Macchia believes, for in spite of the fact that many Pentecostals do in fact observe the rites of water baptism and the Lord's Supper, they typically do so with a truncated vision of their theological import. In his own words,

> … though [Pentecostals] do observe baptism and the eucharist, [they] have often regarded them theologically more as acts of repentance or symbolic testimonies than as 'sacraments' in the sense of events in which the dynamic presence of Christ through the Spirit is encountered.[163]

---

[160] Frank D. Macchia, 'The Church of the Latter Rain: The Church and Eschatology in Pentecostal Perspective' in J.C. Thomas (ed.), *Toward a Pentecostal Ecclesiology* (Cleveland, TN: CPT Press, 2010), p. 258.

[161] Macchia, 'Eucharist: Pentecostal', p. 190.

[162] Frank D. Macchia, 'Is Footwashing the Neglected Sacrament? A Theological Response to John Christopher Thomas', *Pneuma* 19.2 (Fall 1997), pp. 239-49.

[163] Macchia, 'Is Footwashing the Neglected Sacrament?', p. 241.

Macchia believes Thomas' view of the footwashing rite as a sacrament provides an instructive and imitable paradigm for Pentecostal theological reflection on the (other) sacraments. First, he applauds Thomas for not mechanizing the rite.[164] Second, he appreciates Thomas' eschatological emphasis. He believes that the 'ultimate horizon' of the sacraments is Christ's *parousia*, 'when the master returns as the crucified and resurrected Servant/Lord to assert once and for all the Lordship of love and liberation over hate and oppression'.[165] Further, he suggests that perhaps footwashing may serve as a 'link' between water baptism and the eucharist that can 'bridge the original confession of faith found in baptism with the Eucharistic meal that celebrates the cross by looking ahead explicitly to the messianic banquet'.[166] Third, Macchia affirms Thomas' christocentrism, agreeing that the sacraments receive their meaning from Christ, particularly his death and resurrection, and direct the church's attention to Jesus and his past, present, and future work.[167] These three points of emphasis seem to form the basic conceptual framework for Macchia's developing sacramental theology.

Richard Bicknell

In a contribution to a treatment of distinct Pentecostal doctrines, Elim Pentecostal theologian Richard Bicknell takes up Pentecostal sacramental thought and practice for consideration. Like Harold Hunter, *et al.*, Bicknell attempts to articulate the characteristic shape of Pentecostal sacramentality. He finds that Pentecostals do have an incipient and inchoate sacramental theology, one that needs further development and more careful articulation. First, he holds that Pentecostals do insist on the observation of these ordinances, even though they do not regard them as essential to salvation. Instead, 'obeying Jesus' serves as the motivating force. Also, Pentecostals reject any notion of a 'mechanical transfer of saving grace' – one of

---

[164] Macchia, 'Is Footwashing the Neglected Sacrament?', p. 246.
[165] Macchia, 'Is Footwashing the Neglected Sacrament?', p. 247.
[166] Macchia, 'Is Footwashing the Neglected Sacrament?', p. 248.
[167] As Macchia (Macchia, 'Is Footwashing the Neglected Sacrament?', p. 247) notes, 'This transitory nature of religious experience means that biblical teachings on the crucified and risen Lord not only determine the theological meanings of the sacraments, but sacramental experience will serve to further illuminate the meaning of the crucified and risen Lord for our lives'.

the points that nearly every Pentecostal feels compelled to make.[168] In this, Bicknell believes that Pentecostals are simply following an Evangelical/Pietistic impulse that 'supplies a general anti-sacramentalist outlook by which acts are seen as symbolic and non-effectual'.[169] Consequently, like the majority of Evangelicals, Pentecostals insist on the use of symbolic terminology – hence, the use of the term 'ordinance' – expressly to defend against a slide into sacramentalism.[170] Bicknell maintains that Pentecostals reject any notion of a real bodily presence, whether in the form of the transubstantiation of the Catholic tradition or the consubstantiation of the Lutheran tradition. Christ is, quite simply, 'not in the emblems', not 'localised in the bread and wine'.[171] It is 'not through the *elements* that the believer is strengthened' but through the sharing of the meal and Spirit-led reflection on its meaning. Pentecostals typically refrain from referring to the symbols of bread and wine as 'body and blood', and never speak of them as 'host', for they do not believe that grace is in any sense imparted through the actual eating and drinking of these elements. Instead, salvation comes through 'the physical act of Christ dying' and through 'the normal channels of communication'.[172] As Bicknell sees it, for Pentecostals the Lord's Supper is, above all, a *memorial feast*. This is so in two distinct but inseparable senses: the bread and wine are taken 'in memory of the Lord's death' and the Communion meal 'carries us back to the most vital moment in our lives, the moment when Jesus became real to us'.[173] This *anamnesis* intends a recalling of initial commitment for the sake of a renewal and furthering of dedication. Further, Pentecostals remember not only what Christ has done at the cross, but also who he is, and what he is doing presently.

All this notwithstanding, Pentecostals *do* expect Christ himself 'to be present at the communion service'; although Bicknell insists it is not the 'real presence' (in the loaf and the cup) but the 'realized presence' (in the congregation and to the celebrants) that they antic-

---

[168] Richard Bicknell, 'The Ordinances: The Marginalised Aspects of Pentecostalism' in Keith Warrington (ed.), *Pentecostal Perspectives* (Carlisle: Paternoster, 1998), p. 207.
[169] Bicknell, 'The Ordinances', p. 211.
[170] Bicknell, 'The Ordinances', p. 208.
[171] Bicknell, 'The Ordinances', pp. 208-209.
[172] Bicknell, 'The Ordinances', p. 210.
[173] Bicknell, 'The Ordinances', p. 207.

ipate and experience. Christ is personally present via the work of the Holy Spirit in response to the faithful gathering and communing of the saints, so that Pentecostals can speak of the Supper so understood and experienced as a 'Divine contact point', a moment of 'encounter', even the 'focal point of fellowship' with Christ through the Spirit.[174]

In another essay, Bicknell traces more carefully the sources and outcomes of the 'Eucharistic expression' of the Elim Pentecostal tradition,[175] the roots of which, Bicknell believes, are to be found in the Reformed tradition that 'sprang' from the thought and practice of the Swiss Reformers, Zwingli and Calvin, and even more particularly and recently from the memorialistic theologies of the 'Nonconformist bodies' of Congregationalists and the Plymouth Brethren, also known as Free Churches.[176] Bicknell insists that the present-day Elim Pentecostal sacramental thought and practice derives from the nineteenth-century Free Church adaptations of Calvin's and Zwingli's views, although he admits that in most instances Zwingli's memorialism won the day, so that Calvin's sacramental theology plays much less a part in Elim Pentecostals' understanding and practice of the Lord's Supper than does Zwingli's.[177] In fact, in actual practice if not in theological statement Elim Pentecostals reduce even Zwingli's 'bare commemoration' to nothing more than retrospection,[178] a tendency Bicknell knows some Pentecostals find lamentable. Bicknell himself characterizes the view as 'extreme memorialism'.[179]

---

[174] Bicknell, 'The Ordinances', p. 209.

[175] Richard Bicknell, 'In Memory of Christ's Sacrifice: Roots and Shoots of Elim's Eucharistic Expression', *JEPTA* 27 (1997), pp. 59-89.

[176] Bicknell, 'In Memory of Christ's Sacrifice', p. 59. Bicknell ('In Memory of Christ's Sacrifice', p. 64) finds that the sacramental theology of Elim founder George Jeffreys took its shape under the influence of the Congregationalism he encountered in his upbringing and a brief time spent at the Pentecostal Missionary Union Bible School under the tutelage of Thomas Myerscough, who was associated with the Plymouth Brethren. The Elim tradition of weekly Sunday-morning Communion apparently also derives from the practice of the Brethren, and seems to have come to Elim through Jeffreys under Myerscough's influence.

[177] Bicknell, 'In Memory of Christ's Sacrifice', p. 81. Bicknell believes this is mainly because Elim Pentecostals have little to no sense of the church as Christ's body, a well-developed tenet in Calvin's thought.

[178] Bicknell, 'In Memory of Christ's Sacrifice', p. 67. Bicknell finds that his extreme emphasis on the memorial aspect of the Eucharist shows up in Elim Pentecostals' 'purely symbolic' view of the Eucharistic elements.

[179] Bicknell, 'In Memory of Christ's Sacrifice', p. 67.

Much of Elim's treatment of the Lord's Supper is 'anti-sacramental', Bicknell insists, and he provides this example: when candidates apply for entry into Elim Pentecostal ministry they are asked to distinguish between four main interpretations of the Eucharist, and they 'know better than to espouse any form of sacramentalism'.[180] As a matter of fact, Bicknell identifies anti-Catholic sentiment as one of the 'major forces active in shaping Elim's Eucharistic expression'.[181] Given the symbolic nature of the Meal, 'it matters little that real bread and wine are used', so crackers often substitute for unleavened bread and fruit juice for fermented wine. Elim Pentecostalism distances itself from talking of the 'real presence' in either transubstantiationist or consubstantiationist terms, decrying both views as equally unscriptural. Again, Bicknell makes the argument that Christ is present not in the emblems but 'in the dynamic activity of the Holy Spirit'. On his view, not 'real presence' but 'realised [*sic*] presence' is what makes the Sacrament what it is.[182]

One might argue, Bicknell admits, that since Elim Pentecostals hold that 'Christ is not in the emblems' and that 'reception of Christ cannot be via the emblems' that Christ is not present in the Communion service. But such a conclusion would be mistaken, he says, for again and again the testimonies of Elim Pentecostals affirm that Christ is really, if only spiritually, received in the Communion Meal, and the Lord's Supper 'is where the human and divine meet'. Bicknell believes that Elim Pentecostals have no theological justification for these claims. For, while they insist that Christ is present at the Supper, they also contend that his presence is not limited to the Eucharistic context. It is unclear, then, how it is that one might differentiate Christ's presence in the Supper from his presence at other times.[183] In spite of these ambiguities, Elim Pentecostals do hold that the Eucharist promises real benefits to participants, even though it is 'not necessarily effected through the rubrics and setting of the service itself', for 'it is the presence of Christ in the believer that is the source of this strength'. Bicknell concludes, then, that it is difficult if not impossible to imagine or describe what 'special' or unique role can be accorded to the Elim

---

[180] Bicknell, 'In Memory of Christ's Sacrifice', p. 76.
[181] Bicknell, 'In Memory of Christ's Sacrifice', p. 76.
[182] Bicknell, 'In Memory of Christ's Sacrifice', p. 68.
[183] Bicknell, 'In Memory of Christ's Sacrifice', p. 70.

Pentecostal experience of the Lord's Supper, given that they believe 'all of the benefits of the Supper can be gained at any other time, and in differing circumstances, simply through communion with Christ'.[184] In effect, one can discern little difference between a Communion service and any other service: 'both have exactly the same potential to supply exactly the same needs of the believer, for in both, communion with Christ is assured'.[185]

Having laid out this description, Bicknell turns at last to pre-scriptive commentary, offering a few constructive suggestions and criticisms. He regrets that for many communities, the rite of Communion has no real significance; it has been, he says, 'effectively reduced to a token gesture'[186] that lasts only a few minutes. He blames the 'newer style of celebratory service' for this minimalization of the Eucharist. A *'balanced* Eucharistic theology'[187] is needed, one that does not reject the notion of commemorating Christ's death, but includes an emphasis on the church as Christ's body, and arises from a 'meaningful theology of the work of the Spirit in the Supper'.[188] Calvin's theology of the Eucharist would probably provide a 'good starting point', Bicknell believes, for a much-needed revisioning of Elim's Eucharistic faith and practice.

Simon Tan

In a 2003 essay, Simon Tan, an ordained Assembly of God minister and a lecturer in systematic theology, calls for a reassessment of the practice of believer's baptism, which most Pentecostals regard as *'the* biblical position'.[189] Tan's explains that his personal interest in the issue arose from his discerning reflection on the reasons offered against infant baptism. He argues that Pentecostals' adherence to believer's baptism betrays the influence of 'individualistic orienta-tion of the West' and does not fit Asian societies. On his view, in-fant baptism does *not* oppose biblical teachings, in Tan's judgment. In the course of his argument, Tan addresses the different presup-positions that underlie the various approaches to the 'ordinance' of

---

[184] Bicknell, 'In Memory of Christ's Sacrifice', p. 71.
[185] Bicknell, 'In Memory of Christ's Sacrifice', p. 71.
[186] Bicknell, 'In Memory of Christ's Sacrifice', p. 82.
[187] Emphasis added.
[188] Bicknell, 'In Memory of Christ's Sacrifice', p. 82.
[189] Simon G. H. Tan, 'Reassessing Believer's Baptism in Pentecostal Theology and Practice', *AJPS* 6.2 (2003), pp. 219-34. Emphasis added.

water baptism. One interpretation 'emphasizes the importance of a faith response'. An opposing interpretation emphasizes the 'reality of the grace of God in the life of the individual'.[190] Appreciating the importance of the former position, Tan sides with the latter, finding infant baptism the more appropriate practice. He worries that the typical Pentecostal emphasis on personal faith response threatens to overemphasize human 'heroics' and to collapse into subjectivism. Further, he believes that the question is not whether the church may baptize infants but 'whether we have any legitimate reason to *withhold* baptism from them'.[191] Refusing to baptize infants may disclose a 'loss of confidence in the truth of the gospel'.[192]

Although Tan does not address the Eucharist specifically, the implications of his position for a theology of the Lord's Supper appear readily applicable. First, it seems he would affirm a strongly sacramental view of the Supper, given that it would emphasize the 'objectiveness' of God's grace in the believer's life. Second, it seems that he would hold that the burden of proof rests on those who reject a sacramental view of the Supper. Third, it would appear that he would reject a strictly biblicist account of the Eucharist's meaning and purpose in the Christian life.

Daniel Albrecht

In his work on Pentecostal/charismatic ritual published in 1999,[193] the liturgist Daniel Albrecht, then a Professor of Christian History at Bethany College in San Francisco, attempts to identify and describe the shape of Pentecostal worship.[194] Albrecht carefully observes and analyzes the rituals and spirituality of three Pentecostal/charismatic communities,[195] with careful attention to their ap-

---

[190] Tan, 'Reassessing Believer's Baptism', p. 219.

[191] Tan, 'Reassessing Believer's Baptism', p. 233. Emphasis added.

[192] Tan, 'Reassessing Believer's Baptism', p. 234.

[193] Daniel E. Albrecht, *Rites in the Spirit: a Ritual Approach to Pentecostal/Charismatic Spirituality* (JPTSup 17; Sheffield: Sheffield Academic Press, 1999).

[194] Albrecht claims that although charismatics and classical Pentecostals share a basic experience of the Spirit, charismatics are more likely than classical Pentecostals to desire and formulate a sacramental theology, because the former often come from traditions that practice the sacraments regularly. In fact, this is one of the key distinctives of the charismatic movement.

[195] All of these 'faith communities' were located in Sea City, California: Coastal Christian Center (CCC), a classical Pentecostal church of the Assembly of God denomination; Light and Life Fellowship (L&L), a 'non-traditional' and

propriation of Pentecostal symbols. Albrecht is convinced that Pentecostal and charismatic worship services are designed to provide context for 'mystical encounter, an experience with the divine' that is 'mediated by the sense of the immediate divine presence',[196] a fact that would seem to subvert sacramental thought and practice. Moreover, he notes that in spite of the fact that Pentecostal churches traditionally have included a Communion table as a basic piece of the furniture defining the altar space, they have not focused on the sacrament of Communion,[197] and of the three churches Albrecht studied, only one actually made use of a Table, and then only for its monthly Eucharistic service.[198] Similarly, the baptismal font is in most Pentecostal/charismatic churches a 'minimized center' and baptism a relatively de-emphasized practice. Even though all three communities practice adult/believer's baptism, as well as 'Eucharistic communion', Albrecht notes that neither L&L nor VVCF has a baptistery. In spite of these evidences of de-emphasis or minimization of the sacraments, Albrecht insists that Pentecostal/charismatic churches are in some sense sacramental. In his words, in spite of the fact that Pentecostals and charismatics 'seldom use the sacramental language, they certainly believe and experience their God's gracious acts'.[199] Pentecostal/charismatic sacramentality is unique, of course. For example, the 'manifestation of power' in divine healing and other 'sign and wonder' miracles function with a 'sacramental quality' for Pentecostals.[200]

Adam Ayers

In a *Pneuma* article published in 2000, Adam Ayers sets Pentecostal glossolalic phenomena under the lenses of boundary, art, and sacrament, subjecting the characteristic Pentecostal practice of speaking in tongues to 'theological light' in the hope of exposing persis-

---

'creative' community of the Foursquare denomination; and Valley Vineyard Christian Fellowship (VVCF), a charismatic church and a member of the Vineyard Christian fellowship.

[196] Daniel E. Albrecht, 'Pentecostal Spirituality: Looking Through the Lens of Ritual', *Pneuma* 14.2 (1996), p. 21.

[197] Albrecht, *Rites in the Spirit*, p. 132.

[198] Albrecht, *Rites in the Spirit*, p. 132.

[199] Albrecht, *Rites in the Spirit*, p. 132.

[200] Daniel E. Albrecht, 'Pentecostal Spirituality: Ecumenical Potential and Challenge', *Cyberjournal for Pentecostal-Charismatic Research* 2 (July 1997). Available online: http://www.pctii.org/cyberj/cyberj2/albrecht.html. Accessed January 5, 2011.

tent problems and 'to provide a pattern for pastoral address of the phenomenon of tongues in the day-to-day workings of the church'.[201] Throughout the article, Ayers leans heavily on Aquinas' explanation of the meaning and purpose of sacramental signs as given to accomplish simultaneously the proper worship of God and the gratuitous sanctification of human participants through a divinely-empowered move 'to the unknown by means of the unknown'. He holds that the sacraments recognized by the Church are, as Thomas says, 'ordained of God to the production of a spiritual effect'. However, any 'body' that can be moved 'to produce a spiritual effect' can serve as an instrument of grace, that is, it can serve sacramentally, even if it is not ecclesially recognized as one of the ordained sacraments. As Ayers understands him, Aquinas claims that a 'spiritual, sacramental work of grace is present when a sign ordained by God is employed, "arousing the mind of man"', and whenever this arousal 'involves a reflexive aspect of the human being's grasp of the sacred significance of his actions'.[202] In the light of this Thomistic understanding, then, Ayers believes that the Pentecostal experience of glossolalic speech *can* rightly be called sacramental, exactly as Macchia has suggested. In Ayer's own words,

> Applied to tongues, this would mean that tongues becomes an occasion for a work of grace, arousing the mind of a human being toward God in a certain relational configuration. Its value would not necessarily involve a linguistic situation, although it could. Instead, its value would be that it leads its subject to understanding "from the known to the unknown" by providing for its utterer an avenue through which to grasp the sacred implications of his or her own actions.[203]

He also finds it significant that the Eucharist, like glossolalia, is described in 1 Corinthians as a source of both potential blessing *and* judgment. He concludes that given the 'verifying and validating function of tongues' in both Lukan and Pauline texts, 'it would

---

[201] Adam Ayers, 'Can the Behavior of Tongues Utterance Still Function as Ecclesial Boundary? The Significance of Art and Sacrament', *Pneuma* 22.2 (Fall 2000), pp. 271-301 (273).

[202] Ayers, 'Can the Behavior of Tongues Utterance Still Function as Ecclesial Boundary', pp. 293-94.

[203] Ayers, 'Can the Behavior of Tongues Utterance Still Function as Ecclesial Boundary', p. 294.

seem that, to the early church and to the author of Acts, tongues is perhaps even more distinctly ordained of God than even ritual water baptism'. He wonders: If the (universal) church thinks of baptism as sacramental, then how much more glossolalic speech?[204]

Amos Yong

Amos Yong, a licensed Assemblies of God minister and now J. Rodman Williams Professor of Theology at Regent University (Virginia Beach, VA), has engaged sacramental theology on a variety of fronts. In one of his early works, Yong implores Pentecostals not to take up the 'sacramental baggage' of the Catholic tradition, such as the doctrine of *ex opera operato,* even while they find common ground with Catholics in understanding the Pentecostal experience of the Spirit as in some sense sacramental.[205] In his monograph on theological hermeneutics, published a few years later, Yong engages Peirce's theory of signs to describe the various ways in which the Lord's Supper conveys meaning for Christian celebrants.[206] Acknowledging the diversity of thought and practice in the various Christian traditions – on the one hand, sacramentalists contend that the experienced encouragement results directly from eating and drinking the Eucharistic elements, while on the other hand, nonsacramentalists argue that the grace received comes only *indirectly* through the bread and wine via the community's 'remembering, celebrating, and anticipating of Jesus' life, death, and parousia'[207] – Yong maintains the conviction that in spite of these real differences, 'the *result* [of sharing in Communion] is encouragement for Christian life'.[208] This basic agreement should be taken seriously, Yong believes. He finds that Pentecostal and charismatic experience of the sacraments is rich with meaning, for Pentecostal ritual is 'supremely embodied' and possessed of its own logic of sacramentality.[209] He insists that a comprehensive theology of the sacraments

[204] Ayers, 'Can the Behavior of Tongues Utterance Still Function as Ecclesial Boundary', p. 294.

[205] Amos Yong, *Discerning the Spirit(s): A Pentecostal-Charismatic Contribution to Christian Theology of Religions* (JPTSup 20; Sheffield: Sheffield Academic Press, 2000), p. 166.

[206] Amos Yong, *Spirit-Word-Community: Theological Hermeneutics in Trinitarian Perspective* (Eugene, OR: Wipf & Stock, 2002), pp. 202-203.

[207] Yong, *Spirit-Word-Community*, p. 250.

[208] Yong, *Spirit-Word-Community*, p. 249-50. Emphasis added.

[209] Yong, *Spirit-Word-Community*, p. 250.

must emerge not only from 'reflection on the scriptural witness', but also from reflection on the church's *'actual experience ...* throughout history'.[210] What is more, exegesis of biblical texts is not the *only* task, even if it is the primary one. As he sees it, an authentically Pentecostal theology of the Eucharist must derive 'as much, if not more, from our ritual experiences of it than from consultation of the biblical texts'.[211]

More recently (2005), in his *Spirit Poured Out On All Flesh*, a monograph in which Yong attempts to develop and articulate a 'global Pentecostal theology', he calls for Pentecostals and charismatics to adopt a view of the rites of water baptism and Holy Communion that is more in keeping both with the Scripture and the early church fathers, as well as more properly fitted to an understanding of the Spirit's power of presence.[212] He believes that in spite of what one might expect, Pentecostal/charismatics can appropriate a 'fully sacramental' view of both water baptism and the Lord's Supper, a view that nevertheless remains 'fully consistent with Pentecostal intuitions regarding the Spirit's presence and activity in the worshipping community'.[213] To be sure, he maintains that Pentecostals should not regard the sacraments in 'the classical sense', whereby salvation is *'mediated through* the priesthood, through baptism, or through the (other) sacraments'.[214] Nonetheless, the 'Spirit's reality' can and should be understood as in fact 'mediated through the particularly embodied experiences of the community of saints'. When so understood, one finds a 'unique sort of pentecostal sacramentality at work' that operates with an 'experiential and incarnational logic that acknowledges the Spirit's being made present and active through the materiality of personal embodiment and congregational life'.[215] For example, Yong asserts that the rite of water baptism is not merely memorialistic or symbolic, but actually 'enacts our participation in the death and resurrection of Christ' and as a 'concrete act in a historical point in time' serves as the 'means by which we experience the life of Jesus by the Holy

---

[210] Emphasis added.

[211] Yong, *Spirit-Word-Community*, p. 250.

[212] Amos Yong, *The Spirit Poured Out On All Flesh: Pentecostalism and the Possibility of Global Theology* (Grand Rapids: Baker, 2005), p. 162.

[213] Yong, *The Spirit Poured Out On All Flesh*, p. 160.

[214] Yong, *The Spirit Poured Out on All Flesh*, p. 136. Emphasis added.

[215] Yong, *The Spirit Poured Out on All Flesh*, p. 136.

Spirit'.[216] The baptism ritual is, on Yong's view, an act of 'obedient participation in the death of Jesus'. He is careful to say that the sacramentality of the rite resides not in the 'materiality of consecrated water' but in the Holy Spirit's personal presence and activity.[217] Water baptism, Yong insists, is not to be regarded as 'magically washing away sins', but it can and should be regarded as regenerative – insofar as it is understood to effect the Spirit's work 'pneumatically and mystically', and to include the 'faith response of believers'.[218]

As with water baptism, so with the Eucharist: the personal and intimate activity of the Holy Spirit is central and decisive. Only the Spirit's perlocutionary and illocutionary power guarantees that the Lord's Supper is indeed a genuine 'remembering' of the church's memory of Christ. In the Lord's Supper, Christ is present to the celebrants and they are present to Christ, their 'mutual presence' possibilized by the Spirit being 'invited to reign over the Supper' in the *epiklesis*. For only the Spirit's coming in response to the church's invocation 'mak[es] present the living Christ in the "membered" elements of the bread and cup and in the "members" of the congregation as the living body of Christ'.[219] Yong holds that Pentecostals and charismatics have no *need* for a doctrine of transubstantiation, for everything depends upon the Spirit-possibilized 'inter-subjective mutuality' between Christ and the believing community, a mutuality that, by the Spirit's power, 'becomes a mysterious interpersonal encounter wherein Christ and his body are brought into real relationship'.[220] Given that this is so, the Supper must be regarded as a 'sacramental rite' that in fact 'transforms the worshipping community through word and Spirit'.[221]

Yong includes a treatment of Eucharist and water baptism also in his *Theology and Down Syndrome*, published in 2007. He examines the ways in which the sacraments serve the disabled and diseased, suggesting that one might say that those with intellectual disabilities are '*more attuned* to the sacramentality of the Eucharistic elements at an intuitive and material level' because they are not limited by a

---

216 Yong, *The Spirit Poured Out on All Flesh*, p. 159.
217 Yong, *The Spirit Poured Out on All Flesh*, p. 158.
218 Yong, *The Spirit Poured Out on All Flesh*, p. 158.
219 Yong, *The Spirit Poured Out on All Flesh*, pp. 162-63.
220 Yong, *The Spirit Poured Out on All Flesh*, p. 164.
221 Yong, *The Spirit Poured Out on All Flesh*, p. 163.

merely or dominantly cognitivist approach to the sacrament.[222] To illustrate this point, Yong cites the testimony of a woman named Judy, who suffers from Down Syndrome: 'I want to eat Jesus bread … I can't wait until I eat Jesus bread and Jesus juice. People who love Jesus are the ones who eat Jesus bread … I want to eat it and drink with all the other Christians at church cause I love him so'.[223]

Throughout his work, Yong emphasizes the relation of the Word of God to the sacrament of the Lord's Supper. The rite of Communion is, in his words, a 'physical act wherein the word of God is consumed by the body of Christ through the working of the Spirit'.[224] Also, in the (faithful) Eucharistic celebration, the church anticipates the end-of-all-things 'embodiment of the word of God'.[225] He agrees with the Eastern Orthodox traditions that claim the Spirit both 'recapitulates' the past and proleptically anticipates the future Kingdom, ushering both the past and the future into the present experience of the church gathered at the Table. The Lord's Supper, then, is rightly regarded as the sign par excellence of the eschatological kingdom. Further, the Eucharist is a *pharmakon*, and insofar as celebrants faithfully 'internalize the body and blood of Christ' they 'release its healing virtues for broken bodies'.[226] Pentecostals, given their belief that healing is 'in the atonement', should not find it difficult to accept this proposal. If they can believe that healing power and the gift of the Holy Spirit can be and are given and received through 'material means', such as handkerchiefs, aprons, the laying on of hands, then why would they refuse to accept that the Spirit can work through the Eucharistic elements? Why not accept that 'the material elements of bread and wine or juice somehow mediate the presence of Christ by the power of the Spirit'?[227]

Kenneth J. Archer

Ken Archer, a systematician and ordained minister in the Church of God (Cleveland, TN), believes – with John Christopher Thomas,

---

[222] Amos Yong, *Theology and Down Syndrome: Reimagining Disability in Late Modernity* (Waco, TX: Baylor University Press, 2007), p. 211.
[223] Yong, *Theology and Down Syndrome*, p. 193.
[224] Yong, *The Spirit Poured Out on All Flesh*, p. 163.
[225] Yong, *The Spirit Poured Out on All Flesh*, p. 165.
[226] Yong, *The Spirit Poured Out on All Flesh*, p. 163.
[227] Yong, *The Spirit Poured Out on All Flesh*, p. 163.

Frank Macchia, Steve Land and others – that Pentecostal theology so far has failed to account for the meaning of the ordinances in actual Pentecostal practice, and sets out to put an alternative view on the table.[228] In his words, 'The concept of "ordinances" must be re-visioned because in Pentecostal worshipping communities these rites provide sacramental experiences for the faith-filled participants'.[229] For Archer, Pentecostal spirituality is essentially *storied*, so that a genuinely Pentecostal theology of the 'sacramental ordinances' must fit within the framework of the Pentecostal *via salutis*,[230] a meta-narrative Archer infers from the 'Full Gospel' schema of early Pentecostalism: Jesus is savior, sanctifier, Spirit baptizer, healer, and soon-coming king. Influenced by Stanley Grenz's assertion that Evangelicals must retain the understanding of the rites of water baptism and the Lord's Supper as 'ordinances' while allowing that they function as 'channels' for the Spirit's work, Archer suggests that Pentecostals take up the language of 'sacramental ordinances', in the hope that this language will help Pentecostals to hold together various emphases in a dynamic tension. With Macchia, he finds it unfortunate that 'some Pentecostals deny any "real grace" being "mediated" through the ordinances'.[231] Such a reductionist treatment of the ordinances, he laments, truncates the 'mysteries', diminishing them to 'mere memorial rites' that facilitate nothing more than 'cognitive reflection devoid of the Spirit's presence and power'.[232] He hopes that the Pentecostal understanding of the ordinances will discern the 'mystical significance' that will transform them into sacraments in and through which believers not only communicate but also participate in the realities of the Kingdom. These sacraments are not mere ordinances.[233] But he does not want Pentecostals to fall into 'traditional' sacramentalism, either. To retain the language of 'ordinance' helps to underscore the symbolic power of the sacraments, and keeps attention on the dominical mandate as well.

---

[228] Kenneth J. Archer, 'Nourishment for our Journey: The Pentecostal *Via Salutis* and Sacramental Ordinances', *JPT* 13.1 (2004), pp. 79-96.

[229] Archer, 'Nourishment for our Journey', p. 85.

[230] Archer, 'Nourishment for our Journey', p. 81.

[231] Archer, 'Nourishment for our Journey', p. 84.

[232] Archer, 'Nourishment for our Journey', p. 84.

[233] Archer, 'Nourishment for our Journey', p. 96.

Archer follows John Christopher Thomas' identification of the five-fold gospel as the 'unifying ground' for the sacraments. He believes Thomas rightly identifies five sacramental practices that correspond to the five-fold's several tenets, and in a 2004 article he attempts to develop this scheme in detail. First, he holds that water baptism, which 'proclaims one's new identity with Jesus' and signals the believer's entrance into the holy community and the *via salutis*, serves as the sacramental sign of the *salvation* only Jesus accomplishes. Second, footwashing, a 'ceremony of cleansing', is the sacramental activity that corresponds to the experience of *sanctification*, which is an experience subsequent to conversion – another way station, so to speak, along the way in the journey of salvation.[234] Third, in dialogue with Macchia's proposals, Archer finds that *Spirit baptism* is indeed a sacramental experience, with glossolalic speech signifying and expressing the 'mystical experience of union with and participation in God's triune being'.[235] Fourth, the imposition of hands and anointing with oil serve as the sacramental sign of divine *healing*.[236] Fifth, and finally, the Lord's Supper is the sacramental event that directs believers' attention to the *coming of Christ* and his kingdom.[237]

William De Arteaga

In his *Forgotten Power*, published in 2002, William De Arteaga, a priest ordained in the Communion of Evangelical Episcopal Churches, argues for the centrality of the Lord's Supper in the history of 'revival' in North America and Western Europe. His argument is both descriptively and prescriptively advanced, as he gives wide and deep attention to 'revivals' in which the sacraments, and in particular the Eucharist, operated center stage. He insists again and again that the sacraments can and should remain central to Christian spirituality, and that they do not hinder but in fact advance the Spirit's reviving work. He admits that not all charismatic 'breakthroughs' have been sacramental. In fact, many contemporary revivalists discern no connection between the sacramental practices and the work of the Spirit, if they give any thought to it at all. As he sees it, the contemporary mind deems the liturgical and sacramental

---

[234] Archer, 'Nourishment for our Journey', p. 92.
[235] Archer, 'Nourishment for our Journey', p. 93.
[236] Archer, 'Nourishment for our Journey', p. 93.
[237] Archer, 'Nourishment for our Journey', p. 95.

practices as at best incidental to revival, and at worst, inimical to it. He identifies the events of the so-called Second Great Awakening, and the prominent ministries of evangelists like Charles G. Finney and Dwight L. Moody, as the culprits in the unmaking of the sacramental dimension of revival. American Wesleyans, who had been staunchly sacramental, eventually surrendered to the 'temptation of respectability' and quickly the 'Spirit-empowered sacrament' was a thing of the past. To put it briefly, after the revivalism shaped by Finney and Moody, among others, had taken its toll, 'the Wesleyan mix of evangelical preaching, small-group discipleship, sacramental worship, and personal ministry to the poor unraveled'.[238] After the success of Moody in perfecting Finney's innovations, revival was no longer in any way associated with the traditional sacraments. 'Since then no major evangelist has incorporated the Lord's Supper as part of the revival cycle.'[239]

In spite of the successes of non-sacramental revivalists such as Finney and Moody of the 19th century, and Graham in the 20th century – to say nothing of the successes of the Pentecostal/Charismatic movements – De Arteaga avers that the church should strive for a 'balance of Word, sacrament, and presence'.[240] Rather than seeing the ritual observance of Communion with its attending liturgy as a possible barrier to the dynamic and spontaneous nature of revival, De Arteaga believes that 'the covenant presence of God's graces during sacramental worship reinforces the Holy Spirit's special presence and work during the revival period'.[241] Sacramental worship, he says, 'enhances, sustains, and strengthens revivals', a claim he finds evidence for biblically, the 'biblical pattern of revival', and historically, in the communion cycles of the 17th century Scottish Reformed Church and the Wesleyan revivals of the 18th and 19th century.

John Ceresoli

In 1999, at the 28th annual meeting of the Society for Pentecostal Studies,[242] John Ceresoli, a member of the Church of God of

---

238 William De Arteaga, *Forgotten Power: The Significance of the Lord's Supper in Revival* (Grand Rapids: Zondervan, 2002), p. 209.

239 De Arteaga, *Forgotten Power*, p. 213.

240 De Arteaga, *Forgotten Power*, p. 13.

241 De Arteaga, *Forgotten Power*, p. 13.

242 Held that year in Springfield, MO.

Prophecy, testified of a recent sacramental experience in his home congregation, a testimony that was transcripted, and later edited and published in the *Journal of Pentecostal Theology*.[243] Ceresoli recounts how despite the fact that the church officials were at first hesitant, he had convinced them that they should invite a local Catholic priest, Father Phil Thibodeau, to worship with them. The fact that Father Phil had experienced the baptism of the Spirit and 'speaking in tongues' helped to make the connection for them, so after much deliberation, they invited him to deliver the Sunday morning sermon. They had hoped to share Communion with him, given the Catholic emphasis on the Eucharist; however, Father Phil's holy orders would not allow this. After some discussion, it was decided that Father Phil would be invited to join them and the congregations in an 'old fashioned footwashing service'[244] as a sacramental observance. Father Phil expressed some serious concern with replacing the Communion meal with footwashing, but in the end he gladly accepted the invitation. Ceresoli finds it remarkable that in spite of the fact that 'Pentecostals have been criticized for the infrequency and inadequacy of their Eucharistic observance' it was precisely because of this lack, this 'area of weakness and perhaps ignorance', that room was made for something 'new'. As he says, 'the Holy Ghost was working to bring forth something new – an ecumenical experience through sacramental means. Our Pentecostal 'weakness' made room for the freedom of the Spirit to birth a new thing'. Father Phil was, in a sense, 'limited by holy rites'. While the Pentecostal community, 'with its simplicity and with its deep sense of what it feels like to be excluded from the mainstream of Christian history and traditions', sought for a way to include Father Phil in their worship service. 'This one "lost sheep" should not be turned away from full inclusion in the holy gathering, but a way should be found for him to join in the worship in its totality.' When the time came, Father Phil delivered the sermon, sharing his testimony as well as a few scriptural exhortations. Pastor Black then came to the front and invited the district overseer to join him, Fa-

---

[243] John Ceresoli, 'Critical Mass: "We Had Church" in a Holy Catholic Way', *JPT* 17 (October 2000), pp. 7-11.

[244] Ceresoli explains that this decision was made after a lengthy discussion of John Christopher Thomas' work on footwashing and Frank Macchia's response to that work.

ther Phil, and Ceresoli to join him. Spontaneously, 'crying, weeping, praying, and tongues poured forth', he says, 'yielding a broken, repentant spirit that led us to sense the deep need for reconciliation and forgiveness between these two communities'.[245] During the footwashing observance, a message in tongues was given.

> The entire congregation erupted with groanings and weepings of repentance ... After a moment of silence, Father Phil wept and hugged Brother Summerall's neck (the southern Pentecostal, sacramental sign of hugging). He then asked the Pentecostal Church to forgive the Catholics for the ridicule, persecution, and ignorance they have had toward Pentecostals. The entire sanctuary became a sanctuary of love, peace, repentance, and forgiveness'.[246]

Simon Chan

Simon Chan, a theological historian, liturgist, and Professor of Systematic Theology at Trinity Theological College in Singapore, argues that Pentecostals need to re-vision their ecclesiology, and that this can only be done by, among other things, a reconsideration of the place of the sacraments in the church's liturgical and missional life. 'Only a proper theology of the sacraments and pneumatology can overcome the tendency to turn church services into what Gordon Fee calls "a thousand individual experiences of worship."'[247] Chan is convinced that Pentecostals have much to learn from the sacramental traditions, perhaps especially the Eastern Orthodox, whose worship finds its anchor and axis in the Eucharist.[248]

In the Pentecostal experience of Spirit baptism, Chan discerns a distinct and in some sense 'new' experience of God.[249] For, he believes, '[s]ome kind of doctrine specifying the experiential distinctiveness of Spirit baptism is needed for the long-term survival of the Pentecostal-charismatic reality'.[250] Also, the Pentecostal emphasis on 'subsequence', even if it is 'too simplistic a way of encapsulat-

---

[245] Ceresoli, 'Critical Mass', p. 10.
[246] Ceresoli, 'Critical Mass', p. 11.
[247] Chan, *Pentecostal Theology and the Christian Spiritual Tradition*, p. 15.
[248] Chan, *Pentecostal Theology and the Christian Spiritual Tradition*, pp. 37-38, 107-108.
[249] Chan, *Pentecostal Theology and the Christian Spiritual Tradition*, p. 90.
[250] Chan, *Pentecostal Theology and the Christian Spiritual Tradition*, p. 92.

ing the complex realities within the Christian growth process',[251] should not be abandoned, even while Pentecostals attempt to refine a clearer and more theologically sound articulation of its significance. He believes that a *sacramental* understanding of Spirit baptism, informed by sources of the classical Christian tradition, can help in this regard. To this end, Chan proposes that Pentecostals understand Spirit baptism as the 'actualization' of the sacrament of water baptism',[252] as a distinct 'part of the complex of conversion-initiation', and not a mere *superadditum*.[253] To accomplish this, Chan insists that Pentecostals need to do work on two fronts at once: on the one side, they need to rethink the doctrine of subsequence, which has to this point suffered from the fact that the early Pentecostals received uncritically the Evangelical concept of conversion as a one-off 'crisis experience' and uncritically applied the concept to Spirit baptism so that it was described simply as another of several crisis experiences;[254] on the other side, as already mentioned, Pentecostals need for their own sake to engage with the church's wider theological and spiritual tradition, finding better language for their experience.

The driving force of Chan's project is his concern for 'traditioning', for without this, Pentecostals 'cannot ensure that what they have experienced will be faithfully handed down to the next generation'.[255] What is the best way to guarantee the faithful handing-on of the Pentecostal experience and perspective? A liturgy that finds its center in the Eucharist, Chan believes, promises to do this work best, for 'all the basic elements and dimensions of worship find their proper place' in the Eucharistic celebration, and it 'unites both the charismatic and the evangelical dimensions of worship into a coherent whole'.[256] Without a Eucharistic center and ground, the characteristic charismatic and evangelical forms of worship are 'impoverished' and reductionistic. Pentecostals can and should avoid this error. With this goal in mind, Chan avows that '[i]f Pentecostals would learn to appropriate the "practice" of Eucharistic worship they will be better equipped to preserve both Spirit and word,

---

[251] Chan, *Pentecostal Theology and the Christian Spiritual Tradition*, p. 93.
[252] Chan, *Pentecostal Theology and the Christian Spiritual Tradition*, p. 71.
[253] Chan, *Pentecostal Theology and the Christian Spiritual Tradition*, p. 71.
[254] Chan, *Pentecostal Theology and the Christian Spiritual Tradition*, p. 87.
[255] Chan, *Pentecostal Theology and the Christian Spiritual Tradition*, p. 20.
[256] Chan, *Pentecostal Theology and the Christian Spiritual Tradition*, p. 38.

praise and proclamation in their distinctively Pentecostal way of life'.[257] The original Pentecostal event (narratively described in Acts 2) determined the church as a charismatic community, he says, and this reality is continually renewed 'as the Spirit is called upon in the [Eucharistic] *epiclesis*'. In this way, he believes, the charismatic dimensions of worship are made viable. The 'evangelical dimension', which emphasizes proclamation of the *kerygma,* is preserved, too, for the Eucharist proclaims this message in its own way – and does more than this, besides.[258]

In other, more recent works, Chan addresses the wider Evangelical community, engaging with Pentecostalism indirectly. In his *Liturgical Theology,* published in 2006, he argues that Evangelical ecclesiology is diseased, if not altogether dead, and proposes an alternative view of the church as a missional community, indeed, as the community privileged with participation in the *missio dei,* so that the church's work is understood to be 'the extension of the work of the triune God'.[259] The church fulfills this mission in and through her worship, so that the liturgy gives shape to and provides the energy for her life vis-à-vis the world. Again, as he had done in *Pentecostal Theology,* Chan affirms the celebration of the Eucharist as the heart of the church's liturgy. Especially in the Eucharistic celebrations, believers 'are entering the life of Christ', and through the Sacrament the church is constituted as Christ's body. This is why in the church's tradition the Lord's Supper is called the 'sacrament of sacraments'.[260] Hence, Chan insists it is serious a mistake to consider the Eucharist optional, as a mere supplement to the preached Word that the church may take or leave without consequence.[261] In his judgment, the Eucharist is the 'most distinctive mark of ecclesial existence between the ascension and the parousia'.[262]

In keeping with the Eastern Orthodox tradition, Chan regards the Eucharist as a mediation of the church's past and future: the kingdom's 'already' and 'not yet' merge in the here-and-now moment of the church's feast. As he says, it is in the Eucharistic wor-

---

[257] Chan, *Pentecostal Theology and the Christian Spiritual Tradition,* p. 38.
[258] Chan, *Pentecostal Theology and the Christian Spiritual Tradition,* p. 38.
[259] Simon Chan, *Liturgical Theology: The Church as Worshipping Community* (Downers Grove, IL: IVP, 2006), p. 72.
[260] Chan, *Liturgical Theology,* p. 71.
[261] Chan, *Liturgical Theology,* p. 65.
[262] Chan, *Liturgical Theology,* p. 37.

ship of the church, that 'the Spirit actualizes the past through re-membrance (*anamnesis*) and anticipates the future (*prolepsis*) when created things are transfigured'.[263] In the celebration of Holy Communion, then, the church both remembers in loving faith Christ and his saving life, death, and resurrection, appropriating the benefits, and anticipates in loving hope his *parousia,* the final and complete establishment of God's promised kingdom. The experience of 'feeding on Christ to life eternal' in the Eucharistic rite, Chan believes, is nothing less than 'a *foretaste* of the future: the marriage supper of the Lamb, the healing of a broken creation, reconciliation and face-to-face communion'.[264] The church is the community who exists to call for 'the coming of the Spirit as the *arrabon* (the foretaste or pledge) of the new creation'. Evangelicals, regrettably, often lose sight of this reality, a mistake Pentecostals cannot afford to make.[265]

As a Pentecostal, Chan emphasizes the Spirit's work in the celebration of the Supper, specifically, and in the liturgy, generally. In fact, for him the Spirit's role in the church's worship remains always primary and basic. Worshippers never initiate; that prerogative belongs only to God, and in particular, to the Holy Spirit. Even the church's invocation of and response to the Spirit's initiative is 'made possible by the indwelling Spirit'.[266] Not only that, but Spirit-inspired communion is the issue and not the doctrine of 'Real Presence', a teaching which Chan believes encourages individual piety but does nothing to stimulate the church's communion.[267]

MayLing Tan-Chow

In her 2007 monograph on Pentecostal theology, which began as a Cambridge University PhD thesis, MayLing Tan-Chow brings Scripture and early Pentecostal spirituality to bear in a critique of a Singaporean charismatic movement. She notes that worship, not preaching or the Eucharist, holds place of primacy in Pentecostalism – as Albrecht indicates, the altar space, and not the pulpit or the Communion table, is the place of meeting the divine.[268] However,

---

[263] Chan, *Liturgical Theology*, p. 37.
[264] Chan, *Liturgical Theology*, p. 37.
[265] Chan, *Liturgical Theology*, p. 37.
[266] Chan, *Liturgical Theology*, p. 74.
[267] Chan, *Liturgical Theology*, p. 71.
[268] Albrecht, *Rites in the Spirit*, p. 132.

she sees Pentecostal worship as emerging from a creative blend of both sacramental and biblicist traditions.[269] The participative orientation of Pentecostal worship, the expectation and experience of charismatic ministry in 'signs and wonders' are, she says, 'obviously sacramental'.[270] In fact, Pentecostal worship in its entirety can be called 'feasting', for it is 'a prelude to and a rehearsal of the feast of Heaven – the marriage supper of the Lamb, the messianic feast'.[271] In a sense, then, the Eucharist is a microcosm of the larger reality of the Pentecostal participation in and experience of God in worship.

Wesley Scott Biddy

Wesley Scott Biddy's article, 'Re-envisioning the Pentecostal Understanding of the Eucharist: An Ecumenical Proposal', emerged from his work on his Master's thesis, submitted to the faculty of Duke Divinity School in 2005. In the *Pneuma* article, he begins with a question: Is there in fact anything like a distinctly Pentecostal theology of the sacraments?[272] He answers in the affirmative, although he admits that Pentecostal sacramentality is 'largely undeveloped' and acknowledges that Pentecostals remain wary of 'high church' liturgies that they deem 'frozen by an excessive formality that restricts God's freedom to encounter and bless the faithful'.[273] He nonetheless stands convinced that there are 'resources latent in Pentecostal spirituality' for developing a 'conscious theological appreciation of the sacramental character of worship in general, and of those ecclesial rituals that have historically been explicitly recognized as "sacraments" in particular'.[274] Therefore, it is possible, he believes, for a 'distinctively Pentecostal sacramentology' to bubble up from Pentecostal theological reflection on Pentecostal practice and experi-

---

[269] MayLing Tan-Chow, *Pentecostal Theology for the Twenty-First Century: Engaging with Multi-Faith Singapore* (Aldershot, UK: Ashgate, 2007), p. 143.

[270] Tan-Chow, *Pentecostal Theology for the Twenty-First Century*, p. 143.

[271] Tan-Chow, *Pentecostal Theology for the Twenty-First Century*, pp. 153-54.

[272] Wesley Scott Biddy, 'Re-envisioning the Pentecostal Understanding of the Eucharist: An Ecumenical Proposal', *Pneuma* 28.2 (Fall 2006), pp. 228-51 (228). Biddy's concern is largely ecumenical. He is seeking a way in which a distinctly Pentecostal view of the Eucharist might 'aid doctrinal rapprochement' with other Christian traditions.

[273] Biddy, 'Re-envisioning the Pentecostal Understanding of the Eucharist', p. 230.

[274] Biddy, 'Re-envisioning the Pentecostal Understanding of the Eucharist', p. 228.

ence,[275] as evidenced in Frank Macchia's proposal regarding the sacramental dimensions of glossolalia and the discussion that has sprung up in response.

Although Biddy is convinced that Pentecostals cannot accept the idea that the sacraments effect the forgiveness of sins, as is taught in 'high church' traditions, he finds in the characteristic Pentecostal belief in subsequence – i.e. in second and third 'blessings' of sanctification and Spirit baptism – a way to revision the sacraments along new lines. When this is discerned, it is no longer necessary for Pentecostals to resist the idea of 'sacramental grace'. Pentecostal spirituality, at least as Biddy sees it, is constituted by encounter with the divine reality 'in, with, and under *signs*'.[276] He notes that at least two of the tenets of the five-fold gospel explicitly involve signs (i.e. Holy Spirit baptism signified by glossolalia and divine healing signified by anointing and laying on of hands), and that these signs together point toward the fifth tenet (i.e. Christ as coming King), and so function as eschatological signs, too. It follows, then, that a genuinely Pentecostal sacramentology might begin with an account of sacraments as 'events of a divine-human *encounter* that take place through *symbols*'.[277]

Biddy allows that in the name of 'biblical purism' one may say Christ did *not* promise to be present to his church 'in any special way at the Eucharist'. Nevertheless, he maintains that the biblicists' rejection of 'special Eucharistic presence' as nothing more than a Catholic accretion to the pure gospel of the New Testament church is both theologically and historically mistaken, not least because it fails to account for the fact that in the ancient world sharing a meal was understood as a deeply spiritual and even supernatural event. He cites Paul's forbiddance of the Corinthians' participation in the pagan ritual meals (1 Cor. 10.14-22) as an illuminating example. The logic of Paul's argument there demonstrates that 'if a person participates in the expression, he or she necessarily thereby becomes a

---

[275] Biddy, 'Re-envisioning the Pentecostal Understanding of the Eucharist', p. 228.

[276] In making this difference, Biddy is dependent on Tillich's distinction of *sign* (as something which does not bear any 'necessary relation' to that to which it points) from *symbol* (as something which does 'participate in the reality for which it stands').

[277] Biddy, 'Re-envisioning the Pentecostal Understanding of the Eucharist', p. 231. Emphasis added.

participant in the reality, for the reality is both enabled by supernatural means (whether the agents be God or demons) and concretely effected by the sign'.[278] Unmistakably, this understanding of the meal is deep with sacramental significance, and perhaps provides a clue to how it is that Christian sacramental theology developed.[279]

Kimberly Ervin Alexander

In her award-winning work on Pentecostal models of healing, Kimberly Alexander, at the time an Associate Professor of Historical Theology at the Church of God (Cleveland, TN) Pentecostal Theological Seminary, shows that early Pentecostal spirituality was undergirded by a rich (if non-traditional) sacramentality. As evidence, she points to certain characteristic Pentecostal practices such the use of anointed handkerchiefs for healing,[280] and the laying on of hands, a gesture that she contends signifies the 'transference of the Spirit from one believer to the next, or from God through another believer'.[281] More than rote obedience to an 'ordinance', therefore, 'the action [of laying on of hands in prayer for the sick] was fraught with anticipation of the inbreaking of God's grace and gifts'. Quite simply, these Pentecostals believed healing would come '*through* human touch',[282] a conviction that perhaps betrays an underlying sacramentality.

Alexander shows that the Lord's Supper was regarded and experienced by early Pentecostal as a means of healing. The Communion rite served as a remembrance of 'two-fold salvation', that is, spiritual and physical. She cites the words of William Seymour to make the point: '[Christ] gave His blood for the salvation of our souls and He gave a perfect body for these imperfect bodies of ours'. She explains that early Pentecostals believed the Lord's body

---

[278] Biddy, 'Re-envisioning the Pentecostal Understanding of the Eucharist', p. 233.

[279] Biddy, 'Re-envisioning the Pentecostal Understanding of the Eucharist', p. 233. Biddy also points out that in spite of the fact that Paul has exposed many of the Corinthians' sins, it is *only* the sin regarding the perversion of the Eucharist that leads to this warning about sickness and death.

[280] Alexander, *Pentecostal Healing*, p. 206. According to Alexander, the early Pentecostals also used the Bible in a similar way, and some readers used even periodicals as an 'anointing medium' for healing.

[281] Alexander, *Pentecostal Healing*, p. 206.

[282] Alexander, *Pentecostal Healing*, p. 207. Emphasis added.

was to be eaten[283] not only for healing, but also for *health*,[284] and she notes that 1 Cor. 11.30 was commonly taken to mean that those who do not take the Lord's Supper rightly are in danger of falling ill, or at least of not being healed of their sicknesses. One early Assemblies of God writer referred to the 'divine alchemy' of the Supper, and another said that the way to experience 'abundance of Life' was through 'eating Christ's flesh and drinking His blood', for by doing this, believers 'partake of a powerful, efficacious stimulant, an elixir from the Throne'.[285] However, some warned that an overemphasis on healing in the Supper might detract attention from the Lord, 'the benefit eclipsing the benefactor'.[286]

Keith Warrington

In his recently published *Pentecostal Theology* (2008), the British Pentecostal theologian Keith Warrington explains that Pentecostals share with the wider Christian community a belief in the central practices of water baptism and the Lord's Supper. He makes it clear, however, that Pentecostals do not understand these 'ordinances' in the same way as do most other Christian traditions. He believes that Pentecostals fear ritualism and ceremonialism, generally, and sacramentalism, particularly, because they suspect that it implies a 'self-inducing power'.[287] Prescriptively, he identifies water baptism as a 'normative practice' that is 'expected of all believers as a sign of obedience to the command of Jesus'. In this, Warrington maintains the familiar baptistic, Free Church position: the washing rite *follows* conversion, and is nothing more or less than a 'public affirmation of a previous integration into the family of God at salvation', although it may also provide an *experience* of affirmation and confirmation for the believer. He points out that occasionally those being baptized experience physical healing or Spirit baptism, so that it is possible to suggest that water baptism functions as a 'sacramental encounter' of some kind.[288] So far as he knows, few Pentecostals

---

[283] It is important to note that Pentecostals use this idiom of 'eating the Lord's body' both as a straightforward way of referring to eating the Eucharistic bread and in a more spiritual, mystical way, as well, often in the same context.

[284] Alexander, *Pentecostal Healing*, p. 77.

[285] Alexander, *Pentecostal Healing*, p. 169.

[286] Alexander, *Pentecostal Healing*, p. 169.

[287] Keith Warrington, *Pentecostal Theology: A Theology of Encounter* (London: T&T Clark, 2008), p. 161.

[288] Warrington, *Pentecostal Theology*, p. 163.

practice infant baptism,[289] but he acknowledges that Pentecostal theology and practice retains a 'flexibility' that allows church members 'to explore alternative views and to recognize the value of culture in one's hermeneutic'.[290] Against Hollenweger's claim that the Lord's Supper served as the 'central point of Pentecostal worship', Warrington holds that Pentecostal reflection on and attention to the Supper is modest, at most. He finds, following Bicknell, that Pentecostal Eucharistic faith and practice – inasmuch as it exists all – 'may be traced to the Reformation theology and practice of Zwingli and Calvin via Congregationalism and Brethren traditions'. Pentecostals expect to experience Christ's presence 'at any time', so they expect no special presence at the Lord's Table.[291] Further, Pentecostals staunchly resist the notions of transubstantiation of the elements and the communication of 'salvific grace' via the elements.[292]

In keeping with their rejection of many of the theological and liturgical trappings of the high-church traditions, Pentecostal observance of the rite of Communion, or 'the Breaking of Bread' as it is sometimes called, is marked by 'simplicity of form'. Following no written liturgy, the service nonetheless discloses a 'demonstrable pattern',[293] with participants taking time for 'reflection, thanksgiving and open worship, focusing on the death of Jesus, and the reading of one of the New Testament passages describing the event'. This often if not always means a 'bittersweet experience' for the communicants, so that the Communion service differs considerably from the standard form of Pentecostal worship, as it is 'often a quiet and even sober occasion'. He finds it distressing that within much of Western Pentecostalism the observance of Holy Communion is increasingly 'marginalized and swamped by singing'[294] so that it is no longer a central aspect of Pentecostal worship. Almost invariably, the observance of the Supper proves to be a 'personal and private event', even if it takes place in a congregational setting. Warrington worries that for many if not most Pentecostals 'the event has become so personalized that is value for reminding the participants that they are part of a body ... is overlooked or at least rou-

[289] Warrington cites only the Methodist Pentecostal Church of Chile.

[290] Warrington, *Pentecostal Theology*, p. 164.

[291] Warrington, *Pentecostal Theology*, pp. 166-67.

[292] Warrington, *Pentecostal Theology*, p. 168.

[293] Warrington, *Pentecostal Theology*, p. 165.

[294] Warrington, *Pentecostal Theology*, p. 169.

tinized'.[295] Nonetheless, age-old Pentecostal fears of formalism and ceremonialism stem from genuine concerns that must be kept in mind even while a 'fresh appreciation' and new forms of celebration are considered and implemented so that the Supper's 'vitalizing impact' is not lost.[296]

Gerald Emery

In a recent contribution to *Ecumenism* journal, an organ of the Canadian Centre for Ecumenism, Gerald Emery, a licensed minister in the Pentecostal Assemblies of Canada, attempts to show that Pentecostals retain a deep appreciation for the Holy Communion, a fact thick with ecumenical significance.[297] He holds that from the beginning of the movement the Lord's Supper has held 'an important place in the life of the local church', primarily because Pentecostals understand celebration of Holy Communion is first of all an act of *obedience* to dominical mandate.[298] Also, he finds that at the heart of Pentecostal Eucharistic practice is an emphasis on remembering Christ's passion: in the act of receiving the loaf and the cup, the believer 'remembers what makes him a Christian'. Nonetheless, taking part in Holy Communion is equally 'an act of faith for the present', as evidenced most clearly in the Pentecostal experience of real, spirit-to-spirit communion with Christ and the expectation of bodily healing in the Supper. These present-tense benefits are possible, Emery believes, because Christ

> remains the 'I Am' and although the divided elements are not more than and remain only bread and juice, the Lord's Supper leads us to recognize the privilege of living in the faith, living the words of Jesus when he says, 'I am with you always, until the end of the world'.[299]

Veli-Matti Kärkkäinen

Invited to contribute a chapter representing the Pentecostal view of the Lord's Supper, Pentecostal ecumenist Veli-Matti Kärkkäinen, Professor of Systematic Theology at Fuller University, explains that

---

[295] Warrington, *Pentecostal Theology*, p. 169.
[296] Warrington, *Pentecostal Theology*, p. 169.
[297] Gerald Emery, 'Holy Cene (Lord's Supper): Practice and Significance in the Pentecostal Tradition', *Ecumenism* 170 (Summer 2008), pp. 25-27.
[298] Emery, 'Holy Cene', p. 25.
[299] Emery, 'Holy Cene', p. 26

the Pentecostal movement is 'loaded with antisacramental sentiment',[300] with many Pentecostals simply dismissing the sacramentalism of other traditions as 'unscriptural'. His study indicates that
Pentecostals do not consider the rite of Communion constitutive of
the church, and they do not deem episcopal administration necessary to legitimate the sacrament. What is more, they prefer the term
'ordinance' to 'sacrament' because the latter term is freighted with
implied meanings Pentecostals simply find unacceptable. In his
judgment, the theology of the sacraments accepted by most Pentecostals is a form of the 'typical nonsacramental Zwinglian and free-
church view'; the Eucharistic wine and bread, therefore, are understood to have *only* symbolic reality.[301] Somewhat surprisingly, however, the Lord's Supper nevertheless plays an important role in the
churchly life of Pentecostals.[302] At least a few Pentecostals do affirm
a 'spiritual' dimension to the meal that exceeds the merely symbolic,
even while they reject the classical view of Real Presence.[303] For an
example, Kärkkäinen cites a statement by the Foursquare theologian Nathaniel van Cleave, who first repudiates the 'superstition' of
the classical view, but goes on to speak of the 'real operation of the
Spirit' for strengthening and healing those who partake of the elements in faith.[304]

Kärkkäinen acknowledges his initial surprise that the editors of
the volume invited Baptist and Pentecostal theologians to offer
separate contributions, given their considerable similarities. In his
judgment the idea of a distinctly Baptist or Pentecostal view of the
Lord's Supper sounds 'exotic', given that Pentecostals, like Baptists,
typically reject the sacraments altogether.[305] He finds that Olsen's

---

[300] Veli-Matti Kärkkäinen, 'The Pentecostal View' in Gordon T. Smith (ed.),
The Lord's Supper: Five Views (Downers Grove, IL: IVP, 2008), p. 118.

[301] Kärkkäinen, 'The Pentecostal View', p. 123.

[302] Kärkkäinen, 'The Pentecostal View', p. 130.

[303] Kärkkäinen, 'The Pentecostal View', p. 123.

[304] Kärkkäinen, 'The Pentecostal View', p. 119.

[305] Theologians from four other traditions offer responses to Kärkkäinen's
essay. The Baptist theologian Roger Olsen – who was himself raised a Pentecostal – remarks that the 'only change in my belief about and practice of the Lord's
Supper was with regard to the ordinance's efficacy for healing'. Seeing very little
difference between Pentecostal and Baptist views of the Eucharist, Olsen admits
that both traditions can, at *most*, accept '*semisacramental* interpretations' in which
'Christ is believed to be personally present in a special way as the church celebrates the ordinance'. He urges Pentecostals not to lose this commitment, for it
would not be 'true to its roots if it leaned too far toward sacramentalism', which

description fits Pentecostals in some ways as well as it does Baptists: 'What they have usually rejected is any idea that the grace of God is especially attached to these visible, physical objects or emblems'. Certainly, they did not believe participants 'actually eat Christ's body and drink his blood'. However, after reading Olsen's essay, Kärkkäinen finds that the two traditions do differ significantly,[306] with Pentecostals standing much nearer a sacramental understanding of the Lord's Supper and baptism than do Baptists.

Kärkkäinen is troubled that in spite of the fact that Pentecostals do in fact celebrate the Lord's Supper and practice baptism (and, in some movements, footwashing), they have to this point in the movement's history 'devoted little attention to developing any kind of constructive theology of sacraments in general or the Lord's Supper in particular'.[307] He celebrates the new generation of academic theologians endeavoring to work out a Pentecostal theology of the sacraments, although he suspects that these emerging voices 'cannot be taken as representative of grassroots Pentecostalism'. It seems clear, nonetheless, that he appreciates these new turns to the sacraments as beneficial for the Pentecostal tradition, and expects them to effect short- and long-term positive changes in and for Pentecostal praxis and theology.

Telford Work

For Telford Work, a Foursquare Pentecostal and ecumenical systematician, the sacraments are inseparable from the church's identity and mission. For him, the ecclesial communion is a 'land' whose border is crossed in baptism and whose culture and politics are signified in Communion.[308] The rite of baptism marks the end of a former way of life, as Eph. 4.22 suggests,[309] and the sacrament of the Eucharist reminds believers of their status as brothers and sisters in Christ and their attending responsibilities to one another. The celebration of the Lord's Supper also 'reminds us that Jesus the firstfruits from the dead has still gone before us to complete the

---

Olsen understands as regarding 'Christ as bodily present and eaten together with the bread and wine (juice)'. Instead, Pentecostals, like Baptists, should hold to their traditions, regarding the Supper as 'symbolic without reducing it to "mere symbolism"'.

[306] Kärkkäinen, 'A Pentecostal Response', p. 115.
[307] Kärkkäinen, 'The Pentecostal View', p. 117.
[308] Telford Work, *Deuteronomy* (BTC; Grand Rapids: Brazos, 2009), p. 55.
[309] Work, *Deuteronomy*, p. 143.

Father's mission for his brothers' and sisters' sake'.[310] As a Pentecostal, Work believes that both sacramental and charismatic signs are significant as reminders of the hope of the Eschaton, because they point to those things that last, that endure. 'If baptism and healing anticipate resurrection and Eucharist and marriage anticipate the wedding banquet, then ordination and spiritual gifts anticipate something too.'[311]

James K.A. Smith

Largely in conversation with Radical Orthodoxy, Jamie Smith, Professor of Philosophy at Calvin College, calls for Pentecostals to take seriously the church's traditional sacramental thought and practice. He stands convinced, in fact, that the Christological convictions of the Pentecostal movement make a recovery of traditional sacramentality both fitting and necessary:

> If undergirding a theology of sacramentality is a fundamental affirmation of the Incarnation (that the Infinite is revealed in and through the finite), and Pentecostal theology seeks to affirm that in radical ways, then the Pentecostal community and Pentecostal scholars should seek new roles for 'sacraments' in Pentecostal worship and spirituality.[312]

In Smith's view, the Eucharist is truly a means of grace through which peace, joy, and spiritual nourishment come to the worshipping community, but only insofar as the Supper is experienced as an anticipation of the eschatological 'marriage supper of the Lamb' (Rev. 19.9) and the peace and justice of the new creation. Received in this way, Holy Communion sensitizes participants to the norms of Christian existence and in this way provides a 'basis of critique for the present order'.[313] Consequently, the church's participation in the Eucharist is for Smith nothing less than the training ground of a counter-politics. In proper giving and receiving of the Lord's Supper, Christians learn what it means to live together – and with those

---

[310] Work, *Deuteronomy*, p. 142.

[311] Telford Work, *Ain't Too Proud to Beg: Living Through the Lord's Prayer* (Grand Rapids: Eerdmans, 2007), p. 74.

[312] James K.A. Smith, 'What Hath Cambridge To Do with Azusa Street?: Radical Orthodoxy and Pentecostal Theology in Conversation', *Pneuma* 25.1 (March 2003), p. 113.

[313] James K.A. Smith, *Desiring the Kingdom: Worship, Worldview, and Cultural Formation* (Grand Rapids: Baker Academic, 2009), p. 203.

outside the community – in the righteous peace of God and so they become together a kind of foretaste of the end of all things, the 'firstfruits of new creation'. Not that the Eucharist does anything magically. Smith claims only that 'liturgical practices of reconciliation and forgiveness constitute a training ground for making a start – and they demand that we do so'.[314]

Smith insists that he is not insensitive to the dangers of hyper-sacramentalism. Central as the practice is, the Eucharist-event is not itself the kingdom, but a sacrament of the kingdom. Therefore, Communion should be experienced as 'a sanctified letdown', in a sense, because every week that the church celebrates the Lord's Supper is 'another week that the kingdom and its feast have not yet fully arrived'.[315] Even still, it is a divinely-given 'model of the eschatological order', and for this reason the Eucharist should stand 'at the heart of Christian worship' for all Christians, including Pentecostals.[316]

Wolfgang Vondey

Vondey, an Associate Professor of Systematic Theology at Regent University (Virginia Beach, VA) and founding director of the Center for Renewal Studies, offers a 'theology of bread' that seeks to explicate the 'significance of bread *beyond* its role at the Lord's Supper'.[317] Nonetheless, he does work with a robustly sacramental view of the Supper, which he understands as 'a real and concrete token of the continuing presence of Christ among the disciples'. In the light of his reading of the story of Jesus breaking bread with the Emmaus disciples, Vondey insists that the Eucharistic breaking of bread 'is the divine reality breaking into the present companionship' of the Christian community.[318] He wants also to hold attention on the *absence* of Christ, on the 'empty space' left in the wake of Jesus' ascension, a space that is 'filled with the broken bread as a *token* of his continuing presence' and a '*sacred sign*' of the future realization of the kingdom.[319]

---

[314] Smith, *Desiring the Kingdom*, p. 200.
[315] Smith, *Desiring the Kingdom*, p. 200.
[316] Smith, *Desiring the Kingdom*, p. 202.
[317] Wolfgang Vondey, *People of Bread: Rediscovering Ecclesiology* (Mahwah, NJ: Paulist Press, 2008), p. 3.
[318] Vondey, *People of Bread*, p. 173.
[319] Vondey, *People of Bread*, pp. 172-73. Emphasis added.

All in all, Vondey's is an expansive sacramental vision that extends beyond the rites of baptism and the Eucharist to include the church and indeed all creation.[320] In critical conversation with the insights of Catholic sacramentalists like Louis-Marie Chauvet, Vondey takes care to avoid what he deems an exaggeratedly objectivist account of the sacraments. In finding a way forward, Vondey makes much of Augustine's Eucharistic theology.[321] Throughout his work, Vondey's driving concerns appears to be the *visible* unity of the ecumenical, global church, a unity that he believes the Eucharist calls Christians to desire, follow, and enact. For this reason, in his response to the Faith and Order document, *The Nature and Mission of the Church*, he calls for Pentecostals to 'consider more carefully the role of baptism, the Eucharist, and social justice as part of Christian initiation, vocation, and ministry'.[322]

Mark J. Cartledge

Mark Cartledge, a senior lecturer in Pentecostal and Charismatic theology at University of Birmingham, while supporting Macchia's sacramental account of *glossolalia*, seeks to reframe the description in Reformed rather than Rahnerian terms.[323] Cartledge proposes that the sacramental nature of *glossolalia* is best understood in light of Calvin's conception of a sacrament (outlined in his *Institutes* Book IV) as any 'outward sign' – whether natural (like Noah's rainbow) or supernatural (like Gideon's fleece) – enjoined on God's people 'to render them more certain and confidence of the truth of this promises', and, following Calvin, he seeks to prioritize the intercessory work of the Spirit and the indispensability of the believer's active faith.[324] Cartledge infers from this reformulation a number of practical implications for Pentecostal-Charismatic dialogue about the nature and purpose of 'tongues'.[325]

---

[320] See Vondey, *People of Bread*, pp. 247-48.

[321] See Vondey, *People of Bread*, pp. 232-33.

[322] Wolfgang Vondey, 'Pentecostal Contributions to *The Nature and Mission of the Church*' in Wolfgang Vondey (ed.), *Pentecostalism and Christian Unity: Ecumenical Documents and Critical Assessments* (Eugene, OR: Pickwick, 2010), pp. 256-68 (259).

[323] Mark J. Cartledge, *Charismatic Glossolalia: An Empirical-Theological Study* (Burlington, VT: Ashgate, 2002), pp. 195-97.

[324] Cartledge, *Charismatic Glossolalia*, pp. 195-96.

[325] Cartledge, *Charismatic Glossolalia*, pp. 196-97. Including, *inter alia*, a redefinition contra Macchia of tongue-speech as xenolalic.

In his *Testimony in the Spirit,* published in 2010, Cartledge attempts to work out with an empirical Pentecostal theology an authoritative description of core Pentecostal beliefs. He focuses his study on a single classic Pentecostal congregation in the UK, and his central aim is 'to listen to, record and reflect upon the "ordinary theology" of congregational members' on key theological themes, including the sacraments.[326]

In the course of his studies, Cartledge discerned a basic pattern to the congregation's weekly observance of the Lord's Supper. Either the pastor or a senior member of the church – on rare occasions a leading woman in the church – comes forward after a time of singing and response, and reads one or more scriptural passages in preparation for receiving Communion and then prays over the 'emblems' (bread and grape juice, served in small cups).[327] During the ceremony, the congregation usually sings a song; occasionally, there is silence. Afterward, the congregation is instructed to greet one another or to share a word of encouragement with others. Cartledge found that the dominant text in use during Communion was Isa. 53.4-6, and that it was read to emphasize the connection between divine forgiveness, healing, and participation in the Supper. Other texts, of course, were used as well, and in the end he discerned that Isaiah 53 (and other related texts) were read in light of the interpreters' experience of Communion and that they in turn understand their participation in Communion through the lens of these texts. As he says, 'Isaiah 53 and the rite of Holy Communion mutually inform each other'.[328]

Cartledge concludes from his observation of these services that Pentecostals see the Lord's Supper as more than a memorial meal; in his own words, 'The rite of Holy Communion may function as a memorial of atonement for sin, but it fundamentally reinforces the idea that Jesus can and does deal with our burdens just as he has dealt with the cosmological burden of sin'.[329] He is not oblivious to potential problems with contemporary Pentecostal theologies of worship and raises several sets of concerns, including tendencies

---

[326] Mark J. Cartledge, *Testimony in the Spirit: Rescripting Ordinary Pentecostal Theology* (Burlington, VT: Ashgate Publishing, 2010), p. 10.
[327] Cartledge, *Testimony in the Spirit*, p. 31.
[328] Cartledge, *Testimony in the Spirit*, p. 51.
[329] Cartledge, *Testimony in the Spirit*, p. 51.

toward triumphalism and hyper-individualism. Cartledge believes a 'greater focus on the sacrament of Holy Communion' might correct these concerns, especially if linked to a theology of the cross and an emphasis on divine sovereignty.[330]

Daniel Tomberlin

Dan Tomberlin, a Church of God (Cleveland, TN) ordained bishop and pastor, argues that Pentecostals can and should recognize the sacraments – by which he means water baptism, the Lord's Supper, footwashing, and anointing with oil – as real and really effective means of grace.[331] In his own words: 'The waters of the baptismal pool, the bread and cup of the Eucharist, and the anointing oil can indeed be sacraments, that is, they are means through which believers encounter the Spirit of grace'.[332] He is bold to insist that regular, faithful participation in the sacraments is indispensable[333] to the way of life to which Pentecostals, as all Christians, are called by the gospel. Drawing extensively on the work of early Pentecostal pioneers and a kind of phenomenology of Pentecostal worship and spiritual habitus,[334] Tomberlin argues that a robust sacramentality is entirely in keeping with Pentecostal being-in-the-world. He also engages in critical conversation with fellow Pentecostal scholars, including Kimberly Alexander and Ken Archer.

As the book's subtitle makes clear, the 'altar' serves as a focal image for Tomberlin,[335] as does Christ's priestly ministry. He returns again and again to this image and its complex of themes to make his central point: 'Through Christ the High Priest and the Spirit of grace, sacraments are more than mere reenactments or

---

[330] Cartledge, *Testimony in the Spirit*, p. 46.

[331] Daniel Tomberlin, *Pentecostal Sacraments: Encountering God at the Altar* (Cleveland, TN: Center for Pentecostal Leadership and Care, 2010), p.82, defines a sacrament in this way: 'a sacred act of worship blessed by Christ the High Priest through which the worshiper encounters the Spirit of grace'.

[332] Tomberlin, *Pentecostal Sacraments*, p. 86. Although I had met Dan, I had not read his book until after the principal work of my own thesis had already been completed. After having read his book, I decided I needed to include it in this review of literature. Therefore, any similarities of arguments and sources in his work and mine are in fact accidental and unconnected.

[333] For his treatment of this issue, see Tomberlin, *Pentecostal Sacraments*, pp. 91-93.

[334] Tomberlin (*Pentecostal Sacraments*, p. 87) insists that this is so because 'Pentecostal is a physical spirituality'.

[335] He describes sacramental spirituality as 'an ongoing altar call'.

memorials to God's redemptive acts; the baptismal water, the towel and basin, the bread and wine, and the anointing oil become mediatory gifts'.[336]

Regarding the Eucharist itself, Tomberlin holds that Christ (and the Spirit) are in fact present in the celebration. And, while he stops short of calling for Pentecostals to adopt any particular theory of Real Presence, he speculates that Gregory Palamas' distinction between the divine *energia* and *ousia* provides a way forward for formulating a description of the reality and immediacy of Presence at the Table. As Tomberlin sees it, Pentecostals (en masse) cannot accept the Catholic teaching of transubstantiation that describes the bread and wine becoming Christ's body and blood, but *can* accept the Palamite teaching that the Spirit comes upon – rests upon, 'touches' – the bread and wine of the Eucharist.[337] Showing his pastoral colors, he is careful to take time to sketch out in some detail how a local Pentecostal church might integrate regular Eucharistic celebration into their worship services and way of life together.[338]

Conclusions

What is to be learned from this review of literature? First, there appears to have been in the last decade what can rightly be called a 'turn' to the sacraments among Pentecostals, with the work of John Christopher Thomas, Frank Macchia, and Steven Land opening the way for the movement to revision the Evangelical (anti-) sacramental thought and practice that had become standard after WWII, and the work of Amos Yong, Ken Archer, Jamie Smith, and Wolfgang Vondey, among others, advancing the discussion on a number of fronts in conversation not only with Pentecostals and charismatics, but also with ecumenical partners.

Second, speaking broadly, this turn to the sacraments has moved in one or another of two directions. Some scholars (e.g. Chan and Biddy) have emphasized the need for Pentecostals to learn from the sacramental theology of the wider Christian tradition, while others (e.g. Thomas and Yong) are concerned primarily with developing a

---

[336] Tomberlin, *Pentecostal Sacraments*, p. 86.

[337] He contends for a 'stronger' view than that offered in the Reformed tradition, a view Tomberlin believes most early Pentecostals held.

[338] He does the same with the other sacraments, as well.

uniquely and authentically Pentecostal account of the sacraments. There has also been an attempt (by e.g. Thomas, Macchia, and Archer) to develop this Pentecostal sacramental theology by recovering other sacramental rites and practices, such as glossolalia and footwashing, alongside water baptism and the Lord's Supper.

Third, as the above survey demonstrates, there has been a wide range of scholarly opinions among Pentecostals regarding the value and meaning of the sacraments. Some (e.g. Bond, Horton, Slay) have strongly opposed a sacramental understanding of baptism and the Lord's Supper, insisting that these rites must be understood as mere ordinances. With equal force, others (e.g. Chan, Yong, Biddy, Tomberlin) have put forward a high sacramental view. Unsurprisingly, a majority of scholars have sought to occupy what might be called the middle ground – although here, too, one finds a range of opinion, with some (e.g., Bicknell) coming nearer the non-sacramentalist pole and others (e.g. Land, Thomas, Macchia) approaching the opposite end of the spectrum.

Fourth, regardless of their disagreements, Pentecostals who have given attention to sacramental theological concerns have maintained some common ground. For example, all the reviewed scholars agree in eschewing a 'magical' view of the waters of baptism or the bread and wine of Communion. Also, the vast majority of scholars have been careful to warn against the dangers of liturgical formalism and clericalism.

Fifth, all the theologians, irrespective of their positions, appeal to Scripture for support of their positions. Most of them draw on the Christian dogmatic and exegetical tradition(s) as well, and many of them evince clear ecumenical concerns. Speaking in general terms, it seems that those scholars who decide against a sacramental view of the Supper and the Bath do so on (presumed) biblical and pastoral grounds; that is, they do not find sufficient scriptural support for the sacramental position, and they wish to avoid the dangers of ritualism. Conversely, those who advocate a robustly sacramental view do so by arguing from the church's history and historical Christian practice – including those experiences and practices peculiar to the Pentecostal tradition – as well as from the Scriptures, and they seek to explain the Eucharist's theological significance for the church's life in worship and mission. In short, differences in theological method seem to determine the differences in opinion among Pentecostals on the purpose and meaning of the sacraments.

3

(RE)DISCOVERING THE SACRAMENTALITY OF EARLY PENTECOSTALISM: AN EXPLORATION OF THE EARLY PERIODICAL LITERATURE

This chapter consists of a reading of the early Pentecostal periodical literature for sacramental references, both explicit and implicit, with particular attention to theological descriptions of the Lord's Supper. By a close reading of these texts, I hope to discern the sacramental view(s) these early Pentecostals held, and to identify the critical implications of these views for contemporary Pentecostal theology and practice.

Prolegomena

The Normativity of Early Pentecostal Spirituality

Steven Land, following Walter Hollenweger, argues that the first ten years of the Pentecostal movement serve as its 'heart' and not its 'infancy', insisting that any contemporary attempt at constructing an authentically Pentecostal theology must reckon with the spiritual practice and theological reflection of the earliest Pentecostals,[1] who by virtue of their discerning openness to the work of the Spirit provide the norm by which Pentecostalism's ensuing developments

---

[1] In spite of widespread agreement on certain teachings, practices, and experiences deemed centrally important, early Pentecostalism was not monolithic, so it perhaps is best to talk of early Pentecostal*isms*. See Douglas G. Jacobson, *A Reader in Pentecostal Theology: Voices from the First Generation* (Bloomington, IN: Indiana University Press, 2006), p. 13.

must be judged.[2] Such an assertion is sure to strike some readers as odd if not outrageous, so a few clarifications are in order.

First, to agree with Hollenweger and Land is *not* to disregard later developments in the movement or to assume that these developments are necessarily suspect or less important. It is only to affirm that later developments should not be *deviations* from the original dynamics of the movement but faithful continuations of it. In other words, innovations in theology and practice should arise from and remain true to the spirituality that first generated the movement. Put still another way, contemporary Pentecostals must think and live in ways that make one story with the movement's pioneers, just as they should seek to live and think in ways that make their story one with the *apostles'* story and the story of the one, holy, catholic, and apostolic church.

Second, to regard early Pentecostalism in this way does not entail using it as 'an inflexible standard of correctness'.[3] Instead, what Rowan Williams says of the history of the *ecclesia catholica* applies, *mutatis mutandis*, to the history of Pentecostal churches, as well: Pentecostals remain indebted to the pioneering generation, and acknowledging this indebtedness is entailed by the conviction that the Pentecostal movement *now* is the work of the one, unifying Spirit of God who was at work *then*.[4] In attending to the movement's earliest history, we discover anew that 'we are all … living "in the wake" of something prior to all our thoughts and initiatives … [that] we are not our own authors'.[5]

Third, notwithstanding the movement's restorationism and the attending doctrinal and practical distinctives, early Pentecostalism – at least many of the groups within it – remained grounded in the *ethos* of the historic Christian faith, as evidenced by many Pentecostals' fierce commitment to the doctrine of the Trinity, a high Christology, the canon of Scripture, and the churchly practices of footwashing, water baptism, imposition of hands (for ordination and healing), and the regular celebration of the Eucharist as a means of grace.

---

[2] Hollenweger, *The Pentecostals*, p. 551. Cited in Land, *Pentecostal Spirituality*, p. 47.

[3] Rowan Williams, *Why Study the Past: The Quest for the Historical Church* (Grand Rapids: Eerdmans, 2005), p. 110.

[4] As well as through Israel's, the church's, and *creation's* history.

[5] Williams, *Why Study the Past*, p. 111.

Fourth, and finally, the earliest Pentecostals, in many ways stationed at the cultural 'margin' of modernity, found themselves enfolded in the drama of the last-day restoration of God's people, a dramatic placement that afforded them an unusual perspective on the Scriptures and on their own lives in the world. As John Howard Yoder put it, they occupied a situation vis-à-vis the world and the established church that had remained vacant since the Anabaptists of the 16th century.[6] The marriage – or at least courtship – of Pentecostalism and Evangelicalism in the years following the second World War, whatever benefits it afforded, altered this situation dramatically and effectively stripped Pentecostals of an epistemology and hermeneutic that matched their experience.[7] From that time, much ostensibly Pentecostal theology (whether in the pulpit or from the lectern) has proven little more than an (un)imaginative restatement of 'evangelical fundamentals with a few extra chapters on Spirit baptism and gifts'.[8] By attending carefully to primitive Pentecostalism, Pentecostals can (re)discover categories of thought and modes of practice suitable to their spirituality, their being-in-the-world. They can put away Saul's armor, so to speak.

This question remains, of course: what in fact constitutes 'early' Pentecostalism? Land, like Hollenweger, restricts himself to the movement's initial decade. Carl Simpson, in his treatment of the primitive German Pentecostal movement, limits himself to the first seven years.[9] For my part, I concentrate on the first quarter century of the movement, focusing on the period from 1906 to 1931.

Assessing Early Pentecostal Sacramentality

In most Christian traditions, the sacraments of water baptism and the Eucharist are regarded as basic and indispensable to the churchly life, so they receive the lion's share of attention in ecumenical discussion. However, many if not all of the early Pentecostals did not consider themselves beholden to these categories, so a careful reading of their history cannot limit itself in this way. To be clear,

---

[6] Quoted in Martin W. Mitteldstadt, 'My Life as a Mennocostal: A Personal and Theological Narrative', *Theodidaktos* 3.2 (Sept 2008), p. 11.

[7] See Howard M. Ervin, 'Hermeneutics: A Pentecostal Option', *Pneuma* 3.2 (1981), pp. 11–25.

[8] Land, *Pentecostal Spirituality*, p. 24.

[9] Carl Simpson, 'Jonathan Paul and the German Pentecostal Movement – the First Seven Years, 1907-1914', *JEPTA* 28.2 (2008), pp. 169-82.

then, the aim of this chapter is *not* to determine if or how early Pentecostal sacramentality compares to, say, Anglican, Lutheran, or Catholic sacramentality. Instead, the goal is to determine if and how early Pentecostal spirituality discloses what one might justly identify as a sacramental imagination and praxis.

In light of these considerations, for the purposes of this chapter the following working definitions are assumed: in the broader sense, a sacrament is any recurring, embodied gesture or set of actions believed and expected to occasion or mediate God's effective presence; in the narrower sense, a sacrament is a ritual gesture that serves as a 'sign' that somehow actually effects what it signifies, a 'visible word' that does what it says or 'gives what it talks about', to borrow a phrase from Robert Jenson.[10]

Wesleyan-Holiness and Finished Work Pentecostalism(s)

This reading of early Pentecostal periodical literature draws extensively on the model of Kimberly Alexander, whose research of early Pentecostal theologies of healing has made clear how widely the Finished Work tradition differs from the Wesleyan-Holiness, at least on issues of healing. In her monograph on the healing models of early Pentecostals, she demonstrates how the traditions' conflicting soteriological presuppositions inevitably required differences in practice and belief. Imitating her method provides a way of discerning continuity and discontinuity within and between the classical Pentecostal traditions.

Identifying the Primary Sources

I will engage early Pentecostal spirituality by offering a close reading of the periodical literature of the time, because, as Alexander has argued, that literature affords a representative sampling of the habits of thought and practice common to early Pentecostals in the United States. These periodicals served the early movement as a means, *inter alia*, of evangelistic, apologetic, inspirational, and catechetical proclamation and instruction.[11] Additionally, as Alexander's work shows, reading these periodicals provides insight not only into the teaching of the periodicals' editors and leading contributors –

---

[10] Robert W. Jenson, *Canon and Creed* (Louisville: WJKP, 2010), p. 75.
[11] Alexander, *Pentecostal Healing*, p. 71.

including, in some cases, official denominational leaders – but also into the thoughts and feelings of 'marginal' voices, and those who were involved in day-to-day ministry efforts, at home or abroad. In the periodicals, one gets a glimpse of the 'immediacy of effect' because they consist almost entirely of reports of recently-observed or recently-experienced events and various *ad hoc* explanations or defenses of particular doctrines; in short, 'the reader has the opportunity to look through a window at the movement as it develops on a weekly basis'.[12] It is difficult to overstate the importance of these periodicals to early Pentecostalism, and so any attempt at reconstructing the dynamic of the spirituality can ill afford not to reckon with this literature. Altogether, nine early Pentecostal periodical publications will be examined,[13] and for the sake of space and methodological consistency, any material other than the periodicals (e.g. sermons, tracts, diaries, official denominational statements) will be appealed to only rarely.

This chapter will engage the following Wesleyan-Holiness periodicals:

The Apostolic Faith (Los Angeles, CA)

AF served as the official organ of the Apostolic Faith Movement, and was headed at the time by William Seymour. The four-page paper was published monthly (except for one issue), beginning in September 1906, and continuing until 1908. After that, the paper was published by Florence Crawford from Portland, Oregon.

The Bridegroom's Messenger (Atlanta, GA)

TBM was a four-page paper that was pioneered by G.B. Cashwell for Pentecostals in the southern United States. The first issue appeared October 1, 1907, and from December of the same year, continued as a bi-monthly publication.

The Church of God Evangel (Cleveland, TN)

COGE, published first March 1, 1910, was an institution of the Church of God (Cleveland, TN) denomination,[14] and was edited by general overseer A.J. Tomlinson from its beginning until November

---

[12] Alexander, *Pentecostal Healing*, p. 67.
[13] See Alexander, *Pentecostal Healing*, pp. 67-72.
[14] For a brief account of the history and ethos of the early days of the Church of God, see Alexander, *Pentecostal Healing*, pp. 95-101.

1922. After Tomlinson's impeachment, F.J. Lee, who was elected as General Overseer, began service as the paper's editor.

The Pentecostal Holiness Advocate (Falcon, NC; Franklin Springs, GA)

PHA, edited first by G.F. Taylor, served as an official organ of the Pentecostal Holiness Church. Taylor was formerly a general superintendent of the denomination. First published in May, 1917 from Falcon, North Carolina, the periodical moved to Franklin Springs, Georgia the following year.

Following Alexander's lead, after I have completed the reading of these Wesleyan-Holiness Pentecostal periodicals, I will turn next to examine several periodicals representative of the *Finished Work* stream of Pentecostalism as well. These are:

The Latter Rain Evangel (Chicago, IL)

LRE was a publication of the Stone Church, which hosted the General Council of the Assemblies of God in 1914 and 1919. The church's pastor, William Hammer Piper, edited the paper, with the first issue coming off the press in October 1908. The relatively lengthy publication was published on a monthly basis. Typically, the paper included sermons and short treatises on issues of theological import to the movement.

The Pentecost (Indianapolis, IN; Kansas City, MO)

This monthly, eight-page paper, began in 1908 as a joint publication of two independent congregations, and was published for two years under a team of editors that included J. Roswell Flower (later an official in the Assemblies of God) and A.S. Copley, who in 1911 assumed sole editorship, renamed the periodical (*Grace and Glory*), and began using it to propagate the doctrine of the believer's eternal security.

The Pentecostal Testimony (Chicago, IL)

William H. Durham published *PT* irregularly, mostly during his time as pastor of North Avenue Mission in Chicago, and then from Los Angeles, in the final months of his life. The paper, which he used to further his Finished Work teaching, ran at various lengths (12 to 16 pages), and included theological essays by Durham, texts of his sermons, and news about his ministry particularly, the Pentecostal movement generally.

Word and Witness (Malvern, AR; Findlay, OH; St Louis, MO)

WW, published and edited by former Southern Baptist pastor Eudorus N. Bell, endured a tumultuous and now largely obscured history. The four-page magazine was published for the most part on a monthly schedule. It was adopted along with *The Pentecostal Evangel* as an official organ of the Assemblies of God at the Hot Springs meeting in the Spring of 1914.[15]

The Pentecostal Evangel (Springfield, MO)

PE was launched as an independent paper under the name *The Christian Evangel* in 1913. J. Roswell Flower and his wife, Alice, served as its founders and first editors. As already mentioned, the paper was adopted by the Assemblies of God as one of its official instruments, along with *Word and Witness*. Published concurrently for two years, the papers were merged on January 1, 1916. Except for a few years (1918-1923), when it was published as an eight-page paper on a bi-weekly basis, the editors published the four-page magazine weekly.

Having surveyed the Wesleyan-Holiness and Finished Work periodicals, I will turn to A.A. Boddy's *Confidence* magazine, the British Pentecostal periodical first published from Boddy's vicarage in Sunderland, England, beginning April 1908. Like most of these periodicals, *Confidence* consisted of personal testimonies and prayer requests, news of the movement from around the world, and brief theological articles on pertinent topics. I include this examination of *Confidence* for several reasons. First, it served as a kind of bridging device, bringing North American Pentecostalism into dialogue with the movement in Europe; also, Boddy and his wife, Mary, were esteemed by many North American Pentecostal leaders as important figures, as evidenced in part by the frequent reprinting in American periodical of articles previously published in *Confidence*. For example, Elizabeth Sexton, editor of *The Bridegroom's Messenger*, writes: '*Confidence* is one of our best Pentecostal papers, and its editor, Rev. A.A. Boddy has been greatly used of God in England and other countries'.[16] Most important for my purposes, the Boddys lived and

---

[15] See Edith W. Blumhofer, *Restoring the Faith: the Assemblies of God, Pentecostalism, and American Culture* (Champagne, IL: University of Illinois Press, 1993), pp. 116-19.

[16] *TBM* 4.82 (Mar 15, 1911), p. 2.

taught as Evangelical Anglicans, as did at least some of the contributors to their periodical.[17] Therefore, I believe much can be gained by comparing the sacramentality one finds in *Confidence* with that that one finds in the North American periodicals, which issues from a markedly different religious and cultural provenance.

Reading Strategy

I aim to engage these materials not only critically and scientifically but also in faith, as a form of spiritual discipline.[18] I will read them in chronological order, working through one periodical at a time, beginning with the Wesleyan-Holiness publications. I do so in the hope of allowing the developing views to emerge, leaving space for the discovery of how if at all the passing of time, the rapid growth and widespread influence of the movement, and the always ongoing theological dialogue affected the shape of the sacramentality of the primitive Pentecostal movement(s). Schematically, I will read with an eye for (a) explicit references to or reflections on the sacraments, including but not restricted to the Lord's Supper, water baptism, footwashing, and anointing with oil and laying on of hands for healing and ordination; (b) testimonies of observance of the sacraments, and (c) an implied sacramentality embedded in the movement's rhetoric or praxis, e.g. in the use of eating/drinking metaphors or references to the goodness of embodiment and mediation.

Wesleyan-Holiness Periodicals

In the Beginning: *The Apostolic Faith*

AF, published from 1906 through 1908 by the Azusa St. Apostolic Faith Mission, served as the first theological articulation of the emerging Pentecostal movement in the United States. As such, it provides a way into some of the movement's earliest and most instructive practices and convictions. As one might expect, *AF* focuses on the teachings and events that convinced so many in that time that the revival was nothing less than the Bible-promised 'latter rain', that is, the end-time restoration of God's people for Spirit-

---

[17] For an authoritative account of the Boddys' lives and theological commitments, see Gavin Wakefield, *Alexander Boddy: Pentecostal Anglican Pioneer* (Milton Keynes: Paternoster, 2007).

[18] See Williams, *Why Study the Past*, p. 110.

empowered, world-wide mission. The lion's share of writing belongs (1) to the defense of peculiar Pentecostal doctrines (such as healing in the atonement, entire sanctification, Spirit baptism, and speaking in tongues); (2) to calls for and reports of Spirit-empowered world evangelization, and (3) to testimonies of the Spirit's supernatural work in healings, exorcisms, conversions, dreams and visions, and prophecies. These emphases notwithstanding, one finds numerous references to the sacraments, which suggests that Seymour and his fellow Pentecostals believed that participation in the sacraments was an indispensable aspect of the truly Christian life.

All of the Signs of the Full Gospel: Explicit Treatment of the Sacraments

In the September 1907 issue, Seymour offers a comparatively extensive treatment of what he calls the 'ordinances'. He identifies three: footwashing, the Lord's Supper, and water baptism, and he treats them in that order. He does not give any attention to the metaphysics of the sacraments; the finer theoretical points of the discussion evidently do not concern him. He concerns himself instead with the fact that Jesus *commanded* his followers to observe these three practices. If Jesus ordained them then they *must* be performed – end of discussion. 'What right have we to dictate to our blessed Master?'[19] For all intents and purposes, the dominical mandate is the foundation of Seymour's sacramentality.

Footwashing
The footwashing rite, according to Seymour, serves as a 'type of regeneration'. He marshals quotations from the Fourth Gospel for support of this claim. Intriguingly, he distinguishes Jesus' act from the ritual washings practiced by Israel's priests, washings which were a type or symbolic anticipation of the New Testament ordinance. Washing the feet of his disciples, Jesus was enacting an ancient liturgical tradition. In this way, he both fulfilled and once-for-all *reconstituted* the practice, affording it new meaning and power. Having laid out the scriptural evidence, Seymour appeals to the Pentecostal *experience* of footwashing as support of the validity of

---

[19] *AF* 1.10 (Sept 1907), p. 2.

the practice: '*We find that* it is a service much blest of God ...'[20] Finally, he concludes the section with a few practical considerations: one, the service is for believers, not 'sinners'; two, women wash only other women's feet, and men, only other men's; three, the time given to the rite is a perfect opportunity for 'testimony, song and praise', and, finally, footwashing should be followed by participation in the Lord's Supper.[21]

Laying on of Hands and Anointing with Oil
One finds frequent reference in *AF* to the practice of laying on of hands, both for healing[22] and for Spirit baptism.[23] This is unsurprising given that Seymour and the others at Azusa were concerned to follow Scripture's directions for healing. They prayed in Jesus' name to the Father[24] with the imposition of hands, because they believed Mk 16.18 mandated these actions.[25] Similarly, following the prescriptions of Jas 5.14, the sick were to be anointed with oil.[26] G.B. Cashwell testifies that he was healed of 'rheumatism and catarrh' after he was anointed with oil and prayed for, and a woman recounts receiving via the mail a handkerchief anointed with oil: upon opening the letter, she was instantly healed.[27] The *AF* contributors and editor did not feel bound to *explain* what the oil symbolizes or what in fact occurs when the sick person is anointed. As with footwashing, only simple obedience to the scriptural mandate mattered.[28] In the final analysis, this much remains undeniable: the early Pentecostals who find their voice in *AF* made use of *means* of healing – including the anointing with oil and the laying on of hands, as well as the use of anointed handkerchiefs – and these practices were nothing if not sacramental, even if they were not explicitly described in this way.[29]

---

[20] Emphasis added.
[21] Emphasis added.
[22] For example, see *AF* 1.6 (Feb-Mar 1907), p. 6.
[23] For example, see *AF* 1.5 (Jan 1907), p. 4; *AF* 1.2 (Oct 1906), p. 3; *AF* 1.3 (Nov 1906), p. 2; *AF* 1.7 (Apr 1907), p. 4.
[24] For example, see *AF* 1.12 (Jan 1908), p. 3.
[25] For example, see *AF* 1.2 (Oct 1906), p. 3.
[26] *AF* 1.4 (Dec 1906), p. 2.
[27] *AF* 1.4 (Dec 1906), pp. 1, 4.
[28] Alexander, *Pentecostal Healing*, p. 82.
[29] See Alexander, *Pentecostal Healing*, p. 84.

Water Baptism

Seymour understood the rite of water baptism, like Holy Communion and footwashing, as having been commanded of Christians by Jesus himself, and in a September 1907 article he repeatedly stresses this feature of the ordinances' meaning.[30] Like the majority of his Pentecostal brothers and sisters of the period, Seymour believed that in spite of the fact that the washing rite in and of itself does not accomplish anything 'every true believer will practice it' because it is expressly mandated by the Lord.[31] He appears to be in the minority even among his fellow Pentecostals, however, when he maintains that water baptism should be administered by a 'disciple who is baptized with the Holy Ghost'.[32] Besides this piece, one finds no other explicit treatments of water baptism in *AF*, a fact that presumably indicates a widespread agreement on the meaning of the rite. In the ensuing years, however, controversies would arise and engender differing accounts. In any case, many *testimonies* of baptismal services are found, and these have much to say about what early Pentecostals believed about the rite.

The Lord's Supper

Seymour begins his exposition of the meaning of the Communion meal by referencing Jesus' Last Supper. This meal with his disciples marked the last Passover, Seymour believes, because Jesus, having fulfilled the promise of the Passover's symbolism, 'shoved that table aside'. As he had done with Israel's ritual washings, Jesus brings Israel's ritual meal to its end. The Passover, that 'very type of Jesus', was possessed of a threefold significance: (1) the shed *blood* spread on the doorposts speaks of redemption, (2) the lamb's *body* eaten by the pilgrims speaks of both health and healing, and (3) Israel's *watery exodus* speaks of the power of 'the Blood of Jesus Christ' to triumph over all the powers of the enemy.[33] The Lord's Supper, then, stands as the memorial both of Jesus' Last Supper and Israel's last Passover and as such bears all the symbolic weight of both meals,

---

[30] Seymour cites Mt. 3.16, 28.19-20; Mk 16.16; Acts 2.28, 8.38-39; Rom. 6.3-5; Gal 3.27; 1Pet. 3.21.

[31] *AF* 1.10 (Sept 1907), p. 2.

[32] *AF* 1.10 (Sept 1907), p. 2. Seymour's 1915 *Doctrines and Disciplines* indicated the ways in which his opinions had changed, and the concerns he had for the movement he had helped to found. His view of the ordinances, however, does not seem to have changed in the least.

[33] *AF* 1.10 (Sept 1907), p. 2.

as well as all the significance of Jesus' accomplishments in his final hours of suffering, dying, and death. This means, among other things, that if all of Israel went out of Egypt in health because they ate the Passover meal, then Christians, who are eating the meal that *fulfills* the Passover, should not experience anything less. The Supper also points to the future coming of the Lord, the final Exodus of the children of God. Explaining that the Supper 'teaches … salvation and sanctification through the Blood', Seymour appeals to the experience of the Supper: 'We find as we partake of this ordinance, it brings healing to our bodies if we discern the Lord's body by faith'. He insists that celebrants are 'built up' as they 'eat His flesh and drink His Blood'.[34] On Seymour's reading, Paul's account of the institution of the sacramental rite (1 Cor. 11.23-26) directs attention both to the *future* deliverance of the church at Christ's Second Coming and to Christ's *past* suffering and death on Golgotha. That is to say, the meal has both prospective and retrospective meanings. It simultaneously works both proleptically and recapitulatively. The Lord's Supper 'points us to His coming to catch us away in the glorious liberty of the children of God', while at the same time serving as a 'memorial of the death of our Lord'.[35]

Seymour was not alone among early Pentecostals in connecting the meaning of the Sacrament to the symbolism of Israel's Passover meal. An earlier *AF* article contends that the Passover lamb speaks of the salvation won by Christ's sacrificed body so that the events of Passover serve as a 'real type of the atonement', illustrating that Jesus' blood is given for our *souls* and his body for our *bodies*.[36] Jesus surrendered his 'perfect body for these imperfect bodies of ours', so that now, by the faithful partaking of the Lord's body in the Supper, believers may receive healing. *This* is why Jesus commanded his followers to eat his body: 'He said at the Passover supper, just before He was crucified, "Take, eat, this is my body." What for? For health'.[37] Readers are admonished to 'honor the atonement of our Lord Jesus Christ *in all its fullness*'.[38] This is to say, they are to *expect*

---

[34] *AF* 1.10 (Sept 1907), p. 2. Seymour obviously has Jn 6.53, 56 in mind.

[35] *AF* 1.4 (Dec 1906), p. 2.

[36] *AF* 1.4 (Dec 1906), p. 2. It seem reasonable, given the appeal to the language of John 6, that by using the modifier 'real' the writer means to suggest the Supper is not *merely* symbolic or typological, but genuinely a 'means of grace'.

[37] *AF* 1.4 (Dec 1906), p. 2.

[38] Emphasis added.

that healing of their bodies is promised to come through faithful eating of the bread of the Supper, a healing that is not only prefigured by the rituals of the Passover meal but also anticipated and exemplified in the healing that came to all of those who ate the *first* Passover and were healed (as scriptural texts such as Psalm 105.37 make clear). *Health*, as well as healing, was understood to be received through the faithful reception of the Eucharist. According to *AF*, many believers suffer sickness and even death because of their failure to discern Christ's body, i.e. their failure to engage believingly in the Supper. The problem is expounded in unmistakable terms:

> You come to the Lord's table and yet you do not believe in full salvation for soul and body. You take the cup and eat the bread, and yet deny the body of the Lord for health and salvation. So you are sick because you do not discern the body of the Lord Jesus.[39]

At this point in the argument, an appeal is made to the Fourth Gospel's account of Jesus' difficult words: 'Except ye eat the flesh of the Son of Man and drink His blood, ye have no life in you' (Jn 6.53).[40] Coupled with Seymour's reference to eating Christ's body and drinking his blood, this citation shows that at least a few early Pentecostals understood John 6 in sacramental terms, and perhaps also evidences how strongly sacramental the early Pentecostal imagination in fact was. Of course, healing of the body is not the *only* benefit: the whole work of salvation and sanctification is at least in part mediated through the Meal. 'Let us take the Lamb's body, through faith in our Lord, for salvation and healing of these bodies, as we honor His blood for saving and sanctifying our soul and spirit. Amen.'[41]

As already indicated, Seymour's theology of the Sacrament as it appears in *AF* depends on readings of various biblical passages, especially 1 Cor. 11.23-26 and Jn 6.53-56. Besides these texts, Seymour also appeals to Jesus' rebuke of his tempter: 'Man shall not live by bread alone' (Mt. 4.4 and/or Lk. 4.4). This too is something

---

[39] *AF* 1.4 (Dec 1906), p. 2.

[40] This is a startling reading, for by and large Protestants – including Luther, Calvin, and Wesley – have not read this passage as a treatment of the Supper. See Robert W. Jenson, *Visible Words* (Philadelphia: Fortress Press, 1978), p. 85.

[41] *AF* 1.4 (Dec 1906), p. 2.

of a surprising move. Why quote *this* statement, which speaks of God's word as greater than bread, in a treatment on the meaning and purpose of the Eucharistic bread? Is this simply a case of a poorly-selected proof text? At one level, Seymour draws attention to the fact that God's people live ultimately by God's word of command, so that the emphasis falls not so much on eating the bread as on *adhering to Christ's directive*.[42] At another level, however, Seymour's reading provides a way of rehearing the significance of Jesus' words. Seymour reads it as *promise*. (This in spite of the fact that in the Synoptic accounts of the temptations, Jesus cites Deut. 8.4 as a *warning* against failing to trust God for provision.) By taking Jesus' claim as a promise, and by invoking it in a treatment of the Eucharist, Seymour perhaps manages to disrupt the sometimes too-neat separation of word and sacrament in Protestant sacramental theology.

The Marriage of Heaven and Earth: Testimonies of Sacramental Experience

Reports of sacramental observances, especially water baptism, appear here and there throughout *AF*. Virtually without exception, these reports describe the baptism services as *sacred* occasions, and they rarely fail to mention the Spirit's (or Christ's) presence in the event.[43] According to one exemplary account, 'The Spirit of God was upon the people' throughout the baptism service.[44] At another baptism (convened at Terminal Island), 106 received baptism by immersion in the ocean, with more than 500 celebrating the occasion – a 'singing, shouting, joyful company'.[45] Under the title 'Buried with Him in Baptism', an article recounts how on September 11th 1906 a large group met again at Terminal Island: 'The power of God rested on the baptismal service', the report states simply. 'Heaven and earth certainly came together.'[46] Such a description suggests that in spite of the scarcity of explicit theological state-

---

[42] As proof of this, Seymour cites this statement again in his summation, where he reminds his readers that the 'full Gospel' requires believers to obey *every* command of Christ.

[43] *AF* 1.9 (June-Sept 1907), p. 1.

[44] *AF* 1.4 (Dec 1906), p. 1.

[45] *AF* 1.1 (Sept 1906), p. 4.

[46] *AF* 1.2 (Oct 1906), p. 4.

ment, early Pentecostals *experienced* water baptism as something more than a merely memorialist event.

Feasting on Jesus: Embedded Sacramentality

As witnessed in *AF*, early Pentecostal spirituality was *appetitive*. That is to say, Pentecostals knew and characterized themselves as people of intense hunger for God and God's blessings. This is evidenced perhaps most tellingly by the extensive use of eating and drinking metaphors. For instance, the revival services often are described as a grand banquet; someone testifies that 'the Father is furnishing the music and singing, and supplying the wine of the feast. As the table is spread so freely, they take a small drink of the "new wine"'.[47] Participants expected to be 'fed', so to speak, confident that the more they fed *on* God, the more they would be consumed *by* God.[48]

In their use of feasting metaphors, *AF* contributors draw extensively on biblical texts, some of which refer to the Lord's Supper. For example, those who have come to the revival at the Azusa St. mission are described as having been made by the Spirit '… one lump, one bread, all one body in Christ Jesus',[49] unmistakable allusions to 1 Cor. 5.7 and 10.17. Contributors appeal to other texts that do not refer explicitly to the sacraments, as well; for example, one finds references to 'the living waters'[50] (Jn 4.14 and 7.38)[51] and to drinking from the fountain that gives life (Rev. 21.6).[52] However, it is the Lamb's wedding feast (described in Rev. 19.7-10) that more than any other single biblical figure determines early Pentecostals' understandings of the eating/drinking motif, and to a certain extent, their view of the Eucharist, as well. Mention of the 'marriage supper' appears everywhere. G.B. Cashwell, for instance, writes from Memphis to encourage the believers in Los Angeles: 'I long to see you all in life, but if not I will meet you at the marriage supper

---

[47] *AF* 1.4 (Dec 1906), p. 1.

[48] For example, one brother, who remembers how intensely he had desired his Pentecost, testifies that he now finds himself possessed of a new longing: 'I feel a burning desire to see others possess the same blessing'. See *AF* 1.5 (Jan 1907), p. 4.

[49] *AF* 1.4 (Dec 1906), p. 1.

[50] *AF* 1.8 (May 1907), p. 2.

[51] This image of 'living waters' is not *exclusively* Johannine, of course. See also Song of Songs 4.15; Jer. 2.13, 17.13; Zech. 14.8.

[52] *AF* 1.8 (May 1907), p. 3.

of the Lamb'.[53] Because it is a *marriage* supper, nuptial language plays a major part in the discussion, as well.[54] In the words of one writer, 'So Jesus is coming back again, and He wants us, His bride, to be watching and waiting with the garments of righteousness on, ready to enter into the marriage supper'.[55] An unnamed correspondent adjoins,

> We are Christ's spiritual bride now, but there is to be a real wedding take place and a real marriage supper. Those that sit down to this supper will be His queen; the ones that have made their robes white and have the seal of God in their foreheads. O let us not miss this supper.[56]

The embedded sacramentality of early Pentecostalism reveals itself also in the many typological readings of Old Testament passages. Pentecostal readers discerned the *beneficia Christi* (e.g. justification, sanctification, Spirit baptism) typified in the architecture and furniture of Moses' tabernacle. Sanctification, particularly, finds its figurative expression in the holy place and in the 'bread of the presence' described in Exodus 25.

> All that enter wear holy garments, the white linen of the saints. Here we find the shew bread, which represents feeding upon Christ. When we get a holy heart, it calls for the Word of God. Now you have a holy feast continually. You have the Word, Christ Jesus planted in your heart, and you have faith. You believe every word of God.[57]

Working typologically and allegorically with Old Testament texts, the early Pentecostal imagination envisioned the Christian life as a journey, a passing through a series of exits as entries. Believers continually ascend from 'glory to glory', moving from the 'outward Court' of justification through the 'Holy Place' of sanctification, and into the 'Holiest' of Spirit baptism. In the 'holy place' – that is

---

[53] *AF* 1.8 (May 1907), p. 1.

[54] This nuptial language, whether addressed to the marriage of heaven and earth or Christ and his bride, speaks the same as the feasting language. In both metaphors, the same realities are at play: desire and satisfaction, emptiness and fulfillment, otherness and identity (one-ness).

[55] *AF* 1.3 (Nov 1906), p. 2.

[56] *AF* 1.6 (Feb-Mar 1907), p. 1.

[57] *AF* 1.10 (Sept 1907), p. 3.

to say, after believers have been sanctified – they 'feed upon Christ', for Jesus is the bread of life, as John 6 promises.[58] This is witnessed in the words of one of the songs sung at the mission:

> Beyond, there lies the Holy Place,
> Which all may enter by His Grace,
> And there be sanctified.
> The Bread of Heaven each need supplies ...[59]

In the same vein, the Old Testament feasts also illuminate believers' present-day experience in the Spirit. The four feasts (Passover, First Fruits, Pentecost, and Tabernacles) 'typify what we get through the cross now' – that is, a 'complete redemption' – and they illustrate that the believer experiences now a 'continual feast', even while he or she looks to the time 'when [Christ] shall spread the tabernacle and feed us'.[60] In sum, the entire Pentecostal experience is a continual *feast*, i.e. an unbroken enjoyment of Christ and his benefits. Baptized in the Spirit, receiving entrance to Christ's 'banqueting house', the believer enjoys all God's blessings.[61]

In *AF,* these Old Testament 'types and shadows' are never used to refer to the Eucharist explicitly. The emphasis remains instead on the believer's *mystical* partaking of Christ. For them, 'feeding on Christ' is what matters, not so much eating the bread and drinking the wine. However, this should not be considered a rejection or even as a devaluation of the Supper. For, as has been seen, the Lord's Supper was believed to work both as a *medium of* and a *signum for* mystical or spiritual feasting on Christ. If the importance of spiritual communion with Christ exceeds that of participating in the ritual meal, it does not by any means negate it. In fact, it affirms it. The ultimate sanctifies the penultimate, and grants it its status.

It should also be pointed out that under the Pentecostal spell, the neat epistemological distinctions that kept the world modern simply lost their charm. For this reason, one finds many testimonies of the Spirit's work in everyday experiences. A single but singularly brilliant example makes the point:

---

[58] *AF* 1.4 (Dec 1906), p. 2.
[59] *AF* 1.12 (Jan 1908), p. 2.
[60] *AF* 1.9 (June-Sept 1907), p. 2.
[61] *AF* 1.3 (Nov 1906), p. 1.

One morning in the cottage on the Mission grounds, two were healed before breakfast. Another morning at the family worship two were slain under the power and one received the baptism with the Holy Ghost. The dining room is a blessed place. The power comes down so upon the workers that we can scarcely eat. We sing, speak in tongues and praise God at the table. The food from heaven is the best part of the meal.[62]

The 'food from heaven' comes down on those who are serving and dining at the table so that they can scarcely eat or serve. The very activity required *for* the blessing to occur finds itself disrupted *by* the blessing that occurs. This incident in some ways characterizes the tenor of early Pentecostal spirituality, generally, and their sacramentality, specifically; it even perhaps works as a key to unlocking the meaning of early Pentecostal sacramental thought and practice.

Conclusions

After this close reading of the sacramentality witnessed to in *AF*, the following features stand out.

First, although not bound to traditional categories, early Pentecostal spirituality as witnessed by *AF* was unquestionably and at least in some sense robustly sacramental. Seymour and other contributors forcefully and repeatedly insist upon the importance of the ordinances of footwashing, water baptism, and the Lord's Supper.

Second, notwithstanding the fact that they remained unconcerned with metaphysical subtleties, the early Pentecostals whose voices are heard in *AF* clearly held to the belief that the Lord *personally acted* upon the participants in and through their observance of these rites. Even if they did not believe the baptism rite was regenerative, they clearly *did* believe baptism was a God-mandated practice, and their testimonies show that they experienced baptism as an occasion of the Spirit's work. Similarly, the laying on of hands and anointing with oil were common practices and regularly experienced as *means* by which the Spirit pours out God's grace on the church. In *AF*, the accent always falls on Christ's (and/or the Spirit's) *personal* presence and the *power* of the Spirit to heal, to convict of sin, to draw believers into God's presence.

---

[62] *AF* 1.8 (May 1907), p. 2.

Third, at least some of the Pentecostals of this period apparently regarded the Lord's Supper as the greatest of the several divinely-ordained means of healing. They were convinced that if taken in faith the Eucharistic bread and cup somehow mediated the soteriological power of the body of Jesus broken for the healing of the saints and his blood shed for their salvation and sanctification. Although Pentecostal preaching and instruction made much of the Supper's *symbolism*, observance of the meal was never *merely* symbolic or memorialistic. Certain scriptures, especially passages from 1 Corinthians and John 6, gave shape to the theological descriptions of the Eucharist, as did believers' shared *experience* of the Lord's Supper, as evidenced most clearly in Seymour's phrasing: '*We find that* …' The prevalent use of eating and drinking metaphors also suggests the early Pentecostal imagination was determined in large part by sacramental experiences, as well as by the readings of Scripture that illuminated these experiences.[63] All this to say, the Lord's Supper was basic, even *central*, to the experience of the Pentecostal spirituality witnessed by *AF*.

Fourth, the sacramentality of the Pentecostal pioneers was *not* restricted to the traditional rites of water baptism and Holy Communion. They expected God to act at the dinner table as well as at the sacramental altar; for them the dining room was no less sacred than a cathedral.

Fifth, the sacramentality one finds in *AF* often distorts normal referential distinctions, so that certain images and phrases work in multiple dimensions at once, something like Ezekiel's wheels-within-a-wheel. Often, statements that appear at first glance to refer to the sacraments in some straightforward sense turn out at a second glimpse to be allusions to a mystical experience. Because of this dynamic, it can be difficult at times to determine what reality in fact is being described – if indeed it is only one reality. This allusiveness/elusiveness remains one of the critical components of the grammar of early Pentecostal spirituality and sacramentality.

---

[63] Significantly, Pentecostal readings of John 6 diverge from the mainstream Protestant reading, which historically does not regard the discourse as a reference to the sacrament of the altar, in reaction to anti-sacramentalists' use of the saying, 'the flesh profits nothing'.

Azusa South and East: *The Bridegroom's Messenger*

G.B. Cashwell, returning to North Carolina after his experience at the Azusa St. Mission,[64] founded *TBM* as a vehicle for promoting Pentecostalism in the south.[65] Over the years, concern with 'false doctrine' both without and within the movement figured with increasing prominence in *TBM*. In Cashwell's own judgment, '… the late Pentecostal movement stands alone in the world, and is now fronting every heresy of hell and earth'.[66] As the movement extended its boundaries, new controversies arose and older ones persisted and intensified, with debates about Trinitarian doctrine, the application of Christ's 'Finished Work' to the believer in the *ordo salutis*, the meaning and purpose of glossolalia, and the organizing and establishing of governance for the Pentecostal churches appearing at every turn. Through all of this, Cashwell's and Sexton's paper speaks both of and to the sacraments, even if most often in indirect or indefinite ways.

'Come and Dine': Explicit Treatment of the Sacraments

Many in the developing Pentecostal movement(s) feared formality and organization, as did many non-Pentecostal revivalistic and restorationist movements of that period. Cashwell, formerly a Methodist Episcopal minister, remained deeply sympathetic with their concerns.[67] Like them, he believed the churches' histories proved beyond question that *organization* undermined the work of the Spirit, who was quenched by the traditionalism and formalism that they believed organization entailed.[68] This fear could at times give rise to a rejection of the notion of church altogether, and even of all things human or worldly. 'We have had human, soulish, psychical, natural religion so mixed in that it is a great task to come up into the wor-

---

[64] See Doug Beacham, *Azusa East: The Life and Times of G.B. Cashwell* (Franklin Springs, GA: LifeSprings Resources, 2006), pp. 35-58, and Vinson Synan, 'Gaston Barnabas Cashwell', *DPCM* (rev. ed.), pp. 457-58.

[65] Synan, *The Holiness-Pentecostal Tradition*, pp. 117-18. For a detailed examination of Cashwell's reasons for founding the periodical, see Beacham, *Azusa East*, pp. 129-31.

[66] *TBM* 2.33 (Mar 1, 1909), p. 2.

[67] *TBM* 2.33 (Mar 1, 1909), p. 2. See also *TBM* 2.29 (Jan 1, 1909), p. 4.

[68] See, for example, *TBM* 2.30 (Jan 15, 1909), p. 2. 'There is not a council of men on earth today that is able to set down rules and write out a discipline that will be able to govern the church of God. Men have tried to do that but they have failed.'

ship of God in the pure spirit. It is the ramification of these human earthly conceptions that hinders the great power of God among us. Oh! God, deliver us from the earthy.'[69]

Predictably, this repudiation of human and earthly means often entailed a rejection of the sacraments, too.[70] It is unsurprising that unlike many of the prominent leaders of the burgeoning Pentecostal movement, Cashwell did not regard the ordinances as mandatory rites. In point of fact, he feared contentions about the sacraments would splinter the emerging Pentecostal movement. In a late 1907 editorial, he addresses concerns arising within the movement. *First* among the divisions he lists is the battle over the value and purpose of the ordinances.[71] Understanding that those peopling this new movement hailed from various denominations and so held to different schools of thought, Cashwell called for patience and generosity. These issues, in his estimation, were at best of *penultimate* importance, because, as his experience told him, people were filled with the Spirit apart from these practices: 'the Holy Ghost takes up His abode in our being *before and after* we practise [*sic*] them'.[72] Nonetheless, the ordinances can and perhaps should be practiced by believers. At least, no one who has the Spirit of God rejects others for practicing them. Cashwell makes his own preferences clear:

> I love to take the bread and wine in remembrance of our Lord and Savior Jesus Christ, for I expect to see Him soon, and I love to wash feet with the Saints of God for I am not only willing, but I will do the humblest act possible to show my love and fellowship for them for we are all baptized into one body ...[73]

The most direct treatment of the sacraments comes in the third year of publication. In the headline article, Elizabeth Sexton draws readers' attention to a tract entitled 'The Doctrine of the Pentecostal Movement', a tract that advances in ten brief statements the teachings of 'special prominence' among Pentecostals.[74] The eighth

---

[69] *TBM* 1.22 (Sept 15, 1908), p. 2.
[70] See for example *TBM* 2.42 (July 15, 1909), p. 4.
[71] *TBM* 1.4 (Dec 15, 1907), p. 1.
[72] Emphasis added.
[73] *TBM* 1.4 (Dec 15, 1907), p. 1.
[74] *TBM* 2.37 (May 1, 1909), p. 1. Besides traditional Protestant doctrines such as the doctrine of the Trinity, vicarious atonement, the verbal inspiration of Scripture, justification by faith, and the eternal rewards for the faithful and faith-

is devoted to the ordinances. It is the briefest of the ten statements, and mentions only the Lord's Supper and water baptism.[75] Nonetheless, that the statement warrants a place in such a concise list speaks to the high value early Pentecostals placed on the sacraments, and the fact that Sexton afforded this tract special attention in subsequent issues[76] only serves to underscore the point.

Footwashing

Cashwell and Sexton counted themselves among those Pentecostal who did *not* consider footwashing one of the church's sacraments, although Cashwell did find the practice meaningful. Other contributors agreed. Hattie Barth, for example, explains Jesus' washing of his disciples' feet both as an ongoing work of Christ the intercessor and as a once-for-all paradigmatic example of the attitude required to live as the Lord's disciple. In her own words, Christ 'continues to wash in His own precious blood the feet of His disciples from every taint of sin gathered in this earthly walk'; therefore, imitating him, believers' love must demonstrate its authenticity in continuous self-giving ministry to others,[77] rather than in occasional ritual observance. At least a few readers of *TBM did* observe the rite, however, as at least one contributor makes clear: 'In accordance with His word (John 13), He definitely had shown us at the assembly of God at Cambridge, Mass., we should observe the Lord's Supper and the washing of feet on April 4th, the time God set for the passover [*sic*] to be eaten by the children of Israel'.[78] Obviously, this instance also points to the widespread practice of observing the Lord's Supper and footwashing together, and shows how tightly the connection between the church's Eucharist, Christ's Last Supper,

---

less, the tract also affirms teachings peculiar to Pentecostals: the 'baptism of the Holy Ghost and fire subsequent to cleansing', speaking in tongues as 'the distinguishing evidence' of Spirit baptism, and the restoration of 'all the gifts of the Spirit' to the end-time church. Additionally, the tract avows the teaching of divine healing 'provided for all in the atonement' and the pre-millennial return of Christ preceded by the 'catching away of the Bride', doctrines shared by other revivalist and holiness groups who could not accept one or all of the distinctly Pentecostal doctrines.

[75] Tellingly, the statement on justification by faith is relatively abbreviated, too. The statements on glossolalia and divine healing are relatively extensive.

[76] *TBM* 3.60 (Apr 15, 1910), and *TBM* 5.109 (May 1, 1912), p. 1.

[77] *TBM* 1.2 (Nov 1, 1907), p. 1.

[78] *TBM* 2.38 (May 15, 1909), p. 2.

and Israel's Passover meal was drawn frequently by early Pentecostals.

Laying on of Hands and Anointing with Oil
Like *AF*, *TBM* regards the practice of laying of hands and anointing with oil for healing as normative for Christian life and ministry.[79] For instance, a Brother Lehman writes, 'Two were healed instantly through the laying on of hands and the prayer of faith and the precious blood of Jesus'.[80] Sometimes, *both* healing and Spirit baptism were experienced *at once*, and, besides the laying on of hands, anointed handkerchiefs also were used to mediate healing.[81] Healing often took place at the altar, but in keeping with what one finds in *AF*, the means of healing were exercised outside official church gatherings as well, with some testifying of being healed in their homes.[82] The witness of *TBM* is clear: healing often if not always came about through *means*.[83]

Water Baptism
The editors and contributors to *TBM* regarded water baptism as a symbolic rite that does not in its own power effect any real change.[84] Nonetheless, they held that Christians should appreciate and observe the practice. The call to follow Christ *necessarily* leads to the waters of Christian baptism. Scripture is unmistakably clear on the matter.[85] In the opinion of a few, at least, water baptism, when observed faithfully, does in some sense actually accomplish 'the death and burial of the old man', and everyone seemingly agreed that the washing of baptism signifies burial with Christ in his death, as Romans 6 makes clear.[86]

The lengthiest treatment of baptism's meaning and purpose comes in the form of J.H. King's response to readers' questions about Paul's description of the baptism into Christ's death (Romans

---

[79] See for example *TBM* 1.1 (Oct. 1, 1907), pp. 3-4; *TBM* 1.2 (Nov 1, 1907), p. 3; *TBM* 1.6 (Jan 15, 1908), p. 1; *TBM* 4.77 (Jan 1, 1911), p. 3.

[80] *TBM* 5.114 (July 15, 1912), p. 2.

[81] *TBM* 2.31 (Feb 1, 1909), p. 3. See also, for example, *TBM* 3.56 (Feb 15, 1910), p. 4. '... as Brother Schoonmaker anointed Winnie with oil, he told her to expect Him to fill her with His Spirit as well as to heal her.'

[82] *TBM* 1.7 (Feb 1, 1908), p. 4; *TBM* 1.23 (Oct 1, 1908), p. 2.

[83] See for example *TBM* 1.1 (Oct 1, 1907), p. 4.

[84] See, for example, *TBM* 3.51 (Dec 1, 1909), p. 4.

[85] *TBM* 6.134 (June 1, 1913), p. 3.

[86] *TBM* 8.171 (June 1, 1915), p. 1; *TBM* 6.136 (July 1, 1913), p. 3.

6), and, more specifically, its relation to the rite of water baptism and its significance for believers' experience of entire sanctification. In King's opinion, water baptism, as a churchly act, serves as a public and ceremonial witness to an *already-effected* experience. 'In the act of baptism we publicly declare that we are united to Christ and to His death by being submerged into the element[87] as deeply as our bodies are in water.' The burial into Christ's death in fact is analogous *to* – not the effect *of* – faithful immersion in water. The term 'baptism', King insists, is figurative, and *'merely sets forth* that deep suffering through which the soul passes in being separated from sin, whether actual or original'.[88] The crucial experience – the *real* baptism, so to speak – is existential and not ceremonial.[89]

The Lord's Supper

In 1929, *TBM* published the text of a recently-delivered sermon by Hattie Barth, then the magazine's editor. Using 1 Cor. 5.8 as a text, she preached about 'communion', and in her sermon covered the sweep of human history from the 'open face to face communion' enjoyed by Adam and Eve before the Fall, through the history of Israel's election, the victory of God in Christ, and the ministry of the church, to the final restoration of all things at the ages' end. On her telling, between humanity's first sin and Christ's becoming sin for us, the bloody sacrifice served as a means of continued, spiritual communion, to keep humanity from being 'wholly cut off' from

---

[87] Apparently, King means by 'element' the spiritual reality of Christ's death.

[88] *TBM* 1.4 (Dec 15, 1907), p. 2. Emphasis added.

[89] One must be careful not to pigeonhole King's view of water baptism as strictly non-sacramental, however. In the course of his argument, King appeals to Wesley's notes on Romans, and it is highly unlikely he did not know Wesley's (sacramental) understanding of water baptism. If he disagrees with Wesley, he does not indicate it. Further, even after describing 'baptism into Christ's death' as the 'gradual process of self-annihilation', he goes on to claim that the experience of water baptism actually plays a part in the believer becoming 'more intimately united to Christ'. Obviously, then, King's view admits of various interpretations and cannot be described simply as non-sacramental. Of course, Wesley's view was itself complex – perhaps even inconsistent – and cannot be neatly categorized. For an account of Wesley's view, see Brian C. Brewer, 'Evangelical Anglicanism: John Wesley's Dialectical Theology of Baptism', *Evangelical Quarterly* 83.2 (Apr 2011), pp. 107-32. Paul W. Chilcote (*Recapturing the Wesleys' Vision: An Introduction to the Faith of John and Charles Wesley* [Downer's Grove, IL: IVP, 2004], p. 96) insists that for John Wesley, baptism was not merely a symbolic act, and that it was the ordinary means of salvation in the Christian community. See also Thomas C. Oden, *John Wesley's Scriptural Christianity: A Plain Exposition of His Teaching on Christian Doctrine* (Grand Rapids: Zondervan, 1994), pp. 301-309.

God.[90] Even more than the sacrifice of lambs and rams and doves, however, Israel's *Passover meal* was the principal means of communion.[91] Through the keeping of the Passover and the faithful offering of sacrifices – Israel remained in communion with God.

Other meals shared in this glory. Barth finds the church's Eucharist uniquely foreshadowed in Abraham's eating with Melchizedek: 'That bread and wine', she writes, 'we may be sure stood for the same thing that our communion stands for today, even the body and blood of our Lord Jesus Christ, who was crucified for us'. She suggests that it was in *this* way that Abraham 'foresaw' Christ.[92]

Given this, the church's Communion-meal, which 'replaced' Israel's Passover-feast, is an especially fitting means of grace. It is the greatest by far of all the instituted means of grace. Barth laments that many believers 'see nothing but an empty form in the Lord's supper', failing to 'discern' the Lord's body. Those who *do* discern Christ's body, who see 'back of the emblems the real life of Christ for our life', are enabled 'by faith to feed on Him' and thereby to receive healing for their bodies, 'a foretaste, an earnest of the redemption of the body', as well as spiritual nourishment for their spirits.[93]

The Eucharist is blessed, but there remains a promise of far deeper, even richer blessing:

> Beloved, there is a new, a fuller, sweeter, higher communion for us with Jesus when He comes again and we are reigning with Him in the Kingdom. He has been revealing Himself to mankind from dispensation to dispensation in ever increasing fullness, unfolding Himself more and more, and there are depths of His love and glory yet to be revealed.[94]

In the End, 'open face to face communion between God and man' will be restored, exactly as promised by Isa. 25.6-8. In conclusion, Barth prays to that end: 'Oh, our God, hasten the day, for what we

---

[90]Because it was a prefiguration of Christ's atoning death.

[91] On Barth's view, it was the 'more perfect form of communion' because it was a 'more complete type of Christ'.

[92] *TBM* 22.279 (Jan-Mar 1929), p. 1.

[93] In keeping with the view of Hattie Barth and many other Pentecostals of the time, many if not all contributors to *TBM* regarded the Supper as in some sense a sacrament of healing.

[94] *TBM* 22.271 (Jan-Mar 1929), p. 9.

thy creatures need, is face to face communion with our God, the giver of life, that we may have life and that death may be swallowed up of life'.[95]

TBM's references to the Lord's Supper are often obscure, allusive, and fragmentary. For example, one article insists that the 'show bread' of the Tabernacle 'represents the body of our Lord, by which living bread the saints now live'.[96] It is finally indecipherable whether or not this mention of 'living bread' is a reference to the Eucharist. It seems clear that early Pentecostals felt no need to make hard-and-fast distinctions in these matters. Many of the songs printed in *TBM* seem to prove this same willful inexactness; e.g. one invites: 'See at His table vacant places still/Oh! waiting guests, draw near!'[97] Perhaps the popular chorus 'Come and Dine' illustrates it best:

Jesus has a table spread
Where the saints of God are fed,
He invites His chosen people, 'Come and dine';
With His manna He doth feed
And supplies our every need:
Oh, 'tis sweet to sup with Jesus all the time!

'Come and dine', the Master calleth, 'Come and dine';
You may feast at Jesus' table all the time;
He Who fed the multitude, turned the water into wine,
To the hungry calleth now, 'Come and dine'.[98]

Clearly, *TBM* contributors – like first-generation Pentecostals, generally – spoke of feasting *on* (or *with*) Jesus in ways that exceeded the observance of Communion. Still, that they did talk so often and so fervently of eating (with) the Lord betrays an imagination fed, so to speak, by the Supper. It seems safe to conclude that they understood the biblical language of communion as *principally* and most

---

[95] *TBM* 22.271 (Jan-Mar 1929), p. 9.

[96] *TBM* 6.127 (Feb 15, 1913), p. 1.

[97] *TBM* 5.114 (July 15, 1912), p. 1.

[98] A second verse of the song promise that Jesus 'satisfies the hungry every time' when they obey the Lord's command to come and eat. The final verse looks to the eschatological wedding feast: 'Soon the Lamb will take His bride /To be ever at His side/All the host of heaven will assembled be/Oh, 'twill be a glorious sight/All the saints in spotless white/And with Jesus they will feast eternally'.

importantly a spiritual or mystical experience in and of Christ, even while they admitted that sometimes this experience could be occasioned as well as typified by the community's sharing in the Lord's Supper.[99] For some, at least, the Eucharist served *both* as a symbol of mystical 'eating' *and* as a way of obeying and imitating Jesus, and just so served as a kind of God-given means of grace.

'This is My Table': Testimonies of Sacramental Experience

One finds in *TBM* numerous testimonies of sacramental experiences. The communion service was regarded as an especially sacred time, a sanctity often evidenced by the 'hush of heaven' that fell on the celebrants.[100] The observance of the Lord's Supper apparently often opened up space in the community's life for the Spirit to work. For instance, one sister testifies to a message from God given at the close of the Communion meal by means of tongues and interpretation: 'I am well pleased with thee tonight, little flock, for what thou hast done in my name'. Following that word from the Lord, '[s]inging, praying and speaking in the new tongue were manifested in a beautiful way'.[101]

In 1915, *TBM* published the testimony of E.R. Trussel, whose story had been previously published in Boddy's *Confidence* and Flower's *Weekly Evangel*. Trussel testifies to a dream in which he held a conversation with 'my Lord regarding His Supper'.[102] In the dream, Trussel found himself standing near a small table draped in white. On the table he saw a 'small white loaf of bread' and a little silver cruse, filled with sweet wine. He sensed Jesus was there, although he could not see him. Three times he heard: 'This is My Table'. The last time, the Lord said: 'This is my medicine for my little children'. Trussel then received a vision of a crowd of sick and afflicted believers who, he was told, had come to Christ's Table 'carelessly, heedlessly, faithlessly' and as a result have grown worse 'because they have sinned' by their unworthy participation.[103] Realizing how often he too had failed in this regard, he received this vision a second and a third time.

---

[99] *TBM* 4.86 (May 15, 1911), p. 3.
[100] *TBM* 3.51 (Dec 1, 1909), p. 4.
[101] *TBM* 2.38 (May 15, 1909), p. 2.
[102] *TBM* 9.177 (Dec 1, 1915), p. 4. Previously published in *Confidence* 8.4 (April 1915), pp. 70-71, and *WE* 104 (Aug 21, 1915), p. 3.
[103] *TBM* 9.177 (Dec 1, 1915), p. 4.

Reflecting on these dreams and visions, Trussel ventures to explain what he has learned from the experience:

> I can see now that if we are sick or afflicted in any way and will partake of the bread and wine in faith, we must be healed, and will no longer be weakly and sickly and diseased if we are living in obedience to the will of God in other ways, and we have no right to eat until we examine ourselves and are clear before God, and not then if we are sick, unless we can eat in faith and be healed, for what is not of faith is sin.[104]

Later, Trussel received his healing while partaking of the Supper.[105] On the strength of his experiences, he asserts that the Lord's Supper is *'our Lord's medicine* to keep his children well and free from disease until He shall come again and call us to himself'.[106]

'Beggars at Jesus' Feast': Embedded Sacramentality

Early Pentecostal sacramentality was fertilely imprecise, and nothing illustrates this more clearly than the use of the feasting motif. In *TBM*, Christ is celebrated as the 'milk and honey and fine fruits' on which believers feast continually.[107] 'Hunger has passed away, for He satisfies me with His abiding presence.'[108] The image of the Lord's Table, drawn at least in part from a reading of Psalm 23, appears frequently in *TBM*. A.H. Butler celebrates the God who has 'spread His table for us in the presence of our enemies' and the 'real feast of fat things from our Father's table'.[109] Another brother recounts the joys of a recently-attended conference: 'The blessed Holy Ghost had control and quite a number of saints came from a distance, and how we did feast around our Father's table'.[110] Hattie

---

[104] *TBM* 9.177 (Dec 1, 1915), p. 4.

[105] He tells another story of a woman who, on hearing his testimony, declared she too would 'eat in faith' and immediately received her healing from headaches, after years of suffering.

[106] *TBM* 9.177 (Dec 1, 1915), p. 4. Emphasis added.

[107] *TBM* 1.6 (Jan 15, 1908), p. 1.

[108] *TBM* 1.6 (Jan 15, 1908), p. 3.

[109] *TBM* 1.2 (Nov 1, 1907), p. 2; *TBM* 2.23 (Oct 1, 1908), p. 2; see also *TBM* 1.8 (Feb 15, 1908), p. 3; *TBM* 6.134 (June 1, 1913), p. 2. The phrase, 'a feast of fat things', comes from Isa. 25.6 (KJV): 'And in this mountain shall the LORD of hosts make unto all people a feast of fat things, a feast of wines on the lees, of fat things full of marrow, of wines on the lees well refined'. The phrase appears frequently in early Pentecostal periodical literature.

[110] *TBM* 1.12 (Apr 15, 1908), p. 4.

Barth, reading the tabernacle's layout as a model of the Christian's journey into Christ-like maturity, identifies the 'holy place' with the Wesleyan-Holiness experience of entire sanctification. In her reading, the bread of the Presence typifies 'eating on Christ, putting on the new man', so that to eat Christ is to be wholly conformed to Jesus – to be *consumed* by him.[111] Needless to say, it remains unclear whether she means this in an exclusively existential and mystical sense, or if she also refers to participation in the Lord's Supper.

The Holy Spirit's work is not restricted to the Communion rite or to any of the activities of the community's worship gatherings. For example, even everyday meals sometimes served as media for God's transforming presence. A Sister McIntosh writes from Macao, China to inform the readers of a Christmas dinner she had prepared for some of her Chinese neighbors. Of all the gifts she received that Christmas, the greatest, she says, was from God, who directed her to host this feast for her neighbors. Convinced 'this was God speaking and wanting me to make a feast, just as His word held up, for the poor who couldn't make a feast for themselves', McIntosh set to work. She remembers that God 'ministered to our souls as we ministered to their bodies', and found that the feasting reawakened her desire for the Lamb's marriage supper. No one can attend *that* feast except for 'beggars', she insists – 'those who have begged their way into the fulness [*sic*] of God'.[112]

Whatever else it does, her testimony hints of a worldview shaped by belief that the Eucharist is the foretasting of *the* feast, the Lamb's marriage supper, hosted by the risen, finally triumphant Lord. It is difficult to think that this message was lost on the readers of *TBM*.

Conclusions

Some early Pentecostals apparently refused to practice the ordinances. Others, like Cashwell, stop short of such a position, indicating only that he finds participating in the sacraments personally rewarding, and insisting that Pentecostals must not despise those who do practice them. Elizabeth Sexton and her daughter, Hattie Barth, insist on the binding nature of the sacraments, and Barth provides a robustly sacramental description of the Eucharist. All in all, the sac-

---

[111] *TBM* 1.6 (Jan 15, 1908), p. 2. Another contributor appeals to the same image (p. 4).
[112] *TBM* 1.8 (Feb 15, 1908), p. 1.

ramentality one finds in *TBM* remains always more than merely memorialist. At least some of the contributors believed the Lord presented himself in the Supper and acted through the Supper for bodily healing and spiritual blessing. Many references to eating Christ or feasting at the Lord's Table remain vague so that it is difficult, even impossible, to discern whether they refer only to mystical communion or also to the sacramental experience of the church. Nonetheless, it is safe to say that at least for many of those Pentecostals whose voices are heard in *TBM*, the Eucharist served as a master-symbol for the Pentecostal experience of fellowship, not only with God but also with one another.

Church of God (Cleveland, TN): *Church of God Evangel*

Raised a Quaker and in his early 40's a convert to Pentecostalism, A.J. Tomlinson quickly emerged as one of the young movement's most prominent and influential leaders.[113] He first published his magazine, *The Evening Light and the Church of God Evangel* in March 1910, less than two years after his Spirit baptism.[114] After having been convinced of the Bible evidence for the ordinances, and ridding himself of the 'veil of Quakerism', A.J. Tomlinson plunged readily into the practice of the ordinances, regarding the ordinances as essential to the church's life.[115]

Practices of the Faithful Church: Explicit Treatment of the Sacraments

In the judgment of Tomlinson and the Church of God, observance of the ordinances of water baptism, footwashing, and the Lord's Supper is required of the Christian.[116] This is the unmistakable and irrevocable direction of Christ through the Scriptures. Being the Church of God, the (only) true people of God, meant teaching the 'whole Bible', and this required teaching the following doctrines:

---

[113] For Tomlinson's account of the history of the Church of God, see his *The Last Great Conflict* (Cleveland, TN: Walter E. Rodgers Press, 1913), pp. 184-98.

[114] He provided an explanation for the paper's name: 'The dark and cloudy day has passed. We are now in the evening of this wonderful gospel age'. See *COGE* 1.1 (Mar 1, 1910) p. 1.

[115] *COGE* 8.39 (Oct 6, 1917), p. 1.

[116] A.J. Tomlinson plainly prefers this term, although 'the sacrament' also is used.

Regeneration, sanctification, baptism with the Holy Ghost with other tongues as the Bible evidence, divine healing provided for in the atonement, the Lord's supper and feet-washing, the full restoration of the gifts to the Church, water baptism by immersion, and in fact all that Jesus ever taught, including tithes and offerings.[117]

For his part, Tomlinson puts it bluntly: 'Read where the Bible says wash one another's feet, and do it. Read again where He says, take the Lord's supper, then do it. Read where He says pay tithes, then do it'.[118] Jesus' teaching on footwashing is so clear that no one has an excuse to misunderstand.[119] All those who refuse to 'keep' the 'ordinances of God' cannot hope to prosper.[120] For this reason, Tomlinson and others set themselves against the anti-ordinance movements, making every effort to refute their claims. For example, Tomlinson writes,

> There has been a cry against water baptism and washing the saints' feet by many who have entered the ranks of Pentecost, the truth of water baptism and washing the saints' feet is in the Book, and remains as true and unshaken as if they had never raised their voice against it.[121]

Besides the clear teaching of Scripture, *COGE*, like *AF*, often appeals to believers' *experience* of the sacraments as an argument for the binding nature of the ordinances. 'I know', remarks one contributor, 'certain persons that rejected ordinances and government, and began to go down spiritually'. As a result of their stubbornness and refusal to yield to sound teaching, these anti-ordinance, anti-institutional Pentecostals 'are wandering off from the fold of God and will be forever lost except they repent ...'[122]

---

[117] *COGE* 11.22 (June 29, 1920), p. 1.
[118] *COGE* 8.39 (Oct 6, 1917), p. 1.
[119] *COGE* 1.5 (May 1, 1910), p. 4.
[120] *COGE* 11.30 (July 24, 1920), p. 3.
[121] *COGE* 1.9 (July 1, 1910), p. 1. For other examples, see *COGE* 5.4 (Jan 24, 1914), p. 8; *COGE* 9.16 (Apr 20, 1918), p. 4.
[122] For example, see *COGE* 12.3 (Jan 15, 1921), p. 3.

Footwashing

Like Seymour and other *AF* voices, Tomlinson and the *COGE* contributors maintained that footwashing is a church ordinance.[123] Tellingly, the Pentecostal Holiness church comes under explicit and fierce criticism for the notion of *'optional* foot-washing'.[124] A Tomlinson editorial contends that participants 'rejoice and shout and feel good' in their footwashing services, happy to acknowledge that footwashing is one of the 'orders of our Lord'.[125] Also, he and the Church of God maintained the closest connection between the Supper and footwashing.[126] Sometimes, at least, the churches 'assembled at the altar for the sacrament' at the conclusion of the sermon, and, after this, turned to 'the good old time love feast of feet washing'.[127]

Concerned with exact and complete obedience to the Scripture's dictates,[128] the Church of God's sacramental discussions sound virtually scholastic, at times. For example, a questioner asks, 'In observing the ordinance of feet washing, should one foot be washed or both feet?' The answer, as one would expect, is that *both* feet should be washed; Jn 13.10-14 is adduced as conclusive evidence for this position.[129]

Laying on of Hands and Anointing with Oil

The Church of God believed the laying of hands was often if not always necessary for Spirit baptism,[130] as well as for physical healing, as directed by James 5 and Mark 16.[131] Some insisted that the laying on of hands is *not* required for Spirit baptism, holding that the fact that it sometimes *does* happen that way is no proof that it *must.*[132]

---

[123] Tomlinson (*COGE* 6.15 [Apr 10, 1915], p. 1) insists that footwashing is unmistakably plainly taught in Scripture, as are baptism and the Lord's Supper.

[124] *COGE* 6.5 (Jan 30, 1915), p. 4. Emphasis added.

[125] *COGE* 6.1 (Jan 2, 1915), p. 1.

[126] There were exceptions, however rare. See, for example, *COGE* 1.18 (Nov 15, 1910), p. 1.

[127] *COGE* 12.34 (Aug 20, 1921), p. 2.

[128] One contributor, for example, can say that to fail to observe the ordinances is to 'be guilty of all' wrongdoing. See *COGE* 14.35 (Sept 1, 1923), p. 3.

[129] Minutes of the General Assembly (Jan 9-14, 1912), p. 22. Actually, the text reads 'John 3:10-14', but this is obviously a typographical error.

[130] *COGE* 5.23 (June 6, 1914), p. 5.

[131] See *COGE* 5.24 (June 13, 1914), p. 6, and *COGE* 6.11 (Mar 13, 1915), p. 2.

[132] *COGE* 12.41 (Oct 8, 1921), p. 3.

Some argued that the imposition of hands for healing as ordained by Jesus himself fell within the rights of every 'true believer', indicating that at least some within the Church of God believed only the *ordained* should exercise this ministry.[133] Others took a different tack, finding in Scripture three ways to seek healing for the sick: (1) anointing with oil and prayer, (2) the imposition of hands, and (3) the word of faith. Only the first of these is available to *all* believers. The other ways belong only to those who have the 'gift of healing'. The Spirit who dispenses the *charismata* has determined the different rights of the church's individual members.[134] Certainly, it was a widespread practice to anoint the sick with oil and to pray for them by imposition of hands.[135]

Most in the Church of God agreed that the laying on of hands was necessary for *ordination*.[136] In their judgment, Scripture makes it clear that the careful ordination of ministers (bishops, pastors, deacons) is required of the one faithful church.[137] Therefore, only ordinations performed by Church of God bishops counted as legitimate; all other ordinations were invalid.[138]

Anti-ordinance movements claimed the authority of Scripture had been supplanted by the coming of the Spirit, and considered the New Testament ordinances as superfluous as circumcision and Sabbath observance to the Spirit-filled believer; in the same way, they determined ministerial ordination was as unnecessary as a hereditary priestly order. The Church of God stood against these innovations at every turn, and *COGE* editors and contributors warned against those 'enemies to the Word of God' who are

---

[133] *COGE* 8.5 (Feb 3, 1917), p. 3.

[134] *COGE* 12.28 (July 9, 1921), p. 2.

[135] See e.g. *COGE* 5.14 (Apr 4, 1914), pp. 1- 2.

[136] For an account of an ordination service, see *COGE* 12.26 (June 25, 1921), p. 2. Some accepted this position only reluctantly. One brother writes to explain his own conversion: 'Formerly, I did not believe in the laying on of hands and being ordained to preach the gospel. I always said that God baptized me with the Holy Ghost and called me to preach the gospel and I didn't need to be set apart by the laying on of hands. I prayed to God very earnestly about this and searched the Scriptures and I found where Jesus ordained his apostles and that Paul was set apart by the laying on of hands, and Paul said to follow him as he followed Christ'. *COGE* 8.4 (Jan 27, 1917), p. 3.

[137] *COGE* 5.21 (May 23, 1914), p. 8.

[138] *COGE* 7.20 (May 13, 1916), p. 1.

ignoring the holy commandments of the Lord and declaring that holy baptism was only intended for the Jews, that observing the holy sacrament is not required of the children of God in these days, that washing the saints feet is only practiced by the weak-minded and fanatics; and thus fleecing the Lamb of every visible ordinance that He has left for His true children to remember His example.[139]

Water Baptism

In spite of some confusion over whether biblical references to baptism referred to *water* baptism or *Spirit* baptism, the early Pentecostals whose voices are heard in *COGE* agreed that Scripture mandates even the form: 'there is only one mode that rightly be called baptism', i.e. immersion in water. No other form of the practice is recognizable as baptism.[140] Sprinkling fails to suffice because the symbol must express the reality of *dying with Christ*, as described in Romans 6. In the same way, the rite also must symbolize *rising* with Christ: 'The breaking forth from the watery grave in baptism represents the resurrection'.[141] This conviction that the baptismal rite not only fulfilled the biblical mandate but also served as means of entering into Christ's life[142] is demonstrated by the use of the formula '… followed the Lord in baptism', which appears frequently.[143]

Although they deemed water baptism crucial to the life of obedience, many Pentecostals nonetheless took time to explain that the rite of washing was insufficient by itself. F.J. Lee, who followed A.J. Tomlinson as editor of *COGE,* explains that the 'baptism into Christ' of which Scripture speaks (e.g. Gal. 3.27; Rom. 6.3) refers to something more than the ritual washing of baptism. It means being 'completely immersed in Christ not the water, but absorbed in Him, swallowed up in Him'.[144] Although the true church *does* practice water baptism, along with footwashing and the Lord's Supper, as a

---

[139] *COGE* 9.16 (Apr 20, 1918), p. 4.
[140] *COGE* 7.17 (Apr 22, 1916), p. 1. See also *COGE* 14.2 (Jan 13, 1923), p. 3.
[141] *COGE* 14.13 (Mar 31, 1923), p. 3.
[142] *COGE* 12.36 (Sept 3, 1921), p. 2; *COGE* 13.36 (Sept 9, 1922), p. 2; *COGE* 13.38 (Sept 23, 1922), p. 3.
[143] See for example, *COGE* 1.7 (June 1, 1910), p. 7; *COGE* 1.10 (July 15, 1910), p. 6; *COGE* 1.16 (Oct 15, 1910), p. 7.
[144] *COGE* 14.2 (Jan 13, 1923), p. 3.

God-given ordinance, these prove of no use 'without the power of Jesus Christ'.[145]

The Lord's Supper

COGE contributors did not believe the Sacrament worked salvation directly.[146] F.J. Lee fears for those who trust in their regular partaking of the Eucharist, rather than simple obedience in faith, for, as Scripture warns, not everyone who claims Christ does so truly.[147] The Supper does not work apart from the faithful response of the participants, and believers are instructed against a 'tread-mill use of the means' that cannot truly help them 'advance in grace'.[148] Believers must resist the 'temptation to formality', for in spite of the fact that the 'outward ordinances must be attended to', these will be of no profit 'if the inner heart is not in touch with Jesus the source of all life and power'.[149] The elements of Communion are not really transformed into Christ's body and blood, as Catholics teach; instead, they serve as *emblems* of his death.[150] Like most Pentecostals of the time, the Church of God held that the Eucharistic bread symbolized Christ's broken body.[151] For reasons that are not clear, however, they apparently did not follow other Pentecostals in believing that the Lord's Supper serves as a means of bodily healing – in spite of the fact that the *Evangel* speaks often of healing, and of the means of grace.

It would be a mistake, however, to think that the Church of God was anti-sacramental. To the contrary, there is a robust sacramentality to be found in *COGE*. At the core, there is the conviction that the apostolic church necessarily keeps the *full* gospel, so that keeping the ordinances laid down by divine decree is nothing less than decisive for the church's identity as the true people of God.[152] If the bread and wine of the Supper *could* be taken without profit to the participants, such was not *necessarily* the case, for 'the blessed ordinance is so well established in the minds of all Christian people' that those who fail for whatever reason to participate in the Lord's

---

[145] *COGE* 5.31 (Aug 1, 1914), p. 6.
[146] For example, see *COGE* 5.11 (Mar 14, 1914), p. 7.
[147] *COGE* 5.11 (Mar 14, 1914), p. 7.
[148] *COGE* 12.38 (Sept 17, 1921), p. 1.
[149] *COGE* 6.7 (Feb 13, 1915), p. 3.
[150] *COGE* 12.25 (June 18, 1921), p. 4.
[151] *COGE* 12.25 (June 18, 1921), p. 4.
[152] *COGE* 7.48 (Nov 25, 1916), p. 3.

Supper have 'missed some of the most sacred and hallowed moments in the entire Christian Life'; indeed, 'nothing could take the place of the Lord's Supper'.[153] Further, Pentecostals are exhorted to the regular use of the sacraments, including the Lord's Supper: 'every available means of grace should be utilized'.[154] These means of grace serve to bring about the 'improvement and advancement' of the children of God.[155] Tomlinson goes so far as to level a warning at *COGE* readers: 'I'd be afraid to neglect partaking of the Lord's Supper and the washing of feet according to His Word'.[156] Believers live confidently in the 'overcoming power' of the Holy Spirit who makes it so that believers can function as 'acceptable members of the body of Christ' keeping 'all the ordinances, forms, and ways of the religion of Jesus Christ'.[157]

Tomlinson, Lee, and other Church of God leaders attended carefully to the mechanics of the Eucharistic celebration, a fact that points to the strength of their sacramentality. Although they allowed each congregation to decide *when* to have the Sacrament, they did not leave any question *that* it should be done. They understood that Christians from antiquity observed the Sacrament on the Lord's Day, and they insisted that only Church of God ordained ministers should administer Communion.[158] Non-alcoholic wine was to be used for Communion, never water. As Lee explains, the Scripture in no fewer than three places clearly states that Jesus said *wine* was in the cup he shared with his disciples; and, just as importantly, water simply cannot function as an effective *symbol* of Christ's bloody death – only the fruit of the vine can do that.[159]

---

[153] *Book of Doctrines*, pp. 68-69.

[154] *COGE* 7.31 (July 29, 1916), p. 1. Clearly, the fact that such language enjoyed widespread currency among early Pentecostals suggests that the Pentecostal imagination received its shape in part at least from the influence of traditional Wesleyan sacramentality, even if Pentecostals (following their Holiness predecessors) used the language in ways that exceeded and/or transgressed traditional classifications, at least at points.

[155] *COGE* 1.12 (Aug 15, 1910), p. 2. See also *COGE* 6.9 (Feb 27, 1915), p. 4.

[156] *COGE* 6.4 (Jan 23, 1915), p. 1.

[157] *COGE* 7.2 (Jan 8, 1916), p. 4.

[158] *COGE* 5.28 (July 11, 1914), p. 7; *COGE* 9.15 (Apr 13, 1918), p. 2; *COGE* 12.25 (June 18, 1921), p. 4. Lee appeals to Pliny's letter to Trajan, Ignatius' letters, and the *Apostolic Constitutions* for evidence that early Christians met on Sunday for worship.

[159] *COGE* 12.25 (June 18, 1921), p. 4.

'The Form of the "Fourth"': Testimonies of Sacramental Experience

One finds in *COGE* scores of testimonies of sacramental experience. For the Church of God, there was no doubt about the necessity of observing the ordinances, which were regarded as 'sacred and impressive' rites.[160] Often, launching a new congregation and 'setting the church in order' included the celebration of the Sacrament.[161] A brother writes from Kingston, Jamaica, rejoicing that in the receiving of Communion, 'we had wonderful manifestations through the Spirit, speaking in tongues and interpretation and shouting'.[162] One sister became so 'happy' during the time of footwashing and Communion that she 'danced under the power' until she fell into an hours-long trance and had a vision of heaven.[163] A report of revival services in Cleveland, TN explains,

> Six dear children of God followed Jesus in baptism, and several engaged in the Lord's Supper and the washing of the saints [*sic*] feet. The Spirit fell in this service *as usual*, and those who had never engaged in feet washing, received special blessing.[164]

These experiences led them to the conviction the Lord's Supper was 'the most wonderful of all'.[165] If some congregations did not hold to such a high view of the ordinances,[166] they were the exception, not the rule.

Evidently, many of the members of the Church of God expected the sacramental events to occasion Christ's presence and the Spirit's work in uniquely powerful ways. Participating in washing feet and eating the Supper, they found themselves 'greatly blessed with the presence of the Lord',[167] receiving the Lord's power and

---

160 *COGE* 8.19 (May 19, 1917), p. 2. Relating the successes of an evangelistic endeavor, one contributor remarks: '*Of course* we had the Lord's supper and washed each others [*sic*] feet as Jesus said we ought to do'. See *COGE* 5.41 (Oct 10, 1914), p. 3. Emphasis added.

161 *COGE* 8.27 (July 14, 1917), p. 3.

162 *COGE* 12.31 (July 30, 1921), p. 3.

163 *COGE* 5.42 (Oct 17, 1914), p. 7. For similar stories, see *COGE* 6.3 (Jan 16, 1915), p. 2, and *COGE* 6.3 (Jan 16, 1915), p. 3.

164 *COGE* 1.16 (Oct 15, 1910), p. 4. Emphasis added.

165 *COGE* 6.43 (Oct 23, 1915), p. 3.

166 See, for example, *COGE* 1.19 (Dec 1, 1910), p. 6.

167 *COGE* 1.19 (Dec 1, 1910), p. 6. There is a wealth of similar references; for example, see: *COGE* 5.32 (Aug 8, 1914), p. 8; *COGE* 5.51 (Dec 26, 1914), p. 3;

blessing.[168] If one can testify that 'God was there' in the sacramental service,[169] another can say that 'the Holy Ghost manifested Himself' wonderfully,[170] and another can boast that 'Jesus himself was present'.[171] As they obeyed Christ's command to eat the Supper and wash the feet of the saints, they were 'enveloped in the real glories of heaven'.[172]

Often, Sunday evening services were dedicated to observing the Supper and footwashing.[173] Special services such as revivals, camp-meetings, and church conferences regularly closed in this way, as well.[174] A Sister Barr testifies of such a service:

> Sunday night the Lord's Supper, and the eleventh chapter of First Corinthians was preached from. After the sermon was delivered the Lord led me to read the thirteenth chapter of St. John and explain every verse until I got to the seventeenth verse, and then we went into the performance of the chapter, and *the Lord Himself was there*. Impressions were made the hearts of the people such as had never been before in any of our services. I must say that the children of God are happier since they have obeyed the commands as given in Matt. 28:10 and St. John 13.[175]

Another testimony celebrates a recent July 4th service that was 'wonderfully blest of God'. It was 'one of the most victorious services' as the saints took the Sacrament and washed one another's feet.

COGE 6.33 (Aug 14, 1915), p. 3; *COGE* 7.30 (July 22, 1916), p. 3; *COGE* 7.47 (Nov 18, 1916), p. 3; *COGE* 7.53 (Dec 30, 1916), p. 2; *COGE* 8.2 (Jan 13, 1917), p. 3; *COGE* 8.23 (June 16, 1917), p. 4; *COGE* 9.11 (Mar 16, 1918), p. 3; *COGE* 10.30 (July 26, 1919), p. 3; *COGE* 12.20 (May 14, 1921), p. 3; *COGE* 14.37 (Sept 8, 1923), p. 1.

[168] *COGE* 1.3 (Apr 1, 1910), p. 7.

[169] *COGE* 5.7 (Feb 14, 1914), p. 4.

[170] *COGE* 1.7 (June 1, 1910), p. 7.

[171] *COGE* 1.12 (Aug 15, 1910), p. 7.

[172] *COGE* 14.31 (Aug 4, 1923), p. 2.

[173] See, for example *COGE* 1.12 (Aug 15, 1910), p. 7; *COGE* 5.21 (May 23, 1912), p. 8; *COGE* 5.25 (June 20, 1914), p. 3; *COGE* 5.27 (July 4, 1914), p. 8; *COGE* 8.29 (July 28, 1917), p. 4; *COGE* 8.46 (Nov 24, 1917), p. 3; *COGE* 12.4 (Jan 22, 1921), p. 2; *COGE* 14.30 (July 28, 1923), p. 4.

[174] For other examples, see *COGE* 1.14 (Sept 15, 1910), p. 1; *COGE* 12.34 (Aug 20, 1921), p. 2; *COGE* 12.37 (Sept 10, 1921), p. 2; *COGE* 14.31 (Aug 4, 1923), p. 2.

[175] *COGE* 1.7 (June 1, 1910), p. 7. Emphasis added.

As the bread was broken and mention made of the broken body of Jesus, He seemed to manifest His presence in the midst. As I stood there in the presence of God and before the audience with the broken bread, a piece in each hand, I seemed to get a broader view of the Christ and wonderful scheme of redemption than ever before. The form of the 'Fourth' seemed to be there.

The testimony continues, detailing how the people filled the altars and 'knelt in companies one after another' in waves, while music and singing carried on. Everyone participated reverently. Then, at the proper time, the Lord's Supper was served: all was quiet except for the 'groans and sobs as the deacons passed the bread and wine'. After everyone had participated, they washed one another's feet, the men taking one side of the sanctuary, and women the other side. The service was punctuated with '[t]ears, shouts, praises, embracing, handshaking, talking in tongues, singing', and the contributor recalls how the power fell on his own daughter while she played the organ; 'she played for several minutes under the power of the Spirit'. Some sang in tongues, others prophesied, and many experienced other manifestations of the Spirit as the 'Power began to fall again', with signs and wonders following.

Some began to fall into the altar crying for mercy; some fell back in the congregation down between the benches. When there was room made at the altars by deliverance coming to those who were there, others would take their place, filling up the altar again. The work continued until late at night after a number were converted, backsliders reclaimed, several sanctified, and probably ten or twelve swept through to Pentecost.[176]

It is difficult to appreciate the profoundly imaginative and *affective* dimensions of these early Pentecostal celebrations of the Supper. In the words of one *COGE* contributor, communion is a 'heart rending time' in which believers remember 'our blessed Christ as he hung on the cruel cross on Calvary's bloody brow and his body was broken for us, and his blood shed for you and me'.[177] The celebration of the Lord's Supper and footwashing effects 'a deep feeling of

---

[176] *COGE* 1.10 (July 15, 1910), pp. 1-2. For a similar example, see *COGE* 1.20 (Dec 15, 1910), p. 6.
[177] *COGE* 5.8 (Feb 21, 1914), p. 8.

sacredness and fellowship'. Because Christ is felt to be personally present to the participants, the congregation enters an atmosphere of solemnity, as '[t]he heart melts completely in contemplation of the death and sufferings of Christ' and the 'deepest gratitude and devotion' arises from reflection on the agony in the garden.[178] 'Our sorrow is often too deep for words', and 'often we break into tears'.[179] This affectivity arose from the participants' imaginative participation in the events of Christ's saving death.

> As the unleavened bread is broken can we not hear the beat of the hammer that drove the nails into His hands and His feet? And the spear piercing His side? And as we behold the wine in the cup, does it not better than anything else in the world bring thoughts of the shed blood of Christ – the tears in the Garden that were as great drops of blood? And the blood that trickled down, and flowed from His hands and His feet, and gushed from His side – and He bowed His head, and said, 'It is finished'.[180]

Whatever one makes of the explicit theological statements of the Church of God, these testimonies demonstrate that the experience of the sacraments could not rightly be described as merely memorialist.

'They Who Eat His Word': Embedded Sacramentality

As with the other Pentecostal periodicals of the time, one finds in *COGE* frequent uses of the eating and drinking motif. Several testify that the weekly *COGE* installments serve as God's banquet for them.[181] Worship services, including observance of the ordinances, sermons,[182] and testimonies,[183] also served as occasions for everyone to 'enjoy a feast of fat things and the outpouring of the Spirit'.[184] Each Pentecostal believed he or she was 'feasting with my dear Lord'.[185] Obviously shaped by John 6, members of the Church of

---

[178] *COGE* 1.18 (Nov 15, 1910), p. 1.
[179] *Book of Doctrines*, p. 69.
[180] *Book of Doctrines*, p. 69.
[181] *COGE* 3.14 (Sept 15, 1912), p. 1.
[182] *COGE* 1.18 (Nov 15, 1910), p. 8.
[183] *COGE* 5.1 (Jan 3, 1914), p. 8.
[184] *COGE* 1.3 (Apr 1, 1910), p. 8; *COGE* 5.23 (June 5, 1914), p. 2.
[185] *COGE* 1.17 (Nov 1, 1910), p. 8.

God expected to feast on the Bread of life.[186] '[T]rue worshippers are and let the Holy Spirit have His way because the flesh represents the Word and the blood the Spirit.'[187] Everyone is invited not only to drink but also to drink 'freely'.[188] The language of Acts 2 also informed their experience, although they did not always apply it to the Sacrament of the Table. One brother testifies of a camp-meeting in which everyone 'had all things common, eating at one table',[189] and reflecting on Acts 2.42-47, another contributor exclaims: 'The table of Jesus is spread in the midst of where the poor, the blind, the maimed and the halt can come and eat and drink a satisfying portion, and can stay there and feast all the time'.[190]

In keeping with their fellow Pentecostals' habits of speech, those in the Church of God spoke often and with deep emotion about the eschatological feast.[191] The image of the Lord's Table occurs frequently, as well.[192] And while many speak of it as an *analogy* for the benefit of Christian fellowship,[193] they also could use the title as shorthand for Holy Communion.[194] This indicates that the shared experience of the Sacrament did much to shape the understanding of their communion with God and with one another. It appears the Lord's Supper provided for them a most important symbol of this mystical communion, and in some sense helped to effect this communion.

Conclusions

It can hardly be disputed that the Church of God boasted the strongest ecclesiology of all the early Pentecostal groups, and *CO-GE* makes clear that in its formative years the Church of God believed the Lord had ordained certain practices for his one, true

---

[186] *COGE* 5.13 (Mar 28, 1914), p. 6.

[187] *COGE* 1.14 (Sept 15, 1910), p. 6.

[188] *COGE* 5.23 (June 6, 1914), p. 4.

[189] *COGE* 1.14 (Sept 15, 1910), p. 6.

[190] *COGE* 11.47 (Nov 27, 1920), p. 4. See also *COGE* 1.10 (July 15, 1910), p. 1; also, *COGE* 5.19 (May 9, 1914), p. 5.

[191] See, for example, *COGE* 6.17 (Apr 25, 1915), p. 3; *COGE* 6.20 (May 15, 1915), p. 2; *COGE* 9.8 (Feb 23, 1918), p. 3; *COGE* 14.30 (July 28, 1923), p. 4; *COGE* 14.34 (Aug 25, 1923), p. 2.

[192] *COGE* 1.5 (May 1, 1910), p. 6.

[193] For example, see *COGE* 11.38 (Sept 8, 1920), p. 4; COGE 14.31 (Aug 4, 1923), p. 3.

[194] For example, see *COGE* 14.17 (Apr 28, 1923), p. 2; *COGE* 11.2 (Jan 10, 1920), p. 1.

church, including foot-washing, water baptism, the laying on of hands and anointing with oil, as well as the Lord's Supper. While they fiercely resisted (at least in word, if not practice) temptations to formalism, they constantly urged believers to give themselves wholeheartedly to these sacred practices. Emphasis falls again and again on the unmistakable clarity of Scripture in these matters: if some refuse to observe the sacraments it is due either to ignorance or to willful neglect. Given that the Lord's will is so clearly stated, believers must respond in spirited obedience, following Jesus by observing these sacraments.

Numerous testimonies indicate that they understood themselves as objects of God's personal activity in and through the Lord's Supper and footwashing, as well as other ordinances. The vibrant affectivity of their sacramental experiences witnesses to the sacraments' significance and potency, as well. No one can read these testimonies without concluding that Pentecostals in the early Church of God frequently, even *commonly*, believed Jesus Christ was really, personally present to his church in their observance of the Lord's Supper, and that in these moments, the Holy Spirit also was at work, accomplishing the will of God in and among those gathered at the Lord's Table. Perhaps most interestingly, the Church of God apparently differed from most Pentecostals of the time by not speaking of the Lord's Supper as a means of healing. To be sure, they did not outright reject the notion, but neither did they make use of it, even while they vigorously championed the claim that bodily healing was guaranteed by Christ's atoning death.

The Pentecostal Holiness Church: *The Pentecostal Holiness Advocate*

The 1917 convention of the Pentecostal Holiness Church included the initiation of a weekly periodical to serve as the official literary organ of the church.[195] G.F. Taylor was chosen as editor and business manager of the paper, which was entitled *The Pentecostal Holiness Advocate*.[196] Taylor published the first issue of *PHA* in May 1917.

---

[195] Vinson Synan, *Old Time Power* (Franklin Springs, GA: Life Springs, 1998), pp. 152-53.

[196] Joseph E. Campbell, *The Pentecostal Holiness Church* 1898-1948 (Franklin Springs, GA: Publishing House of Pentecostal Holiness Church, 1951), pp. 536-37.

'All the Means of Grace': Explicit Treatment of the Sacraments

One finds frequent use of 'means of grace' language in *PHA*, perhaps owing to the Wesleyan-Methodist training of the denominational leaders.[197] For instance, a North Carolina pastor suggests that as with armies in war-time, so in the life of the believer: some blessings come only at the cost of 'the greatest self sacrifice, most heroic faith, and tremendous effort', which for the Christian involves prayer, the study of Scripture, and 'all the means of grace of which our whole being is capable'.[198] G.F. Taylor, defending the 'rich heritage' that Pentecostals enjoy as Christians,[199] finds it profoundly troubling that most of his Pentecostal brothers and sisters are not using all the means of grace, unwisely and unnecessarily limiting themselves to only a few.[200] He concludes the piece with an admonition to pursue the same holiness the martyrs modeled. 'What the most perfect Christian has become through grace we may become if we are as diligent in the use of the means of grace.'[201] Without doubt, Taylor understands the means of grace as practices handed down by previous generations of holy men and women and it is inconceivable that he would not have considered baptism and the Lord's Supper as two such practices.

Footwashing

Unlike many other Wesleyan-Holiness Pentecostals, Taylor and the PH Church did not understand footwashing as a binding ordinance. Taylor read Jn 13.1-16 typologically, holding that Jesus' washing of his disciples' feet models an *attitude* that believers must imitate.[202]

---

[197] For example, *PHA* 1.10 (July 5, 1917), p. 1; *PHA* 3.19-20 (Sept 4, 11 1919), p. 3.

[198] *PHA* 1.33 (Dec 13, 1917), p. 3.

[199] In his words, 'every doctrine of our holy religion has been baptized with the blood of millions of martyrs', and Pentecostals, like all Christians, have only what 'the martyred saints bequeathed to us'.

[200] *PHA* 9.27 (Nov 5, 1925), p. 1. Emphasis added.

[201] *PHA* 9.27 (Nov 5, 1925), p. 1. It is not entirely clear what Taylor means by this designation, although he obviously thinks of the devotional reading of Scripture as belonging to it. Presumably, however, he means by it what the Wesleyan tradition means by it: Taylor came to Pentecostalism from a Methodist Episcopal background through the Holiness movement.

[202] He also held that John 13 is not an alternate account of Jesus' Last Supper; in his own words, 'the supper at which the feet were washed was not the passo-

Although he will not object to those who practice the rite, he maintains that it is not required of them. 'We have no objection to those who wish to follow this example by washing each other's feet. Personally, I do not see this as a church ordinance, but I can not [*sic*] object to it among those who wish to practice it.'[203] T.A. Melton held the same position on these matters.[204] Unquestionably, water baptism and the Supper are ceremonies of the new covenant, and *perhaps* footwashing is such a rite, as well. However, if Scripture intends it to be 'literally practiced' as a churchly rite, then it is 'strictly ceremonial', he insists.[205]

Laying on of Hands and Anointing with Oil

A reading of *AF* and *TBM* shows that the early Wesleyan-Holiness Pentecostals held that the imposition of hands was directed not only for healing, but also for Spirit baptism,[206] and (less often) ordination. The witness of the *PHA* is the same. J.O. Lehman writes from Johannesburg to report of several healings through the laying on of hands, a practice he believes mandated by the Scriptures.[207] In his contribution, T.L. Robertson finds that the contemporary church when compared to the earliest Christians, who were 'really in full power', falls short, for the primitive Christians could '*transmit* the baptism of the Spirit by the laying on of hands, ordaining people in power, healing the sick, etc.'[208]

Some assume that Christ's ongoing healing ministry is accomplished via churchly *means*; one brother makes this claim, but quickly points out that he intends *only* those means explicitly described in the Bible: 'I believe in the use of Scriptural means, such as the laying on of hands, the anointing of oil and the prayer of faith'.[209] G.F. Taylor argues similarly. Citing Mark 16, Taylor boasts: 'Here we

---

ver [*sic*] supper, nor the time when the Lord's supper was given'. See *PHA* 1.39 (Jan 24 1918), p. 2. F.M. Britton (*PHA* 9.51 [Apr 29, 1926], p. 2) offers an explanation of what he identifies as the four suppers of Passion Week, with the footwashing happening on the second, and the Lord's Supper, the third.

[203] *PHA* 3.30 (Nov 20, 1919), p. 2. Clearly, this shows that at some in the Pentecostal Holiness Church *did* practice it.

[204] *PHA* 6.45 (Mar 8, 1923), p. 5.

[205] *PHA* 1.16 (Aug 16, 1917), p. 8.

[206] *PHA* 1.23 (Oct 4, 1917), p. 3.

[207] *PHA* 1.20 (Sept 13, 1917), p. 5; *PHA* 11.27 (Nov 3, 1927), p. 13.

[208] *PHA* 14.13 (July 24, 1930), p. 3. Emphasis added.

[209] *PHA* 3.149 (Apr 1, 1920), p. 3.

have the promise direct from Jesus that the sick shall be healed with the laying on of hands by those that believe'. Taylor then moves to consider James 5. He takes the reference to the elders to refer primarily to 'ordained ministers', but acknowledges that it may also refer to 'anyone who has faith in God for healing, minister or layman'. The sick person is anointed with oil, but the oil is not rubbed into the skin, for the prayer of faith and not the oil itself accomplishes the healing. As the Scripture says, this is a time for confession of sins to one another, as well. These are the 'Bible instructions' for healing.[210] As Taylor's sees it, the Divine Physician, like any surgeon, retains certain 'instruments' and uses them as needed. The 'complete set of instruments' includes the prayer of faith, anointing with oil, laying on of hands, the Name of Jesus, and the Blood of Jesus. The patient, of course, must cooperate, confessing his faults – exactly as James 5 directs.[211]

Many, in the midst of their theological reflection, make a point to explain that the laying of hands *by itself* avails nothing. Taylor, for one, takes up the story of Naaman's healing as an example, finding in the prophet's command to wash in the Jordan an analogy to Christ's command to lay on hands and anoint with oil. As it was with Naaman, these gestures in themselves do not effect the healing, he asserts, but the healing will not come without them, for healing depends upon obedience. 'There is no remedy in the laying on of hands. There is no remedy in anointing with oil.'[212] Along the same lines, others argue that the imposition of hands is *never* the means of God's activity, at least not in any straightforward sense.

> Human agency has a part in the dissemination of the gospel, but not in the mysterious power of the Holy Ghost ... Laying on of hands has never healed a sick body, or brought the baptism of the Holy Spirit in its self. We believe God, we obey God, then His power is put into motion that surpasses human reason.[213]

---

[210] *PHA* 1.42 (Feb 14, 1918), p. 4.
[211] *PHA* 3.30 (Nov 20, 1919), p. 7.
[212] *PHA* 4.11 (July 15, 1920), p. 10.
[213] *PHA* 11.3 (May 19, 1927), p. 3. It is necessary to ask why early Pentecostals felt compelled to deliver these assertions, to make clear their conviction that the sacraments did not work apart from faith and that the sacramental signs themselves (e.g. water, bread and wine, oil) did not function on their own power. Evidence suggests that perhaps early Pentecostal experiences of the sacraments

Water Baptism

As Seymour and others had done, Taylor distinguishes between the rites and ceremonies of the Old Testament and the ceremonies of the 'New Dispensation'. Water baptism, like the Lord's Supper, belongs to the new covenant, fulfilling and reconstituting Israel's ritual baptisms and the ceremonial Passover meal. Taylor explains that *both* the Passover and the Supper, as well as the Jewish ritual washings and Christian baptism are 'entirely ceremonial'.[214] He is careful to draw a distinction: water baptism remains a necessary *condition* of pardon of sins, but not the *means* that effects that forgiveness. In Scripture, the term 'baptism', he insists, refers to far more than water baptism – in his opinion, it refers sometimes to water baptism, sometimes to Spirit baptism, and sometimes to suffering[215] – and not every one has to be baptized in water, as the stories of Cornelius and the thief on the cross illustrate. Taylor insists that water baptism is nothing more or less than the fitting symbol of the 'real' baptism; as a result, the rite of washing is *not* for the remission of sin.[216] In his words, repentance is 'more than a handshake and water baptism'.[217] In response to a query about the meaning of 1 Pet. 3.21, he writes,

> The parenthetical expression refers to water baptism, and this has its place, and is right and proper, but mere water baptism alone has no saving virtue. The baptism that counts is the inward work of grace, the regenerating forces and virtues of the atonement and resurrection of Jesus Christ'.[218]

For Taylor and apparently many others in the Pentecostal Holiness Church, 1 Cor. 12.13, Col. 2.12, and Rom. 6.3-6 do not refer so much to the *rite* of washing as to a personal spiritual/existential *experience* that accomplishes both the loosing from sin and the flourishing of a great joy and unity among believers. On this reading, 'baptism in Jesus' name' is the baptism the Lord asked James and

---

were so potent and lively that their leaders found themselves required to warn against misunderstandings and overestimations of the sacraments.

[214] *PHA* 1.18 (Aug 30, 1917), p. 4. Taylor uses this phrase, 'entirely ceremonial', three times in the one-page article.

[215] *PHA* 2.17 (Aug 22, 1918), p. 8.

[216] *PHA* 1.35 (Dec 27, 1917), p. 16.

[217] *PHA* 5.51 (Apr 20, 1922), p. 2.

[218] *PHA* 5.5 (June 2, 1921), p. 10.

John if they were ready to undergo (Mt. 20.23).[219] All this notwithstanding, the Pentecostal Holiness Church refused to downplay the need for and meaning of the rite of water baptism. In fact, Taylor, speaking for the denomination, maintains that 'pardon is merited through the blood of Jesus alone, but granted to us on the condition of works and faith', so that, for those able to receive it, water baptism is nothing less than a condition of pardon.[220] It is, he explains, '*the door* into the church militant, or an entering into membership and fellowship with the church he joins'.[221]

Of course, not everyone in the Pentecostal Holiness Church held such a high view of the rite. One contributor, for example, goes out of his way to insist that water baptism – unlike baptism in the Spirit – is a thoroughly ' human act', even if it is done in the name of God.

> It is often administered to unfit subjects, and almost as often administered by preachers who are equally unfit to baptize a child of God. But the baptism of the Holy Spirit is never given to an unfit subject nor by one that is unfit for His office … Water baptism is an act in which God may not take part. The baptism of the Holy Ghost is a supernatural act in which God and the recipient only have part.[222]

In the case of water baptism, virtually all first-generation Pentecostals considered water baptism a symbolic ritual; it is possible to submit to the ritual washing without in fact being cleansed by the Spirit. Breaking with the Augustinian tradition, some also insisted that the purity of the minister was a matter of concern. Even so, they maintained that the rite was necessary, and allowed that God *could* act in it. This view of water baptism needs to be considered in light of both the history of Pentecostalism's emergence from the Wesleyan-Holiness revivals and movements, many of which emphasized the radical subjectivity of the believer and accepted members with or without water baptism, and the rising controversies within the movement regarding the significance of water baptism.[223]

---

[219] *PHA* 1.7 (June 15, 1917), p. 3.
[220] *PHA* 1.29 (Nov 15, 1917), p. 5. He offers the thief on the cross as an example of one whose circumstances would not allow baptism.
[221] *PHA* 4.30 (Nov 25, 1920), p. 2. Emphasis added.
[222] *PHA* 11.3 (May 19, 1927), p. 3.
[223] *PHA* 4.47 (Mar 24, 1921), p. 9.

The fact that the Pentecostal Holiness Church *required* water baptism for membership indicates something of a move away from these Holiness roots. Further, it should be remembered that the Pentecostal Holiness churches sanctioned the practice of infant baptism – although even this was understood as a kind of 'believer's baptism'.[224]

Lord's Supper

Most often, *PHA* identifies the Lord's Supper as 'the sacrament'. In fact, the term appears dozens of times, and in various contexts. Frequently, one finds announcements of upcoming meetings in which ministers are requested to come early to the conference so the sacrament can be administered.[225] Announcements and testimonies of celebrations of the Lord's Supper at quarterly meetings, Sunday morning worship services, and Sunday night 'devotional services' are also plentiful.[226]

As seen often in *AF* and *TBM*, one finds clear reference to the Lord's Supper as a means of bodily healing. In response to a submitted question, G.F. Taylor answers:

> Healing for the body goes with the sacrament of the Lord's supper, as well as blessing for the soul. Many eat without discerning the Lord's body, and they do not get healed, and so they are weak and sickly. Some actually go to sleep in Jesus; that is, they die, when they could be healed if they discerned the Lord's body in the sacrament'.[227]

Taylor also provides some specific directions for receiving the Supper, and offers a few explicit statements on the official position of the Pentecostal Holiness Church. First, Communion is acknowledged as the 'second ordinance' of the church, instituted by Christ himself, and, second, all those who partake in the meal receive the blessings promised in Scripture. Third, in light of these facts, all

---

[224] See *PHA* 1.31 (Nov 29, 1917), p. 5. Taylor claims that infants are regenerated in the same way confessing adults are regenerated, although *when* God chooses to regenerate no one can tell. In this light, he concludes that there is no reason for Christian parents *not* to baptize their infants.

[225] For example, see *PHA* 2.15 (Aug 8, 1918), p. 13; *PHA* 2.28-29 (Nov 7, 14, 1918), p. 5; *PHA* 3.21 (Sept 18, 1919), p. 1.

[226] For example, see *PHA* 4.15 (Aug 12, 1920), p. 11; *PHA* 4.16 (Aug 19, 1920), p. 5.

[227] *PHA* 5.5 (July 2, 1921), p. 10.

Christians should partake of the meal joyfully, 'not so much because they are commanded to do so, but because it is their privilege'.[228]

Taylor includes an extended statement on the 'metaphysics' of Communion, which is obviously framed as a rejection of the views of other Christian traditions, Catholic and Protestant:

> We do not believe that the bread is the body of Jesus Christ, nor that the wine is His blood; we do not believe that the bread represents his body, and the wine represents His blood and that when blessed, His body and blood accompany them. We do not think that our literal bodies feed on His body and blood, but that as we partake of the bread and wine, our souls feed on the flesh and blood of Jesus Christ, brought to us through the Holy Ghost.[229]

Clearly, Taylor – and presumably the majority of the readers of and contributors to *PHA* – repudiates both the Roman Catholic and Lutheran understandings of real presence, holding some form of the Calvinist view, instead. This much is certain: the Sacrament, in his estimation, does *not* effect grace mechanically. 'Like everything else in the church, the Lord's Supper may be taken without imparting any grace or blessing.' He also warns against *overemphasizing* the importance and power of the Supper. Those who believe that in the taking of the emblems one receives 'divine life and grace' and that water baptism and continual celebration at the Lord's Table in themselves win salvation deserve the charge of 'extreme formalism'. However, he is equally opposed to those who have rejected the ordinances altogether. Believers are to avoid both extremes, he insists, for there remains 'a spiritual blessing to be derived from taking the Lord's Supper when it is taken in the proper spirit'.[230] Among these promised blessings, one should expect to receive healing, according to 1 Cor. 11.30.[231]

Celebrants can and must come to the Table *prepared* to receive rightly. In Taylor's judgment, several hours of meditation on Jesus' death are needed to put one in the proper frame of mind for receiv-

---

[228] *PHA* 3.11 (July 10, 1919), p. 2.
[229] *PHA* 3.11 (July 10, 1919), p. 2.
[230] *PHA* 3.11 (July 10, 1919), p. 2.
[231] *PHA* 5.5 (June 2, 1921), p. 10.

ing the Meal. While eating, one should 'endeavor to see Jesus on the cross', for in this way the Supper effects blessing for the participant. Taylor finds it disturbing that many celebrate communion without drinking from the same cup, using individual cups, instead. Such a practice distorts the 'features and purposes of the Supper'. For the real purpose of Communion is 'to humiliate us, to teach us the spirit of Jesus, and to unite us as a church in the spirit of fellowship'.[232] When the congregation uses a single cup, and all drink from it, then these truths are made plain; however, when individual cups are used, the symbol of the church's fellowship is distorted.[233] Further, participants are to use unfermented juice only, and unleavened bread. As with the one cup, so with these elements: the sign must in fact signify what it is intended to signify. Further, the church is to follow Jesus as closely as possible in these matters, as well as in all others. If Jesus used unleavened bread, then so should we; it is as simple as that. It is difficult from reading of *PHA* to determine when, or how often, PH churches observed the Sacrament; sometimes the service was held after Sunday school and before the Sunday morning sermon;[234] at other times, at the close of prayer meeting;[235] a Wednesday night service at conference;[236] or a Friday night service to open a conference.[237] Finally, the Table is open for all 'regenerated people', without regard to their 'belief, sect, or degree of grace'. As a rule, unsaved persons should not be allowed to partake, for even if a few come to the Table to repent, that happens only infrequently.[238]

J.H. King, like Taylor, laments that some Pentecostals fail to give the Communion its proper due. For instance, he recalls a recent conference communion service, a 'sacred hour', which too many did not recognize as a moment of opportunity:

> How sad indeed that preachers treat the holy communion with indifference, yea with contempt. A conference communion ser-

---

[232] *PHA* 3.11 (July 10, 1919), p. 2.
[233] *PHA* 3.11 (July 10, 1919), p. 2.
[234] *PHA* 6.40 (Feb 1, 1923), p. 5; *PHA* 6.46 (Mar 15, 1923), p. 4.
[235] *PHA* 6.42 (Feb 15, 1923), p. 3.
[236] *PHA* 7.15 (Aug 9, 1923), p. 6.
[237] *PHA* 7.23 (Oct 4, 1923), p. 3.
[238] *PHA* 3.11 (July 10, 1919), p. 2.

vice can only be held and enjoyed once a year, and such should be esteemed a great privilege by all the members of the same ...

As King sees it, those who truly love each other *'delight to commune with each other around the sacred table'*.[239] Those who do not delight in this time fail in their loving. Communion is 'solemnly sweet' and an 'exalted privilege', King finds, as the saints 'humbly bow at the Lord's table, celebrating His suffering and death, drinking in His love, and touching each other in hallowed fellowship around one common mercy seat'.[240] It is deeply painful for him that so many treat the sacramental Meal with 'cold indifference'.[241] King's concern for 'touching each other in hallowed fellowship' raises a key feature of early Pentecostal spirituality. In that period, at least, Pentecostalism was not a hyper-individualist movement. King's statement suggests that it was the *practice* of the sacraments, including the Eucharist, which kept the members of the churches in touch with one another – literally and otherwise.

'Crowned with Glory': Testimonies of Sacramental Experience

As in the other Pentecostal literature of this period, one finds in *PHA* accounts of water baptism scattered through the entries,[242] including numerous uses of the language of 'following the Lord in baptism'.[243] An evangelist writes of recent successes in revival services: 'Sunday evening there were eight baptized in water. God gave witness to and blessed the same. Praise the Lord for the sweetness of His sacred presence'.[244] One missionary reports the dramatic baptism of a native African chief and his wife,[245] and another, J.O. Lehman, tells of a Good Friday baptism service.[246] Lehman recounts another occasion when someone received his Spirit baptism as he came out of the water.[247] The testimonies continually strike a note of joy:

---

[239] Emphasis added.

[240] *PHA* 2.33-34 (Dec 19-26, 1918), p. 6.

[241] *PHA* 2.33-34 (Dec 19-26, 1918), p. 6.

[242] *PHA* 1.9 (June 28, 1917), p. 6.

[243] For example, *PHA* 1.4 (May 24, 1917), p. 13; *PHA* 1.51 (Apr 18, 1918), p. 6.

[244] *PHA* 2.16 (Aug 15, 1918), p. 7.

[245] *PHA* 2.19 (Sept 5, 1918), p. 4

[246] *PHA* 2.12 (July 18, 1918), p. 10.

[247] *PHA* 2.12 (July 18, 1918), p. 10.

[W]e had had a baptismal service today, Aug. 19th, in which five expressed their faith in water baptism and went down into the water, as did Jesus, and were baptized, coming up straightway out of the water, praise the Lord, the witness of the Spirit agreeing thereto shown upon their faces.[248]

One finds a wealth of testimonies of experiences at the Table, also. Someone witnesses to the 'precious time around the Lord's Table'[249] and the 'blessed feast of the Lord'.[250] Another testifies to a sermon on the sufferings of Christ, which was followed by observance of the Lord's Supper and footwashing, recalling that 'God smiled upon us as we went through this part of the service. The saints shouted, danced, and talked in tongues as in days of old'.[251] Another report celebrates the story of a terminally ill woman who asked the church to bring the sacrament to her home and while partaking of it received her healing.[252] A Sunday morning service 'devoted to the holy Communion' included a 'very impressive sermon on the Lord's Supper, and many were moved to joy expressed either in shouting or in weeping'.[253] A series of services closed on Sunday morning with a sermon and the celebration of Communion. 'During this time', the brother recalls, 'it seemed that I was about as near heaven as I have ever been. The real power of God was present'. After the service, everyone shared 'another feast' on the grounds.[254]

As already mentioned, conferences often began and ended with celebration of the sacrament. A typical testimony comes from the Georgia conference:

Rev. J.H. King preached a good sermon Sunday morning at eleven o'clock from the prophecy of Haggai during which time he emphasized several Hebrew words in regard to God's dealings with the Jews. At the close of the sermon the Sacrament was taken by a large audience. This being done the power of the

---

[248] *PHA* 1.22 (Sept 27, 1917), p. 5.
[249] *PHA* 1.29 (Nov 15, 1917), p. 13.
[250] *PHA* 2.27 (Oct 31, 1918), p. 13. See also *PHA* 1.37 (Jan 10, 1918), p. 6.
[251] *PHA* 1.45 (Mar 7, 1918), p. 14. For similar accounts, see *PHA* 2.7 (June 18, 1918), p. 2; *PHA* 2.18 (Aug 29), p. 11; *PHA* 4.11 (July 15, 1920), p. 4.
[252] *PHA* 4.5 (June 3, 1920), p. 5.
[253] *PHA* 8.30 (Nov 20, 1924), p. 5.
[254] *PHA* 1.45 (Mar 7, 1918), p. 16.

Lord fell on quite a number of the saints and some shouted, danced and talked in tongues, while still others laughed and wept. It was indeed a blessed time for those present.[255]

King himself remembers a special service in which the 'Sacramental Service was crowned with Glory'. He recalls the intensity of the worship ascending 'to the Lamb on the Throne', as the congregation 'remembered His death on the Cross'. As if to explain why the Sacrament occasioned such a response, King adds: 'The cleansing Blood thrills the heart with unspeakable ecstasy *as its efficacy is applied*'.[256] It appears that, in King's judgment, the act of 'remembering' Christ's death in the Sacrament actually *effects* the application of the atonement. In the same vein, missionaries recount Rev. Lehman's final service with the congregation in South Africa and time of Holy Communion, which they describe as 'the most precious part of the service'. During the celebration, they explain, 'heaven seemed to have come down' and everyone rejoiced to 'feel the efficacy of the blood of Jesus'.[257] In this last claim, one hears yet again the conviction that the Lord's Supper serves more than a merely memorialist function.

As has already been seen, the Eucharist was expected to occasion nothing less than Christ's *real presence*, although the mode of presence was never clearly defined. For example, a brother writes from Krugersdorp to report that the Quarterly Conference closed with 'the sacrament service', and that 'all departed feeling God had been with us'.[258] A similar testimony comes from Krugersdorp a few years later: 'At 3:00 P. M, we had the sacrament, and we can say the presence of the Lord was so very real and near to us'.[259] In the view of many *PHA* contributors, because Christ is present to the celebrants, the Spirit is always at work, effecting God's will and applying the benefits of Christ's death and resurrection – which means not only healing for the body, but also healing and rectification for the soul. One brother testifies that while his little girl was

---

[255] *PHA* 5.30 (Nov 23, 1921), p. 4.
[256] *PHA* 2.49 (Apr 3, 1919), p. 6. Emphasis added.
[257] *PHA* 2.27 (Oct 31, 1918), p. 12.
[258] *PHA* 4.18 (Sept 2, 1920), p. 12.
[259] *PHA* 7.31 (Nov 29, 1923), p. 7.

'on her knees at the altar sacrament', she received Christ's blessing. In his words, 'just as she drank the wine the Lord sanctified her'.[260]

The Father's Table: Embedded Sacramentality

As one might expect, *PHA*, like the other Pentecostal periodicals of the time, makes frequent use of eating and drinking metaphors. For example, one author celebrates the fact that anyone can enjoy 'good feasts at our Father's table' because that 'table' is 'spread' all the time.[261] *PHA* contributors also put to use familiar readings of Israel's first Passover meal, believing that the typology illustrates, among other things, that no one can truly eat Christ until one is purged of sin.[262] Sometimes, this was connected to readings of John 6. The Passover lamb was understood as a prefiguring of Christ – believers must eat *him*, as he commanded: 'Eat my flesh and drink my blood'.[263] *PHA* contributors rejoiced in a continual 'feast' of God's presence,[264] the gospel,[265] the gathering and fellowship of believers,[266] and especially the preached and explained Scripture.[267] Editor Taylor, in reflections on Proverbs, rejoices that believers enjoy the blessings of the 'feast' spoken of in the 23rd Psalm as well as in John 6, where Jesus invites his followers to feed on him. 'It is the words of Jesus that contain His life, and we may feed on Him by a careful and prayerful study of His Word.'[268] Preaching was like the killing of the 'fatted calf'.[269] A special edition of *PHA* celebrated N.J. Holmes, founder of Holmes Bible and Missionary Institute, and someone recalled how Holmes expertly 'broke the bread of life' providing 'feasting' for 'hungry souls'.[270]

---

[260] *PHA* 2.14 (Aug 1, 1918), p. 7.
[261] *PHA* 4.6 (June 10, 1920), p. 16. See also, *PHA* 2.36-37 (Jan 2-9, 1919), p. 14.
[262] *PHA* 2.38 (Jan 16, 1919), p. 2.
[263] *PHA* 3.38 (Jan 15, 1920), p. 5.
[264] *PHA* 2.24 (Oct 10, 1918), p. 8.
[265] So one contributor (*PHA* 5.39 [Jan 25, 1923], p. 5) explains, 'The truth of the gospel is the bread upon which the servants or ministers must feed the members of the household of God'. See also *PHA* 7.1 (May 3, 1923), p. 5.
[266] *PHA* 6.43 (Feb 22, 1923), p. 10. See also *PHA* 1.38 (Jan 17, 1918), p. 2; *PHA* 6.40 (Feb 1, 1923), p. 7.
[267] *PHA* 9.40 (Feb 11, 1926), p. 2. See also *PHA* 7.24 (Oct 11, 1923), p. 6.
[268] *PHA* 4.18 (Sept 2, 1920), pp. 8-9. At least one other contributor took a similar tack. See *PHA* 4.10 (July 8, 1920), p. 3.
[269] *PHA* 5.36 (Jan 4, 1923), p. 12.
[270] *PHA* 3.39 (Jan 22, 1920), p. 9.

References to the eschatological banquet abound in *PHA*, at least as much as in the other Pentecostal periodicals of the day.[271] For example, a contributor shares her vision of the Marriage Supper in which she saw the Lord's Table spread for all: 'I cannot describe the beauty and grandeur of the table, it was most wonderful. The table reached from one end of the heaven even to the other, as the rainbow, and a bright light shone on the table from the throne above'.[272]

Conclusions

As with the other Pentecostal periodicals, one finds in *PHA* scores of references to sacramental thought and practice, many of which bear witness to a relatively 'high' sacramentality, although, of course, other witnesses stand in tension with these views. As seen in other literature of the period, *PHA* contributors rejected the notion of baptismal regeneration, emphasizing instead the importance of obeying the divine mandate and imitating the Lord's example. Unlike the Church of God (Cleveland, TN), the Pentecostal Holiness church did not consider foot-washing a church ordinance, although many within the denomination did practice it, obviously, and the church never officially forbade it or even discouraged the practice.

As was common among Pentecostals of the time, *PHA* editors and contributors made no careful distinctions between the actual eating of the Supper and mystical communion with Christ, and while they *did not* hold to anything like a developed doctrine of transubstantiation (or its equivalents), they clearly *did* expect God to act on them through the Supper, and not merely in the mental recollection of Christ's crucifixion. In their view, the Supper occasions Real Presence – mysteriously, somehow – at least to those who come in faith, believing. And, like virtually all of the Pentecostals of the period, *PHA* insisted on an open table and the *communal* nature of the sacraments, especially the Lord's Supper.

---

[271] *PHA* 6.51 (Apr 19, 1923), p. 4; *PHA* 7.4 (June 24, 1923), p. 3.
[272] *PHA* 6.48 (Mar 29, 1923), p. 6.

Early Wesleyan-Holiness Sacramentality: Summary and Conclusions

The early Wesleyan-Holiness Pentecostal periodicals testify in plainest terms to a full-bodied, richly-textured sacramentality – even if it sometimes voices itself in untraditional language. In fact, on the strength of the witness of numerous voices in this literature, it is not too much to speak of a distinctive early Wesleyan-Holiness Pentecostal sacramental theology and praxis. It is fairly easy to sketch the basic contours of this sacramentality.

First, although they did not devote any considerable energy to articulating *how* it might be so, first-generation Pentecostals unquestionably did believe the Lord was personally present at his Table. The Lord's Supper was not primarily – still less *only* – a memorialistic rite. Instead, the congregation's celebration of the Communion meal was believed to be a means of Christ's on-going ministry, a sacred moment in which the risen Lord in all his power gave himself to his church, nourishing it with his own life. This is evidenced most vividly, perhaps, in the widespread belief that the Lord's Supper served as a means of healing and spiritual nourishment, although, in some cases, the conviction that the bread was a symbol of Christ's body broken for the healing of the saints led to a genuinely sacramental view of the *bread* and a rather memorialist view of the *wine*, regarded as a symbol of Christ's blood shed for sins.

Second, a trio of basic convictions fired the Pentecostal sacramentality of the period. One, the Lord had *mandated* observance of water baptism and the Lord's Supper (and, for some in the Wesleyan-Holiness camps, footwashing and the imposition of hands for healing or ordination, as well). Two, in faithfully enacting the sacramental rites, participants were *imitating* Jesus. Three, inasmuch as they obeyed the Lord's command and obediently imitated him, they received assurance of his liberating and salutary *presence*. The sacraments – and in particular the Lord's Supper – were quite explicitly understood by many, including most of the more prominent figures, as God-ordained means of and opportunities for both this imitation and this participation.

Third, there are signs that early Pentecostals *experienced* more in the rite than their theology accounted for. This is perhaps especially true of water baptism.

Fourth, early Wesleyan-Holiness Pentecostals devoted serious attention to the mechanics of sacramental administration, which is another unmistakable sign of a deep sacramentality. Disputes arose about whether multiple immersions were necessary for the baptism to be acceptable, and whether wine, water, or grape juice was the most fitting element for the Eucharistic cup. They debated at length the biblical evidence for and against footwashing and ordination. They argued about whether everyone had the right to anoint the sick with oil, or if that remained the privilege of the ordained.

Fifth, first-generation Pentecostals in the Wesleyan-Holiness stream relied heavily on Scripture for elucidation of their sacramental experience and praxis, frequently appealing to typological readings of Old Testament passages, and especially the design of Israel's Tabernacle. No passage received more attention than 1 Cor. 11.23-33, especially verses 28-30. The Lukan formula, 'the breaking of bread', was used often as well. Departing from the mainstream Protestant tradition, many Pentecostals read John 6 as at least in part a reference to the Eucharist.

Sixth, the Wesleyan-Holiness Pentecostal sacramentality of this period did not work with clear terminological distinctions, using 'sacrament' and 'ordinance' interchangeably, and employing a variety of names for the Lord's Supper, including 'Holy Communion', 'the Communion', and 'the Sacrament', and speaking of the presence of Christ and the Spirit at/in the Supper without drawing a clear or consistent distinction.

Seventh, perhaps because the sacraments remained at the center of the life of the worshipping community, Pentecostal worship managed to resist devolution into *hyper-individualism*, even if it did emphasis personal encounter with Christ through and with the Spirit. As Alan Lewis explains, 'sacrament happenings', even while 'full of personal significance', in fact 'liberate us from interior, individualistic preoccupation with ourselves and turn us outward to the world as visualizations of the gospel's communal and global range'.[273] Although they would not have put it in these terms, this describes early Pentecostal sacramentality well, for it was very much 'turn[ed] outward to the world', as Lewis phrases it.

---

[273] Alan E. Lewis, *Between Cross and Resurrection: A Theology of Holy Saturday* (Grand Rapids: Eerdmans, 2003), p. 394.

Of course, Wesleyan-Holiness Pentecostalism was not *uniformly* sacramental. Some within the movement were rigidly anti-sacramental, apparently fearful of the excesses of the 'high church' traditions with their so-called 'dead formalism'. Some simply concerned themselves with other matters, and gave little or no attention to the sacraments, either in thought or practice.[274] Nonetheless, it is safe to conclude that early Wesleyan-Holiness Pentecostalism was *characteristically* sacramental, and to say that many early Pentecostals considered observance of the Lord's Supper the least dispensable and most sacred part of the church's worship.

Finished Work Periodicals

Introduction
For the first decade, Pentecostals were more or less unanimously Wesleyan-Holiness in teaching a second, definitive work of grace. This consensus began to erode, however, as waves of converts from non-Holiness groups entered the movement.[275] Many of these new Pentecostals hailed from baptistic backgrounds and had not been trained in holiness theology.[276] William H. Durham, a former Baptist pastor, served as one of the leading spokespersons for an emerging group of Pentecostals who sought to maintain an emphasis on Spirit baptism while disavowing the traditional Pentecostal (and holiness) teaching on sanctification. It would be a mistake to attribute the movement solely to Durham's influence; after all, one finds examples of what would come to be known as Finished Work doctrine *prior* to Durham's 1910 sermon at the Chicago conference, nonetheless, Durham did do much to spread the message and his open attacks on the accepted view of sanctification effectively opened the way to a new form of Pentecostal spirituality.[277] Convinced he had received the revelation directly from God, Durham regarded all his opponents as in fact enemies of God, and he used his considerable rhetorical skills to further the movement, insisting

---

[274] Among Wesleyan-Holiness periodicals, Cashwell's *Bridegroom's Messenger* stands out in this regard.

[275] Synan, *The Holiness-Pentecostal Tradition*, p. 149.

[276] Synan, *The Holiness-Pentecostal Tradition*, p. 149.

[277] Synan, *The Holiness-Pentecostal Tradition*, p. 150.

those who disagreed with him were not truly Pentecostal at all.[278] In spite of virulent opposition to the new teaching from prominent Pentecostals, including Seymour, C.H. Mason, Tomlinson, and King, the 'Finished Work' doctrine effected drastic and lasting changes on the movement. By at least one estimate, no less than 60 per cent of North American Pentecostals had embraced the new doctrine by 1914.[279]

As was true of the Wesleyan-Holiness stream, the cause of the early Finished Work movement was advanced by periodicals featuring the work of major editors and contributors such as E.N. Bell, A.S. Copley, and J. Roswell and Alice Reynolds Flower. Understanding early Finished Work Pentecostalism requires engagement with these texts. I will read them chronologically, beginning with periodicals that predate the Assemblies of God and concluding with the Flowers' *Pentecostal Evangel*. As for reading method, I will continue to attend to explicit references to or treatments of the sacraments first, and then move to testimonies of sacramental experiences, and conclude with the implied sacramentality embedded in various phenomena such as the prevalence of the eating and drinking motifs.

Early Independent Finished Work Periodicals

In this section, I engage four leading Finished Work Pentecostal periodicals – *Word & Witness, Latter Rain Evangel, The Pentecost,* and *Pentecostal Testimony* – from the early days of the Finished Work movement, prior to the rise of the Assemblies of God.

'Our Melchezedik Refreshes Us': Explicit Treatment of the Sacraments

Like the majority of Wesleyan-Holiness Pentecostals, Finished Work Pentecostals considered ritual performance of the ordinances of water baptism and the Lord's Supper obligatory for believers. For instance, an author in *WW* explains that an ordinance is a *law*, which means that observance of the washing rite and the Eucharist are 'binding on all Christians'.[280] The author insists that those who

---

[278] Jacobsen, *A Reader in Pentecostal Theology*, p. 12.
[279] Allan Anderson, *An Introduction to Pentecostalism: Global Charismatic Christianity* (Cambridge, UK: Cambridge University Press, 2004), p. 47.
[280] *WW* 9.6 (June 20, 1913), p. 2.

refuse to practice 'these two commands' are in rebellion, 'walking disorderly and in disobedience'; as a result, they should and must repent and 'get a salvation that will cause them to love the ways of the Lord better than their own ways'.[281] Readers are warned against claims of self-promoting teachers who claim the Lord's Supper and baptism are not to be observed any longer.[282] Any revelation that contradicts the word of Scripture simply 'cannot be from the Holy Spirit', for it is axiomatic: 'the Spirit and the Word agree'. As is clear from Jesus' great commission and Peter's Pentecost sermon, baptism is a *scriptural* injunction, and so it follows that '[t]hese passages forever settle two points: First, that the baptism in the Holy Spirit does not take the place of baptism in water. Second, that water baptism was administered by the apostles after Pentecost'.[283] Similarly, the Lord's Supper should be done until Christ's return, as Scripture directs.

Footwashing

References to footwashing in these periodicals typically deal exclusively with the 'spiritual' significance of the story of Jesus washing his disciples feet (Jn 13.1-17). Elizabeth Sisson's contribution is illustrative. She offers a typological reading of the account: 'What do you mean by washing the feet? An exceeding tenderness in our hearts, over the failures of our brothers and sisters, that retires into God, and there, by faith and love, washes them with the blood of Jesus'.[284]

Footwashing, then, works for Sisson as a kind of symbol of Christ's intercessory work, his ongoing application of the sanctification won at his cross. But more than that, Jesus works through the corporate body of believers, allowing them to cooperate in this work. So, she asks,

> Will we let Jesus through us continue daily the foot-washing of the disciples? Shall we let Him take off us all superfluous robes of our rights, our dignity, our opinions, etc., and gird us with the

---

[281] *WW* 9.6 (June 20, 1913), p. 2.
[282] *WW* 10.6 (May 20, 1914), p. 3.
[283] *WW* 10.6 (May 20, 1914), p. 3.
[284] *LRE* 9.11 (Aug 1917), p. 15.

towel of His humility, and wash through us the dust of human
infirmities off the feet of our faulty brethren?[285]

She concludes: Jesus' example serves as a call to take on even the
most menial service.[286]

Another view does make itself known, if only rarely. In Spring
1922, Pastor Glover delivered a sermon at the Stone church on the
relation of holiness to humility. In it, Glover laments that many
Pentecostals have become 'too high-toned' and he imagines that the
practice of the foot-washing rite best subverts this arrogance. 'Jesus
did it, and it would do you good, provided you would go and sit
alongside of someone with whom you cannot get along and wash
his feet and make up with him.'[287] He does not call for routine observance, or speak of the rite as an ordinance or sacrament; however, his esteem for the rite is perhaps unparalleled among prominent
Finished Work Pentecostals of the time.

Laying on of Hands and Anointing with Oil
Countless testimonies make clear that early Finished Work Pentecostals practiced the rites of laying on of hands for both divine
healing and Spirit baptism, as did their Wesleyan-Holiness Pentecostal siblings.[288] True, many of them apparently did not consider
imposition of hands *necessary* for healing to take place or for one to
receive one's Pentecost; nonetheless, they found that the Scriptures
(e.g. Mk 16.18 and especially the many instances in Acts) plainly do
call for these practices, a fact that settled the issue for them.[289] They
attended carefully to the shape of the biblical mandate. For example, some warn against laying hands on the demonized because it is
not explicitly called for in the Scriptures: 'It is not scriptural to lay
hands on a demon-possessed person. We are told to *cast out* demons, and to *lay hands* on the sick'.[290] To put it briefly, Finished
Work Pentecostals, like their Wesleyan-Holiness brothers and sisters, practiced the imposition of hands in submission to what they
believed the clear direction of Scripture.

---

[285] *LRE* 9.11 (Aug 1917), p. 15.
[286] *LRE* 13.6 (Mar 1921), p. 19.
[287] *LRE* 15.10 (July 1922), p. 17.
[288] See for example *LRE* 1.5 (Feb 1909), pp. 10, 19.
[289] *LRE* 5.9 (June 1913), pp. 20-21; *TP* 1.12 (Nov 1, 1909), p. 2.
[290] *LRE* 2.8 (May 1910), p. 18.

What is more, in laying hands on the sick and on those who have not received their Pentecost, believers were believed to be *imitating* Jesus and the apostles. So, F.F. Bosworth explains that '... when I pray for the sick I have no living faith *until I lay my hands upon them* and begin to pray. While I am doing what Jesus said the believer should do, the faith comes both to me and to the sick one'.[291] Bosworth believes the embodied act works as a *medium* for the Spirit's work; it is only in the event of imposing hands, in the very act, that the Spirit collaborates with the faith of the obedient participants.

Even if they agreed on the need for laying on of hands for healing and Spirit baptism, many early Pentecostals did *not* consider ordination by imposition of hands either necessary or beneficial. The evidence is mixed; unlike the imposition of hands for healing, the early Pentecostals in the United States apparently did not come to anything like a common opinion on the need for and meaning of laying on of hands for ordination to ministerial office. For example, Minnie Abrams recalls ministers in India who rejected the Pentecostal movement because unordained women were allowed to preach; for them, ordination was a churchly rite accomplished only by the bishop laying his hands on the candidates. Abrams' response to their critique was incisive: 'I said, "Yes, you should have received the baptism of the Holy Ghost at that time, but did you? Is there any fruit in your lives?"'[292] Often, 1 Tim. 4.14 was read as applying to *all* believers, rather than strictly to a clerical class.[293] However, a report of the 1917 General Council of the Assemblies of God indicates that many discerned the need to correct some excesses: 'The matter of more precautions being taken in the ordination of the ministry was emphasized, also the great necessity of qualifying for such an high and holy calling'. This document identifies ordination as a 'sacred rite'.[294]

Water Baptism
Water baptism proved to be a major point of contention in the emerging Finished Work movement, due largely to the theological innovations of 'Oneness' Pentecostals. In 1915, Pastor Fraser writes

---

[291] *LRE* 5.9 (June 1913), p. 10. Emphasis added.
[292] *LRE* 1.12 (Sept 1909), p. 5.
[293] *LRE* 2.8 (May 1910), p. 10.
[294] *LRE* 10.10 (Oct 1917), p. 10.

from the Stone Church to warn against 'new light' that he believes is threatening the integrity of the Pentecostal movement. Fraser inveighs, first, against the 'new formula' for baptism that insists on baptizing only in Jesus' name. 'At one fell swoop', he says, the innovating teachers 'demolish the doctrine of the Trinity'. He continues by providing a lengthy rebuttal of the Oneness position, contesting in particular their reading of the Scripture.[295] He finds their practice of re-baptism absolutely unwarranted and unacceptable.[296] *One* baptism is sufficient, he believes, for when we were baptized 'it was into all the truth the ordinance contained, whether we understood it or not'.[297] Obviously, such a disavowal of re-baptism suggests a vigorous sacramentality, one that believes the rite of washing always accomplishes more than the participants can express or understand theologically.

In Fraser's judgment, the teachers of the new doctrines fail on two fronts: they not only take water baptism to accomplish something it in fact does not, but also they tie it too closely to baptism in the Spirit.[298] Fraser admits that one *might* take 1 Pet. 3.21 to teach baptismal regeneration, but only if one reads uncarefully. On closer examination, one sees easily enough that water baptism is for the sake of a 'good conscience'. Unlike Episcopalians and the Campbellites, Pentecostals practice water baptism as a sign of an already-accomplished regeneration, Fraser insists. They deem water baptism *necessary*, but do not regard it as salvific. Ritual washing in water is required of the converted, but it does not *accomplish* the conversion. As Fraser puts it, water baptism is 'simply the outward witness of the inward process, simply the outward profession of that which has already taken place inside the man, in the very core of his being'. For, 'if a man has been truly washed from his sins, his next business is to run to the baptismal waters and go down there, *indicating to the world* the process that has taken place inside the man'.[299]

---

[295] *LRE* 11.8 (May 1915), p. 3.

[296] Not everyone in the Finished Work movement agreed with Fraser. For a counter-example, see *LRE* 11.8 (May 1915), p. 3.

[297] *LRE* 11.8 (May 1915), p. 6.

[298] *LRE* 11.8 (May 1915), p. 5.

[299] In this, Fraser sounds like Zwingli, who held that Communion's meaning and purpose was first to unite Christians to one another and thereby to express this unity to the watching world. See Gregory J. Miller, 'Huldrych Zwingli' in Carter Lindberg (ed.) *The Reformation Theologians: An Introduction to Theology in the Early Modern Period* (Malden, MA: Blackwell, 2002), p. 163.

Regarding the water rite, Durham sounds a familiar Pentecostal note: the rite in water does not convert but nonetheless serves as the divinely ordained sign of an already-accomplished regeneration, so the rite is nonetheless required. In Durham's words, conversion 'makes [the believer] a candidate for water baptism, which is the only thing required of him between conversion and the baptism in the Holy Spirit'.[300]

Durham sharply distinguished water baptism and Holy Communion from all other such practices, including, for example, foot-washing: 'We recognize only two ordinances in the Gospel – the Lord's supper and baptism'. He does accept that other rites, ceremonies, and customs are biblical and so have their 'proper places', but nonetheless maintains: 'we do not believe anointing with oil or laying on of hands, or foot-washing to be ordinances'.[301] As Durham sees it, 'The Gospel is briefly summed up in these few words: the believer in Christ, and Christ in the believer'. For him, this summation explains the need for *two* – and *only* two – ordinances: one that symbolizes 'getting into' Christ, and another that symbolizes 'His coming into us'. Through baptism, then, believers are 'buried ... into his death', as Paul declares.[302] In the same way, the Supper symbolizes believers' receiving Christ into themselves as they 'commune of the body and blood of the Lord'.[303]

The Lord's Supper

One finds in the early Finished Work publications numerous strong assertions that divine healing comes through faithful participation in the Eucharist. F.F. Bosworth, for one, explains that the Supper with its 'two emblems' serves to keep before our minds 'the two great benefits purchased for us by the death of Jesus'; namely, forgiveness of sins (symbolized by the wine) and the healing of our bodies (symbolized/effected by the bread). In Bosworth's judgment, many Christians come wrongly to the Table – and so fail to receive their healing – because even in eating the bread they do not really 'discern' Christ's body; they eat the bread 'not knowing that it is an emblem of the Lord's body broken for their healing'.[304] To

---

[300] *PT* 1.8 (1911), p. 5.
[301] *PT* 1.5 (July 1, 1910), p. 15.
[302] *PT* 1.5 (July 1, 1910), p. 15.
[303] *PT* 1.5 (July 1, 1910), p. 15.
[304] *LRE* 6.9 (June 1914), p. 3.

illustrate what happens for those who *do* rightly discern the body, Bosworth shares the story of a brother who, having been convinced of the truth of Bosworth's teachings on the issue, 'put the bread in his mouth really appropriating the Lord's body for the first time in his life' and immediately received his healing.[305] If normally the healing waited on the actual eating of the bread, Bosworth believed that at times one might be healed even *before* or entirely *apart from* taking the bread in one's mouth – if only one genuinely believes what the bread symbolizes and so discerns the Lord's body truly.[306]

In early 1912, Durham reports on a recent ten-day conference in Los Angeles; participants shared in the Supper on several occasions, and Durham testifies that he had never seen 'more glorious and wonderful communion services than those'. He invites his readers to imagine more than 500 people gathering at the Table with the 'power of the Holy Spirit resting so mightily upon them that they are speaking in tongues and singing in the Spirit much of the time, with the most blessed unity existing'. Durham personally oversaw these Communion services, and he recalls how powerfully the Spirit affected everyone:

> After we had partaken of that which by living faith *becomes unto us His Body and Blood*, the Spirit seemed to take complete control, and for a long time the Heavenly Anthem poured forth like a mighty torrent of holy Heavenly melody, until our very souls were ravished, Glory to God. If we can have such fellowship and blessing here, what must Heaven be?[307]

Perhaps it would not be fanciful to gather from Durham's report at least a few building blocks of his theology of the Sacrament. First, he clearly believes that the church's celebration of the Lord's Supper, at least on this occasion, lifts the celebrants up into the presence of God, opens them to heaven, so that they enjoy loving communion with God.[308] Second, he stresses the importance of 'liv-

---

[305] *LRE* 6.9 (June 1914), p. 3.

[306] *LRE* 6.9 (June 1914), p. 3.

[307] *PT* 2.1 (Jan 1912), p. 13. Emphasis added.

[308] His use of 'ravished' is particularly striking. Perhaps it derives from Song of Songs 4.9, a text that was used in relation to the Eucharistic celebration by American revivalists, including Gilbert Tennent during the so-called First Great Awakening. See Kimberly Bracken Long, *The Eucharistic Theology of the American Holy Fairs* (Louisville: WJKP, 2011), pp. 94-104.

ing faith' to make the Supper truly sacramental. Third, he clearly believes that in order for the blessings of the Eucharist-event to be received, the Spirit must act on the believers, awakening in them an affective response, a response of joy, even ecstasy in the divine presence. Fourth, he also claims that those who receive the bread and wine in 'living faith' receive in fact Christ's 'body and blood' in those elements. With the possible exception of this last claim, Durham is simply articulating in brief what many, and perhaps most, of his fellow (Finished Work) Pentecostals believed. Perhaps some of them would not have agreed with Durham that the bread and wine become by faith Christ's body and blood; nonetheless, they *did* believe that the Supper occasioned, even mediated intimacy with God. As Fraser insists, the ordinance is 'intended to be a *real communion* of the soul with Christ'.[309]

> By forms and ceremonies and resolutions one can never become acquainted with God. With penance and persecution one does not come to know God. Much and systematic giving does not bring us to a knowledge of Him. Regular church-going and attendance on every means of grace, as a mere form, acquaints not with Him.[310]

Perhaps the clearest evidence of the fervency and extent of early Pentecostal sacramentality comes in the exaggerated forms of Eucharistic devotion that continually emerged and required address. The fact that the early Pentecostals maintained the centrality of the Supper even at the risk of such extremes indicates a profound commitment to the Eucharist. To take but one example: in late 1912, an unnamed member of the *LRE* staff wrote a 'candid criticism of spurious writings', warning against overvaluing the Sacrament. In larger part due to the effect of these 'spurious writings', some Pentecostals had been convinced to partake of the Supper daily in their homes. Troublingly, the contributor finds that some 'go so as to carry the bread and wine in their pockets or handbags that they may be able to partake at any season and in any place'. This is an alarming matter, for it is 'ultra-Spiritual' and eventually such imbalance yields disastrous results. 'Who knows but what the doctrine of transubstantiation leading to the Romish worship of the

---

[309] *LRE* 11.9 (June 1915), p. 8. Emphasis added.
[310] *LRE* 1.5 (Feb 1909), p. 20.

sacrament in the "elevation of the host" had its rise in some such exaggeration of the value of the Eucharist?"[311]

Often, the discussions of the sacraments in these periodicals remain playfully elusive and multivalent. For example, a 1910 article in *The Pentecost* provides a comparison of Abraham's encounter with Melchizedek to the believer's encounter with Christ:

> That bread and wine with which our Melchizedek refreshes us are a memorial of those sufferings by which alone we are enriched, and one who has tasted that the Lord is gracious, implies in so doing that he refuses any portion in this world.[312]

The relation of eating the bread and drinking the wine of Holy Communion to the spiritual 'tasting' of the Lord through the Spirit (e.g. in reading Scripture or meditating on the Word) remains unclear, and the writer employs memorialist language; nevertheless, he obviously believes that the Eucharist *actually* 'refreshes' and enriches the celebrants, so that the Supper has more than a merely memorialistic function. It appears plausible that a strong sacramentality is at play.

The contributor's use of Scripture also deserves attention. In his efforts to express the meaning of the bread and wine, he appeals to texts that at least at one level do *not* refer to the Eucharist. First, he takes up the offering of Melchizedek, 'king of Salem [and] the priest of the most high God', to Abraham (Gen. 14.18-19), and he steals a phrase from 1 Pet. 2.3, as well. His reading of these texts suggests that he understands the Eucharistic bread and wine as gifts of Jesus, the true priest of God and king of peace. Not only that, but his reading also suggests that he believes the church participates in Christ's kingly and priestly ministry in the observance of the Eucharist, for according to 1 Peter 2 those who have 'tasted that the Lord is gracious' are in fact the 'holy priesthood' who together 'offer up spiritual sacrifices, acceptable to God by Jesus Christ'.[313]

Early Pentecostal affectivity takes perhaps its strongest forms of expression in reflections on the meaning of the Lord's Supper. For example, in August of 1909, *LRE* published a sermon from that year's *Homiletic Review*. The sermon, entitled 'The Empty Seat at the

---

[311] *LRE* 5.3 (Dec 1912), p. 19.
[312] *TP* 2.11-12 (Nov-Dec, 1910), pp. 2-3.
[313] *TP* 2.11-12 (Nov-Dec, 1910), pp. 2-3.

Master's Table', anticipates the joys of the future Marriage Supper of the Lamb, truly the *Last* Supper, a final, joyous celebration of the Sacrament with all the redeemed. The saints will '... enjoy this sacrament side by side with Paul and Timothy and Saint Augustine and Luther and Calvin and David Livingstone and our own promoted kith and kin whom the angel, black-winged, tore from our embrace. Oh, we shall enjoy!'[314]

Given the nature of things in the sin-wrecked world, not all God's people can gather at once to the Table, but Jesus personally 'has planned one final communion service', a festival all the saints shall enjoy in company.

> Then Jesus the glorified, Jesus the High Priest, with nail-pierced hands, will break the bread and say 'This is my body', and pour out the cup anew saying 'This is my blood', and with Abraham and Isaac and Jacob, with the whole Israel of God, shall we sit down in the kingdom of the Father, rehearsing from Eden below to Eden above the transporting glory of redemption.

'The Lord's Table, Not Ours': Testimonies of Sacramental Experiences

One finds an abundance of testimonies of life-changing experiences at the Table and in the baptismal waters. A.A. Boddy writes from Sunderland, recalling the experience of Christ 'fully' converting him: 'He met me there within the Communion Rails, suddenly and unexpectedly'.[315] Participants commonly prepared themselves for these moments of sacramental observance by times of focused prayer. According to one report, 'most of our women' spent the whole of Good Friday in the church, fasting and praying, 'preparatory to receiving the Sacrament of the Lord's Supper'.[316] That they would *prepare* themselves for the Supper strongly suggests that they shared a conviction of the sanctity and power of the Meal. Whatever they did not say about the Eucharist, actions such as these indicate a sacramentality of the strongest order.

---

[314] *LRE* 1.11 (Aug 1909), p. 20. Although not written by a Pentecostal, the fact that *LRE* published the sermon remains instructive. It is not unthinkable that some Pentecostal pastors and evangelists took this sermon, or at least parts of it, to their pulpits.

[315] *LRE* 1.5 (Feb 1909), p. 9.

[316] *LRE* 9.2 (Oct 1916), p. 23.

Evidently, this robust sacramentality was shared by Pentecostals abroad as well, as numerous missionary reports and testimonies make clear. Mary Caroline Holmes writes from 'the Moslem World', testifying of her encounters with 'hidden disciples' of Jesus who seemed at first glance to be devout Muslims. She details her experience with a certain government official who came weekly to discuss the Scripture with her. She explains how he was hesitant to identify himself as a Christian, although he did allow himself to be identified as a 'Jesus lover'. He came to the worship services, too, but did not participate in the Eucharistic celebration. Nonetheless, he revealed his love for Christ in these moments. Once, during Communion, Holmes noticed his 'hungry longing look', and afterwards he admitted to her he could hardly restrain himself from coming to the Table: 'I almost cried out, "Let me come too"'. On another occasion, she saw him

> pick up from the ground a fragment of bread some careless hand had dropped, carefully wipe from it every trace of soil and then reverently kiss it, saying as he did so, 'I never can see bread on the ground to be trodden under foot. Our Lord said of bread, "This is my body broken for you". It is sacred to me'.[317]

Obviously, Holmes interpreted and applauded this act as a sign of devotion to Christ, and this is likely an indication of *her* estimate of the Supper's importance.

Another missionary rejoices that he has been able to baptize more than thirty 'Hindoos' and share the Lord's Supper with them. 'We had the communion and I taught them what it meant, and you should have seen how reverently they partook of that bread and wine.' At the close of the service, 'the power of God came down and seemed to fill the place where we were kneeling'.[318] Marie Stephany writes from north China, explaining how she and her team celebrate the Lord's Supper on the first Sunday of the month and how they are 'very careful to instruct the natives not to partake of the Lord's Supper if there is anything between them and the Lord, or their fellow men'. They are vigilant, she says, not to let observance of the Supper descend to mere habit. Once, nearly five years prior to her writing this report, one of the locals who had

---

[317] *LRE* 17.11 (Oct 1924), p. 7.
[318] *LRE* 18.1 (Nov 1924), p. 22.

been standing outside observing their Communion service, approached her, weeping, and asked to receive the bread and wine. 'I want to take that bread and wine and I believe it will drive this opium devil out of me', he said. After explaining to him that he must believe in Jesus, and praying with him, she 'gladly gave him the Lord's Supper'. Stephany rejoices that not once from that time has he returned to either opium or morphine.[319] A missionary to Russia remembers a service in Moscow during which a woman, a local professor's wife, 'saw the Lord Jesus Himself standing by the communion table with outstretched hands blessing the bread and wine'.[320] Far from the exception, this seems to have been the *rule*: early Pentecostals, whether from the Wesleyan-Holiness or Finished Work stream, expected the Lord to present himself to his people in their Eucharistic celebration, to preside over the meal, to work with them and upon them through it.

'Jesus is the Food': Embedded Sacramentality

As one would expect in light of the reading of other materials from this period, there is an implicit sacramentality smoldering in the rhetoric and practices at use in these early Finished-Work periodicals. First, numerous eating and drinking metaphors are in play. For instance, one contributor avows that in the as-yet unrealized Kingdom, 'Jesus and his gentile wife will be feasting on the good things of heaven'.[321] And speaking of the believer's present-day experience, Copley declares: 'Jesus is the food, the Holy Ghost the feeder. We are the instruments or vessels which He uses'.[322] Also, one finds testimonies of the *physical* dimension of the encounter with Christ and the Spirit. Ruth Angstead of Zion City testifies to the anguish she experienced while receiving the sufferings of Christ in a dream or vision. 'I went to rest at 12:30, and before me was the thorn-crowned pierced and bleeding Lamb of God.' The Spirit directed her to extend her arms and legs, and doing this she felt the 'cruel nails' pierce her body. She was taken in the Spirit to Gethsemane and there 'tasted the cup of His suffering'. She recalls: 'It seemed my very heart would break and the blood oozed from the pores of

---

[319] *LRE* 19.5 (Feb 1926), p. 19.
[320] *LRE* 8.8 (May 1915), p. 21.
[321] *TP* 1.2 (Sept, 1908), p. 6.
[322] *TP* 1.2 (Sept, 1908), p. 7.

my body'. Visions of heaven and of Christ's ascension followed; then, entrance to 'the abode of damned spirits'; and, finally, a vision of 'the great final judgment with nations on the right and left'. She resisted the Devil's attack and eventually 'sank out of self', and 'many waters' seemed to surge through her. After singing four songs in an unknown tongue, she delivered a message in tongues, 'each time interpreting, magnifying Father, Son and the precious blood'.[323]

Finally, the language of *desire* factors prominently, as well. Many of the contributors to these early Finished Work periodicals report the experience of finding themselves possessed with 'a panting hunger',[324] a desire for a 'richer and closer walk'[325] with Christ as the Spirit 'bears the soul forward with desire'.[326] All of this suggests a spirituality that remains open to and hungry for mediation, for the presence and work of God in and through the sacramental *media gratiae* ordained for this purpose.

Conclusions

As evidenced above, the early Finished Work periodicals, like the Wesleyan-Holiness papers of the same era, point to a richly textured sacramental practice, and much of what one finds remains consistent with that discovered in the Wesleyan-Holiness literature, although one can perhaps discern lines of divergence as well.

First, water baptism is carefully distinguished from Spirit baptism, and regarded by many as crucial to Christian obedience even though the rite of washing does not effect regeneration. This is virtually identical to what one finds in the Wesleyan-Holiness literature of the time.

Second, in contrast to some Wesleyan-Holiness literature (especially *AF* and *COGE*), footwashing receives comparatively little attention in Finished Work literature, and by and large most contributors do not regard it as an ordinance. Similarly, laying on of hands and anointing with oil are never explicitly described as sacraments, although they are unquestionably treated as God-directed and God–sanctioned means of healing.

---

[323] *TP* 1.2 (Sept, 1908), p. 1-2.
[324] *TP* 1.2 (Sept, 1908), p. 1.
[325] *TP* 1.6 (Apr-May, 1909), p. 11.
[326] *TP* 1.2 (Sept, 1908), p. 7.

Third, many contributors to these early Finished Work periodicals apparently expected Jesus to be personally present at the Table. Participants testify again and again of God's presence and activity mediated through the rite of eating and drinking. Like many of their fellow Pentecostals in the Wesleyan-Holiness stream, they also believed that the Lord's Supper, if received faithfully, is believed to be a means of healing.

Fourth, the relatively 'high' view of the Supper evidenced in these periodicals often is supported by surprising readings of unexpected biblical texts, including passages from the Old Testament.

In conclusion, then, it is perhaps not too much to say that at least at a few points the view of the Eucharist one finds in this early Finished Work literature is as vigorous as anything one might discover in the larger Protestant tradition, or indeed the entire catholic Christian tradition, even if it never takes on the metaphysical subtleties that have dominated much of the discussion through the centuries. In the final analysis, it is safe to conclude that the Lord's Supper was a central locus of early Finished Work Pentecostal spirituality and piety.

The Assemblies of God: The Pentecostal Evangel

J. Roswell Flower and his wife, Alice Reynolds Flower, began publishing *PE* July 1913 and the magazine quickly earned wide readership.[327] The Flowers helped form a loose network of churches into the Assemblies of God, and their periodical became an official organ of the denomination, along with E.N. Bell's *Word and Witness*. On January 1, 1916, Bell's *WW* merged with Flower's *Weekly Evangel*.

'Jesus Brought Very Near': Explicit Treatment of the Sacraments

Often, it is assumed that early Pentecostals had no sense of Christian history, no sense of connection to the wider churchly theological-spiritual tradition. Those who assume this also often imagine that early Pentecostal spirituality was not – and indeed *could not*

---

[327] This magazine has operated under several names in the course of its (ongoing) history. First, it was known as *The Christian Evangel* (July 19, 1913-March 6, 1915), then the *Weekly Evangel* (March 13, 1915-May 18, 1918), the *Christian Evangel* (June 1, 1918-October 4, 1919), the Pentecostal Evangel (Oct 18, 1919-June 9, 2002), *Today's Pentecostal Evangel* (June 16, 2002-July 19, 2009), and, finally, *Pentecostal Evangel* (June 26, 2009 – present).

have been – sacramental. However, closer examination exposes both of these assumptions as mistaken. For example, the Flowers' *Evangel* published an advertisement for a 10-volume edition of the Ante-Nicene Fathers with a list of teachings deemed crucial to the Christian faith, including divine healing, speaking with tongues, prophecy, foot-washing, water baptism, and Holy communion and the love feast. 'In short', the advertisement boasts, 'these books constitute a complete history of primitive Christian doctrines'.[328] To say that the list is *complete* is obviously an overstatement, but such a list spells out quite plainly what Pentecostals of the time considered principal matters for discussion and reflection, and shows that they knew *their* practices (especially footwashing, laying on of hands, water baptism, and Holy Communion) belonged to the ancient Christian tradition. In the same way, B.F. Lawrence, perhaps the first historian of Pentecostalism, in an attempt at providing a defense of the 'apostolic faith restored', argues that the Quakers were 'in many respects, our true fathers in the faith', for 'the burden of their preaching and practice was identical with our own'. Lawrence notes that they 'neither baptized nor took the Lord's Supper', but maintains that this was not so much from 'objection to the sacraments' as due to a limitation forced on them by the spiritual dryness and doctrinal compromises of their time.[329] That Lawrence would not only note the difference but even attempt to explain it expresses the fact that at the founding of the movement Pentecostals considered the sacraments central to their spirituality. It is only in this light that one can rightly read *PE's* sacramentality.

Footwashing

One finds in *PE* many reports of footwashing services, suggesting those in the Finished Work movement within the Assemblies of God considered footwashing an important if not essential churchly practice. One also discovers statements that qualify, more or less severely, the significance of the rite for the Christian life. In fact, some contributors do not regard it as a rite in any sense; for them, the story of Jesus washing his disciples feet serves as an example, an enacted metaphor of sorts for the humble readiness to do even menial service that characterizes the Christ-like life. For instance, one

---

[328] *WE* 129 (Mar 4, 1916), p. 9.
[329] *WE* 123 (Jan 15, 1916), p. 5.

article, published in 1917, laments that some Pentecostal congregations *do not* celebrate the Supper, and the article's author, Mary Chapman, judges that these congregations neglect the Sacrament in large part because they believe it should be observed always with footwashing, a logistically complicated rite that proves impracticable and so makes regular Eucharistic celebration difficult if not impossible. Many brothers and sisters, she insists, are forced to attend *other* (non-Pentecostal?) churches to 'get the Communion' because it is not observed in their home 'Assembly'. Obviously, if Pentecostals felt compelled to attend other churches in order to receive the Eucharist, then they must have believed that it had more than merely symbolic value; surely, it seems incontrovertible that at least many of them believed that the Sacrament was indispensable to the fruitful and faithful Christian life.

Chapman reserves judgment on whether footwashing should be regarded as an ordinance, but insists that one finds 'no scriptural grounds for attaching it in any sense to the communion of the Lord's Supper', because 'in the four places we have explicit directions for partaking of the bread and wine' one finds no mention of foot-washing. 'The washing of feet', she concludes, 'is mentioned in one place and there is room for a great deal of difference of opinion about what it means, and one should not judge another in regard to it'. Communion, conversely, is 'plainly taught in four places', and the need for and importance of it 'plainly stated and emphasized'.[330] Holy Communion should be observed as a ritual, nothing more or other than that.[331] Similarly, E.N. Bell disputes the teaching that footwashing remains binding on all Christians. Jesus did not *command* his disciples to wash feet, but he did say it 'ought' to be done. 'All Christians worthy of the name', Bell avers, 'believe in obedience to Christ ... but all do not understand His teaching alike on this point'. This lack of consensus takes many forms:

> Some think He meant to wash one another's feet in times of sickness or need and not as a church ordinance, and we leave such free to obey as they understand. Others believe He meant for all to wash feet as a church ordinance, and we leave these free to obey as they understand. But strictly speaking, an 'ordi-

---

[330] *CE* 61 (Oct 3, 1914), p. 3.
[331] *CE* 61 (Oct 3, 1914), p. 3.

nance' is a law, something 'commanded,' which will result in a penalty if not done as commanded; and there is no explicit 'command' to observe such as a church ordinance.[332]

Obviously, these instances, and others like them, intimate a move away from the regular practice of footwashing and from the understanding of it as an ordinance, especially as witnessed in *AF* and *COGE*. Just as clearly, however, the fact that Bell has to insist against it indicates that many within the movement were in fact practising it. Besides, *PE* includes testimonies of footwashing services.[333] Alice Wood writes from Argentina testifying of a recent celebration of the Lord's Supper and footwashing – 'a time of rich blessing', she recalls.[334] Someone else sends a testimony of a recent service in which three were baptized in water, after which they received 'the sacrament' and washed one another's feet; he remembers that 'The Lord wonderfully blessed' the service.[335] Many other testimonies like these prove that both the celebration of the Supper and the observance of footwashing rite were believed to be confirmed by the presence and power of the Lord, illustrating that those in the Assemblies of God in this early period expected God to act on them through their celebration of the churchly rites.

Laying on of Hands and Anointing with Oil
The evidence shows that Pentecostals in the Assemblies of God regarded laying on of hands as a way of obeying and imitating Jesus, just as they did footwashing, baptizing in water, and sharing the Eucharistic cup and the loaf. Asked the meaning of 'laying on of hands' in Heb. 6.2, E.N. Bell explains that the practice served three purposes in the apostolic churches: *ordination* (Acts 6.6; 13.3; 1 Tim. 4.14), *healing* (Mark 16.18; Acts 28.8), and *Spirit baptism* (Acts 8.17; 9.17; 19.6).[336] As Scripture directs (Jas 5.14), the laying on of hands was accompanied often if not always by anointing with oil.[337] Nonetheless, laying on of hands and anointing with oil are not requisite for receiving the Spirit, Bell believes, arguing not only from Scrip-

---

[332] *PE* 474-475 (Dec 9, 1922), p. 8.
[333] See, for example, *WE* 123 (Jan 15, 1916), p. 15; *WE* 128 (Feb 26, 1916), p. 4; *CE* 270-271 (Jan 11, 1919), p. 1.
[334] *WE* 214 (Nov 10, 1917), p. 13.
[335] *CE* 290-291 (May 31, 1919), p. 9.
[336] *WE* 128 (Feb 26, 1916), p. 8.
[337] *PE* 316-317 (Nov 29, 1919), p. 8.

ture, but also on the strength of his experience: 'But neither Scripture nor present day observation justifies us in the conclusion that the fulness [*sic*] comes only by the laying on of hands'.[338] Nevertheless, the imposition of hands *may* serve as a 'means' for Spirit baptism.[339] Although every believer has the right to lay hands on the sick and to pray for healing,[340] at least some early Finished Work Pentecostals recognized (in the light of 1 Tim. 5.22) the danger of praying for healing *rashly*, without proper discernment. The same principle applied to prayers for ordination and Spirit baptism.[341] As with other Pentecostal periodicals, *PE* turns again and again to Scripture and the example of Jesus and his apostles to support their points. For example, one contributor holds that: '… the apostolic way to appoint one officially was after he was selected by the Church, to lay hands on him officially, pray over him and thus publicly set him apart to his appointed work. *Of course we should do the same* until Jesus returns'.[342]

Water Baptism

As already seen, early Pentecostals found themselves beset with questions about water baptism and the rite's meaning and purpose, and the difficulties only intensified after 1910 and the rise of an identifiable Finished Work movement. Within the Finished Work ranks, some allowed for re-baptism, and others regarded the rite entirely unnecessary if one had already received Spirit baptism. They argued this on the grounds that John's baptism was rendered superfluous by Pentecost, for after Christ baptized one in the *Spirit* what need could there be for the one to receive baptism in *water*? In their judgment, all rituals were finally put away by the inauguration of the New Covenant. Rev. and Mrs. Flower, as well as E.N. Bell, among others, argued against these positions. J.R. Flower avers that because baptism in water typifies the death, burial, and resurrection of Christ, which were once-for-all events, so baptized believers 'die with him in the likeness of his resurrection' only *once*. 'This is not to be repeated lest we put Christ to an open shame', he insists.[343]

---

338 *WE* 122 (Jan 8, 1916), p. 7.
339 *WE* 187 (Apr 28, 1917), p. 9.
340 *WE* 138 (May 6, 1916), p. 8.
341 *WE* 127 (Feb 19, 1916), p. 10.
342 *CE* 246-247 (June 29, 1918), p. 9. Emphasis added.
343 *WE* 100 (July 24, 1915), p. 1.

Likewise, Bell maintains that in spite of the fact that Christ did do away with the ordinances of the Old Testament, the ordinances of the New Testament retain their binding force. In his judgment, any Christian who claims water baptism is unnecessary is both ignorant of Scripture and disobedient to the Lord's clear command.[344] The official position adopted by general council of the AG in 1916, makes the same basic point:

> The Ordinance by a burial with Christ should be observed as commanded in the Scriptures, by all who have really repented and in their hearts have truly believed on Christ as Savior and Lord. In so doing, they have their body washed in pure water as an outward symbol of cleansing, while their heart has already been sprinkled with the blood of Christ as an inner cleansing. Thus they declare to the world that they have died with Jesus and that they have also been raised with Him to walk in newness of life.[345]

PE, like the other Pentecostal periodicals of the time, expounds a theology of water baptism that carefully discriminates ritual washing from the Spirit's renewing work in the 'heart' of the believer. Although he insists that water baptism is necessary, Bell agrees that water baptism and Spirit baptism are radically different from one another – as virtually every Pentecostal of the time would have said. This is so because of the different ways Christ acts in these events. In the latter event, he is actively the Spirit-baptizer. 'Christ baptizes with the Spirit, never with water. The preacher baptized with water – never with the Spirit. In one Christ is the active agent, in the other the preacher is the active agent. One is in the element of the Spirit, and in the other the element used is water.'[346]

Such a reading of the ritual washing seems strictly non-sacramental, apparently allowing no room for the churchly act of baptism to collaborate in the Spirit's act of cleansing and initiating the believer into the *corpus Christi*. Bell's reading of Jn 3.5 continues this line of thought. He admits that the church from the early se-

---

[344] *PE* 312-313 (Nov 1, 1919), p. 5.
[345] *WE* 170 (Dec 16, 1916), p. 8.
[346] *PE* 326-327 (Feb 7, 1920), p. 5.

cond century read this as a reference to water baptism,[347] and that this remained the accepted reading until the Reformation. Calvin, he says, broke with the tradition. While the Episcopal churches remained adherent to the 'ancient view', most Protestants have followed Calvin, and some Baptists have deserted even *this* position. As for Pentecostals, Bell finds that they generally teach water baptism as 'an external purifying symbol while the real internal birth is done by the Holy Spirit'.[348] For his part, Bell believes water baptism has the same relation to regeneration that the ancient rite of circumcision had to membership in Israel's covenant.[349] To begin, he establishes a rigid duality between 'flesh' and 'spirit', between external rites and the internal work of God. Citing Titus 2.5, Col. 2.11-12, Heb. 10.22, and Acts 2.38, Bell affirms: 'Now in all these passages there is a reference both to water baptism and to work of the Spirit, a reference to the outward token and to the inward reality', and he hurriedly adds: 'These two lines should not become confused lest we take one for the other, lest we see the outward token and lose sight of the inward work of the Spirit'.[350]

As soon as he has drawn this distinction, however, he mitigates it, if only slightly. He admits that 'in the mind of God' the token of baptism and the work of regeneration are 'closely related', as made clear in the lives and teaching of the apostles. What is more, the regular practice of delaying water baptism for converts – a practice Bell fears has become more and more frequent – is 'wholly unwarranted by Scripture'. We should seek, then, to hold the two in close relationship without confusing them. The 'old body' of sin is 'put off' by both 'outwardly and inwardly', *both* by work done by the church, in the ritual of baptism, *and* work done by Christ, in the 'circumcision of the heart', the 'raising up in the newness of life through the power of the Holy Spirit'.[351] In all truth, Bell's reflections are somewhat tortured, as he struggles to explain the *why* and

---

[347] Bell briefly outlines two other views of this passage; first, that Jesus refers to natural birth ('of water'), and then to spiritual birth ('and the Spirit'); second, that Jesus alludes to what Paul elsewhere names 'the washing of the water by the Word' (Eph. 5.26).

[348] *WE* 121 (Jan 1, 1916), p. 8. Bell's choice of words is striking; perhaps he only means to say that ritual washing is a symbol of the purifying accomplished by the Spirit; however, he in fact says that the symbol itself purifies.

[349] This position has an ancient pedigree.

[350] *WE* 118 (Dec 4, 1915), p. 4.

[351] *WE* 118 (Dec 4, 1915), p. 4.

the *what* of water baptism. Nonetheless, this remains clear: he, along with the overwhelming number of early Pentecostals, insists that water baptism is necessary and that 'following Jesus in baptism' is integral to the life of obedience that leads to salvation. In the final analysis, his view remains something more than memorialistic, even while much of what he says seems staunchly non-sacramental.

The Lord's Supper
According to the Statement of Fundamental Truths adopted by the general council of the Assemblies of God in October 1916, the Lord's Supper is far more than merely a memorial feast:

> The Lord's Supper, consisting of the elements, bread and the fruit of the vine, is the symbol expressing our sharing the divine nature of our Lord Jesus Christ, 2 Pet. 1:4; a memorial of his suffering and death, I Cor. 11:26; and a prophecy of His second coming, I Cor. 11:26; and is enjoined on all believers 'until He comes.'[352]

This statement alone goes a long way in affirming the robust nature of Finished Work sacramentality. It is also important to note that nothing in this statement stands at odds with the claims of the Wesleyan-Holiness Pentecostals of the time.

Of course, the Assemblies of God's official statement does not stand alone. There are many explicit treatments of the Lord's Supper in *PE*. For example, in response to a reader's question about the possible benefits of taking the Supper, sometime editor and frequent contributor E.N. Bell provides a detailed explanation of his view of the Sacrament, complete with a brief overview of four historical positions. Catholics, he says, believe that the bread when it is blessed by the priest is 'transmuted into the literal living body of Christ', so that 'in partaking we actually eat the body of Christ and literally drink His blood, and so get eternal life by partaking of the supper'. Bell rejects this teaching. He rejects the doctrine of consubstantiation, as well, which he attributes to the Episcopalians.[353] The third position, proposed by 'the noted theologian Zwingle' [*sic*], understands Communion as '*simply* a Memorial Feast', in which 'the *only good* received in partaking [is] in bringing vividly to memory the

---

[352] *WE* 170 (Dec 23, 1916), p. 8.
[353] He notes that the Lutherans hold this view as well.

truths of Christ's atoning death'.[354] In this view, as Bell understands it, neither Christ's body nor his blood are present at the Table, but are only 'remembered and appropriated'. Bell acknowledges some truth in this position, but he finally rejects it, too: 'It lowers our view of the Lord's Supper and makes it a thing too common'. The fourth stance Bell attributes to Calvinists, especially Presbyterians, who maintain, he says, that the elements remain unchanged, but Christ is truly, *spiritually* present to the celebrants. Having provided this overview, Bell ventures his own view:

> ... there is a good deal of truth in this spiritual view. In fact there is some truth in nearly every view of it. But I do not believe the physical Christ is present in the bread nor in the cup. I believe the loaf is still real bread and the cup still only the fruit of the vine. I believe it is a memorial, for Jesus said, 'This do in MEMORY of me.' But it is *more* than a memorial feast. *Jesus is there* in the Spirit to bless, quicken, uplift and heal; but what benefit the partaker will receive depends much on his spiritual discernment; his faith and his appropriation from the spiritually present living Christ.[355]

In these claims that the Supper is 'more than a memorial feast' and that 'Jesus is there', Bell shows himself in league with many if not most Pentecostals of his time, in both Finished Work and Wesleyan-Holiness camps, and with the wider Christian tradition as well. While he does not uncritically assume any of these views, he clearly does come nearer to those traditions that emphasize Real Presence than those that do not. He insists that celebrants should examine themselves before partaking of the sacred meal, should prepare themselves for partaking, and then 'by faith realize His spiritual presence and power'; they should 'appropriate spiritual life, real health, communion and fellowship with the living risen Christ'.[356] These verbs – 'realize' and 'appropriate' – raise the point again: Bell's view of the Supper seems robustly sacramental.

Of course, Bell is not alone in making these claims; J. Roswell Flower assumes an almost identical position. For him, as for Seymour and others, the church's Meal, as the 'supper of remem-

---

[354] Emphasis added.
[355] *WE* 146 (July 1, 1916), p. 8.
[356] *WE* 146 (July 1, 1916), p. 8.

brance', *replaces* Israel's Passover;[357] it is an ordinance entirely fitted to the New Covenant. Memorialistically, it 'shows forth the Lord's death', serving as the 'continual reminder of a blood sacrifice', but *not only* that; it *also* serves as a 'reminder of the coming of the Lord', a 'perpetual sign-post' to the Advent. Flower notes that each Gospel account of the institution of the Supper includes reference to Jesus' promise to drink the cup 'anew in the kingdom of God' with his disciples.[358] In the final analysis, the Lord's Supper 'embodies so much and typifies such wonderful truths, that God's people cannot afford to pass it by as non-essential'.[359] Like Bell, Flower believes Jesus is *'brought very near'* as God's people eat the Supper, and Christ's 'redemptive work' is 'attested to' by the fact that communicants often receive their healing while they partaking of the bread and wine.

Similarly, Flower's wife, Alice Reynolds Flower, holds that the Lord's 'last supper' marked the 'passing of the old order', this new rite fulfilling and superseding the Passover, which belonged so distinctly to what she calls 'the old dispensation'. Pentecostals, she insists, should not lose sight of the vital importance of the Sacrament both for the individual believer and the corporate life of the community.[360] Like E.N. Bell and her husband, as well as many Pentecostals of the time, Sister Flower insists that the Lord's Supper directs believers' attention to the *future*, as well as to the past, bringing into the present-day experience of believers a 'taste' of the future messianic banquet. In fact, as she works it out, while the *bread* promises healing for sick and diseased bodies, it is specifically the Eucharistic *cup* that serves as a pledge of the coming kingdom, a time in which 'we shall taste in all its purity and sweetness the "new" cup of his joy'. Also, in keeping with her contemporaries, Flower argues that the way in which participants receive the Supper determines what the Supper in fact does for them. Partaking *wrongly* of the Supper brings sickness and death, as Scripture warns. Partaking *rightly*, however, brings 'life and health'. Therefore, because of the Supper's life-giving or death-dealing power, believers should eat

---

[357] Bell agrees. Christ's last supper was the *final* Passover meal; Christ himself is the Passover for Christians. See *WE* 129 (Mar 4, 1916), p. 8.

[358] *WE* 100 (July 24 1915), p. 1.

[359] *WE* 100 (July 24 1915), p. 1.

[360] *CE* 61 (Oct 3 1914), p. 2.

the sacramental Meal expectantly. What is more, if they eat and drink faithfully, they are sure to 'feel with renewed blessing the power of Christ's sacrifice', for Christ has conquered death and therefore he is present now to those who take 'the bread of life in truth'. Not only is he present to them, but also he himself is in fact 'the food that causes our spiritual nature to be nourished and strengthened'.[361] She concludes her article by quoting a stanza of a Eucharistic hymn:

> See, the feast of love is spread,
> Drink the wine, and break the bread;
> Sweet memorials, till the Lord
> Calls us round His heavenly board;
> Some from earth, from glory some
> Severed only, 'Till He come'.[362]

In this early period, Finished Work Pentecostals, just like their contemporaries in the Wesleyan-Holiness stream, consistently and apparently intentionally blurred the boundary between the ritual eating of the meal and the mystical 'feasting' on Christ. In this, they were proving true to a reading of John 6, and the tensions of that text. As in the Fourth Gospel, feasting on Christ always means more than *merely* receiving the bread and wine:

> He gave His flesh and blood for you and for me, and He de-clares that I have no life in me unless I eat His flesh and drink His blood. Now this means more than the ordinance of the Lord's Supper. It means that you and I must partake of the liv-ing Person of our Lord Jesus Christ through the Holy Ghost.[363]

In her widely-published tract, 'Our Health, His Wealth', Eliza-beth Sisson insists that believers' communion with God is not re-stricted to the moment of observing the Lord's Supper, although it is not entirely independent of it, either.

---

[361] Clearly, her theology of the Eucharist is informed here by a reading of John 6 and the so-called 'Bread of Life discourse'.

[362] Although Flower provides no documentation, presumably because her readers would readily have recognized it, this is the last stanza of Edward H. Bickersteth, Jr.'s 'Till He Come', first published in 1862.

[363] *CE* 274-275 (Feb 8, 1919), p. 3.

Ah! Not more truly in that hour, happily called 'Holy Communion', in that service, blessedly named 'the Lord's Supper', are the emblems of the Saviour's [*sic*] broken body and shed blood, passed around, than is the SUBSTANCE always being passed to us. 'You may feast at Jesus' table all the time.'[364]

She readily admits that it is 'fitting to have memorial hours for receiving the emblems', while insisting it is 'normal to be feeding on the Substance *every hour*'.[365] Some object to her teaching, she knows, accusing her of profaning the sacred. But she insists that what is needed is '*Sacramental living*; for it makes continually holy, common things'.[366] Sisson quotes from the Book of Common Prayer and invites her readers to 'change the formula into a daily living reality'. She rejoices that God will 'transmute the faith-act into very real spiritual feeding on the body and blood of your Lord', recalling a young girl who boasted: 'morning by morning I eat His flesh and drink His blood before I go to work'.[367] Sisson avows that 'our life in its entirety is constantly partaking of nourishment from the King's table'. And she appeals (without citation) to Neh. 8.10:

Eat the fat, drink the sweet, and send portions to them for whom nothing is prepared. Oh, how rich the food! the very flesh of our Lord! Oh, how holily sweet the drink! the life-blood of our Lord coursing through all our being, quickening every part with the vitality now on the victory-throne!'

In conclusion, she celebrates believers' continual communion with God through the Spirit, and describes in a kind of poetry the rapturous end promised to those who eat Christ faithfully: 'As we uninterruptedly feed and drink, through the "holy communion" we change from grace to grace and from glory to glory, till in us "He shall fully see His seed'.[368]

---

[364] Emphasis in original.

[365] Emphasis added.

[366] Emphasis added.

[367] *PE* 582 (Jan 31, 1925), p. 6. First published in *Confidence* 9.10 (Oct 1916), p. 166.

[368] *PE* 582 (Jan 31, 1925), p. 6. It would be a mistake to take her reference to 'the very flesh of our Lord' as a *metaphysical* claim. Nonetheless, it also would be a mistake of equal degree not to take her claim seriously, for whatever it does not signify, it clearly *does* suggest a deep and richly textured theology of the Sacra-

Holy and salutary though the rite of the Sacrament is, Sisson maintains that it remains possible to eat it *without benefit*. 'Many today are partaking of the Lord's Supper who are going down in death in body and soul', she says, because they are failing daily to 'recognize the body and blood of the Lord Jesus as their life', above and beyond the sharing the cup and the loaf. The ritual participation happens 'only once a week or once a month',[369] but believers 'may and should partake of it in Spirit [*sic*] every moment in our daily life'.[370] Even so, feasting on Christ *includes* the 'ordinance of the Lord's Supper', although that rite does not entail *all* that it means to 'eat His flesh and drink His blood'.[371]

Sisson's reading of John 6 – and in particular the claims of vv. 53-56 – is matched by several other contributors' readings of this and similar passages. For example, a Christological reading of Exodus 12 suggests for a Brother McCafferty the connection between Israel's eating of the Passover lamb and the church's feeding on Jesus, as promised in Jn 6.53: 'During the "night" we are to eat the "flesh" of the Lamb. By it we have our strength – yea, our life'.[372] This language of 'eating Christ' appears frequently in *PE*, as in other Pentecostal periodicals of the time, often to refer to a spiritual/existential 'feasting' on Christ by faith,[373] a reading in keeping with the Protestant tradition, Lutheran and Reformed. Sometimes, however, Jn 6.53-56 is taken in a more directly Eucharistic sense. Carrie Judd Montgomery, for example, uses it in just this way. As other Pentecostals of the time had done, she connects the passage with divine healing, insisting that the call to eat Christ's flesh and drink his blood is difficult only for those not illumined by the Spirit. In her judgment, 'In the Lord's Supper we receive the bread and wine, and if by faith we receive Him then His life springs up in us', just as John's Gospel promises.[374]

---

ment, underscored by the conviction that the risen crucified Christ is personally present to and in the church's sharing in the sacred meal.

[369] This is one of the best clues we have to the frequency with which early Pentecostals observed the Supper.

[370] *CE* 274-275 (Feb 8, 1919), p. 3.

[371] *CE* 274-275 (Feb 8, 1919), p. 3.

[372] *WE* 214 (Nov 10, 1917), p. 3

[373] See *CE* 254 (Sept 7, 1918), p. 5; *PE* 350-351 (July 24, 1920), p. 4; *PE* 414-415 (Oct 15, 1921), p. 4; *PE* 582 (Jan 31, 1925), p. 7 (this is reprint of Sisson's article, 'Our Health, His Wealth').

[374] *PE* 715 (Sept 17, 1927), p. 4.

Other Scripture passages also come out in the theological reflection. Acts 2.42-47 and the characteristic Lukan formula, 'breaking bread', are put to frequent use, sometimes in non-sacramental senses (as when it is used to describe church dinners)[375]. E.N. Bell, for one, uses it to refer to the Sacrament, and indicates that he reads the Lukan passages as references to the Eucharist, as well.[376] He also uses the phrase to describe the believer's mystical intimacy with Christ, in one instance, appealing to the story of Christ breaking bread with the Emmaus disciples (Luke 24) to make just this point. 'If you talk of Him, He will draw nigh, He will come in, He will break bread with those tender hands.'[377] One contributor, explaining what it means to 'discern Christ's body' (1 Cor. 11.29), insists that 'the body which we discern in the breaking of bread is not the Church, but the body that bare our sins on Calvary before Christ rose and was glorified'. Nehemiah 8.10 is also used, because it provides an illustration of, as well as an invitation to, a renewed sense of the Sacrament's power and value for the church. The 'Old Testament saints' partook of the 'Living Portion' in their day, and now 'we can partake of the present meal ourselves, and then we can send portions, not cooled off, but steaming hot, to others'.[378]

In a 1931 article, the British Pentecostal Donald Gee responds to the request of a young American pastor for an account of the way in which the weekly 'Breaking of Bread' ceremony is performed in Britain's Pentecostal churches.[379] Gee reports that this service, often called a 'fellowship meeting',[380] is in fact an 'open' meeting, meaning that the pastor retains his role as leader but is not obtrusive, tactfully allowing for 'the sacred liberty of the whole body'.[381] Gee remarks that he has become convinced that if there is any truth to the claim that the British Assemblies display a remarkable spiritual depth it is due more than anything else to these Sunday morning fellowship meetings. He also reports that the celebration of the Lord's Supper is the focal point of these weekly meetings. In his words, the Communion rite is 'the central feature' of the

---

[375] For example, see *CE* 256-257 (Oct 5, 1918), p. 14.
[376] See *PE* 316-317 (Nov 29, 1919), p. 5.
[377] *PE* 334-335 (Apr 3, 1920), p. 5. See also *PE* 547 (May 17, 1924), p. 11.
[378] *WE* 162 (Oct 28, 1916), pp. 4
[379] *PE* 894 (April 18, 1931), pp. 2-3 (2).
[380] *PE* 894 (April 18, 1931), p. 2.
[381] *PE* 894 (April 18, 1931), p. 2.

service. The lead-up to the Lord's Supper – a time of prayer, the reading of Scripture and/or hymn singing – is the 'most favorable opportunity for the exercise of certain of the Gifts of the Spirit, such as Prophecy, or Tongues and Interpretation'. If all is right, and the participants have expressed themselves in a 'true spirit of worship', then 'the place should be charged with the power and Presence of The Spirit to such an extent that exercise of His Gifts should be both easy and edifying'.[382] Requests for prayer may be put forward, and if they are done 'tactfully' such requests are 'means of grace and blessing to all'. The celebration of the Sacrament may precede or be preceded by 'some ministry of the Word'. Regardless, '[t]here need be no rule'.[383] The 'full spiritual benefit' would be lost if left for the end of the meeting 'when everybody is tired and duties call for a speedy journey home'.[384]

Gee insists that participants of the Supper expect 'fellowship with Christ Himself' in the breaking of the bread. The 'mere breaking of bread' must not 'degenerate into a fetish'; it must 'never be regarded as the end, but only the means to an end'. Only a 'fresh Unction' can preserve the weekly Communion celebration from becoming 'mere custom'. However, when properly observed, the Lord's Supper 'provides real point [*sic*] and helpfulness to the meeting by definitely centering the thought upon Christ'.[385]

'Identified with Christ': Testimonies of Sacramental Experience

Testimonies disclose something of the richness and complexity of early Assemblies of God experiences of the sacraments of water baptism and the Lord's Supper. Often, testimonies show that these baptisms proved occasions for the Spirit's wonders. For example, Bell notes:

> A good many are receiving when baptized in water at the time or a few minutes afterwards as they kneel in prayer and look for Him. Many of these receive without laying on of hands and many others receive with the laying on of hands after obeying the Lord in water baptism.[386]

---

[382] *PE* 894 (April 18, 1931), p. 2.
[383] *PE* 894 (April 18, 1931), p. 2.
[384] Emphasis original.
[385] *PE* 894 (April 18, 1931), p. 2.
[386] *WE* 122 (Jan 8, 1916), p. 8.

A report from Canalou, Missouri rejoices that 'eight were buried with Christ in water baptism',[387] and another contributor celebrates that three have 'identified with Christ in water baptism'.[388] Still another testimony announces that eight 'obeyed the Lord', being baptized in water.[389] These formulae ('buried with Christ', 'identified with Christ', 'obeyed the Lord') indicate plainly the conviction that in water baptism believers follow the Lord's direct command and imitate him and just in this way enjoy fellowship with him.

Testimonies of experiences at the Lord's Table abound as well. One sister writes of a special service in her local church devoted to preparing missionaries for upcoming work in Mexico. After the sermon, the congregants shared the Holy Communion and found themselves caught up in the Spirit: '… the melting, strengthening power and presence of the Holy Ghost' was unforgettable, and the participants found themselves overcome with joy: 'The song ['They Were in an Upper Chamber'] just burst forth from us all', she recalls; 'and the Lord gave us a fresh pledge and assurance that He would go forth with His servants, confirming the Word with signs following'.[390]

Among the many testimonies, one stands out. The *WE* report of the 1916 General Council of the Assemblies of God includes a lengthy treatment of the sermon preached by D.W. Kerr in preparation for the Communion celebration that closed the meeting.[391] Repeatedly, the article – recounting Kerr's remarks – emphasizes the *present-tense* effectiveness of the Supper.

> This meal is intended not only for our spiritual, but for our physical benefit. Here is good news for the sick. You are invited to a meal for your health. As you are eating in faith you can receive healing for your body. If you cannot use the past tense and say 'By His stripes ye were healed', turn it into the present tense and declare, 'By His stripes I am healed'. You say perhaps 'I hope to be healed'. What time in the future will you be healed? God brings the future down to the present tense.

---

[387] *WE* 141 (May 27, 1916), p. 14.
[388] *WE* 139 (May 13, 1916), p. 11.
[389] *WE* 218 (Dec 8, 1917), p. 3.
[390] *WE* 181 (Mar 31, 1917), p. 13.
[391] *WE* 162 (Oct 28, 1916), pp. 4.

The Eucharist does work as a memorial, and the emblems do in fact symbolize Christ's broken body and shed blood.[392] Also, the feast points both *back*, to Christ's death, and *forward*, to his return. However, participants' focus must remain always on the Supper's 'distinct present aspect', which is paramount: '*Here* is the present tense of Calvary. We have come to a place of freshness, the result of Calvary. What is it? Life and life more abundant!'[393]

> There is nothing old or stale about this memorial feast, the fruit of the vine is not old, the shed blood is not aged, the bread is not stale, the Lord's body is not a mere thing of the past, the way is *new and living*. The thing most striking about the character of the feast is its *presentness*, not its pastness or its futureness. It has a present aspect, there is a sign of warmth, the blood is not cold and coagulated but flowing fresh from the wounded side of Jesus, 'recently killed and yet living'.[394]

These assertions point to a critical fact: even the early Pentecostals' use of memorialist and symbolic language does *not* prohibit sacramental meanings, for in their theology the Lord of the Supper is risen and through the Spirit makes himself present to the church, not least in the church's celebration of the Sacrament. For many of them, the emphasis lies not so much on what Christ *has done* as it does on what Christ *is doing*, here and now, through the shared Meal.[395]

Further, according to the *WE* report of Kerr's sermon, the Supper remains ineluctably *mysterious,* and it is only faith that grasps meanings otherwise mystifying and inexplicable: 'Faith enters into a realm far beyond the sphere of understanding, and can extract the good and joy out of that which soars high above our reasonings'. As a result, Pentecostals, as they are striving to live by just this kind of faith, 'have no need to preach a doctrine of consubstantiation or transubstantiation'. Instead, they 'just receive Jesus' words and act on them'.[396] In other words, they felt no need to explain *how* Christ

---

[392] Emphasis added.

[393] *WE* 162 (Oct 28, 1916), pp. 4-5.

[394] *WE* 162 (Oct 28, 1916), p. 5. Emphasis added.

[395] That this position is expounded in a Finished Work periodical makes it all the more striking.

[396] *WE* 162 (Oct 28, 1916), pp. 4. This claim makes clear, first, that Pentecostals did not feel beholden to traditional categories, and, second, reiterates the

is present in the Supper, but only to appreciate and enjoy that presence.

Guests at God's Feast: Embedded Sacramentality

Feasting motifs appear again and again in *PE*. Many readers regarded the weekly paper as a kind of feast.[397] 'Its precious truths are food for my hungry soul.'[398] An advertisement for a Bible school extends an invitation:

> Do you need a refreshing? Do you need a deeper death to the self life that 'Christ in you' may be more richly manifest? Is your heart hungry for God? Come up to this gathering of the saints before the Lord. Let us put His promises to the test. Let us see what God will do. Let us believe God for a real feast of fat things. Glory.[399]

As seen in other Pentecostal periodicals of the era, *PE* refers often to the marriage supper described in Rev. 17. Indeed, to be converted and Spirit-filled means nothing less than to 'set [one's] face toward the Marriage Supper'.[400] The joys of this future feast are experienced even now in the present life, if only partially and anticipatorily. Believers enjoy already the blessings that await them; they experience 'God's feast' throughout the course of their lives together. The saints must invite as many as possible to this feast,[401] for God desires 'a Love-feast on earth, ere He takes His loved ones with Him to His throne', and this feast should not lack for guests.[402] Spirit-baptized believers, then, must show hospitality, not only in sharing their meals together and in taking food to the hungry and the invalid but also in inviting others to enjoy the Lord's spiritual blessings. Reading Mt. 25.35-36 and Neh. 8.10, Alice Flower makes the point forcefully: 'Not only may this [hospitality] apply to a literal feast, but spiritually interpreted, should move us to seek out and feed the hungry souls instead of lingering about those who know so

---

heart of Pentecostal spirituality as imitation of and precisely in this way participation in the life of Jesus Christ.
   [397] *WE* 126 (Feb 12, 1916), p. 7.
   [398] *WE* 127 (Feb 19, 1916), p. 11.
   [399] *WE* 131 (Mar 18, 1916), p. 13.
   [400] *WE* 129 (Mar 4, 1916), p. 3.
   [401] *CE* 2.13 (Mar 28, 1914), p. 8.
   [402] *CE* 2.13 (Mar 28, 1914), p. 7.

well the way of salvation, even at the sacrifice of our temporal benefits'.[403] Obviously, 'God's feast' names the entire Christian life, and in the same way, 'love-feast' refers to more than the shared ritual meal, but clearly such descriptions reveal an imagination fired by experience of Communion and grounded in a regular observance of the rite.

Conclusions

PE provides unmistakable witness to a strong sacramentality, a sacramentality at least on par with that evidenced in earlier Finished Work periodicals and in the writings of Wesleyan-Holiness Pentecostals of the era. The view of the meaning of the ordinances/sacraments (footwashing, water baptism, and laying on of hands) are very much in keeping with that found in other Pentecostals periodicals. For example, they agree that the rite of water baptism, while not regenerative, is both necessary and profitable. The same is true of the reflections on the Eucharist and testimonies of Eucharistic experience. Contributors reiterate on numerous occasions how necessary and beneficial the Supper is for the church's life in the Spirit.

What are the major features of the view of the Eucharist witnessed to in *PE?* Three bear mentioning.

First, Bell, the Flowers, and other contributors to *PE* clearly felt no obligation to adhere strictly to the traditional theological categories or provide answers to the definitive sacramental controversies, Reformed or Catholic, although they are familiar with them. For example, they speak of the Spirit's presence in the Supper as well as Christ's, and no attempt is made to explain in philosophical terms how the Lord works through the Meal, although clearly he *is* expected to do so.

Second, *PE* contributors, like other Pentecostals of the time, make extensive use of Scripture in their reflections on the ordinances, often in surprising ways. They regularly appeal to texts that at first glance seem unrelated to the Eucharist – e.g. Neh. 8.10 – but they depended especially on Paul's instructions (1 Corinthians 11) and Jesus' teaching on the Bread of Life (John 6).

Third, there is in *PE* a consistent emphasis on the present-tenseness of Christ's presence in the Eucharist-event; the symbolic

---

[403] *CE* 2.13 (Mar 28, 1914), p. 7.

virtues of the ordinance are not overlooked, but certainly do remain secondary. The point of stress is the immediacy of blessing in the sacramentally-realized Presence.

Early Finished Work Sacramentality: Summary and Conclusions

Speaking broadly, early Finished Work Pentecostalism was no less sacramental than was early Wesleyan-Holiness Pentecostalism, although certain slight differences perhaps appear. For sure, the Finished Work movement at this early stage remained richly textured and diverse, and the sacramentality one discovers in the periodical literature is far from monochromatic. For all this diversity, however, a set of core convictions remained more or less established.

First, Finished Work Pentecostals, no less than their Wesleyan-Holiness brothers and sisters, rejected any notion of baptismal regeneration. Even so, they acknowledged water baptism as a churchly ordinance, and held that no true believer would refuse it as a matter of simple obedience. Not only that, numerous testimonies indicate that the experience of water baptism often belied their theological articulations of the rite's meaning.

Second, many Finished Work Pentecostals did not consider footwashing a churchly ordinance, with some (notably, William Durham) arguing that the practice must not be classed with water baptism and the Lord's Supper, even insisting that it should not be practiced ritually. Many Finished Work Pentecostals did observe the practice in spite of these protests, and some prominent leaders, including E.N. Bell, contended for its importance, although they stopped short of describing it as a sacrament. This marks a difference from some, but not all, Wesleyan-Holiness Pentecostals.

Third, like their brothers and sisters in the Wesleyan-Holiness stream, Finished Work Pentecostals resisted the idea that the sacraments worked magically, and they vigilantly opposed formalism, even while they regarded the Lord's Supper as in many ways the crux of Pentecostal worship. Communion services were for them deeply sacred occasions, times in which the Spirit worked forcefully. Rejecting Catholic and Lutheran articulations of Real Presence, they nevertheless adamantly affirmed that Christ was in some sense present to the celebrants at the Table. Not by any means did they experience the Supper as merely a memorial feast, even if they did believe that it had been given as a means of remembering the

Lord's atoning death. The 'present-tenseness' of the Supper remained foremost.

Fourth, like Wesleyan-Holiness Pentecostals, Finished Work Pentecostals justified their sacramental thought and practice by appealing to biblical texts, including, most prominently, 1 Cor. 11.23-33. Other passages, such as Jn 6.53-56, Acts 2.42-47, and Neh. 8.10, were used as well.

Fifth, like most Wesleyan-Holiness Pentecostals, they came to the Lord's Table trusting that if they rightly discerned the body of Christ, then they would receive bodily healing as well as spiritual nourishment.

Sixth, and finally, it is no exaggeration to claim that early Finished Work Pentecostalism was *characteristically* sacramental. More or less exactly like their brothers and sisters in the Wesleyan-Holiness movement, Finished Work Pentecostals regarded the Lord's Supper as an essential, even definitive rite of Christian worship and a source of blessing for the gathered congregation, including healing for both the body and the soul.

The Boddys and British Pentecostalism: *Confidence* Magazine

Introduction

The Anglican vicar A.A. Boddy, widely considered the founder of British Pentecostalism, established *Confidence* magazine in 1908, not long after his congregation, All Saints' Church in Sunderland, England, found itself swept up in the storms of Pentecostal revival.[404] He intended the magazine to serve as nothing less than a 'means of grace',[405] and as a 'Pentecostal paper for Great Britain and other lands'. He retained his membership in the Anglican Communion after his Spirit baptism, continuing as vicar of All Saints' in Sunderland.

The orientation of Boddy's theology, as well as that of other regular *Confidence* contributors, remains a matter of debate. Cartledge argues *contra* Faupel that Boddy's theology was largely if not

---

[404] See Gavin Wakefield, 'The Human Face of Pentecostalism: Why the British Pentecostal Moment Began in the Sunderland Parish of the Church of England Vicar Alexander Boddy', *JEPTA* 28.2 (2008), pp. 158-68.

[405] *Confidence* 1.1 (Apr 1908), p. 3.

essentially *Wesleyan*, and faithful to the 5-fold Gospel – in spite of the fact the phrase itself is never used.[406] Regardless, Boddy's magazine is included in this chapter primarily because it helps to cast into relief the depth and breadth of sacramentalism in the literature of the North American Finished Work and Wesleyan-Holiness camps of the period.

'Give Us Thy Real Presence': Explicit References to the Sacraments

The sacramentality one discovers in *Confidence*, like that found in the North American periodicals of the time, is textured and variegated, often exceeding the boundaries of traditional sacramental thought. For example, there are references not only to *Christ's* presence in the Supper, but also of the presence of the Spirit and the Father, as well. So, some can speak of Eucharistic participation as 'partaking of the Holy Spirit',[407] and can describe themselves at the Table as 'children in the Father's presence'.[408] While it is not advisable to make too much of them, unembellished statements like these, startling in their suggestiveness, indicate something of the unexplored depth of Pentecostal sacramental experience and reflection.

Footwashing

A.A. Boddy takes a position on footwashing similar to that held by many in the Finished Work tradition, and some in the Wesleyan-Holiness movement. He reads the account as a description of a necessary attitude, a willingness to serve humbly even in the most menial of ways. Surprisingly, he also assumes that John 13 should be read in conjunction with the Synoptic accounts of Jesus' 'last supper', as matched puzzle pieces.[409] At least one other *Confidence* contributor also understood footwashing as symbolic of Christ's ongoing work of sanctifying his people.

> Jesus looks after the feet of the saints. What care He takes that your walk and mine may be clean, that our feet may go into no defilement, that we may walk nowhere that will not be pleasing to our God, and so we read in that verse that He poured water

---

[406] Mark J. Cartledge, 'The Early Pentecostal Theology of *Confidence* Magazine (1908-1926): A Version of the Five-Fold Gospel?' *JEPTA* 28.2 (2008), pp. 117-30.

[407] *Confidence* 10.2 (Mar-Apr, 1917), p. 17.

[408] *Confidence* 3.1 (Jan, 1910), p. 20.

[409] *Confidence* 4.3 (March 1912), pp. 56-57.

into a basin and began to wash their feet. I like these words, 'and began.' It was only the beginning, not the end of that washing. It is going right on to-day [*sic*]; He is cleansing the feet of His saints. That is the application of the water of the Word through the power of the Holy Ghost. It was only the beginning; He is carrying it on to-day, and will only be satisfied when He lands the Church right up in Heaven, sanctified and cleansed in His Presence.[410]

Laying on of Hands and Anointing with Oil

Like most of his North American Pentecostal brothers and sisters, A.A. Boddy read the directives of Jas 5.14 as normative for healing practices. Both men and women can serve as 'elders', as 'channels of the quickening Spirit'; 'the Lord has given these gifts of healing'.[411] The call for prayer must come from the sick, exactly as the Scripture directs, and confession of sins is 'very advisable', for the prayer is for complete healing of body, soul, and spirit and not the removal of the sickness only. Boddy held that laying on of hands, as directed by Mk 16.18, was also an acceptable practice. However, in spite of the fact that it is scripturally sanctioned and so 'might be exercised by any Baptised [*sic*] person, if [he or she is] clearly led by the Spirit', some Pentecostals nonetheless insisted that it should never be done 'indiscriminately', as if it were 'only a form'.[412] The oil used in anointing does not possess healing powers, but symbolizes the Holy Spirit and signals the 'complete consecration to God of the body'.[413]

Testimonies indicate at least many *Confidence* readers shared Boddy's convictions on these matters. J.O. Lehman reports the instantaneous healings of a blind man and a young, deaf girl through the laying on of hands.[414] One woman, celebrating her 'wonderful healing', recounts how she received 'laying on hands for casting out and healing and for the Holy Ghost to come'.[415] A brother testifies of a service in which all those who desired to 'have the Word of God carried out, and be anointed with oil' were invited forward for

---

[410] *Confidence* 7.10 (Oct 1914), p. 193.
[411] *Confidence* 3.8 (Aug 1910), p. 178.
[412] *Confidence* 2.8 (Aug 1909), p. 174.
[413] *Confidence* 1.3 (June 30, 1908), p. 18.
[414] *Confidence* 2.5 (May 1909), p. 121.
[415] *Confidence* 5.1 (Jan 1912), p. 9.

prayer.[416] It suffices to say, then, that *Confidence's* teaching on the imposition of hands harmonizes with the teaching of North American Pentecostal periodicals in virtually every respect.

Water Baptism
Given the Boddys' Evangelical Anglican theology, one might expect their view and the views of the majority of *Confidence* contributors regarding water baptism to differ from that of most North American Pentecostals. Most of the time, however, that turns out not to be the case. For instance, in a lengthy exposition of Jn 3.2, A.A. Boddy says *nothing* of water baptism, instead inviting those who doubt their salvation to act in 'simple Faith', to 'Ask the Holy Spirit to make your Union with Christ your Head in His Death and Resurrection Life very real in your experience'.[417]

It is not surprising that *Confidence* assumes a difference between water baptism and Spirit baptism, in keeping with the Pentecostal experience, or that it regards baptism as a form of imitating Jesus.[418] In these ways, the theology of baptism in *Confidence* differs not at all from that found in the North American Pentecostal periodical literature. However, there appears to be a point of difference in the Boddys' belief about the relationship of the *external rite* of washing and the *internal work* of the Spirit. Although they could speak of baptism as the 'outward act of immersing in water connected with repentance' and believed that the washing rite serve as 'the outward sign of cleansing from sin, death to self, and resurrection to new life in Christ', they nonetheless maintained the conviction that the Spirit comes into the believer through – or at least 'alongside' – the service of ritual washing.[419] It would appear that not many American Pentecostals would have held the same opinion.

The Lord's Supper
There is in *Confidence* a deep and richly textured theology of the Lord's Supper – and not only in the Boddys' writings. For example, one contributor champions the reputation of a Brother Cook, 'a black saint', by reporting that Cook arises from his spending 'whole

---

[416] *Confidence* 4.7 (July 1911), p. 165.
[417] *Confidence* 2.4 (Apr 1909), p. 96.
[418] *Confidence* 5.6 (May 1913), p. 90; See also *Confidence* 1.1 (Apr 1908), p. 11. They, too, speak of 'following the Lord in baptism'.
[419] See *Confidence* 1.5 (Aug 15, 1908), p. 4; *Confidence* 8.12 (Dec 1915), p. 230.

nights in prayer' to partake of the 'Holy Sacrament with fear and trembling'.[420] Another writer reports on the work in Basutoland, remarking on the 'healthy fear of God' that characterizes the congregation there, a 'healthy fear' due, in large part, to the death of two men who 'dared to eat the Lord's Supper whilst being in sin' and were 'slain by the Lord'.[421]

This robust theology of the Eucharist is perhaps strongest and clearest in the Boddys' contributions, however. In a March 1912 article exploring the 'closing scenes in our Lord's earthly life', A.A. Boddy explains how just before or just after Judas had abandoned Jesus, 'the Omniscient Lord instituted the Holy Communion in the most solemn way', surely knowing in that moment this institution would be observed through the centuries 'until His great Advent'.[422] Boddy himself recalls having shared 'the blessed bread and holy wine' with 'Canaanitish Christians in the Syrian Church dedicated to St Paul'. They recited the prayer of consecration and the words of administration in 'Syrian Arabic', yet he knew 'that this same Lord Jesus was again with us as of old when he reclined in that upper chamber in that same Holy City'. He rejoices that many find Jesus 'at His Holy Table in a new and unexpected way'.[423] Concluding his thoughts on the Last Supper, Boddy wonders if it might not be while the church is gathered at the Table 'that the brilliance of His glory will stream upon us', so that the celebration on earth is once-for-all transposed by Christ's *parousia* into the 'wondrous and blessed Marriage Supper of the Lamb'.[424]

Like her husband, Mary Boddy insisted on the centrality of the Eucharist, and if anything with greater emphasis and sophistication. In one article, apparently judging that many of her fellow Pentecostals were *not* properly receiving the Supper and the 'wonderful power of His precious Body being given for us', she asks, 'Are we appropriating *all* that our Lord has obtained for us?' She abjures her readers to take the Sacrament with a greater seriousness, to come to the Table *expectantly*: 'As we take part in the blessed Holy Com-

---

[420] *Confidence* 10.1 (Jan-Feb 1917), p. 9.
[421] *Confidence* 8.12 (December 1915), p. 237.
[422] *Confidence* 5.3 (March 1912), pp. 56-59.
[423] *Confidence* 5.3 (March 1912), pp. 56-59.
[424] *Confidence* 5.3 (March 1912), p. 58. In saying this, Boddy brilliantly displays the continuity Pentecostals perceive between the church's celebration of Holy Communion and the 'marriage supper of the Lamb'.

munion, do we fully realise [*sic*] that is a real participation in the body of Christ?' She appeals to a few biblical passages, including John 6 and 1 Corinthians 10 to support her claims. 'If we would "dwell or abide in Him" we must eat His flesh and drink His blood.' She insists that nothing less or other than this is 'the true union with Christ'.[425] In another place – again reflecting on Jn 6.51-53 – Boddy pronounces her gratitude for the gift of the Eucharist: 'We thank God for the Holy Communion, which is a continual remembrance of this wonderful salvation'. Having said this, she is not content, but pushes on to insist that the Eucharist-event is 'nay, more than a remembrance' and is in fact nothing less than a 'continual feeding upon the Heavenly Manna, the hidden manna which cometh down from Heaven – even Christ Himself'.[426] In that line, 'nay, *more than a remembrance*, a continual feeding',[427] she gives voice to a theology of the Eucharist that, judging from the bulk of the evidence, most North American Pentecostals of the time would have agreed to. Again and again, she insists that if properly received Holy Communion effects transformation into Christ:

> … if we believe and receive the word of death to our old body of sin, and receive His word in the Holy Communion as 'spirit and life' ('the flesh profiteth nothing'), the Holy Spirit will quicken that seed of the Word and it will become flesh in us. So shall we be of the same substance or seed as His blessed Body.[428]

The outlines of a robust (Reformed) theology of the Sacrament shine through these claims. Clearly, Mary Boddy believes that in order for Communion to be everything it has been promised to be, then the celebrants must 'believe and receive', must put their faith in the promise of God so that the Holy Spirit can enliven the rite – and the bread and wine? – so that the Word ingested/'ingested' in the receiving of the elements can be 'quickened' and believers can be transformed into Christlikeness – made to be 'of the same substance' as the 'blessed Body' of Christ himself. In other words, when rightly received, the Eucharist by the Spirit's power becomes for the believer an ontologically-transforming event, one in which

---

[425] *Confidence* 7.8 (Aug 1914), p. 150.
[426] *Confidence* 7.12 (Dec 1914), p. 232.
[427] Emphasis added.
[428] Here, she references Heb. 2.14.

the celebrant is 'at-oned' with Christ, and made to share in his nature.

Excursus: the Boddys' Cranmerian Theology of the Eucharist

The Boddys made constant use of the *Book of Common Prayer* (*BCP*), an act thick with implications for this project because of *BCP*'s unquestionably high sacramentalism. *BCP* gives liturgical expression to Thomas Cranmer's 'indirect theology',[429] which varied by degrees through the years, but remained always Reformed. Sometimes Zwinglian, at other times Bucerian (especially in the later versions),[430] Cranmer's thought about the Eucharistic presence of Christ was always set over against the traditional Roman Catholic view, and, to a lesser degree, the Lutheran.[431] Nonetheless, Cranmer *did* hold to a belief in real presence, even while he by and large rejected the Thomistic and Lutheran articulations of it.[432]

For good reasons, it may be assumed that the Boddys retained a view more or less compatible with Cranmer's. For example, one article provides the text of a New Year's sermon Mary had delivered in which she explains how she came to understand Christ's life as 'proof against all disease for all time'. The body, as well as the soul, received its redemption in Jesus' death and resurrection. In explication, she appeals to a turn of phrase from *BCP:* 'My body made clean by His Body, and my soul washed in His most precious Blood'.[433] Obviously, the 'Body' that makes clean is Christ's *Eucharistic* Body, and the Blood, the Communion wine. Mary Boddy ex-

---

[429] For the most part, Cranmer gives liturgical expression to the theology of the reformers, including Luther, Calvin, Zwingli, and Martin Bucer, a personal friend. There is controversy as to which reformer Cranmer remained most faithful. See Roger E. Olsen, *The Story of Christian Theology* (Downers Grove, IL: IVP, 1999), p. 436. As Olsen notes, Cranmer's friendship with Bucer was not the only intimate source for his theology; Cranmer's wife was Lutheran, and she was the niece of the (somewhat inconsistent) Lutheran theologian, Andreas Osiander.

[430] Willem Nijenhuis, *Ecclesia Reformata: Studies on the Reformation* (Leiden: Brill, 1972), argues for three phases in Cranmer's view of the Eucharist: first a Catholic view, then a Lutheran, and finally a view akin to the Swiss Reformers.

[431] Byron D. Stuhlman, *A Good and Joyful Thing: the Evolution of the Eucharistic Prayer* (New York: Church Publishing Inc., 2000), pp. 114-21.

[432] Certainly, the first version of *BCP* (1549) – published on Pentecost Sunday – was considered too 'Catholic' by most reformers, especially in its doctrine of the Eucharist; the succeeding version (1552) vindicated itself as a more properly 'Protestant' book. See R.C.D. Jasper and G.J. Cuming, *Prayers of the Eucharist: Early and Reformed* (Collegeville, MN: Liturgical Press, 1990), pp. 232-49.

[433] *Confidence* 7.1 (Jan, 1914), p. 11.

cerpts this phrase from the well-known 'Prayer of Humble Access', offered by the administering priest while kneeling at the Lord's Table.[434] The prayer reads:

> We do not presume to come to this thy Table, O merciful Lord, trusting in our own righteousness, but in thy manifold and great mercies. We are not worthy so much as to gather up the crumbs under thy Table. But thou art the same Lord, whose property is always to have mercy: Grant us therefore, gracious Lord, so to eat the flesh of thy dear Son Jesus Christ, and to drink his blood, that our sinful bodies may be made clean by his body, and our souls washed through his most precious blood, and that we may evermore dwell in him, and he in us. *Amen.*

Following Cranmer, the Boddys believed that the sacraments – and in particular, Holy Communion – served as means to real, spiritual communion with Christ through the Spirit. The Boddys' daughter, Jane, recalls her confirmation and first Communion, and its effect on her: it 'filled me with new spiritual life'.[435] Boddy himself acknowledges also the symbolic value of the Eucharist, agreeing that 'The Lord's Supper was instituted by Christ, and is a memorial of His death and Passion'. However, this memorialist dimension does not exhaust the Supper's reality, for 'by partaking of it we have communion with Christ till He comes'.[436] He cites an excerpt from an Andrew Murray sermon, which climaxes in a prayer: 'Blessed Lord! how wondrously Thou hast provided for our growing likeness to Thyself, in giving us Thine own Holy Spirit. Thou hast told us that it is His work to reveal Thee, to give us Thy Real Presence within us'.[437]

Perhaps the clearest proof of the Cranmerian character of the Boddys' theology comes in A.A. Boddy's interpretation of his Spirit baptism. He recalls that while administering an early morning Communion Service, September 21st, 1892, 'the Holy Spirit in infinite love came upon me' just as he was reading the text for the day,

---

[434] It is not clear whether Mary intends to draw attention to the Eucharist, although there is no reason to assume otherwise. Many Pentecostals, then and now, consider the Lord's Table a place of healing.

[435] *Confidence* 1.2 (May 1908), p. 8.

[436] *Confidence* 9.4 (Apr 1916), p. 74.

[437] *Confidence* 129 (Apr-June, 1922), p. 26.

2 Cor. 4.6. Boddy appeals to a line from *BCP* to explain the event. The moment, he says, overwhelmed him:

> I knew He had come, and that I was 'fulfilled with His grace and heavenly benediction'. It seemed as if my vocal organs were affected, and that it was 'Another' who was reading those precious words through me. When the service was over I praised Him in the words of the Doxology. The longing of my heart was satisfied; my constant prayer was answered.[438]

Such use of the *BCP* almost certainly suggests more than a familiarity with its language. It implies a deeply held conviction that what the *BCP* describes as happening in the Eucharist-event is in fact what the participants are experiencing.

Jesus in the Midst: Testimonies of Sacramental Experience

Pentecostals from across Europe, as well as from the United States and other parts of the world, came to the Sunderland church for Pentecostal conferences, and shared together in Eucharistic celebration. T.B. Barratt's wife, Margaret, reports on one of these conferences,[439] recounting how every one attending the conference, irrespective of denominational affiliation, received an invitation to the Sunday morning celebration of the 'Sacrament of the Lord's Supper'. All 'gathered together as one family, namely, God's children', she boasts.[440] Even if the service differed ceremonially from what many expected, its significance for them remained unchanged: 'the form was different, but the spirit was the same'.[441] Indeed, she believed that sharing in the Eucharist not only reflected this unity, but actually *effected* it. Even if the Boddys belonged to the Church of England and others hailed from other denominations, they found themselves in one Spirit because there is 'one cup of which we drink, and one bread of which we eat; so we are one body'.[442]

In the same vein, a North American believer reports on another international conference, hosted at Sunderland:

---

[438] *Confidence* 7.2 (Feb 1914), p. 24.
[439] Her article was published originally in T.B. Barratt's magazine, *Christiania*; Boddy reprints it for his readers.
[440] *Confidence* 1.4 (July 15, 1908), p. 5.
[441] *Confidence* 1.4 (July 15, 1908), p. 5.
[442] *Confidence* 10.5 (Sept-Oct 1917), p. 67.

One morning, very early, a large number of us were assembled at
All Saints' Church, by Mr. Boddy's invitation, to partake of the
Lord's Supper, and it was a service of unusual sweetness and solemnity. Many different nationalities were represented. Some of
our German brethren could not speak English, but one could
read the language of their shining faces. Brothers and sisters
were present who knew nothing of the ritual of the Established
Church of England, but as it was read by Rev., Mr. Boddy (as-
sisted by a curate) in tones of deepest reverence, and in the
power of the Holy Spirit, a marvellous [*sic*] hush fell upon us,
and we realized that though in some cases religious training had
been different, yet we were all blessedly one in Christ, one bread,
one body, all having been made to drink into the one Spirit.[443]

As seen in this example, writers and readers of *Confidence* employed biblical images and turns of phrase to explain their sacramental experience. C.H. Hook writes to admonish those who are
wrongly participating in the Supper, appealing to Jesus' promise
(John 6) and to Paul's warning (1 Corinthians 11). Many are sick or
have died because of the failure 'to discern the Lord's body in the
sacrament, in other words – not feeding on Christ enough to keep
[them] alive'. 'Jesus is the life; then feed on Him.'[444] In a talk that
had been delivered in California before being published in *Confidence*, Carrie Judd Montgomery expounded Jesus' command to eat
his flesh and drink his blood as a call to the 'truth that is too deep
and mystical' for natural understanding. 'That which is not compre-
hensible to the natural man, the spiritual man obeys.'[445]

Again and again, testimonies in *Confidence* demonstrate that the
Communion rite was understood as a time for Christ to present
himself and to act on the celebrants. A.A. Boddy remembers a
prayer meeting that climaxed with celebration of the Lord's Supper:
'Pastor Paul saw Jesus in the midst',[446] an experience that took place
during the December 1908 conference in Germany.

Before the last meal there was the solemn Breaking of the Bread,
when pastor Paul acted as our Presbyter, and the Chalice and the

---

443 *Confidence* 2.8 (Aug 1909), p. 177. Emphasis added.
444 *Confidence* 1.7 (Oct 15, 1908), p. 11.
445 *Confidence* 7.7 (Sep 1914), p. 175.
446 Supplement to *Confidence* 1.9 (Dec 15, 1908), p. 4.

large plate of bread were solemnly passed round after he had reverently used the words of Institution and Blessing. *The Lord Himself was seen by him standing in our midst*, as at the Last Supper. Then the Pastor turned to me and said, 'Let the Englishmen sing the song of the Blood', so we sang, and all joined in their own tongue or in English:

Oh, the Blood, the precious Blood,
It cleanses me, I praise the Lord;
From sin and guilt it sets me free,
The precious Blood, it cleanses me.[447]

Times of corporate worship devoted to the celebration of Holy Communion often yielded moments of renewal, as the Spirit began to move some to prophesy, others to speak in tongues; some were instantly healed, and others were impelled to ecstatic celebration. Many received their Spirit baptism while partaking of the Lord's Supper,[448] and outbreaks of the Spirit in the course of the Communion celebration were anything but an uncommon experience. One sister, bedfast for nearly six years and for a long time at the edge of death, requested the Lord's Supper brought to her in bed and immediately on receiving it with the church's prayers began to improve and eventually revived and received a complete healing.[449]

European Pentecostals, like their brothers and sisters in the United States, held the Supper in the highest regard, and attended carefully to the details of the ritual. They insisted on open communion, for they believed 'this is the Lord's Table, not ours'.[450] Pentecostal churches in Amsterdam, for instance, refused to allow anyone to partake of 'the Bread and Wine' until they had signed a paper verifying that they were in fact 'right with God and man and have perfect love towards all'. One visitor to a service describes how one or two came forward to 'get right with God' before Communion; the service was strikingly 'simple', and a 'most restful, quiet spirit' pervaded the moment. A missionary writes from China, explaining how the team taught the converts to engage the sacraments: 'They even had to be told how to partake of the Lord's

---

[447] *Confidence* 2.1 (Jan 1909), p. 4. Emphasis added.
[448] *Confidence* 4.8 (Aug, 1911), p. 177.
[449] *Confidence* 6.6 (June, 1913), p. 112.
[450] *Confidence* 1.5 (Aug 15, 1908), p. 10.

Supper, i.e., how much to eat and how much to drink, as it was all so strange and new to them'.[451]

'Too Deep and Mystical': Embedded Sacramentality

The language of hunger and feasting factors significantly in *Confidence,* as it did in the North American Pentecostal literature of the time. One testifies of the 'pleasure' and 'sweetness' of his experience of Christ, and boasts: 'no wonder we say to others "taste and see that the Lord is good" [and] " His mouth is most sweet; yea, He is altogether lovely"'.[452] The entire Pentecostal experience is satisfying, for

> It tastes just like the best of Bread, it looks like the purest Bread, it strengthens us exactly as does Heavenly Bread, and the Father tells us in our hearts that it is the very Bread He promised. It has upon it all the Hall-Marks of being Heavenly Food given by our beloved Father.[453]

Every believer should set aside time each day with the Scripture: 'Devour the Word, feed upon it'.[454]

> When we do, we will get so strengthened and so sustained and so filled that it is bound to flow over, and the Word, the living Word which came down from Heaven, shall be revealed to us through the written Word by the Spirit of God, and thus the true manna shall feed us day by day until we lack no more.[455]

As with the North American periodicals, the dinner table, as well as the Eucharistic altar, was regarded as a sacred space: 'After supper we had a profitable time of prayer and fellowship together. Our brother is hungry for God's best, and the Lord enabled me to satisfy him upon some points that had troubled him'.[456] Also, one finds frequent mention of the marriage supper.[457]

---

[451] *Confidence* 9.7 (July 1916), p. 122.
[452] *Confidence* 7.12 (Dec 1914), p. 227.
[453] *Confidence* 2.8 (Aug 1909), p. 182.
[454] *Confidence* 2.7 (July 1909), p. 150.
[455] *Confidence* 2.3 (Mar 1909), p. 69.
[456] *Confidence* 3.8 (Aug 1910), p. 181.
[457] See, for example, *Confidence* 2.5 (May 1909), p. 120; *Confidence* 3.12 (Dec 1910), pp. 288-89; *Confidence* 4.1 (Jan 1911), p. 8; *Confidence* 128 (Jan-Mar 1922), p. 4.

Conclusions

Because of the Boddys' Anglicanism, one is not surprised to find frequent meaningful references to the sacraments. One might be surprised however, to find that when the sacramentality is compared to that of, say, *AF, COGE,* or *PE,* little difference appears, either in degree or in kind. Boddy's *Confidence* differs from other Pentecostal literature of the time in its treatment of the sacraments mainly if not only in this regard: it makes use of the *Book of Common Prayer.* Because of this, the *descriptions* of the sacraments in *Confidence* often adheres formally to the Reformed (Cranmerian) tradition, but it does not seem to hold a markedly different *notion* of the sacraments than that expressed in North American Pentecostal periodicals. Insofar as *Confidence* provides a clear window on the life of early Pentecostals not only in the United States and Britain but also in Western Europe, it is no exaggeration to say that for at least many Pentecostals in the Western world the sacraments were vital, even fundamental, to their spirituality.[458]

Like their Pentecostal brothers and sisters in the U.S., the Boddys and other principal contributors to *Confidence* practiced the laying on of hands for healing and Spirit baptism in submission to the clear direction of Scripture, and although they never described it in sacramental terms they obviously expected this practice to occasion the Spirit's work. For at least a few of the contributors, including Boddy and his wife, Holy Communion was genuinely a unique means of grace, effecting the presence of Christ for the celebrants. It was medicine for the sick and nourishment for the spiritually hungry.

Early Pentecostal Sacramentality: Summary and Conclusions

What, then, has been learned from this reading of the early periodical literature? It has come clear that a great many if not the vast majority of early Pentecostals in the United States engaged in sacramental practice and thought, although a small, always marginalized minority in and alongside the Pentecostal movements opposed the

---

[458] At the least, it is safe to say that Boddy himself, as the magazine's editor, selected and disseminated articles that leave this impression.

sacraments in any form. Pentecostals were not uniform in their sacramental beliefs and praxis; however, there was widespread agreement that water baptism and Holy Communion, as well as laying on of hands – and, to a lesser extent, footwashing – remained critical and even central to Pentecostal worship. Early Pentecostals celebrated the sacraments not only as a matter of obedience to the dominical mandate but also in full expectation that God would act uniquely and powerfully in and through these rites.

It is impossible to appreciate early Pentecostal spirituality generally, or their sacramentality specifically, unless one discerns that they arose from a form of *imitatio Christi*. It was a following of Jesus 'to fulfill all righteousness' that fired their experience of the sacraments. They observed the ordinances of water baptism, Holy Communion, and footwashing as occasions for encountering and imitating the risen Jesus and mediation of the grace of divine transformative presence. These rites were never merely ceremonial or memorialistic, although their rich symbolism was not lost on the practitioners. The evidence indicates first generation Wesleyan-Holiness and Finished Work Pentecostals experienced these rites as 'sacred occasions', unique opportunities for the Spirit to work in the community. For them, these were moments in which heaven met earth and believers found themselves overwhelmed by God's real, active presence. Hence, it is not surprising that one finds at least an incipient theology of the sacraments embedded in and emerging from early Pentecostal prayer and preaching. Above and beyond the explicit references to the sacraments, one finds a multifaceted sacramentality embedded in the rites and practices, as well as the idiom of early Pentecostals. For instance, the extensive use of eating/drinking metaphors reveals an *appetitiveness*, a hunger for God and the work of God; the Supper served as the sign par excellence of this hunger. As Jamie Smith explains, Pentecostal spirituality is an 'extension of the Reformed intuition about the goodness of creation', and the characteristic emphasis on physical healing is an implicit 'affirmation that God cares about our bodies', an 'affirmation of the goodness of embodiment'.[459] This is borne out again and again in the sacramentality of early Pentecostals, as well.

---

[459] James K.A. Smith, *The Devil Reads Derrida* (Grand Rapids: Eerdmans, 2009), p. 30.

To be sure, Pentecostals of the first generation rejected anything that tended toward formalism, and vigorously refused all descriptions of the sacraments operating automatically.[460] Further, they did not restrict themselves to traditional sacramental categories, although they did not avoid use of explicitly sacramental terminology, as later Pentecostals seem to have done, instead using many names for the Meal, including Holy Communion, the Sacrament, and the Lord's Supper. They did not find themselves compelled to explain the *metaphysics* of Christ's presence in the Supper, even though plainly many of them did believe that Christ himself was present to the church through, or at least *with*, the observance of the Meal. For them, the Lord's Supper was never *merely* a memorial feast. Numerous accounts of dreams or visions about the Supper illuminate in an inimitable way how formative the Eucharist was for early Pentecostal spirituality.

Their experience of the Supper and their articulation of its meaning and purpose also received their shape from reflection on key biblical passages, including Paul's account of the institution of the Supper (1 Cor. 11.23-33) and the so-called Bread of Life discourse in John 6, as well as the 'breaking bread' passages in Luke-Acts, Neh. 8.10, and references to the 'bread of the presence' in Exodus 25, among other passages. John 6.53-56 received special attention, both by those who insisted on the importance of obeying Jesus in sharing the meal and those who claimed Christians were called to 'feast' on Jesus mystically, as a way of life, and not merely ritually. Apparently, most did not regard these as mutually exclusive alternatives, but as parallel dimensions of the sacred reality.

---

[460] They would agree with Wesley's stance, as expounded in his sermon on the 'Means of Grace': '… all outward means whatever, if separate from the Spirit of God, cannot profit at all, cannot conduce, in any degree, either to the knowledge or love of God. Without controversy, the help that is done upon earth, He doeth it himself. It is He alone who, by his own almighty power, worketh in us what is pleasing in his sight; and all outward things, unless He work in them and by them, are mere weak and beggarly elements. Whosoever, therefore, imagines there is any intrinsic power in any means whatsoever, does greatly err, not knowing the Scriptures, neither the power of God. We know that there is no inherent power in the words that are spoken in prayer, in the letter of Scripture read, the sound thereof heard, or the bread and wine received in the Lord's Supper; but that it is God alone who is the Giver of every good gift, the Author of all grace'.

In this, Pentecostals of the first generation fit nicely with many in the ancient and medieval Christian tradition. Their ambiguous talk of eating Christ fits nicely with, for example, Origen: 'We drink the blood of Christ not only in the sacramental rite, but also when we receive his words in which are life, as he himself says: "The words that I have spoken are spirit and life" (Jn 6.63) ...' Origen continues, teasing out further implication of this controlling metaphor:

> Just as Christ is the living bread, so is his enemy, death, the dead bread. Every rational soul is nourished by one or the other of these ... Thus, every word through which we receive spiritual drink, or every story through which we are nourished, is a vessel of food and drink. We are admonished therefore not to worry about words and stories which come from the outside but only about those which come from within so that our heart will be filled with pure, drinkable and eatable senses, and not with mere words or fancy speeches; for the 'kingdom of God does not consist in talk but in power'.[461]

As these readings suggest, the first-generation Pentecostal imagination was deftly metaphoric, deploying, encoding, and deciphering (biblically-informed) metaphors in an almost inexhaustible variety of ways. For instance, the bread of the presence could and did serve as a way of identifying Christ himself, as a way of explicating the benefits he affords (e.g. salvation, sanctification, healing, Spirit baptism), and as a way of describing the believers' intimate fellowship with Christ through the Spirit. These meanings were rarely if ever neatly distinguished. To take another example, the Passover meal was taken often as a *signum* of Israel's deliverance from Egypt, and both the Passover and the Exodus were regarded as *signa* of Christ's last supper (and the first of the church's Suppers) that in turn served (and serves) as a sign of his death on the cross and the benefits it effects, as well as referring backward to the entire system of signs that pre-figured it, and forward to the future 'marriage supper of the Lamb' – which itself is a metaphor for believers' eternal fellowship with God in Christ. This imaginativeness not only

---

[461] Quoted in Hans Urs von Balthasar (ed.), *Origen, Spirit and Fire: A Thematic Anthology of His Writing* (Washington DC: Catholic University of America Press, 1984), p. 264.

shaped how Pentecostals engaged the Supper, but emerged from their shared experience of Communion. For them, the Eucharist served both as a *signum* and a medium, a way of obeying the Lord's commands and bringing to mind the events of his saving death, but also a means of the Spirit making the participants like the one who ordained the meal. It seems likely that the Eucharistic rubrics and practice of the larger Christian tradition helped to shape early Pentecostal spirituality, informing their use of eating and drinking metaphors, at least at some remove.

These observations and conclusions call into question certain historical analyses and secondary accounts of early Pentecostalism that overlook or downplay its sacramentality, inviting new engagement and assessment of the spirituality that gave rise to the movement. To put it briefly, the sacramental thought and practice of early Pentecostals has not received the attention it deserves. Even where it has been addressed, it often has been underappreciated, if not altogether misunderstood.

4

THE LORD'S SUPPER IN THE CHURCH'S SCRIPTURE

Introduction

Given that Pentecostals have been from the first and remain a people devoted to the authority of Scripture, a proposed Pentecostal theology of the Eucharist should show how it makes sense in light of the 'whole counsel' of Scripture. This is not simply a matter of amassing proof texts, of course, and requires more than a careful exegesis of key passages: the biblical texts must be engaged in a way that rings true to the form of life recognizable to Pentecostals as devotion to the God of the gospel. My objective in this section is to develop an interpretive model that meets these standards. After developing a Pentecostal hermeneutical model, I will select three representative texts from the Scripture's witness to the meaning and purpose of the Eucharist-event, and then read these texts using the schema developed in the previous chapter for reading the early Pentecostal periodicals, drawing first on explicit theological statements about the Eucharist, then testimonies of Eucharistic experience, and, finally, texts whose sacramental theology remains embedded and suggestive.

(Re)Imagining a Pentecostal Hermeneutic

Introduction

Over the past twenty-five years or so, Pentecostal scholars have turned their attention to hermeneutics, asking how readers can and should engage the Christian Scriptures, attempting to identify and describe in detail what in fact makes a reading of the Scriptures genuinely *Pentecostal*. In the course of this development, it has become increasingly clear that Pentecostal interpretative strategies stand apart from those of the 'liberal' Protestant tradition on the one hand and those of the Evangelical tradition on the other hand – in spite of the fact that Pentecostals share with Evangelicals a high view of Scripture. Influenced to a considerable degree by postmodern literary theory[1] and the insights of post-critical theology, Pentecostal scholars are forging hermeneutical models better fitted to the ethos of the movement. Not everyone agrees on every point, of course. Nonetheless, several themes and emphases have won widespread acceptance. To be more exact:

1. The work of the Spirit in making faithful interpretation possible, inspiring the readers to make gospel sense of the texts.

2. The authority and sufficiency of the Scriptures' final, canonical form.

3. The role of the worshipping community in the process of interpreting the Scriptures.

4. The need for confessional, theological readings concerned primarily with how the Scriptures work as God's address to God's people here and now.

5. Respect for the irreducible diversity of theological and literary 'voices' in the Scriptures.

6. Regard for the over-arching 'story' of the history of salvation as a hermeneutical key.

7. The priority of narrative, literary readings of a text over against historical-critical readings.

8. The significance of the history of effects for the contemporary interpretative process.

Most if not all of these themes have been gathered under a simple and often-used rubric – Spirit, Word, and community – and perhaps it is no exaggeration to say a definitive interpretative model

---

[1] See Hannah K. Harrington and Rebecca Patten, 'Pentecostal Hermeneutics and Postmodern Literary Theory', *Pneuma* 16.1 (Spring 1994), pp. 109-14.

is emerging under this heading.[2] In the following section, I will take up this rubric to explore the developments and emerging scholarly consensus among Pentecostals. In my conclusion, I will attempt to show what difference the various assumptions and claims of the model make for discerning the import of the Scriptures' manifold witness to the value and meaning of the Communion rite.

The Inspiring, Interpreting Spirit

Pentecostals believe the Spirit is the Scripture's definitive interpreter,[3] the one who makes faithful 'hearing' of the Word possible.[4] The Spirit promises to 'lead and guide the community in understanding the present meaningfulness of Scripture',[5] enabling us to read the Scripture with a 'new clarity that could not be possible without his aid'.[6]

Pentecostals typically distinguish between Spirit and Word, so that the community's *charismatic* participation is judged to be fundamentally indispensable to the work of rightly discerning the will of God in light of the written Word.[7] Land describes the authority

---

[2] Many have used this rubric, including Rick D. Moore, 'Canon and Criticism in the Book of Deuteronomy', *JPT* 1 (Oct 1992), pp. 75-92; Land, *Pentecostal Spirituality*, pp. 39-40; John Christopher Thomas, 'Women, Pentecostals, and the Bible: An Experiment in Pentecostal Hermeneutics', *JPT* 5 (1994), pp. 41-56; Amos Yong, *Spirit-Word-Community: Theological Hermeneutics in Trinitarian Perspective* (Eugene, OR: Wipf & Stock, 2002), and Kenneth J. Archer, *A Pentecostal Hermeneutic: Spirit, Scripture and Community* (Cleveland, TN: CPT Press, 2009), pp. 213-15 (originally published as *A Pentecostal Hermeneutic for the Twenty-First Century* [New York: T&T Clark, 2004]).

[3] It is one thing to insist *that* the Spirit is active in the interpretative process, but quite another to explain *how*. The more difficult question is, then, by what *means* does God influence and direct the interpretation of Scripture? What is needed to answer this question is a hermeneutic that 'seeks to articulate what the Spirit's role is and how the Spirit works specifically', as Thomas ('Women, Pentecostals, and the Bible', pp. 41-42) says.

[4] In this, Pentecostals are not distancing themselves from the *ecclesia catholica*, but attempting to put into practice a conviction shared by all Christians. For the ecumenical confession of Pentecostals and Roman Catholics on this issue, see Veli-Matti Kärkkäinen, 'Authority, Revelation, and Interpretation in the Roman Catholic-Pentecostal Dialogue', *Pneuma* 21.1 (Spring 1999), pp. 89-114.

[5] Archer, *A Pentecostal Hermeneutic*, p. 248.

[6] John McKay, 'When the Veil is Taken Away: The Impact of Prophetic Experience on Biblical Interpretation', *JPT* 5 (1994), p. 21.

[7] So Archer (*A Pentecostal Hermeneutic*, p. 248) drawing principally on the work of Rick Moore, John Christopher Thomas, and Stephen Fowl, argues that 'the Spirit does speak and has more to say than just Scripture. This requires the

and efficacy of Scripture as finally dependent on the relation of the Spirit to Christ. This means that Word and Spirit are 'married' so that no thought or action is truly scriptural if it is not 'communicated out of the fullness of the Spirit'.[8] It is this that makes the Scriptures authoritatively effective: 'as the Spirit formed Christ in Mary, so the Spirit uses Scripture to form Christ in believers and vice-versa'.[9]

Discerning in his reading of Deuteronomy a 'theology of revelation' that calls for 'two revelatory channels, that of canonical writing and charismatic speech',[10] Rick Moore contends that occasional Spirit-impelled *speech* is divinely purposed to keep Israel from losing touch with the God who speaks and is spoken of in the *written* texts. While he readily acknowledges that a 'close linkage' remains between the scripted Word and the 'charismatic utterance', Moore believes Deuteronomy teaches that 'each revelational medium would have its own respective function'.[11]

Deuteronomy here seems to see the essential and distinct contribution of charismatic revelation in terms of the manifesting of God's nearness in a way that counters an idolatrous manufacturing of divine presence, on the one hand, and a legalistic distancing of divine word, on the other.[12]

Moore draws from this several applications for contemporary Pentecostal life, the most telling of which is the need to hold in tension Word and Spirit and so avoid 'a Spirit-less word (rationalism), on the one hand, and a Word-less Spirit (subjectivism), on the other'.[13] In other words, Pentecostal hermeneutics depends in part on the willingness and ability to allow the Spirit's '*dynamic* word' expressed through the charismata to illuminate the '*enduring* word' of the biblical texts.[14]

---

community to discern the Spirit in the process of negotiating the meaning of the biblical texts'.

[8] Land, *Pentecostal Spirituality*, p. 100.

[9] Land, *Pentecostal Spirituality*, p. 100.

[10] Moore, 'Canon and Charisma in the Book of Deuteronomy', p. 79.

[11] Moore, 'Canon and Charisma in the Book of Deuteronomy', p. 80.

[12] Moore, 'Canon and Charisma in the Book of Deuteronomy', p. 89.

[13] Moore, 'Canon and Charisma in the Book of Deuteronomy', p. 91. For example, Yong (*Spirit-Word-Community*, p. 257) can speak of a 'necessarily healthy tension between Spirit and Word'.

[14] Emphasis added.

Pentecostals characteristically maintain that the Holy Spirit is no less active in present-day biblical interpretation than in the ancient composition of these texts.[15] In fact, Clark Pinnock dismisses altogether the distinction of 'inspiration' and 'illumination',[16] insisting there are only two modes of the same inspiration – 'contemporary' and 'original'.[17] In any case, the witness of countless Pentecostals indicates that the interpretative process is a supernatural event:

> They tell of passages illuminated in new ways, of texts that take on new meaningfulness, of verses that burn themselves into the memory, of completely new appreciations of whole books of the Bible, of a positive urge to read page after page of the text, of exciting new discoveries about God's self-revelation in Scripture, and so forth.[18]

In sum, the Spirit's role is believed by Pentecostals to enliven Scripture so that it acts on the readers as God's Word *pro nobis*. That is, the Spirit makes possible confessional, spiritual, and theological readings that seek to discover what God is saying to the churches in the here-and-now of their historical and socio-cultural situations, and in this way to make God's will known.[19] Apart from the Spirit's help, the faithful and effective reading of Scripture as God's Word is, quite simply, impossible.

Pentecostals also characteristically insist that their *experience* of God in community is indispensable to the interpretive process.[20] In

---

[15] Wesleyan New Testament scholar Robert Wall ('A Response to Thomas/Alexander, "And the Signs Are Following" [Mk 6.9-20]', *JPT* 11.2 [2003], pp. 176-77) argues that 2 Tim. 3.15-17 suggests that 'God inspires the *performance* rather than the production of Scripture'. As he reads it, Paul teaches that the biblical texts are always 'presently inspired by God'.

[16] This is a familiar distinction utilized by many Pentecostals. See for example Roger Stronstad, 'Pentecostal Experience and Hermeneutics', *Paraclete* 26.1 (1992), p. 18.

[17] Clark H. Pinnock, 'The Work of the Holy Spirit in Hermeneutics', *JPT* 2 (1993), p. 5.

[18] McKay, 'When the Veil is Taken Away', p. 21.

[19] This is not far removed from what Ellen F. Davis ('Teaching the Bible Confessionally in the Church' in Richard B. Hays and Ellen F. Davis [eds.], *The Art of Reading Scripture* [Grand Rapids: Eerdmans, 2003], p. 11) describes as readings that 'tell us about the nature and will of God, to instruct us in the manifold and often hidden ways in which God is present and active in our world'.

[20] N.T. Wright (*The Last Word: Beyond the Bible Wars* [San Francisco: HarperCollins, 2005], p. 101) criticizes the uses of the so-called 'Wesleyan quadrilateral' that regard experience as 'a separate source of authority to be played off against

fact, Pentecostals see experience as both the *means* to the right interpretation of Scripture and its promised *effect*. They come to the Scriptures in the first place because they expect God to act on them and for them.[21] The goal of Pentecostal readings is nothing less than 'theophany, a divine encounter, a revelation, an experience with the living God': through the reading and performance of Scripture, believers expect to be formed by God via the Spirit into the image of Christ'.[22] Similarly, the Pentecostal view of Scripture arises from a 'theology of biblical experience' that assumes believers' lives now are no less available to the presence and power of God than were the lives of the prophets, apostles, and the life of Jesus himself.[23] Because of this, the Pentecostal interpreter is 'more like a producer or performer on stage' than a reviewer who criticizes the performance.[24]

But experience of God is not only an outcome of reading the Scripture rightly. It is also a necessary hermeneutical key. Drawing on the events of Acts 15,[25] John Christopher Thomas argues that on the strength of the Scripture alone, the council had no reason to

---

scripture itself'. If some Pentecostals do speak of their experience in this way, that is certainly not what Thomas, Archer, Moore, and Waddell, *et al.*, intend. Instead, experience in the Spirit leads *to* the Scripture, making the Scripture 'hearable', so to speak. Experience is not another 'source of authority', but the necessary condition for receiving the Scripture's authority rightly.

[21] Pinnock ('The Work of the Holy Spirit in Hermeneutics', p. 16) insists, 'The Spirit ... actualizes the word of God by helping us to restate the message in contemporary terminology and apply it to fresh situations. The result is that salvation history continues to take effect in us'.

[22] Robby Waddell, *The Spirit of the Book of Revelation* (JPTSup 30; Blandford Forum: Deo Publishing, 2006), pp. 111, 118. In agreement with Cheryl Bridges Johns and Steven Land, et. al., he argues that 'participation in the Spirit' is indispensable to the process of meaning-making, summing up his position in a motto: 'Unless we believe, we shall not understand'.

[23] McKay, 'When the Veil is Taken Away', p. 26.

[24] McKay, 'When the Veil is Taken Away', p. 19.

[25] As we have seen, Acts 15 has often been used by Pentecostals (e.g. Thomas and Archer) as a paradigm for faithful interpretation. Perhaps the time has come to build on the strength of this model by bringing this story into dialogue with other similar stories in the Lukan corpus, including Jesus' reading of Isaiah (Lk. 4.16-21), the eye-opening experience of the Emmaus disciples (Lk. 24.13-35), and the story of Philip and the Ethiopian (Acts 8.26-40), allowing these different accounts to help give further shape and definition to a genuinely Pentecostal hermeneutical model. By allowing these other accounts in Luke-Acts of early Christian interpretation to inform the discussion, Pentecostals perhaps will find ways of augmenting the strengths of the interpretive model they have put forward in light of Acts 15.

decide for the inclusion of the gentiles. Instead, Peter's testimony of the conversion of gentiles and Paul and Barnabas' witness to the 'signs and wonders' performed among them made possible James' decision for and reading of the passage from Amos and the community's Gospel-faithful decision that followed. Clearly, 'the Spirit's witness heavily influenced the choice and use of Scripture', and that in this way the Spirit 'helped the church make its way through this hermeneutical maze'.[26] In the final analysis, then, Pentecostals believe their experience opens up the text, and that the newly-opened text in turn makes possible truer obedience and fuller blessing,[27] creating an ascending spiral of transformational readings of Holy Scripture.

The Inspired, Interpreted Word

A growing number of Pentecostals are distancing themselves from traditional Evangelical descriptions of the nature and authority of Scripture, including the notion of *sola Scriptura*.[28] Ken Archer, for example, speaks of the biblical text as a 'full-fledged' and 'interdependent dialogical participant',[29] which means in effect that the text waits on the community's and the Spirit's engagement, and that without these, it simply is not itself. This move is not intended to undermine the authority of the Scriptures, but to avoid reductionistic accounts of how that authority works. By playing up the importance of the Spirit's and community's shared roles in interpretation, Pentecostals are seeking to avoid treating Scripture as an 'object' rather than 'a living Word which interprets us and through

---

[26] Thomas, 'Women, Pentecostals, and the Bible', p. 50.

[27] E.g. Larry R. McQueen (*Joel and the Spirit: The Cry of a Prophetic Hermeneutic* [Cleveland, TN: CPT Press, 2009], p. 5; [first published by Sheffield Academic Press as JPTSup 8, 1995]) prefaces his reading of Joel with this methodological explanation: 'On the one hand, my Pentecostal pre-understandings will illuminate aspects of the text of Joel left undiscovered by other interpreters. On the other hand, a fresh critical reading of Joel will facilitate a clearer articulation of Pentecostal eschatology and ecclesiology. The dialogical role of experience opens up the text of Joel for questions otherwise left unaddressed'.

[28] Arguably, this arises from a fundamental misunderstanding of what this slogan does and does not mean. Popularly, it means something like, 'The Bible is the *only* authority', but in fact it means (at least, it meant in the Reformers' formulations) something more like, 'The Bible is the sole, *primary* authority'.

[29] Archer, *A Pentecostal Hermeneutic*, p. 218.

which the Spirit flows in ways that we cannot dictate, calculate, or program'.[30] The aim is to allow Scripture to be truly *God's* Word.

This school of thought also emphasizes the essential narrativity of divine revelation, seeking both to read the Scriptures and to imagine the whole of the Christian life as fundamentally *storied*.[31] For Pentecostals, Christian thinking and living is not only about 'story-*telling* but also [about] participation in and performance of the Christian story in new and different contexts'.[32] Hence, the scriptural Word 'functions as a meta-narrative and is the foundational story for belief and practice',[33] which means that Christian interpreters should read the Scriptures as cohering as and in a single story, i.e. the drama of salvation-history. Only in this way can interpreters read rightly or live faithfully.[34] Obviously, Pentecostals are not alone in championing narrative readings; nonetheless, Jamie Smith suggests Pentecostal spirituality is perhaps perfectly attuned to narrative as 'a fundamental and irreducible mode of understanding' and so uniquely situated to hear Scripture testify of the 'overall plot of God's rescue of his creation'.[35]

Finally, there is also an emerging consensus that Pentecostals can and should concern themselves with the final, canonical form of the text.[36] 'The final canonical form of the biblical narrative is what shapes the reader and enables the reader to develop a praxis-oriented understanding of life.'[37] Pentecostal readings of the Scripture are 'synchronic, focusing on the final form of the text, and theological, allowing the ethos and experience of the tradition to

---

[30] Rick D. Moore, 'A Pentecostal Approach to Scripture', *Seminary Viewpoint* 8.1 (1987), p. 4.

[31] Land (*Pentecostal Spirituality*, p. 71) talks of 'Pentecostal narratives', of 'participating in the story of God', of the 'Biblical drama', of the 'salvation-history drama of redemption'.

[32] Wolfgang Vondey, 'Review of Kevin VanHoozer's *The Drama of Doctrine*', *Pneuma* 30.2 (2008), p. 365.

[33] Archer, *A Pentecostal Hermeneutic*, p. 229.

[34] Kenneth J. Archer, 'A Pentecostal Way of Doing Theology: Method and Manner', *IJST* 9.3 (July 2007), p. 311.

[35] James K.A. Smith, *Thinking in Tongues: Pentecostal Contributions to Christian Philosophy* (Grand Rapids: Eerdmans, 2010), p. 69.

[36] This is not to say that 'behind the text' concerns do not matter. It is to say, as Lee Roy Martin (*The Unheard Voice of God: A Pentecostal Hearing of the Book of Judges* [JPTSup 32; Blandford Forum: Deo Publishing, 2008], p. 14) puts it, that 'the world within the text takes priority over the world behind the text'.

[37] Archer, *A Pentecostal Hermeneutic*, p. 228.

inform the interpretation'.[38] This confidence in the text's canonical form is made unmistakably clear in early Pentecostal readings of Mk 16.9-20, for example.[39]

The Inspired, Interpreting Community

Increasingly, Pentecostal scholars are insisting on the authoritative role of the community in the interpretative process.[40] So much so that a consensus seems to have emerged: interpretation is ultimately a *communal* undertaking.[41] For many Pentecostals, the local, worshipping community is the 'spiritual cultural context in which interpretation takes place',[42] and it is necessarily in the community's discussion of Scripture that God's intended meaning is negotiated.[43] Right interpretation is 'the result of a creative transaction of meaning' in the community's effort to make sense of the Scriptures' meaning for its life and the lives of its members.[44] Along the same lines, it is precisely in and through the community's dialogue about the Scripture in light of their shared experience that the Spirit makes right interpretation possible.[45] That is to say, the community

---

[38] Waddell, *The Spirit of the Book of Revelation*, p. 101.

[39] John Christopher Thomas and Kimberly Ervin Alexander, '"And the Signs are Following": Mark 16.9-20 – A Journey into Pentecostal Hermeneutics', *JPT* 11.2 (2003), pp. 147-70.

[40] Kärkkäinen ('Authority, Revelation, and Interpretation in the Roman Catholic-Pentecostal Dialogue', p. 103) holds that this is due, perhaps, to the fact that historically Pentecostals have maintained (more often than not, *implicitly*) that Scripture is 'clear' for the Spirit-led individual so that the believer's 'private judgment' is sufficient for right interpretation. Those who are arguing for a greater emphasis on the community's role in interpretation do so in part because they hope that this will alleviate that old problem.

[41] Pentecostals would agree with Hauerwas, who contends that '... reading scripture in community serves a constitutive purpose by shaping the way persons-in-community come to see the world and themselves. In sum, the church is the *irreplaceable locus* of authority for reading scripture'. See Michael G. Cartwright, 'Stanley Hauerwas's Essays in Theological Ethics: A Reader's Guide' in John Berkman and Michael G. Cartwright (eds.), *The Hauerwas Reader* (Durham, NC: Duke University Press, 2001), p. 641.

[42] Archer, *A Pentecostal Hermeneutic*, p. 213.

[43] 'Community' should be taken to mean both the local church and the *ecclesia catholica*, although the emphasis falls on the local congregation as it gathers in worship.

[44] Archer, *A Pentecostal Hermeneutic*, p. 181.

[45] Thomas makes this argument in light of the Acts 15 account of the Jerusalem community's decision, and concludes that as it was then, so it is now. 'It is the community that is able to give and receive testimony as well as assess the reports of God's activity in the lives of those who are part of the community'

serves as the vital context for good (i.e. faithful and transformation-al) interpretation.[46] Of course, individuals participate in the discus-sion.[47] But it is only the (local, catholic, worshipping, Spirit-led) community that truly authors interpretations.[48]

The importance of the history of effects (*Wirkungsgeschichte*) to the interpretive enterprise for Pentecostals follows naturally from this emphasis on the role of the community,[49] and numerous schol-ars are teasing out how this discipline might prove beneficial for contemporary Pentecostal interpretation. John Christopher Thomas compares studying the history of effects to hearing and discerning testimonies of others in the community,[50] and he holds that Pente-costals stand to gain much from the practice of hearing these testi-monies. In other words, the effective history of a text is a surer sign of the Spirit's work than are the findings of historical-critical analy-sis.[51]

This is not all a matter of academic theory. Larry McQueen was the first to devote a careful and sustained consideration of early Pentecostal readings of biblical texts,[52] and many others have fol-

---

(Thomas, 'Women, Pentecostals, and the Bible', p. 55). In this, Thomas antici-pates Luz (quoted in Emerson B. Powery, 'Ulrich Luz's *Matthew in History*: A Contribution to Pentecostal Hermeneutics?', *JPT* 14 [1999], p. 17), who puts it pithily: 'truth *is* the dialogue'.

[46] Frank Macchia ('The Book of Revelation and the Hermeneutics of the Spir-it: A Response to Robby Waddell', *JPT* 17 [2008], p. 20) suggests that Waddell should have 'more clearly and forcefully' acknowledged the 'priority' of the text over the community.

[47] As Martin (*The Unheard Voice of God*, p. 15) explains, Pentecostals recog-nize and celebrate the fact that '[m]ultiple voices do not diminish the meaning of the text', but 'enhance, deepen, and strengthen it'.

[48] Like John Christopher Thomas, Archer (*A Pentecostal Hermeneutic*, p. 213) draws on the Acts 15 story as a model for interpretation.

[49] The work of Ulrich Luz has been influential among Pentecostals, not least because of Thomas' influence. For an assessment of the possibilities of Luz's approach for Pentecostal studies, see Powery, 'Ulrich Luz's *Matthew in History*: A Contribution to Pentecostal Hermeneutics?', pp. 3-17.

[50] John Christopher Thomas, *The Spirit of the New Testament* (Blandford Fo-rum: Deo Publishing, 2005), p. 18 (First published as John Christopher Thomas, 'Pentecostal Theology in the Twenty-First Century', *Pneuma* 20 (1998), pp. 3-19). Waddell (*The Spirit of the Book of Revelation*, p. 113) also adopts the metaphor of testimony for this use.

[51] Wesleyan scholar Robert Wall ('A Response to Thomas/Alexander', p. 177) expresses this point exactly: 'the canonical authority of a biblical text is discerned by the church not in consideration of its originality when critically appraised, but by its performance in Christian formation when spiritually attested'.

[52] McQueen, *Joel and the Spirit*, pp. 68-103.

lowed him in this practice. To cite but two examples, Robby Waddell draws on the witness of Pentecostal readers before him who had offered scholarly treatments of the Apocalypse[53] and Lee Roy Martin sets aside a section of his monograph to the pre-critical readings of the book of Judges.[54] The effective history of 1 Cor. 13.8-12[55] and 3 Jn 2[56] have received extended treatments from Pentecostal scholars, as well.[57]

With Land[58] and McQueen, John Christopher Thomas maintains the witness of early Pentecostalism has particular and primary significance for contemporary Pentecostal hermeneutics. In his article on the role of women in ministry,[59] Thomas draws on this witness, as well as in his and Alexander's argument for the authority of the longer ending of Mark.[60] Ken Archer has taken perhaps an even stronger stance: 'The early Pentecostal hermeneutic must be retrieved and retained in order for the movement to mature as a Christian theological tradition'.[61] This hermeneutic – which Archer characterizes as a 'pre-critical commonsense' approach designed to let the text speak for itself – enabled first-generation Pentecostals to 'create new theological mosaics',[62] and to recover much of which traditional Christianity had lost sight. For his part, Thomas does not restrict his vision to early Pentecostalism, even if that remains his focus. He also wants to listen to the testimony of those from the wider Christian community, including, for example, the impact of Romans on Augustine, Luther, Wesley, and Barth and the influence of the Sermon on the Mount on Wesley, Tolstoy, Bonhoeffer, and

---

[53] Waddell, *The Spirit of the Book of Revelation*, pp. 119-22.

[54] Martin, *The Unheard Voice of God*, pp. 17-30.

[55] Gary Steven Shogren, 'How Did They Suppose "The Perfect" Would Come? 1 Corinthians 13.8-12 in Patristic Exegesis', *JPT* 15 (1999), pp. 99-121.

[56] Heather L. Landrus, 'Hearing 3 John 2 in the Voices of History', *JPT* 11.1 (2002), pp. 70-88.

[57] It should perhaps be observed that John Christopher Thomas has been behind much of this emphasis on effective history in recent Pentecostal scholarship. He served as joint-supervisor for Waddell's PhD thesis; at the time her article was published, Landrus was his MDiv student; and McQueen, Martin, and Archer have worked or do work closely with him at the Centre for Pentecostal Theology at the Pentecostal Theological Seminary (Cleveland, TN).

[58] Land, *Pentecostal Spirituality*, p. 13.

[59] Thomas, 'Women, Pentecostals, and the Bible', pp. 41-56.

[60] Thomas and Alexander, '"And the Signs Are Following"', pp. 147-70.

[61] Archer, *A Pentecostal Hermeneutic*, p. 2.

[62] Archer, *A Pentecostal Hermeneutic*, pp. 125-26.

King. Waddell, in instructive dialogue with Thomas and Ulrich Luz, suggests that the testimony of the early church and 'premodern' interpreters deserve special attention.[63]

Perhaps no Pentecostal has put more emphasis on the viability and imitable quality of patristic and medieval hermeneutics than Telford Work,[64] especially in his recent commentary on Deuteronomy. He champions and attempts to appropriate the pre-critical model of reading for the fourfold sense of Scripture,[65] which Work believes will still serve to guide present-day readers 'into a more accurate, clearer, and fuller sense of the import of biblical texts ...'[66] In this, Work is (perhaps unknowingly) following in the footsteps of several early Pentecostals, including prominent figures like William G. Schell,[67] G.F. Taylor,[68] and J.H. King.[69]

Conclusions

What difference does all of this make for reading those New Testament passages that speak of the Lord's Supper? What difference does it make, more generally, for the work of constructing a theology of the Eucharist? It calls for literary/theological readings of Scripture in the context of the worshipping and God-experiencing community, readings that remain sensitive to a text's canonical fit and that take seriously the history of effects, always remaining focused on how the Spirit uses Scripture to transform the community

---

[63] Waddell, *The Spirit of the Book of Revelation*, p. 113.

[64] A close reading of his work suggests that his hermeneutic increasingly has been shaped by his Pentecostal experience. For example, he seems less beholden to the historical-critical method he deemed 'necessary' in his earlier work (*Living and Active: Scripture in the Economy of Salvation* [Grand Rapids: Eerdmans, 2002]? See Telford Work, *Ain't Too Proud to Beg: Exercises in Prayerful Theology* (Grand Rapids: Eerdmans, 2007), pp. 31-32.

[65] Telford Work, *Deuteronomy* (BTC; Grand Rapids: Brazos, 2009), pp. 18-22.

[66] Work, *Deuteronomy*, p. 19.

[67] See, for example, Schell's article on the ante-Nicene fathers in *LRE* 7.4 (Jan 1915), pp. 7-11.

[68] Taylor (*PHA* 15.21 [Sept 17, 1931], pp. 1, 8) acknowledged the need for 'doctrinal guides by which the Scriptures may be interpreted' and that these guides were established by the early church fathers. In the same vein, he spoke (*PHA* 15.23 [Oct 1, 1931], pp. 1, 4) of the creeds as 'ancient landmarks' that must not be removed.

[69] See, for a particularly illuminating example, J.H. King's interpretation of Prov. 8.22-32 in *PHA* 20.13 (July 30, 1936), pp. 3, 9.

into Christ's *ecclesia*. In the readings that follow, then, I will seek to enact this model.

Eating the Word: Eucharistic Theology in the New Testament

Reading Strategy

In this section, I read three representative texts, utilizing the interpretative method sketched in the previous section. In each case, I begin first with consideration of the literary context of the passage, then I proceed to read it literarily and theologically with an ear for canonical resonances and an eye on the text's effective history, as well. I conclude each reading by drawing conclusions that will come into play in the following, constructive chapter. As with the early Pentecostal periodical materials, I first treat an *explicit* treatment of the Lord's Supper (1 Cor. 10.14-22), move to a *testimony* of Eucharistic celebration (Acts 2.42), and, finally, take up a text whose sacramentality appears to be *embedded* (Jn 6.52-59). Taken together, the readings of these representative texts will (a) offer a model for how Pentecostals can and should read Eucharistic texts as they appear in the canonical Scriptures and (b) supply an initial move toward an authentically Pentecostal and robustly biblical theology of the Lord's Supper.

The Eucharist as Divine-Human Love Feast: 1 Cor. 10.14-22

[14]Therefore, my dear friends, flee from the worship of idols. [15]I speak as to sensible people; judge for yourselves what I say. [16]The cup of blessing that we bless, is it not a sharing in the blood of Christ? The bread that we break, is it not a sharing in the body of Christ? [17]Because there is one bread, we who are many are one body, for we all partake of the one bread. [18]Consider the people of Israel; are not those who eat the sacrifices partners in the altar? [19]What do I imply then? That food sacrificed to idols is anything, or that an idol is anything? [20]No, I imply that what pagans sacrifice, they sacrifice to demons and not to God. I do not want you to be partners with demons. [21]You cannot drink the cup of the Lord and the cup of demons. You cannot partake of the table of the Lord and the table of demons. [22]Or are we provoking the Lord to jealousy? Are we stronger than he?

Introduction

1 Corinthians 10.14-22 (and especially vv. 16-17) stands out as one of the most explicit statements about the theological significance of the Lord's Supper, not only in the Pauline corpus[70] but also in the entire biblical canon; for this reason alone it deserves thorough examination and exposition. Although this passage – unlike the others I intend to read – did not receive much attention from early Pentecostal interpreters, I am convinced the passage is critically important to any attempt to hear what the New Testament has to say about the Lord's Supper and the church's Eucharistic thought and practice.

The Interpretive Context

Paul intends to address several deeply troubling issues brought to his attention by envoys from Corinth, as the reader learns early in the letter (1.11). Later in the letter (7.1), the reader discovers that the apostle also has received a letter from the Corinthian congregation, a letter full of questions that require detailed and nuanced answers. Among other bad news, Paul is disturbed to hear that many Corinthian Christians, claiming moral and spiritual superiority,[71] are

---

[70] It is important not to make too much of the lack of references to the Eucharist in Paul's other extant letters, as Jerome Murphy O'Conner ('Eucharist and Community in First Corinthians', *Worship* 50.5 [Spring 1976], p. 370) explains:

> Paul's allusions to the eucharist are concentrated in Chapters 10-11 of First Corinthians. His silence regarding this central sacrament in other letters is due to the occasional character of his communications with the churches for which he was responsible. He was not a speculative theologian principally concerned with the interrelationship of concepts within an ideal structure, but a pastor whose attention was focused by the real problems of Christian living in a concrete situation ... The fact that he devotes so much space to the eucharist in the Corinthian correspondence is a clear indication that there was something radically wrong with the Corinthians' approach to this sacrament. The fact that he does not touch on the topic in other letters signifies only that the same problem did not arise in other communities.

I stand in basic agreement with Denis Farkasfalvy ('The Eucharistic Provenance of New Testament Texts' in Roch A. Kereszty (ed.), *Rediscovering the Eucharist: Ecumenical Conversations* (Mahwah, NJ: Paulist Press, 2003), pp. 27-51), who argues that not only does the New Testament provide a theology *of* the Eucharist, but that the entire New Testament – in form and content – arises in part from Eucharistic experience of the worshipping community.

[71] For an examination of Paul's treatment of the 'strong' and the 'weak', see Volker Gäckle, *Die Starken und die Schwachen in Korinth und in Rom: Zu Herkunft und Funktion der Antithese in 1 Kor 8.1-11.1 und in Rom 14.1-15* (Tübingen: Mohr Siebeck, 2004).

engaged in εἰδωλοθύτων (i.e. banqueting in the pagan temples, and/or buying and eating food previously offered to idols),[72] and he devotes a major section[73] of the epistle to address this outrage.[74] The passage I have selected to read, 10.14-22, fits in the third and final part (10.1-11.1) of this major section (8.1-11.1).

Even a hasty reading of 1 Corinthians makes it clear that the Corinthian Christians regularly participated in the Lord's Supper,[75] and that they did so in the context of a larger meal.[76] What is more, as the rhetoric of 10.16-17 makes clear, the Corinthian Christians also already believed[77] that the Eucharist was in fact a 'communal participation'[78] in Christ's body and blood – no doubt because this was something Paul himself had previously made clear to them.[79] For

---

[72] Richard B. Hays (*First Corinthians* [Interpretation; Louisville: WJKP, 1997], p. 135) explains that these were 'hot-button issues' in Corinth for three interrelated reasons: 'the problem of boundaries between the church and the pagan culture, the strained relationship between different social classes in the community, and the relation between knowledge and love as the foundation of the church's life'. For a fuller examination of the issues arising from food offered to idols, see Anthony C. Thiselton, *The First Epistle to the Corinthians: A Commentary on the Greek Text* (NIGTC; Grand Rapids: Eerdmans, 2000), pp. 612-20, 660-61; John Fotopoulos, *Food Offered to Idols in Roman Corinth: A Socio-Rhetorical Reconsideration* (Tübingen: Mohr Siebeck, 2003); David E. Garland, 'The Dispute Over Food Offered to Idols (1 Cor. 8.1-11.1)', *Perspectives in Religious Studies* 30.2 (Sum 2003), pp. 173-97.

[73] Following the outline of Thiselton, *The First Epistle to the Corinthians*, pp. 607-12, which is itself indebted to Kenneth E. Bailey, 'The Structure of 1 Corinthians and Paul's Theological Method Also With Special Reference to 4.17', *Novum Testamentum* 25.2 (1983), pp. 152-81. See also Hays, *First Corinthians*, pp. 159-73.

[74] According to some commentators, Paul acknowledged the Corinthians' right to eat meat offered to idols, but nonetheless insisted that they should refuse to make use of this right in deference to the 'weak' among them. See, for example, E. Coye Still III, 'The Meaning and Uses of EIDŌLOTHYTON in First Century Non-Pauline Literature and 1 Cor 8.1-11.1: Toward a Resolution of the Debate', *Trinity Journal* 23.2 (Fall 2002), pp. 225-34.

[75] If we can take Paul at his word (1 Cor. 4.17; 7.7; 11.16), then the same was true for *all* the Pauline communities.

[76] Dennis Edwin Smith, *From Symposium to Eucharist: The Banquet in the Early Christian World* (Minneapolis: Fortress, 2003), pp. 173-218.

[77] Rudolph Bultmann (*Theology of the New Testament* [Waco: Baylor University Press, 2007], p. 151) concludes that 1 Cor. 10.16 speaks of Holy Communion as 'self-evident for Christians'.

[78] This is Thistelton's translation of κοινωνία (*The First Epistle to the Corinthians*, p. 104).

[79] See Raymond F. Collins, *First Corinthians* (Sacra Pagina; Collegeville, MN: Liturgical Press, 1999), p. 375-82.

whatever reason, however, they had not allowed that conviction to influence their day-to-day life together. As a result of this failure, Paul has to show them in the starkest terms that the shared partaking of the Lord's Supper makes any dabbling in idolatry not only scandalous and risky, but also *absurd*.[80] Because they are one at the Lord's Table with Christ and his community, it simply makes no sense for them to partake of the 'table of demons' – it is nonsensical in the way all sin necessarily must be. He hopes to save them from this nonsense by directing their attention to the definitive 'counterreality' of Christ encountered in Christian worship, particularly in the celebration of the Lord's Supper.[81]

The Eucharistic Tapestry of 1 Corinthians

An incipient theology of the Eucharist threads through and holds together the whole fabric of 1 Corinthians.[82] This is perhaps due to the fact that the Eucharist gave Paul a language, so to speak, with which he could both diagnose the Corinthians' disease and prescribe its cure. If such claims seem overstated, one has only to consider how the motifs of 10.16-17 show up in various places throughout the letter and color the entirety of it. Not only Paul's response to the issues of εἰδωλοθύτων (chs. 8-10), but also his diatribe against carnal factionalism (chs. 1-4), sexual disorder and immorality (chs. 5-7), as well as his correctives for the Corinthians' worship (chs. 11-14) arise from and work back to the claim that the Corinthians are in fact one body in Christ because of their sharing in his body and blood at the Eucharistic meal.[83] The failure to dis-

---

[80] Collins (*First Corinthians*, p. 381) says it well: 'To participate in idol worship is, implicitly, to deny the sovereignty of the Lord Jesus. Hence there is radical incompatibility between the worship of idols and sharing the table of the Lord'.

[81] As Hays (*First Corinthians*, p. 173) explains, 'This is the positive counterreality set over against the danger of idolatry: authentic Christian worship draws us together around the table of the Lord in such a way that we become a covenant people, receiving the blessing of fellowship with God and sharing our lives with one another'.

[82] Aquinas certainly saw it this way: he read 1 Corinthians as an extended treatment of the sacraments, singling out chapters 8-11 as an exposition of the Eucharist. For an extended treatment of Aquinas' comments on 1 Corinthians, see Daniel A. Keating, 'Aquinas on 1 and 2 Corinthians', in Thomas Gerard Weinandy, Daniel A. Keating, and John Yocum (eds.), *Aquinas on Scripture: An Introduction to His Biblical Commentaries* (London: T&T Clark, 2005), pp. 127-48.

[83] His statements about the resurrection and the resurrected body (chapter 15) resonate to 10.16-17, as well. For example, Paul says Christ, the 'last Adam', is a 'life-giving spirit' precisely because he has been raised a 'spiritual body'

cern and embody this basic reality is in fact at the root of the many sins plaguing the Corinthians' community. To put it another way, if the Corinthians had discerned the Lord's body, if they had recognized what it means to share in Christ's body and blood, they would not – and indeed could not – have split into factions, or given themselves to promiscuity, or dared to flirt with idols, or despised the weaker members of the community, or abused the *charismata*.[84]

A literary reading of 1 Corinthians shows how tightly the threads of Paul's arguments are interwoven. Having been told in the letter's introduction (1.9) that believers have been called into the 'fellowship of God's Son' (κοινωνίαν του υἱοῦ αὐτοῦ), the reader later finds that this κοινωνίαν[85] comes about, at least in part, through participation in the church's sacred meal (10.16-17).[86] Having first heard that Paul wants only to 'proclaim' Christ crucified (1.23), the reader later discovers that this is *the very message* the Lord's Supper itself delivers (11.26),[87] indicating that for Paul the preaching of the Gospel – which was a necessity (9.16) – remained connected inextricably to the church's Eucharistic observance. Again and again in the letter, Paul appeals to Israel's Exodus narrative and to Israel's tabernacle/Temple cult,[88] frequently with an emphasis on Israel's

---

(15.44-45); this, apparently, explains how the Corinthians can share in and be enlivened by Christ's body in the present, even while they await the future resurrection – so long as they rightly discern the Lord's body (11.17-34).

[84] Interestingly, by reversing some of the claims of the letter – i.e. by stating them in positive rather than negative terms – one perhaps uncovers other signs of a robust sacramentality. As believers eat the loaf and drink the cup in a *worthy* manner, they participate in the body and blood of the Lord (11.27), and if they eat and drink while *rightly discerning* the body, they receive salvation, rather than judgment (11.29). Because Christ has indeed been raised from the dead, the Christian community can eat and drink, not in despair, but in *hope* (15.32).

[85] For an examination of two of the key terms in 1 Cor. 10.14-22, κοινωνία and μετέχειν, see Harm W. Hollander, 'The Idea of Fellowship in 1 Corinthians 10.14–22', *New Testament Studies* 55.4 (Oct 2009), pp. 456-70.

[86] Collins (*First Corinthians*, p. 379) explains that in the beginning of the letter 'he reminded the Corinthian Christians that they were called to fellowship with Jesus Christ our Lord. Now he specifies that fellowship with the Lord is realized through participation in his blood and body'.

[87] See Victor Paul Furnish, *The Theology of the First Letter to the Corinthians* (NTT; Cambridge: Cambridge University Press, 1999), p. 83.

[88] Collins (*First Corinthians*, p. 376) suggests that Paul's *lexis* 'expresses the significance of the Christian Eucharist in a way that would be familiar with Hellenistic mystery religions'. In one form or another, such claims are frequently made by commentators on 1 Corinthians. It seems to me, however, that while

meals: the first Passover, the manna in the wilderness, the sacrifices of the altar. Two examples demand consideration. First, in 10.1-4, where Paul speaks of the 'spiritual' food and drink[89] that sustained Israel in the years of wandering, he affirms that God is a God of meals, a God who ordains spiritual food and drink for his people, giving the lie to the Corinthians' belief that eating and drinking have nothing to do with bringing us close to or estranging us from God (8.8).[90] Even if the apostle's talk of drinking the one Spirit and being baptized into the one body (12.13) is not explicitly sacramental, the phrasing unquestionably brings to mind the language of 10.1-4, and resonates with the assertions of 10.16-17. Second, when Paul talks of celebrating 'the festival' rightly (5.8),[91] he is not only drawing on the story of the first Passover, but almost certainly employing the term as another name for the κυριακὸν δεῖπνον (11.20), and calling for the Corinthians to consider how it is that this Supper is to be observed. This means not only that Christ deserves the honor that belongs to YHWH, as Fee acknowledges,[92] but also that the church's Communion meal is significant as a covenant-making rite, as well. If the Passover constituted Israel as God's people, then so does the Eucharist constitute the church as renewed Israel.

The formula employed in 6.13 – 'the body is for the Lord and the Lord for the body'[93] – draws together the several crucial themes (eating and drinking, sexual intercourse,[94] and participation with the

---

such background information may prove illuminating, it also threatens to obscure Paul's concern with *Israel's* cultic meals, and, in particular, with Jesus' institution of the Supper.

[89] *Didache* 10 uses this very language to name the Eucharist.

[90] For an argument that this is indeed the Corinthians' formula, see Hays, *First Corinthians*, p. 141.

[91] Not everyone agrees that this is reference to the Eucharist, of course. However, see Rodrigo J. Morales, 'A Liturgical Conversion of the Imagination: Worship and Ethics in 1 Corinthians' in Scott W. Hahn and David Scott (eds.), *Letter & Spirit* (Vol. 5; Steubenville, OH: St Paul Center for Biblical Theology, 2009), p. 109.

[92] Gordon Fee, *Pauline Christology: An Exegetical-Theological Study* (Peabody, MA: Hendrickson, 2007), p. 123.

[93] Almost certainly, this is Paul's counter to the Corinthians' maxim that food is meant for the stomach and the stomach for food (10.13). For an examination of the slogans in 1 Corinthians and their importance of identifying them for the interpretive process, see Jay E. Smith, 'Slogans in 1 Corinthians', *Bibliotheca Sacra* 167.665 (Jan-Mar 2010), pp. 68-88.

[94] Hays (*First Corinthians*, p. 164) points to the fact that sexual misconduct is a key theme in the letter (5.1-13; 6.12-20; 7.2-5), but he does not explore how

Lord) that prepare the reader for the bold assertions of 10.16-17 and 10.21. What is more, it is hardly out of the question that the second half of the formula, 'the Lord [is] for the body', should be taken sacramentally. It is possible and perhaps even necessary to understand it to mean that the way in which the Lord is 'for' the ecclesial body is by the offering of his sacramental body and blood to be consumed Eucharistically, as 10.16-17 implies.

The Eucharist and Israel's Love Story

Richard Hays has persuasively argued that Paul's argument in 1 Corinthians works to narrate the Corinthians into Israel's story, to show them that they belong to the one people of God and so must live in loving faithfulness to God.[95] It cannot be insignificant, then, that the (apparently) sacramental claims of 1 Cor. 10.16-17 follow directly from Paul's recounting of the *baptism* of 'our fathers' into Moses in the waters of the Exodus and their *Eucharistic* experiences in the wilderness (1 Cor. 10.1-3).[96] Seen in this way, the Lord's Supper is shown to be nothing less than a continuation of Israel's feastings, so that as the Corinthians gather at the Lord's table they are being Israel-ized, so to speak. Receiving 'bread from heaven' from God just as Israel had received manna in the wilderness, they, as the true Israel, are celebrating the offering to God of the Passover Lamb, as 1 Cor. 5.8 makes clear. In the same way, 1 Cor. 11.17-34 narrates the Corinthian Christian community into *Jesus'* story: 'on the night he was betrayed …' Israel's story, tragically, is one of frequent betrayal and of unrequited love, a story of flirtation and intrigue with strange gods; Jesus, however, saves that story, and the Corinthians are invited to share in his victory by sharing in his way of life.

The Eucharist as Romantic Gesture

Clearly, Paul believes the Corinthians are flirting with idols, and that they are just so in danger of committing *adultery* against God. In eating this meat offered to other gods, entertaining themselves in

---

Paul works this out in light of the 'one body' of Christ received and signified in the Lord's Supper.

[95] Richard B. Hays, *The Conversion of the Imagination: Paul as Interpreter of Israel's Scripture* (Grand Rapids: Eerdmans, 2005), pp. 1-24.

[96] See Mark D. Vander Hart, 'The Exodus as Sacrament: the Cloud, the Sea, and Moses Revisited', *Mid-America Journal of Theology* 12 (2001), pp. 9-46.

pagan temples, the Corinthians are arousing YHWH's jealousy,[97] exactly as their 'ancestors' in the wilderness did.[98] Seeing this connection, one discovers the logic of 10.14-22: eating at the table of demons is *adulterous* because coming to the table of the Lord is — *nuptial*. It can be argued, then, that for Paul the Eucharist is an intimate, even *romantic*, gesture of Christ, the church's bridegroom. In offering the Corinthians his body and blood, Christ, the jilted lover, is wooing them back from other lovers, offering his best gifts in the attempt to recapture his lover's heart.[99]

As surprising and provocative as such a reading may seem, the reader has been prepared for it. Besides drawing in the immediate context on Israel's history of 'going after' idols — which, again, the Old Testament consistently identifies as adultery — Paul earlier in the letter explicitly links the bodily oneness enjoyed by and enjoined on husband and wife with the mystical oneness of Christ and the believer (6.12-20). If by the joining of their bodies husband and wife are made 'one flesh', then in the same way to be 'united' (κολλώμενος) with Christ[100] is to be made one body with him.[101] Just as the husband and wife belong to one another, so do Christ

---

[97] As Ex. 34.14 says, God's *name* is Jealous.

[98] Collins (*First Corinthians*, p. 381) explains, 'In the biblical tradition God's jealousy is associated with idol worship (Exod. 20.5; 34.14; Deut. 5.9; 1 Kgs 14.22; Ezek. 8.3, etc). Jealousy leads God to judge the people severely when they abandon him for some god or goddess (Deut. 6.14-15; Josh. 24.19-20; Ps. 78.58-64; Zeph. 1.14; Nah. 1.2, etc.)'.

[99] John Chrysostom, *Homilies on 1 Corinthians* 24.3 (NPNF 1.12, p. 139).

[100] Following F.F. Bruce's suggestion (*Paul: Apostle of the Heart Set Free* [Grand Rapids: Eerdmans, 1979], p. 114), we can read this not as a contrast between bodily oneness, on the one hand, and an immaterial, spiritual oneness, on the other hand, but as a contrast between a bodily oneness controlled by the 'flesh' and a bodily oneness effected by the same Spirit who has raised Christ from the dead. To say, then, that believers are made 'one spirit' with Christ is to say that they belong to the same new creation order as he does, as the resurrected *kyrios*; the 'body' they are as a community already participates in and in some sense anticipates the resurrected body promised in 1 Corinthians 15.

[101] Nijay K. Gupta ('Which "Body" Is a Temple (1 Corinthians 6:19)? Paul Beyond the Individual/Communal Divine', *Catholic Biblical Quarterly* 72.3 [July 2010], pp. 518-36) is right to argue that 'body' in Paul's thought goes beyond an easy individual/communal divide. Strangely, however, he does not explore how Paul's reflections on the Eucharist inform this discussion. It seems possible, even likely, that this notion of 'body' might have occurred to Paul in his reflections on the Eucharist, or, more particularly, on Christ's claim at the Last Supper that his body is somehow identifiable with and received through the Eucharistic bread.

and the church.[102] To be sure, this relationship is not perfectly symmetrical; neither husband nor wife has authority over the other's body (7.4), but the Christian has been 'bought with a price' (6.20a), and must submit to Christ's authority and glorify God with his body (6.20b). Nonetheless, because Christ and the church belong to one another they can and do hand over their bodies to one another in mutual submission. Christ does not 'hand over' (παραδῶ) his body lovelessly (13.3), but gives himself up in the 'more excellent way', laying down the example the church should follow. In this light, the Lord's Supper shows itself to be one of the ways in which Christ's body is 'there' for the church, and we can see that the nuptial joining of the bodies of Christ and his church is realized *Eucharistically*, exactly as 10.16-17 suggests.

Eucharist as Community-Making Meal

Paul's emphasis in 1 Cor. 10.16-17, as throughout the letter, falls on the responsibility of the members to the community vis-à-vis God and the watching world. The promise of sharing in Christ's body and blood is a promise to the community *qua* community. Therefore, Conzelmann is right to conclude that for Paul, 'partaking of the Lord's Supper does not first and foremost serve the edification of the individual, but unites the individuals to form the body of Christ'.[103] Perhaps no one has articulated this truth more forcefully or clearly than the Thomist theologian and philosopher, Herbert McCabe, O.P.:

> It is because the Eucharist is the sign of our unity that the Body of Christ is present there. Christ is present precisely as the sign of our unity and not in any other way … The Eucharist is first of all about our unity with each other, a profound and mysterious unity which is only in the body of Christ.[104]

---

[102] This seems to be the import of Eph. 5.22-33.

[103] Hans Conzelmann, *A Commentary on the First Epistle to the Corinthians* (Philadelphia: Fortress Press, 1975), p. 171. Similarly, Herman N. Ridderbos (*Paul: An Outline of His Theology* [Grand Rapids: Eerdmans, 1975], p. 473), 'The Supper is no personal affair between the individual believer and Christ. It is the covenant meal, the congregational meal, *par excellence*. And it points to the sacrifice made by Christ, the reconciliation that takes place in his blood, as the only ground of this communion between God and his people and of the unity of the church'.

[104] Hebert McCabe, *God Matters* (London: Continuum, 1987), p. 84.

This is clearly how pre-modern interpreters read 1 Cor. 10.16-17. Tellingly, Cyril of Alexandria assumes that the Pauline formula originates from these verses.[105] Similarly, Cyril of Jerusalem argues that it is via participation in the Eucharist that the church becomes a Christ-bearing community, 'one body and one blood with Christ'.[106] This emphasis appears in the liturgical formulae of *Didache* 9-10.[107] John Damascene explains how the Eucharist effects 'participation' with fellow believers:

> Participation is spoken of; for through it we partake of the divinity of Jesus. Communion, too, is spoken of, and it is an actual communion, because through it we have communion with Christ and share in His flesh and His divinity: yea, we have communion and are united with one another through it. For since we partake of one bread, we all become one body of Christ and one blood, and members one of another, being of one body with Christ.[108]

Contemporary interpreters also acknowledge that the Eucharist gives definitive shape to the community's life. At the Table, the community is not only reminded of the Lord, his death, and his *parousia*, but also is '*reconstituted* as community that lives from his cross and manifests its meaning'.[109] The bread is by the holy, vivifying Spirit made one with the resurrected body of Christ, and through the Spirit's intercession the church is made one with Christ by feasting on the bread. This is why the bread symbolizes *both* the crucified Christ *and* the one church that belongs to him.[110] Paul himself says that 'The bread ... [is] a sharing in the body of Christ'. Hence, it is possible to insist that this sharing is (at least) one of the

---

[105] George Panikulam, *Koinonia in the New Testament: A Dynamic Expression of Christian Life* (Rome: Biblical Institute Press, 1979), p. 27.

[106] Cyril of Jerusalem, 'Mystagogic Catechesis 4', in Edward Yarnold, *Cyril of Jerusalem* (Early Church Fathers, London: Routledge, 2000), p. 179.

[107] For example *Did.* 9.8: 'Even as this broken bread was scattered over the hills, and was gathered together and became one, so let your church be gathered together from the ends of the earth into your kingdom'.

[108] John of Damascus, *De Fide Orthodoxa* 4.13. Available online: http://www.orthodox.net/fathers/exactiv.html#BOOK_IV_CHAPTER_XIII. Accessed November 15, 2010.

[109] Furnish, *The Theology of the First Letter to the Corinthians*, p. 83. Emphasis added.

[110] Furnish, *The Theology of the First Letter to the Corinthians*, pp. 85-86.

ways in which the church becomes the *soma Christou*. As Conzelmann explains, 'The sacramental participation in Christ's body
makes ... the body of Christ'.[111] Perhaps it would not be wrong to
say that as the church comes to embody the Eucharist – itself an
embodiment of Christ crucified – the church shares in Christ's incarnation,[112] becomes his Spirit-formed and Spirit-baptized body.
Needless to say, for the stronger reading to work, the 'because' of v.
17 must bear maximum theological weight.

Some interpreters accept the claim that the Supper is a community-making meal, but nevertheless reject the idea that it does this
work *sacramentally*. Fee and Richard Horsley,[113] for example, play up
the socio-political dimensions of the Eucharist, insisting that the
meal symbolizes a reality it does not itself directly create or sustain.
Fee takes 1 Cor. 10.16-17, in particular, to mean that the Lord's
Supper binds individuals together to form a community whose 'singular existence' as God's people is in some sense 'experienced regularly at his Table'.[114] For whatever reason, he makes every effort to
downplay the sacramental reality of the Supper, arguing that it
merely *commemorates* the church's already-established fellowship.[115]
He will not countenance the idea that 1 Cor. 10.17 means believers
'*become* that body *through* this meal'.[116] Instead, 'they affirm what the
Spirit has already brought about through the death and resurrection
of Christ'.[117] Such a reading can be made to work, of course; but, on
balance, it fails to do justice to the depth and breadth of Paul's
thought, to say nothing of the power of the church's Eucharistic
experience, and is unnecessary in any case. Although Paul does not
say *how* believers share in Christ's body and blood or in what way
the one bread makes the church one body – he has no metaphysical

---

[111] Conzelmann, *A Commentary on the First Epistle to the Corinthians*, p. 171.

[112] This resonates strongly to Irenaeus' theology of the Eucharist. See D. Jeffrey Bingham, 'Eucharist and Incarnation: The Second Century and Luther', in
Kereszty (ed.), *Rediscovering the Eucharist: Ecumenical Conversations*, pp. 116-41.

[113] See Richard A. Horsley, '1 Corinthians: A Case Study of Paul's Assembly
as an Alternative Society', in Richard A. Horsley [ed.], *Paul and Empire: Religion
and Power in Roman Imperial Society* (Harrisburg, PA: Trinity Press International,
1997), p. 248.

[114] Fee, *The First Epistle to the Corinthians* (NICNT; Grand Rapids: Eerdmans,
1987), p. 469.

[115] Fee, *The First Epistle to the Corinthians*, p. 467.

[116] Emphasis added.

[117] Fee, *The First Epistle to the Corinthians*, p. 470.

theories to put forward – , it seems unmistakably clear that Paul is claiming *that* these things happen. Certainly, that has been the influence of the text on many Christian interpreters. Hence a stronger, fully *sacramental* reading of 1 Cor. 10.16-17 makes better sense in light of the larger context of the letter, and its effective history.

The Eucharist as/and Imitation of Christ

The communion meal sacramentally brings about churchly unity, but only as it includes the purposeful efforts of the church's members to make and keep the peace. After all, as Paul reminds the Corinthian hubrists, the people of Israel had sacraments, yet they died in the wilderness (10.1-13)! In fact, the reality of the sacramental feast forces on the community the responsibility to live in love, with creativity, humility, and longsuffering patience. Those who fail to live just so in the Christian community are 'answerable for the body and blood of Christ' (11.27) and suffer the gravest consequences (11.29-30).[118] They stand guilty of crucifying Christ afresh, because what is done to the 'least' is done to him, what is done to a member of the body, is done to the body and its head.[119] Insofar as believers

> fail to manifest the love by which they have been graced and formed into a community through Jesus' life-giving death, they are violating the body of the Lord himself, who is present in and with the gifts of bread and wine'.[120]

The Eucharist-event, therefore, not only symbolizes and effects believers' receiving of the *beneficia Christi*, but also calls for the day-to-day imitation of Christ. Perhaps this is why Paul is careful to say that to receive the Eucharist faithfully is to share in Christ's *body and blood*,[121] i.e. in his sufferings and humiliating death,[122] as Thisel-

---

[118] For a Pentecostal examination of this passage, see Thomas, *The Devil, Disease, and Deliverance*, pp. 43-54. See also Furnish, *The Theology of the First Letter to the Corinthians*, pp. 77-86.

[119] This perhaps suggests an understanding that resulted from Paul's Damascus road encounter (Acts 9.3-9)?

[120] Furnish, *The Theology of the First Letter to the Corinthians*, p. 84.

[121] To speak of the Eucharist as in invitation to share in Christ's 'sacrificial lifestyle' suggests the image of the cup of suffering Christ has to drink, which his disciples must also drink (Mk 10.35-40). Collins (*First Corinthians*, p. 379) points out that it also resonates with the language of the Psalms that speak of the cup of salvation (e.g. Ps. 16.5), as well as the cup of divine wrath (e.g. Ps. 116.13). Alt-

ton suggests: '[c]ommunal participation in the body and blood of Christ entails manifesting publicly the sacrificial lifestyle of Christ, as seen in his blood (i.e. his death) and his body (i.e. self-giving public life)'.[123]

To take the Supper rightly, then, is to be drawn into a cruciformed life, to be stamped with the *character* or 'mind of Christ' (à la 1 Cor. 2.16 and Phil. 2.5-8). It is to receive the Christomorphic 'vision of life distributed with the bread'.[124] To partake of Christ's body and blood is to be made like Christ in his life-giving death, to be empowered by the same Spirit to live as he lived, pray as he prayed, believe as he believed, obey as he obeyed until one's life like his is taken, blessed, broken, and given out for the world. Those who love him want nothing more and can accept nothing less.

Toward a Pauline Theology of the Eucharist: Conclusions

Read literarily-theologically, 1 Cor. 10.16-17 shows itself inexhaustibly rich with implications for Pentecostal theological reflection on the Eucharist.

First, this reading makes indisputable the fact that the Corinthians regularly celebrated the Lord's Supper; that they did so in compliance with Paul's express direction,[125] and that they took the rite

---

hough Paul himself does not exploit the connection, any reader sensitive to intertextual resonances will observe that the 'cup of blessing' (1 Cor. 10.16) is a source of blessing precisely because it signifies and effects the church's sharing in Christ's redemptive suffering. See John D. Laurence, 'The Eucharist as the Imitation of Christ', *Theological Studies* 47.2 (June 1986), pp. 286-96.

122 Certainly, such an emphasis would work as a powerful refutation of the triumphalist and elitist enthusiasm that seems to have plagued the Corinthian Christians. If anyone imagines a glorified life is possible apart from the cross, Paul means to show in no uncertain terms that it is not. For an examination of these tendencies in Corinth, see Calvin J. Roetzel, *The Letters of Paul: Conversations in Context* (Louisville: WJKP, 2009), p. 92; also, Furnish, *The Theology of the First Letter to the Corinthians*, pp. 10-12.

123 Thiselton, *The First Epistle to the Corinthians*, p. 767.

124 Vondey, *People of Bread*, p. 240.

125 A direction he claimed to have received 'from the Lord' (11.23). Roetzel (*The Letters of Paul*, p. 76) reads this as a direct citation of a Eucharistic liturgy Paul had received from other Christians, perhaps in Antioch or Jerusalem. Stanley B. Marrow (*Paul: His Letters and His Theology* [Mahwah, NJ: Paulist Press, 1986], p. 145) does not believe it is a reference to a 'private communication' from the Lord, but a 'consecrated formula for the Christian tradition'. Bruce (*Paul, Apostle of the Heart Set Free*, p. 283) is more modest: 'When he tells the Corinthians that he "received from the Lord" the account of what Jesus did and said "on the night when he was betrayed", he does not say when or where he received it.

to be a means of communion with Christ. This has enormous import for contemporary Pentecostal thought and practice, and coupled with the witness of those early Pentecostals who insisted on the regular and faithful observance of the Supper, it can be stated boldly that Pentecostal worship can and should include the Eucharistic celebration.

Second, the literary-theological interpretation of 1 Corinthians points to the fact that the Eucharist does not work 'magically', that a high *theology* of the Sacrament does not automatically translate into a way of life true to and reminiscent of the Lord who presides at the sacramental Meal. At least a minority of the Corinthian Christians (seemingly) trusted that because they believed the Supper made them one with the glorious Christ, they could continue to live with the divisions enforced by the mores of the surrounding 'world' in which they found themselves enmeshed.

Third, in context, the claims of 1 Cor. 10.16-17 suggest that it is helpful to see the church's receiving of the Lord's Supper as a *romantic gesture*, as a gift between lovers, a tryst with Christ who is jealous for his bride, and a way in which Christ, God fleshed, is bodily present to and for his church.

Fourth, these verses indicate that the Lord's Supper is a community-making meal. Pentecostals desire ever-deeper intimacy with God and neighbor, and these verses make clear that the Spirit uses the (faithfully-celebrated) Sacrament to do this by grounding the reader in the *story* of God's redemption of all things, the story of Israel, the story of Israel's messiah, the story of the apostles' and those who submit to follow them. The 'body' the Eucharist makes is the one people of God.

Fifth, a literary-theological reading of 10.16.17 suggests that the Eucharist accomplishes this (better: the *Spirit* accomplishes this through the Eucharistic celebration) by making possible the community's shared participation in Christ's 'body and blood', allowing the community not only to receive the benefits of atonement, but also to receive Christ himself, and his character as the one who humbled himself even to death on a cross.

He received it "from the Lord" in the sense that it is in the crucified and exalted Lord that all true Christian tradition has its source, as it is by him that it is perpetually validated. The probability is that he received it at the outset of his Christian career ...'

The Breaking of Bread, the Making of Community: Acts 2.41-47

[41]So those who welcomed his message were baptized, and that day about three thousand persons were added. [42]They devoted themselves to the apostles' teaching and fellowship, to the breaking of bread and the prayers. [43]Awe came upon everyone, because many wonders and signs were being done by the apostles. [44]All who believed were together and had all things in common; [45]they would sell their possessions and goods and distribute the proceeds to all, as any had need. [46]Day by day, as they spent much time together in the temple, they broke bread at home and ate their food with glad and generous hearts, [47]praising God and having the goodwill of all the people. And day by day the Lord added to their number those who were being saved.

Introduction

The next text to be read is a New Testament *testimony* of Eucharistic experience, again following the paradigm that emerged in the historical section (Chapter 3) of this thesis. Of the possible texts to be read (e.g. Jude 12 or Acts 20.7), I have chosen Acts 2.41-47, in part because of how frequently early Pentecostals used the passage.

The Interpretive Context

Acts 2.41-47 stands as the conclusion to the first major section of Acts (after the prologue of 1.1-5).[126] True to the Lukan style,[127] this summary ties together separate literary units. Immediately *before* this summary, the reader is given Peter's Pentecost sermon (Acts 2.14–

---

[126] Following the outline of John Christopher Thomas, *The Spirit of the New Testament*, p. 230 (work first published as 'The Charismatic Structure of Acts', *JPT* 31.1 (2004), pp. 19-30). Also, Douglas A. Hume (*The Early Christian Community: A Narrative Analysis of Acts 2.41-47 and 4.32-35* [Tübingen: Mohr Siebeck, 2011], p. 91) sees a chiastic structure to the Pentecost story (2.1-47), with the outer elements describing 'how the community is gathered together in one place'. In this way, 2.41-47 serves to explain how those who at Pentecost were gathered together in one *place* were made by the Spirit a genuine community, one in *spirit*. For still other outlining possibilities, see Ben Witherington, *The Acts of the Apostles: A Socio-Rhetorical Commentary* (Grand Rapids: Eerdmans, 1998).

[127] On the narrative unity of Luke and Acts, see Robert C. Tannehill, *The Narrative Unity of Luke-Acts: A Literary Interpretation* (2 Vols.; Minneapolis: Augsburg Fortress, 1990); William S. Kurz, *Reading Luke-Acts: Dynamics of Biblical Narrative* (Louisville: John Knox Press, 1993).

40) and a brief account of the response to it (Acts 2.41), and immediately *after* this summary, the narrative gives us the account of Peter and John healing the lame man (Acts 3.1-11) and another speech by Peter in the Temple (Acts 3.12-26).[128] Hearing of the astonishing response to Peter's sermon, the reader is impressed by the effectiveness of the apostolic witness. The community did work to maintain continuity with Jesus' teachings and the way of life he handed on to his followers,[129] giving themselves to the matrix of practices described in v. 42: adherence to the apostles' teaching,[130] fellowship,[131] prayers,[132] and the breaking of bread. Luke tells the reader that they 'devoted themselves' (προσκαρτεροῦντες)[133] to these practices, emphasizing the believers' energetic intentionality and diligence in these activities.[134] Not that this made the community impervious to trouble. Disputes, scandals, persecutions continued to arise; nonetheless, the way of living structured by this 'fourfold

---

[128] William H. Willimon, *Acts* (Interpretation; Louisville: John Knox Press, 1988), p. 42.

[129] Luke Timothy Johnson, *The Acts of the Apostles* (Sacra Pagina; Collegeville, MN: Liturgical Press, 1992), p. 58.

[130] As he did in the story of Jesus teaching the two on their way to Emmaus (Lk. 24.13-34), Luke tells us nothing of the content of the apostles' teaching. He does this, perhaps, to force the reader to ask – and then seek to discover – what in fact Jesus and the apostles *did* teach.

[131] Scholars disagree on what is meant by κοινωνία in this passage. Witherington (*The Acts of the Apostles*, p. 160) holds that it is a kind of catchall term, entailing everything from common prayer and worship to sharing their goods, and David G. Peterson (*The Acts of the Apostles* [TPNTC; Grand Rapids: Eerdmans, 2009], p. 161) agrees. Johnson (*The Acts of the Apostles*, p. 58) interprets it more narrowly, taking it to refer specifically to the sharing of material possessions. Although a strong case might be made for the more inclusive reading, Luke's characteristic concern for the poor suggests that the narrower reading is likely the correct one.

[132] It is not clear why Luke uses the plural with the article; perhaps it implies that the first Christians did not only pray, but continued to use certain prayers, such as the Lord's Prayer. On the general significance of prayer in the Third Gospel and Acts, see P.T. O'Brien, 'Prayer in Luke-Acts', *Tyndale Bulletin* 24 (1973), pp. 111-27; Kyu Sam Han, 'Theology of Prayer in the Gospel of Luke', *JETS* 43.4 (Dec 2000), pp. 675-93; Stephen S. Smalley, 'Spirit, Kingdom and Prayer in Luke-Acts', *Novum Testamentum* 15.1 (Jan 1973), pp. 59-71.

[133] This verb or its cognates appears four other times in Acts (1.14; 2.46; 6.4; 8.13; 10.7), always with this implication.

[134] Willimon (*Acts*, p. 39) observes, 'The crowd, formed from the ranks of the "crooked generation", was not to be left to its own devices'. The 'crookedness' does not straighten itself out on the strength of a 'spiritual experience' alone, but requires constant correction from habit-forming and so character-building practices.

embodiment of the gospel'[135] continually animated their life together in the world.[136] As the disciples gave themselves to these practices, they found that the Spirit worked powerfully among them, not
only by holding them together in heartfelt unity and deep joy as
they lived and worshipped together (v. 46), but also in combating
sickness[137] and poverty (vv. 43-44). As their numbers swelled, they
found themselves blessed with the favor of 'all the people' (v. 47).

'Blessed is the One Who Breaks Bread': The Eucharist and Jesus' Table-Fellowship in Luke-Acts

Opinion has long been divided on what κλάσει τοῦ ἄρτου in fact
means in Acts 2.42, 46.[138] Does it refer to the *Eucharist*, or merely to
ordinary meals shared in the believers' homes? In the effort to let
Luke-Acts speak for itself, it is best to ask how the breaking of
bread is characterized elsewhere in the two volumes of Luke's
work.

Eating and Drinking and the Kingdom of God
Luke the Evangelist often pictures Jesus at table,[139] frequently with
the poor to whom the kingdom is said to belong.[140] The Gospel

---

[135] Willimon, *Acts*, p. 40.

[136] Perhaps no theologian has given more attention to the significance of this
passage for churchly Eucharistic practice than John Calvin. Elsie Anne McKee
(*John Calvin on the Diaconate and Liturgical Almsgiving* [Geneva: Librairie Droz,
1984], p. 85) shows that, for Calvin, these four marks serve as the always-
recognizable 'face' of the true church and that 'no gathering of the Church
should ever be held without the Word, alms, the participation in the Supper,
prayers'.

[137] Acts 2.43 speaks of 'signs and wonders', perhaps implying some were
healed in the taking of the bread and wine. On the miraculous in Luke-Acts, see
Peterson, *The Acts of the Apostles*, pp. 83-86.

[138] McKee (*John Calvin on the Diaconate and Liturgical Almsgiving*, pp. 82-83)
provides examples from the ancient and medieval church of differing opinions
on the question of whether or not Acts 2.42 has any sacramental reference.

[139] Barbara Rossing ('Why Luke's Gospel? Daily Bread and "Recognition" of
Christ in Food-Sharing', *Currents in Theology and Mission* [June 2010], pp. 225-29
[225]) explains, 'Jesus in Luke's Gospel is a Jesus who loves to eat. One scholar
notes that "Jesus is either going to a meal, at a meal, or coming from a meal ..."
The way Jesus eats even leads to his death'.

[140] E.g. Lk. 5.29; 7.33-34, 36-50; 10.38-42; 11.37-52; 14.1-24; 22.14-38; 24.20-
49. Andy Johnson ('Our God Reigns: the Body of the Risen Lord in Luke 24',
Word & World [Spring 2002], p. 137) has it right: 'Remarkably, [Jesus] includes at
the same table people who were mortal enemies in the normal order of things.
For example, he was regularly host at a table that included both a tax collector
(Levi), "a collaborator with the Romans", and a Zealot (Simon), a kind of "Jewish

describes Jesus sharing in ten separate meals, sometimes as host, sometimes as guest. Narratively, these meals provide critical context for the account of breaking bread with his disciples at the Last Supper, and prepare the reader for Acts' description of Jesus' post-resurrection meals and church's post-Pentecost practice of breaking bread.[141] In fact, Jesus' table fellowship and its relation to the kingdom of God[142] works as perhaps *the* definitive theme in Luke-Acts.[143] Without question, a link between eating and drinking with

---

freedom fighter" who struggled to liberate Israel from the Romans. Jesus' table fellowship, therefore, dramatically depicted the reconciliation that characterized the kingdom he was proclaiming.' Joel B. Green (*The Gospel of Luke* [TICNT; Grand Rapids: Eerdmans, 1997], p. 227) explains that this kingdom is 'a new world order where the demonized, the sick, women, and others living on the margins of society are embraced in the redemptive purposes of God'. For an introduction to how scholars read Luke-Acts' treatment of the poor and the outcast, as well as the issues of wealth and poverty, see Thomas E. Phillips' taxonomic and bibliographic essay 'Reading Recent Readings of Issues of Wealth and Poverty in Luke and Acts', *Currents in Biblical Research* 1.2 (Apr 2003), pp. 231-69.

[141] Eugene LaVerdiere (*Dining in the Kingdom of God: The Origins of the Eucharist in the Gospel of Luke* [Chicago: Liturgy Training Publications, 1994]) describes the first six meals as shared with Jesus the *prophet*, the next two, including the Last Supper, as shared with Jesus the *Christ*, and the final two as shared with Jesus the *Lord*. See also Michael Joncas, 'Tasting the Kingdom of God: The Meal Ministry of Jesus and Its Implications for Contemporary Worship and Life', *Worship* 74.4 (July 2000), pp. 329-65.

[142] The Third Gospel is at every point concerned with the kingdom of God. For example, Jesus' birth is heralded as the birth of Israel's rightful king (Lk. 1.32-33), and, later, the mature, Spirit-baptized Jesus identifies himself as the authoritative messenger of the 'good news of the kingdom of God' (Lk. 4.43; 8.1; 16.16), a message he calls his disciples to announce, as well (Lk. 9.1-2; 10.1-16). The prayer he models for his disciples (Lk. 11.2) is nothing if not a calling for the eschatological reign of God to come, and Christ's miracles (as well as his disciples') – especially the healings and exorcisms – are said to signal the kingdom's in-breaking (Lk. 11.14-20). On many occasions, the Gospel narrates accounts of Jesus explaining the nature of the βασιλεία (e.g. Lk. 13.18-21), and Acts reports that this was the heart of his message to the apostles after his resurrection, as well (Acts 1.3). Through these accounts, the reader learns that the kingdom, though already present, remains presently hidden, unobservable (Lk. 8.9-10; 17.20-21; 23.3, 37-38). Similarly, in spite of the fact that the Father gives the kingdom, it must be sought out and claimed by violent effort (Lk. 12.31-32). The reader also discovers that although in some sense already 'realized', Jesus' βασιλεία is not yet fully established. When the disciples ask if the resurrected Christ will 'now restore the kingdom to Israel', his response is to direct them to prepare themselves for mission: 'It is not for you to know the times ...' (Acts 1.6-8).

[143] See, for example, Dennis E. Smith, 'Table Fellowship as a Literary Motif in the Gospel of Luke', *JBL* 106.4 (Dec 1987), pp. 613-38; Philip Francis Esler, *Community and Gospel in Luke-Acts: The Social and Political Motivations of Lucan Theology* (Cambridge: Cambridge University Press, 1987), pp. 105-109; Craig L.

the establishment of God's reign is made repeatedly, especially in the first of Luke's volumes.[144] In the Gospel, Jesus' mother celebrates the goodness and power of the One who fills the hungry with good things (Lk. 1.53), and Jesus himself later pronounces a blessing on 'those who hunger now', promising that they shall be filled (Lk. 6.21) as God's kingdom is established.[145] By the practice of eating bread and drinking wine, Jesus differentiates himself from John the Baptist and his disciples (5.33; 7.33-34),[146] and to the surprise of his contemporaries, he departs in yet another way from John's example by not requiring his disciples to follow scrupulously traditional table customs; in one instance, he defends his disciples' plucking and eating grain on the Sabbath (6.1-5) by drawing on the story of David's eating the bread of the Presence, identifying himself as Lord of the Sabbath. The disciples are instructed to pray for their 'daily bread' (τὸν ἄρτον ἡμῶν τὸν ἐπιούσιον)[147] and for the kingdom to come – a prayer that, in light of the Third Gospel's portrayal of Jesus, strikes the reader as two forms of a single petition: *Marana tha.*

Jesus' Hospitality and Menial Service
In Luke's Gospel, Jesus' table fellowship is marked by a radical hospitality[148] and willingness to serve menially yet lovingly. These themes are brought to focus in the story of the feeding of the five

---

Blomberg, 'Jesus, Sinners, and Table Fellowship', *Bulletin for Biblical Research*, 19.1 (2009), pp. 35-62. Wilson C.K. Poon ('Superabundant Table Fellowship in the Kingdom: The Feeding of the Five Thousand and the Meal Motif in Luke', *Expository Times* 114.7 [Apr 2003], pp. 224-30 [230]) 'Luke does rather uniquely give high prominence to the theme of food and feeding'.

[144] In short, when the *Didascalia Apostolorum* speaks of the Eucharist as 'the likeness of the body of the kingdom of Christ' it perhaps gives voice to a distinctly Lukan theology of the Meal. See Scott W. Hahn, 'Kingdom and Church in Luke-Acts: From Davidic Christology to Kingdom Ecclesiology' in Craig G. Bartholomew, Joel B. Green, and Anthony C. Thiselton (eds.) *Reading Luke: Interpretation, Reflection, Formation* (Grand Rapids: Zondervan, 2005), p. 310.

[145] Luke Timothy Johnson, *The Gospel of Luke* (Sacra Pagina; Collegeville, MN: Liturgical Press, 1991), p. 106.

[146] See Otto Böcher, 'Ass Johannes der Taufer kein Brot (Luk 7:33)', *New Testament Studies* 18.1 (Oct 1971), pp. 90-92.

[147] Lk. 11.2-4. On possible translations of the Greek phrase, see Johnson, *The Gospel of Luke*, p. 178; Johnson personally decides for 'the bread we need'.

[148] For a reading of Luke's Gospel in light of this theme, see Brendan J. Byrne, *The Hospitality of God: a Reading of Luke's Gospel* (Collegeville, MN: Liturgical Press, 2000).

thousand (Lk. 9.12-17)[149] – an account bracketed by descriptions of Herod's perplexity at Jesus' claims (9.7-9) and Peter's confession of Jesus as God's messiah (9.18-20). Viscerally moved by concern for the multitude, Jesus insists on feeding them,[150] and his characteristic radical hospitality leads Jesus to violate the standard dietary rules and social customs of the time, allowing *everyone* to share in the meal.[151] For these reasons, the miracle works as more than an extraordinary demonstration of his compassion for the hungry and his power to care for them; it serves as nothing less than a parabolic enactment of his larger mission to bring about the cosmic Jubilee (4.16-21).[152]

Informed by these recurring themes, careful readers find in Jesus' parable of the master returning from a wedding banquet (12.36-37) something more than a parable: they discern that he is in fact *directing* his disciples to live in expectation of his 'return', that is, his establishing of the eschatological kingdom of God. The readers also hear in this parable the promise that when he does in fact come to them bringing the kingdom, he will not only eat with them, but in fact *serve* them the meal, the messianic banquet. Even in the End, Christ's reign is one of hospitality, humility, and service-in-love.

---

[149] Poon ('Superabundant Table Fellowship in the Kingdom', p. 224) argues that the story of the feeding of the five thousand is central to the Gospel of Luke, and that the meal signifies the superabundance of Jesus' table fellowship as opposed to the conventions of the Pharisees. He also suggests (p. 229) that the Feeding looks forward not so much to the Last Supper as to the story of Jesus' encounter with the disciples on the road to Emmaus because 'the similarity in wording between thanksgivings for the bread in 9.16 and 24.30 is at least as strong as that between the former and 22.19', and 'Luke talks about the day "wearing away" in each case in reporting the time of the meal'.

[150] Johnson, *The Gospel of Luke*, p. 206.

[151] Green (*The Gospel of Luke*, p. 365) makes much of the fact that nothing is said about the uncleanness/cleanness of the meal and participations: 'Here are thousands of people, an undifferentiated mass of people, some undoubtedly unclean, others clean, some more faithful regarding the law, others less so. The food itself – is it clean? Has it been properly prepared? Have tithes been paid on it? Where is the washing in preparation for the table? Such concerns are so lacking from this scene that we might miss the extraordinary character of this meal ...'

[152] Green (*The Gospel of Luke*, p. 365) notes that this miracle among other things shows Jesus' standing in the tradition of miraculous meals provided by Israel's prophets (e.g. Elisha's feeding of a hundred men in 2 Kgs 4.42-44).

The Messianic Banquet

Besides the emphasis on Jesus' hospitality and service, the Gospel also frequently points the reader to the promise of the future messianic banquet. For example, Jesus shows himself to be Israel's true prophet when he foretells the gathering of the nations to the great banquet in the kingdom of God (Lk. 13.29), and an unnamed companion of Jesus – *while breaking bread with him* – ecstatically declares the blessing sure to be enjoyed by all who share in this future messianic feast: 'Blessed is anyone who will eat bread in the kingdom of God!' (Lk. 14.15).[153] These are yet further signs that Jesus is the one whose life and death and resurrection bring about God's promise of a restored world, a world in which bread is broken and wine poured out in everlasting justice and peace.

The Last Supper

All of this interweaving of themes in the earlier chapters of Luke's Gospel prepares the reader for Luke's account of the Last Supper. As the Gospel tells it, on that night, the night of his betrayal, Jesus confesses that he has 'longed' (ἐπιθυμίᾳ ἐπεθύμησα) – in the same way that the prodigal desired to eat the swine's food (Lk. 15.16) and Lazarus desired to eat the crumbs that fell from the table of the wealthy man (Lk. 16.21) – to eat this 'last' Passover[154] with his disciples (Lk. 22.15), and promises not to eat it again 'until it is fulfilled in the kingdom of God' (Lk. 22.16), obviously evoking again the hope of the future messianic feast. As Jesus shares this meal with the apostles, he confers on them his Father's kingdom, assuring them that as heirs of the kingdom they may 'eat and drink at [his] table' (Lk. 22.28-30). He also proclaims that he is 'one who serves' (22.27), and in this way shows the nature of authority in his

---

[153] This provokes Jesus to deliver a parable (Lk. 14.16-24), in part to explain that only the 'uninvited' – that is, the sick and poor, the nameless and faceless – will 'get a taste of my banquet' (v. 24). J. Lyle Story ('All is Now Ready: An Exegesis of "The Great Banquet" [Luke 14.15-24] and "The Marriage Feast" [Matthew 22.1-14]', *American Theological Inquiry* 2.2 [July 2009], p. 69) points out that 'Jesus proceeds to share with the ecstatic guest at his side … the incredible news that the Messianic feast is present, here and now, thus correcting the guest's mistaken oversight'.

[154] Green (*The Gospel of Luke*, p. 759) points out that Jesus' promise anticipates 'the completion of God's purpose' and speaks of 'the coming eschatological banquet in which his own meal practices would be the norm'.

kingdom.[155] Christ is *kyrios* precisely as one who serves. The disciples submit to this lordship precisely by serving, and in serving like him, they reign with him. The kingdom is borne by Jesus' – and the *disciples'* Jesus-like – hospitality.

Jesus' Post-Resurrection Meals and the Church's Post-Pentecost Fellowship
This table fellowship with his disciples continues even *after* his resurrection; the resurrected but not yet ascended Jesus often sits at table with his disciples (Lk. 24.13-35, 36-53; Acts 1.4), revealing not only the nature of his resurrected body,[156] but also preparing his followers for the new realities they will experience after his ascension.[157] The Gospel and Acts carefully and repeatedly draw attention to the basic continuity between Jesus' pre-resurrection table fellowship, these post-resurrection meals, and the church's ongoing Sunday fellowship meal, revealing that in Luke's theology the cosmic, heavenly lordship of the resurrected Christ is as bound up with eating and drinking as was his pre-Easter messianic ministry.[158]

'Breaking Bread'
Finally, it should be noted that three times in the Gospel Jesus explicitly is said to break bread – at the feeding of the five thousand (9.16), at the Last Supper (22.19), and at Emmaus (24.30) – and that each time the meal in question is occasioned by specific, ritual-like acts.[159] Obviously, then, these are no ordinary meals, but miraculous feasts occasioned by the Lord's specific, ritualized acts of taking, blessing,[160] breaking, and giving the bread.[161] Significantly, Jesus'

---

[155] As Johnson (*The Gospel of Luke*, p. 206) puts it, 'Authority is here expressed in table service'.

[156] See Peter's sermon (Acts 10.34-43) in which he insists that the nature of Jesus' resurrection is revealed in the fact that the risen Jesus ate and drank with his disciples.

[157] LaVerdiere, *Dining in the Kingdom of God*, pp. 170-71.

[158] Michael G. Lawler, 'Christian Rituals: An Essay in Sacramental Symbolisms', *Horizons* 7.1 (Spring 1980), p. 31.

[159] Contra Green (*The Gospel of Luke*, p. 364), who insists that these were *not* significant gestures, but actions expected at '*any* meal among pious Jews, in preparation for the eating of the food itself'.

[160] On the variant form of 'to bless' in Lk. 24.30, see Louis-Marie Chauvet, *The Sacraments: The Word of God at the Mercy of the Body* (Collegeville, MN: Liturgical Press, 2001), p. 25.

[161] Tannehill, *The Narrative Unity of Luke-Acts*, II, p. 334.

true identity and vocation are made known in these acts.[162] As already noted, Peter confesses Jesus as 'the Messiah of God' (9.20) immediately *after* the feeding of the five thousand, and the eyes of the Emmaus disciples are opened in the very moment of the breaking of the bread.[163]

The Church's Eucharist in Context of Lukan Feasting Themes

With all of this in mind, it is difficult to imagine that readers would not take Acts 2.42, 46 to describe the Eucharist, even if also it is judged to fit within or alongside an ordinary meal. Accordingly, LaVerdiere is right to identify 'the breaking of bread' as a Lukan name for the Eucharist,[164] and to hold that when the early Christian communities broke bread together (as described in 20.7, as well as 2.42, 46), they were purposefully and self-consciously reenacting the Last Supper and the post-Easter, pre-Ascension meals, liturgically and ritually imitating Jesus' (symbolic) words and gestures with them – both before and after his passion.[165] It seems plausible to conclude, then, that while any and every meal they shared – whether with other believers or with the marginalized and poor 'outside' – was in some sense a continuation of the now-risen Jesus' table fellowship, the Eucharist was the *hub* of the community's life together, so that the Lukan Pentecostal community understood their sharing of the rite of the Lord's Supper not only as an analeptic reminder of Christ's covenant-making death and a proleptic anticipation of the

---

162 As Hume (*The Early Christian Community*, p. 106) explains, 'Through the repetition of key words and motifs that recall Luke's accounts of the Lord's Supper and the shared meal with the disciples at Emmaus, the narrator is continuing the theme of the recognition of Jesus' identity in communal meals'.

163 Chauvet (*The Sacraments*, pp. 22-28) proposes that the story of Jesus' meal with the Emmaus disciples is 'a catechesis in the form a story' intended to teach the readers of the Gospel that Jesus' post-Pentecostal presence – even while it cannot be found, seen, or touched – is nonetheless real and effective. Also, he points out how closely this resembles a key theme in the Fourth Gospel: Jesus' 'going away' is necessary and profitable for the community.

164 LaVerdiere, *The Breaking of Bread*, p. 17.

165 Oscar Cullmann (in his essays published in Oscar Cullmann and F.J. Leenhardt, *Essays on the Lord's Supper* [Cambridge, UK: James Clarke & Co., 2004], pp. 5-23) famously argued that the early church Eucharist emerged not from a remembrance of Jesus' table fellowship or his Last Supper, but from meals shared with the spiritually-present Risen (not-yet Ascended) Christ. It seems to me, however, that Cullmann at times exaggerates the difference between the pre-paschal and post-paschal meals, and between the ontology of the presence of Christ before and after his resurrection.

future eschatological banquet, but also a most important means of the Spirit's enforcing among them and on their behalf the kingdom and its blessings.[166] For them, the Eucharist was the first means of 'sacramentally continuing [Jesus'] hospitality down the ages'.[167]

To show that the breaking of bread refers to the Eucharistic Meal is not enough, however. It still needs to be shown what Luke believes happens in this Meal, and other meals as well. For that, we must turn to Luke's theology of the kingdom.

The Mysteries of the Meal(s)

Carefully tracking the narrative of Luke-Acts, the reader begins to sense that *all* meals are theologically significant, from Jesus' fellowship with outcasts and undesirables, to the Last Supper he shared alone with his apostles. Apparently, no neat and clean difference is maintained in either the Gospel or Acts between '*merely* breaking bread and the church breaking bread as a sacramental religious activity'[168] – and the ambiguity surely is intentional.[169] According to Luke-Acts, then, *every* meal shared by the primitive Christian community was at least an echo of the Eucharist,[170] eaten in thanksgiving for Christ and in anticipation of the final messianic banquet.[171] It can be stated as a rule that at least in Lukan theology, hard-and-fast distinctions between 'ordinary' meals and the church's sacramental meal are virtually impossible to make and unnecessary in any case.

This harmonizes nicely with early Pentecostal thinking and acting, which, like Luke's narrative, typically felt no need to separate – in thought or in practice – the Eucharistic rite from other meals. Numerous testimonies from the early literature show that Pentecostal fellowship meals were believed to have extraordinary, supernatural significance – in much the same way as the sacred Supper itself. To be sure, the regular religious celebration of Communion as a symbolic meal remained decisively important for them, but this did

---

[166] Johnson, *The Gospel of Luke*, p. 405.

[167] Byrne, *The Hospitality of God*, p. 172.

[168] Willimon, *Acts*, p. 41. Emphasis original.

[169] See LaVerdiere, *Dining in the Kingdom of God*, pp. 192-93.

[170] Or, from a different perspective, the Eucharist-event was itself an echo of Jesus' table-fellowship, either in his pre-resurrection ministry or at the end of days.

[171] Willimon, *Acts*, p. 41.

not overshadow the fact of their conviction that the Spirit moved no less powerfully among them in 'ordinary' meals as well.[172]

All Things Common: The Economics and Politics of 'Breaking Bread'

The Eucharist was from the beginning an *economic* and *political* force. Jesus' eating with the poor and the outcast had socio-economic and political ramifications, so it is unsurprising that the early church's shared meals – ritual and otherwise – did as well.[173] As Daniela Augustine shows, the descent of the Spirit at Pentecost 'induces an economic model of distributive justice as witness of Christ's resurrected life',[174] so that the Lukan Pentecostal communi-ty gives shape to an exemplary economic model, not least in their habit of breaking bread together.[175] On her reading, the sharing of material possessions is in Acts 'the first sign of this divinely induced reality of healing all creation'. Because they broke bread together as their Lord had done, because they believed the risen Christ and his kingdom were present to them at their meals, they came to see that they could also share their possessions fearlessly and that 'worldly' rank and status were meaningless signifiers.[176] Therefore, now as then, the common Table *must* be understood to require '*some* kind of sharing, advocacy, and partisanship in which the poor are privi-leged, and in which considerations of merit and productivity are subjected to the rule of servanthood'.[177] This economics is the em-

---

[172] It is important not to reduce Luke's stories of eating and drinking so that they speak *only* to the church's Eucharistic practice. Nevertheless, interpreters are wise to ask what Luke has to teach us about the Eucharist, as well as about table fellowship of other kinds.

[173] Rossing ('Why Luke's Gospel?', 227) is on target: '… Luke makes clear that the opposite of sharing – excessive greed and hoarding – imperils salvation'. Rossing also points out that Luke's view of wealth and poverty is rooted in Isra-el's history, and particularly in the story of manna in the wilderness. See also Christopher R. Bruno, '"Jesus is Our Jubilee" … But How? The OT Background and Lukan Fulfillment of the Ethics of Jubilee', *JETS* 53.1 (Mar 2010), pp. 81-101; Paul Hertig, 'The Jubilee Mission of Jesus in the Gospel of Luke: Reversals of Fortunes', *Missiology* 26.2 (Apr 2008), pp. 167-79.

[174] Daniela C. Augustine 'Pentecost, Communal Economics and the House-hold of God', *JPT* 19.2 (Fall 2010), p. 232.

[175] Augustine, 'Pentecost Communal Economics and the Household of God', p. 233.

[176] John Howard Yoder, *Body Politics: Five Practices of the Christian Community Before the Watching World* (Scottsdale, PA: Herald Press, 2001), p. 17.

[177] Yoder, *Body Politics*, p. 22.

bodiment of Jesus' proclamation of the Jubilee (Lk. 4.18-19),[178] and reveals the true significance of the Sabbath, as Jesus explained it (Lk. 6.1-11).[179] Most of all, it is the embodiment of the communion received and given at the Lord's Table. The church 'experiences the fullness of the life of the community of the Trinity' in the Eucharist,[180] learns to overcome the 'urge to consume and store for consumption', and so becomes able to live as food for the world.'[181]

A connection also obtains between the community's politics and the 'gladness of heart' (2.46) that characterized their sharing in the Lord's Supper.[182] Like the household at the return of the prodigal son (Lk. 15.11-23), the disciples ate their bread with *joy*[183] because they knew that '[a]lready they were dining in the kingdom of God'.[184] In their lives, 'the celestial wedding supper had begun, the kingdom of God was come, blissful communion with the Lord already existed'.[185] It is perhaps not without significance that this matches early Pentecostal spirituality, which, as seen in the previous chapter, was vitalized by the apocalyptic affections engendered in shared Eucharistic celebrations. Like the Lukan Pentecostal com-

---

[178] See Johnson, *The Gospel of Luke*, pp. 79-81.

[179] See Green, *The Gospel of Luke*, p. 253. For the possibility that Luke refers to Second Isaiah and not to the Jubilee described in Leviticus, see Tannehill, *The Narrative Unity of Luke-Acts*, I, pp. 67-68. On the significance of Israel's Jubilee tradition, see John Sietze Bergsma, *The Jubilee from Leviticus to Qumran* (Leiden: Brill, 2007).

[180] And, one might add, in the 'everyday' meals that echo the Eucharist.

[181] Augustine, 'Pentecost Communal Economics and the Household of God', p. 235.

[182] Joy is one of the dominant Lukan themes. The reader 'hears' of those who joy in the coming of Jesus and/or those who bear witness to him. Zechariah is promised that his son will bring 'joy and gladness' (χαρά … καὶ ἀγαλλίασις), and that many will rejoice (χαρήσονται) at his birth because he will prepare the way for Christ (Lk. 1.14). Elizabeth exults in Mary's news and the child dances joyously (ἀγαλλιάσει) in her womb (Lk. 1.44). Even Herod – for all the wrong reasons – is 'very glad' (ἐχάρη λίαν) to see Jesus (Lk 23.8). According to Hume (*The Early Christian Community*, p. 96), the narrator of Luke-Acts 'often portrays characters reacting with joy when they experience God's presence'.

[183] Bultmann (*Theology of the New Testament*, p. 339-40) is right: early Christian joy was *eschatological*, arising from conviction about 'the Christian's relatedness to the future'. What is more, this joy was realized in their life together, in the 'fellowship and mutual helpfulness' they enjoyed.

[184] LaVerdiere, *Dining in the Kingdom of God*, p. 195. Peterson (*The Acts of the Apostles*, p. 163) believes they were 'aware that God was at work in their midst in a new way and that they were enjoying the benefits of the messianic salvation'.

[185] Ernst Benz, *The Eastern Orthodox Church: Its Thought and Life* (Garden City, NY: Anchor Books, 1963), pp. 22-23.

munity, primitive Pentecostals in the U.S. found their political and economic imaginations transformed as their affections were enflamed. By the witness of both the Scripture and early Pentecostalism, it seems, then, that 'the breaking of bread' gives rise to eschatological joy, a deep and self-sustaining happiness that sets the believing community free from the anxieties that dominate the 'world', thus allowing them to live generously, sharing their goods without reserve.

Toward a Lukan Theology of the Eucharist: Conclusions

First, Acts 2.41-47 shows that the earliest Christians, those closest to the apostles, regularly and joyfully celebrated the Lord's Supper, a fact replete with important and far-reaching implications for Pentecostals, given the pride of place many Pentecostals afford the narratives of Luke-Acts.

Second, read in the light of the Lukan emphasis on the kingdom of God and its link to eating and drinking, the passage shows that the 'breaking of bread' serves as the sign *par excellence* that the kingdom has come and is coming, because at the Eucharist the risen Christ is present as *host*, even now present by the Spirit to break the bread and prepare the community to live as bread for the world.

Third, Luke's vision of the Spirit's transformative work is not limited to the church's liturgical life, although it remains centered and grounded there. This suggests that even 'ordinary' meals are imbued with supernatural significance, that every meal can and should be sacramental in a way analogous to *the* meal, because Christ is in fact *kyrios* of all things and no rigid distinction between 'sacred' and 'secular' can be maintained.

Fourth, this reading of Acts 2.41-47 suggests that the Eucharistic celebration always should be contextualized by apostolic teaching, by fellowship, by liturgical and spiritual prayer if it is to remain authentic. By itself, the Lord's Supper cannot hold the community in Christian fellowship.

Fifth, it seems Jesus' practices of table fellowship not only prepared the church to understand the Lord's Supper, but also provided a paradigm for the church's engagement with the poor and marginalized, both within and without the believing community. This implies that all Christian fellowship – and *table* fellowship is and must remain at the heart of this – comes from and leads back to the

Eucharist. Sharing in the Eucharistic 'breaking of bread' prepares the community for fellowship with 'outsiders', and vice versa. Further, in the light of Jesus' habit of eating with undesirables and using the table as a sign of the universal kingdom of God, it only makes sense to maintain an 'open' Communion.

Eating is/as Believing: John 6.25-59

[25]When they found him on the other side of the sea, they said to him, "Rabbi, when did you come here?" [26]Jesus answered them, "Very truly, I tell you, you are looking for me, not because you saw signs, but because you ate your fill of the loaves. [27]Do not work for the food that perishes, but for the food that endures for eternal life, which the Son of Man will give you. For it is on him that God the Father has set his seal." [28]Then they said to him, "What must we do to perform the works of God?" [29]Jesus answered them, "This is the work of God, that you believe in him whom he has sent." [30]So they said to him, "What sign are you going to give us then, so that we may see it and believe you? What work are you performing? [31]Our ancestors ate the manna in the wilderness; as it is written, 'He gave them bread from heaven to eat.'" [32]Then Jesus said to them, "Very truly, I tell you, it was not Moses who gave you the bread from heaven, but it is my Father who gives you the true bread from heaven. [33]For the bread of God is that which comes down from heaven and gives life to the world." [34]They said to him, "Sir, give us this bread always." [35]Jesus said to them, "I am the bread of life. Whoever comes to me will never be hungry, and whoever believes in me will never be thirsty. [36]But I said to you that you have seen me and yet do not believe. [37]Everything that the Father gives me will come to me, and anyone who comes to me I will never drive away; [38]for I have come down from heaven, not to do my own will, but the will of him who sent me. [39]And this is the will of him who sent me, that I should lose nothing of all that he has given me, but raise it up on the last day. [40]This is indeed the will of my Father, that all who see the Son and believe in him may have eternal life; and I will raise them up on the last day." [41]Then the Jews began to complain about him because he said, "I am the bread that came down from heaven." [42]They were saying, "Is not this Jesus, the son of Joseph, whose father and mother we

know? How can he now say, 'I have come down from heaven'?" [43]Jesus answered them, "Do not complain among yourselves. [44]No one can come to me unless drawn by the Father who sent me; and I will raise that person up on the last day. [45]It is written in the prophets, 'And they shall all be taught by God.' Everyone who has heard and learned from the Father comes to me. [46]Not that anyone has seen the Father except the one who is from God; he has seen the Father. [47]Very truly, I tell you, whoever believes has eternal life. [48]I am the bread of life. [49]Your ancestors ate the manna in the wilderness, and they died. [50]This is the bread that comes down from heaven, so that one may eat of it and not die. [51]I am the living bread that came down from heaven. Whoever eats of this bread will live forever; and the bread that I will give for the life of the world is my flesh." [52]The Jews then disputed among themselves, saying, "How can this man give us his flesh to eat?" [53]So Jesus said to them, "Very truly, I tell you, unless you eat the flesh of the Son of Man and drink his blood, you have no life in you. [54]Those who eat my flesh and drink my blood have eternal life, and I will raise them up on the last day; [55]for my flesh is true food and my blood is true drink. [56]Those who eat my flesh and drink my blood abide in me, and I in them. [57]Just as the living Father sent me, and I live because of the Father, so whoever eats me will live because of me. [58]This is the bread that came down from heaven, not like that which your ancestors ate, and they died. But the one who eats this bread will live forever." [59]He said these things while he was teaching in the synagogue at Capernaum.

Introduction

The final text I have selected to consider is one whose sacramentality is *embedded*, rather than explicit. While other texts merit consideration,[186] I have chosen to read Jn 6.25-59, and I will continue to employ the reading strategy explained above.

---

[186] Including, for example, Heb. 6.4-5; 13.10; 1 Jn 5.6-8, and 1 Cor. 10.1-4. This list can and should include numerous Old Testament passages, such as Neh. 8.10 and Isa. 25.6, as well.

The Interpretive Context

Jesus' Bread of Life Discourse (6.25-59) is situated in the Fourth Gospel's book of signs[187] (1.19-12.50), one of the Gospel's two major sections, in addition to its prologue (1.1-18) and epilogue (21.1-25).[188] Early in the so-called book of signs, Jesus' ministry is met with all but universal acclaim and affirmative, believing response;[189] but chapter 5 marks a transition in the narrative,[190] as the reader discovers a sudden, drastic turn against Jesus and his ministry. After Jesus heals the man at the pool (5.6-9), 'the Jews' question the man and then condemn the healing as a violation of the Sabbath and Jesus as a lawbreaker (5.9-18). In response, Jesus offers an extended discourse on his relation to the Father and the judgment sure to fall on all who refuse to acknowledge him as the Father's Son (5.19-47). A similar pattern plays out in chapter 6. Jesus performs a 'sign'[191] – in this case, the feeding of the five thousand (6.1-13) – that convinces some to attempt to make him king (6.14). However, discerning their faithlessness, Jesus eludes the crowds (ὄχλος πολὺς) for the evening (6.15), and on the next day confronts them for their lack of genuine belief in him (6.26-27):

---

[187] Andrew T. Lincoln (*The Gospel According to Saint John* [BNTC; London: Continuum, 2005], p. 6) rejects this title for the section because it is 'not precise enough to describe the public mission, since it makes the specific signs more dominant than they in fact are and does not do justice to the speech material'. On 'signs' in John's Gospel, see Rudolf Schnackenburg, *The Gospel According to St John* (New York: Seabury Press, 1990), I, pp. 515-28.

[188] Following the outline of Francis J. Maloney, *The Gospel of John* (Sacra Pagina; Collegeville, MN: Liturgical Press, 1988), pp. 23-24, 194. See also D.A. Carson, *The Gospel According to John* (TPNTC; Grand Rapids: Eerdmans, 1991), pp. 105-108; M.M. Thompson, 'John, Gospel of' in Joel B. Green, Scot McKnight, and I. Howard Marshall (eds.), *Dictionary of Jesus and the Gospels* (Downers Grove, IL: IVP, 1992), pp. 373-74.

[189] Including, for example, the belief of Andrew, Simon Peter, and other disciples (1.35-51; 2.11, 22), and that of the Samaritans who respond to the witness of the woman Jesus encountered at the well (4.27-42).

[190] Thomas, *The Devil, Disease and Deliverance*, pp. 92-93.

[191] The feeding of the five thousand is the fourth of seven signs in the Gospel, and the discourse on the bread of life is the fourth of seven such discourses. See Lincoln, *The Gospel According to Saint John*, pp. 6-7. For an exploration of how the Fourth Gospel uses the Synoptic tradition of the feeding of the five thousand and Jesus' walking on water, see Frederick A. Rusch, 'The Signs and the Discourse – The Rich Theology of John 6', *Currents in Theology and Mission* 5.6 (Dec 1978), pp. 389-90.

Jesus answered them, 'Very truly, I tell you, you are looking for me, not because you saw signs, but because you ate your fill of the loaves. Do not work for the food that perishes, but for the food that endures for eternal life, which the Son of Man will give you. For it is on him that God the Father has set his seal'.

When he insists that they must believe in him, that such belief is the only true 'work of God' required of them (6.28-29), they demand a further 'sign' (σημεῖον) to validate his claims.[192] In response to this demand, Jesus delivers another extended discourse, this time emphasizing his identity ('I am the bread of life') and the need for them to believe on him. The passage can be outlined[193] in this way:

6.1-4   Narrative introduction

6.5-15   Jesus feeds the five thousand

6.16-21   Jesus walks on the water

6.22-24   Further narrative contextualization

6.25-59   Teaching on bread of life

6.60-71   Crisis among disciples created by Jesus' teaching[194]

No doubt, due to the abundance of narrative markers, any pericope in the Gospel is difficult to outline; it is virtually impossible to determine where exactly any given passage begins or ends. It seems fairly clear, however, that the discourse moves toward the (Eucharistic?) claims of the conclusion (vv. 49-58).[195]

Jesus' teaching, which the reader learns is delivered in the days before the Passover feast (6.4),[196] can be read as a kind of *midrash*[197]

---

[192] Given the recent miraculous feeding of the multitudes, the crowds' appeal to the story of manna in the wilderness as the example of what a validating 'sign' must be strikes the reader as strange and unwarranted. Has Jesus not already given them a 'sign' of just this kind?

[193] Chapter 6 is notoriously difficult to organize neatly, as is more or less the entire Gospel. As Stephen Fowl ('John 6.25-35', *Interpretation* [July 2007], p. 316) explains, the widespread disagreement on the breakdown of John 6 is due at least in part to the fact that 'Each passage [in John's Gospel], particularly its images and ways of identifying Jesus, is intimately connected to a web of other passages'.

[194] Maloney, *The Gospel of John*, p. 194.

[195] John Dominic Crossan, 'It is Written: A Structuralist Analysis of John 6', *Semeia* 26 (1983), p. 15.

[196] Some scholars hold that in the Book of Signs John is also drawing attention to various festivals of the Jewish calendar, using the feasts' liturgical and ritual imagery as an interpretive lens for Jesus' own self-identifying actions and words. See, for example, Thompson, 'John, Gospel of', p. 373; Maloney, *The*

on the words of Scripture – 'he gave them bread from heaven to eat'[198] – , so that the entire Discourse is framed, informed, and energized by plays on the language and imagery from this text.[199] For example, discerning the crowds' intentions, Jesus admonishes them to 'work for ... the food that endures for eternal life', food only he can give because he himself is 'the bread of life', the 'true bread from heaven', and 'the living bread that came down from heaven'. The reader encounters it as a single piece, but the discourse actually addresses two audiences in turn – the crowds, first, and then 'the Jews'. While Jesus is speaking to the crowds, answering on his own terms their demand for a 'sign' like that given to wandering Israel in the wilderness to prove his authority and power[200] (vv. 25-40), 'the Jews' 'grumble' against him,[201] so he turns his teaching to them (vv. 41-58).[202] In effect, then, the reader traces a development of thought in the discourse. As he teaches and responds to his interlocutors, Jesus' claims become increasingly provocative and more

---

Gospel of John, pp. 164-65; Gerald Wheaton, *The Role of Feasts in John's Gospel* (PhD thesis; St Andrews, Scotland; 2009); Michael A. Daise (*Feasts in John: Jewish Festivals and Jesus' 'Hour' in the Fourth Gospel* [Tübingen: Mohr Siebeck, 2007]. Others see no such connection. See, for example, Gerald L. Borchert, *John 1-11* (TNAC; Grand Rapids: Broadman & Holman, 1996), pp. 226-27.

[197] Following Peder Borgen, *Bread from Heaven: An Exegetical Study of the Concept of Manna in the Gospel of John* (Leiden: Brill, 1965), pp. 20-27, 59-98. See also Peder Borgen, 'Observations on the Midrashic Character of John 6', *Zeitschrift für die neutestamentliche Wissenschaft* 54 (1963), pp. 232-40. For an alternative view, see P.N. Anderson, *The Christology of the Fourth Gospel: Its Unity and Disunity in the Light of John 6* (Tübingen: Mohr, 1996), pp. 174-78.

[198] Daise (*Feasts in John*, p. 139-40) points out that scholarly opinions differ on the source of the quotation in v. 31; the primary candidates are Ps. 78.24b; Exod. 16.4b; Exod. 16.15d, and Neh. 9.15a. For the use of the Old Testament in John 6, see Jean Zumstein, 'La réception de l'écriture en Jean 6', in Camille Focant and André Wénin (eds.), *Analyse narrative et Bible* (Leuven: Leuven University Press, 2005), pp. 147-66.

[199] Maloney, *The Gospel of John*, p. 207. Jerome H. Neyrey (*The Gospel of John* [TNCBC; Cambridge: Cambridge University Press, 2007], pp. 124-28) contends that Jesus' discourse is an extended re-narrating of each term in this scriptural text. For example, the crowds believe the 'he' of the text is Moses, but Jesus contends that he himself is the true referent; in the same way, Jesus' hearers assume that the 'bread' of the text is the manna given in the wilderness, but Jesus again insists that he himself is that bread.

[200] Maloney, *The Gospel of John*, p. 207.

[201] As Israel had 'grumbled' in the wilderness.

[202] According to Crossan ('It is Written', p. 12), Jesus speaks very differently to 'the Jews' than to the crowds. His teaching was at first primarily an 'I-You' dialogue, but in response to 'the Jews' grumbling and complaining, the language shifts to predominantly 'I-He'.

and more difficult for his hearers to understand, resulting finally in the apostasy of many of his followers. When 'the Jews' take offense at his claims, first because they recognize him as Joseph's and Mary's son (vv. 41-42), and then because they cannot imagine what it might mean to 'eat' his 'flesh' (v. 52), Jesus intensifies his claims: only those eat the flesh and drink the blood of the Son of Man have hope of eternal life, and only they 'abide' in him (vv. 53-56). His disciples respond to these claims in shock and disbelief (v. 60), and Jesus, sensing their 'complaining', turns and asks if his words have offended them and if they are prepared to see 'the Son of Man ascending to where he was before' (vv. 61-62).[203] He reminds them that 'the flesh profits nothing', that only the spirit gives life, insisting that this life and this spirit are bound up with his words (v. 63). This does not assuage them, however, and 'many of his disciples turned back and no longer went about with him' (v. 66).[204] The passage ends with Jesus' prophecy of his betrayal, and the narrator's identification of Judas as the betrayer (vv. 69-71).

Eating and Drinking in the Fourth Gospel and the Bread of Life Discourse

Although concentrated in chapter 6, talk of eating and drinking occurs throughout John's Gospel. From the wider context of the Gospel, for example, we see that Jesus' seven ἐγώ εἰμι claims are bracketed by the first of the sayings, 'I am the bread of life' (6.35), which has to do with eating, and the last, 'I am the true vine' (15.1), both of which play on eating/drinking imagery.[205] Two of the Gospel's seven 'signs' deal with drinking and eating, as well: the turning of water to wine (2.1-12) and the multiplication of bread (6.5-13).[206]

---

203 On whether this is meant to intensify or ameliorate the offense, see Carson, *The Gospel According to John*, pp. 300-301. James F. McGrath (*John's Apologetic Christology: Legitimation and Development in Johannine Christology* [SNTS 111; Cambridge: Cambridge University Press, 2004], p. 178) suggests that this might be a case of characteristic Johannine irony.

204 Gary A. Phillips, '"This is a Hard Saying. Who Can Be Listener to It? Creating a Reader in John 6', *Semeia* 26 (1983), p. 38.

205 Perhaps this constitutes a kind of inclusio? On possible uses of inclusio in the Gospel, see Carson, *The Gospel According to John*, p. 237. Also, see Mark W.G. Stibbe, *John's Gospel* (London: Routledge, 1994), p. 112, and idem, *John as Storyteller: Narrative Criticism and the Fourth Gospel* (Cambridge, Cambridge University Press, 1992), pp. 19-20.

206 Some sacramentalists have made much of the verb 'eat' (τρώγων) used in Jn 6.54-58 and again in 13.18, but this seems unconvincing because *Judas* is the

The Passover motif, threaded throughout the Gospel, also plays on these images. For example, Jesus is identified in the opening chapter (1.29, 36) as 'God's lamb' (ὁ ἀμνὸς τοῦ θεοῦ) who carries away the word's sin, a title the reader later discerns as a reference to Israel's *Passover* lamb, a sacrifice to be *eaten*, and whose death means life for Israel and so for the world.[207] This Passover theme gives way more broadly to the relation of the death and life to eating and drinking, so that it is while Jesus is eating supper with his friends in Bethany, 'six days before the Passover', that Mary anoints Jesus for his burial (12.7).[208] Strikingly, the only time Jesus himself is said explicitly to eat or drink is at the very moment of his death (19.28-30)[209] – the very 'hour' in which he is offered as the Passover lamb for the world. In the same way, the reader should notice that it is precisely *at table* that Jesus is betrayed to his destiny (13.18). This complex of life-giving dying and life- or death-bringing eating is drawn into the bread of life discourse when Jesus speaks of giving the bread that is his flesh for the life of the world (6.51). Tellingly, it is in response to *this* saying of Jesus that many of the disciples abandon Jesus, and precisely at this moment that Peter makes his confession of Christ.[210]

The eating and drinking imagery and its connection to the language of life and death is strongest and most difficult to follow in the conclusion of the discourse. We can outline the passage in this way:

6.50 'This is the bread ... one may eat of it and not die'

  6.51a 'I am the living bread...'

    6.51b 'Whoever eats of this bread will live forever'

      6.53 'Unless you eat my flesh and drink my blood, you have no life'

      6.54 'Those who eat ... have eternal life'

---

only one who is said to 'eat' at the Last Supper! However, if Jesus did *not* mean something more than 'spiritual' eating, the scandal caused by his claims seems strange and disproportionate.

[207] Jane S. Webster, *Ingesting Jesus: Eating and Drinking in the Gospel of John* (Atlanta: SBL, 2003), p. 27.

[208] Webster, *Ingesting Jesus*, p. 93.

[209] Webster, *Ingesting Jesus*, p. 130.

[210] It is perhaps telling that the Corinthians showed their true colors at the Lord's Table, too, or that Jude talks about 'spots' in their feasts.

6.57   '… whoever eats me will live because of me'

6.58   'This is the bread … who eats this bread will live forever'

Within this structure, the claims of 6.53 stand at the center, showing its critical importance. For the first time in the discourse, Jesus speaks of *both* eating *and* drinking, as well as of his *flesh* and his *blood*. The phrase 'this is' (οὗτός ἐστιν) frames the section, forming an *inclusio* that implies the identification of Jesus and his death with his body/flesh and his blood that like the Passover lamb are to be consumed if their benefits are to be received.[211] Again, this points to the critical and even decisive significance of eating and drinking not only for the Discourse, but also more broadly for the Gospel in its entirety.

What, if anything, are contemporary readers to make of all of this talk of eating and drinking Christ in the Fourth Gospel? Does it have any bearing on contemporary sacramental thought and practice? More to the point, what, if any, difference does it make for churchly thinking about and participating in the Lord's Supper? Bluntly put, does the bread of life discourse speak to the Eucharist-event at all, or does it refer exclusively to so-called *spiritual* 'feeding'?[212] Are all of the chapter's references to Christ as 'bread' entirely figurative,[213] merely and exclusively 'vivid metaphors for believing', as some have suggested?[214]

---

[211] Obviously, it also echoes the Synoptic accounts (e.g. Mt. 26.26 and Lk. 22.19): 'this is my body' (τοῦτό ἐστιν τὸ σῶμά μου), although it is impossible to determine if John does this intentionally or not. However, Lincoln (*The Gospel According to Saint John*, p. 232) holds that it is 'highly probable' that the words of institution from the Synoptic tradition have influenced John's account in several ways. He notes that Mt. 26.26-28 comes closest to the Johannine statement about eating Jesus' flesh and drinking his blood.

[212] This is the position of many interpreters. For example, David Gibson ('Eating Is Believing? On Midrash and the Mixing of Metaphors in John 6', *Themelios* 27.7 [Spring 2002], pp. 5-15) contends that 'if "flesh" and "blood" refer to Jesus' person in his death, not the Eucharistic elements, then the verbs "eat" and "drink" in v. 53 have to be understood in the same metaphorical way as "eat" in vv. 50-51b is used in reference to Jesus' person'. Even if John 6 makes use of Eucharistic terminology, he concludes, 'it is used to point to the significance of Jesus' death, not the sacramental elements'.

[213] Borchert (*John 1-11*, p. 263) observes that the Fourth Gospel often appeals to a contrast between two levels of reality to hold up Jesus' superiority: e.g. the difference between the two temples in 2.19, the two births in 3.3, two spirits in 3.8, and two waters 4.10. In this context, it is a contrast between two breads.

[214] Craig R. Koester, *Symbolism in the Fourth Gospel: Meaning, Mystery, Community* (2nd ed.; Minneapolis: Augsburg Fortress Press, 2003), p. 304.

In attempting to answer these questions, it needs to be said that given the hermeneutic that guides our reading, we do not need to decide whether the author(s) of the Gospel *intended* the passage to have sacramental significance;[215] still less do we need to figure out if the 'historical Jesus' could have or would have spoken of Communion in this way. We need only to point out that the text itself, when read narratively and theologically, *can* be heard to speak to the sacraments – and we know from the history of interpretation that it *has been* read in this way.[216]

Such readings are shown to be legitimate for (at least) two reasons. First, the language and structure of the Fourth Gospel is more or less endlessly ambiguous, complex, and multivalent, so that the text of the Gospel is replete with a virtually inexhaustible depth of meaning.[217] What Smith says of the water imagery in John applies,

---

[215] On the modern historical-critical question of whether John is pro- or anti-sacramental, see Stephen S. Smalley, *John: Evangelist and Interpreter* (New York: Thomas Nelson, 1984), pp. 128-30, 204-10, and Brown, *The Gospel According to John I-XII*, pp. 280-94. On John 6 in particular, see Carson, *The Gospel According to John*, pp. 276-82; James D.G. Dunn, 'John VI – A Eucharistic Discourse?', *New Testament Studies* 17 (1971), pp. 328-38; M.J.J. Menken, 'John 6.51c-58: Eucharist or Christology?' in R. Alan Culpepper (ed.), *Critical Readings of John 6* (Leiden: Brill, 1997), pp. 183-85.

[216] Craig R. Koester ('John Six and the Lord's Supper', *Lutheran Quarterly* [Dec 1990], pp. 420-26) provides a brief but helpful overview of the history of interpretation. As he tells it, the most influential Eucharistic readings of John 6 seem to have come from Cyril of Alexandria, Chrysostom, Basil the Great, and Gregory of Nyssa, among a few others, while non-sacramental readings have been championed by many equally prominent figures, including Clement of Alexandria, Origen, Augustine, Aquinas, Erasmus, Luther, Melanchthon, and Calvin. Koester personally holds to the traditional Lutheran non-sacramental line of interpretation, maintaining that a Eucharistic reading creates more problems than it solves. In his judgment, the references to eating and drinking Christ's flesh and blood are best understood as an invitation to faith in Christ and his atoning death. For an examination of Aquinas' reading of John 6, see Michel Corbin, 'Pain de la Vie : La Lecture de Jean VI par S Thomas d'Aquin', *Recherches de Science Religieuse* 65.1 (Jan-Mar 1977), pp. 107-38, and Michael Dauphinais, '"And They Shall Be Taught of God": Wisdom and the Eucharist in John 6', in Michael Dauphinais and Matthew Levering (eds.), *Reading John with St. Thomas Aquinas* (Washington, DC: Catholic University of America Press, 2005), pp. 312-17. For Luther's and Calvin's uses of the passage, see David S. Yeago, 'The Bread of Life: Patristic Christology and Evangelical Soteriology in Martin Luther's Sermons on John 6', *SVTQ* 39.3 (1995), pp. 257-79, and Eleanor B. Hanna, 'Biblical Interpretation and Sacramental Practice: John Calvin's Interpretation of John 6.51-58', *Worship* 73.3 (May 1999), pp. 211-30.

[217] Here I stand in agreement with, among others, Raymond Brown (*The Gospel and Epistles of John*, p. 18): 'In the Fourth Gospel the author frequently intends

with necessary distinctions, to the eating and drinking imagery, as well: 'It is characteristic of the Fourth Gospel that this water imagery is never explicitly limited to, or explained as, water baptism. At the same time, it is hard to imagine that baptism is not somehow in view'.[218] So, even if the Lord's Supper is judged never to be the *primary* referent of John's eating and drinking imagery, it nonetheless seems likely that a Johannine sacramentality lies embedded in the text at some level of significance. Second, the convictions and experiences Christian readers bring to the text make it impossible for them *not* to hear at least allusions to the Eucharist.[219] Consequently, we can reasonably propose that readers of the Fourth Gospel are warranted in taking the discourse as instruction both about *both* believing in Christ (i.e. feeding spiritually on him) *and* about the meaning of the church's sacramental practice and experience.[220] In short, John 6 can and does speak about the Eucharist, if only in a secondary and derived sense.[221]

The interpretative practices of early Pentecostals again prove helpful. As seen in the previous chapter, their readings of John 6 typically worked *with*, rather than *against*, the unsettledness, ambiguity, and many-sidedness of Johannine language. Even while a few

---

the reader to see several layers of meaning in the same narrative or in the same metaphor (figurative language)'. See also Saeed Hamid-Kahni, *Revelation and Concealment of Christ: A Theological Inquiry into the Elusive Language of the Fourth Gospel* (Tübingen: Mohr Siebeck, 2000); Earl J. Richard, 'Expressions of Double Meaning and Their Function in the Gospel of John', *New Testament Studies* 31.1 (Jan 1985), pp. 96-112; D.A. Carson, 'Understanding Misunderstanding in the Fourth Gospel', *Tyndale Bulletin* 33 (1982), pp. 61-91.

[218] D. Moody Smith, *The Theology of the Gospel of John* (NTT; Cambridge: Cambridge University Press, 1995), p. 156.

[219] Contra Koester ('John Six and the Lord's Supper', p. 432), who seems to hold in contempt those readers who hear allusions to the Eucharist in the Fourth Gospel because they are '*already* steeped in the traditions concerning the Lord's Supper'.

[220] Contra Carson (*The Gospel According to John*, p. 279), who asks, '… if the arguments against a thoroughly sacramental interpretation of this chapter are so strong, and the coherence of a metaphorical approach so commanding, what is to be gained by bringing in a Eucharistic interpretation through the back door, as a kind of second layer of meaning'.

[221] In agreement with Gary Burge ('Revelation and Discipleship in St John's Gospel', in John Liermen [ed.], *Challenging Perspectives on the Gospel of John* [Tübingen: Mohr Siebeck, 2006], p. 246) who points out the 'hierarchies of meaning' in John's Gospel. See also Neyrey, *The Gospel of John*, pp. 127-28, and C.H. Cosgrove, 'The Place Where Jesus Is: Allusions to Baptism and the Eucharist in the Fourth Gospel', *New Testament Studies* 35 (1989), pp. 522-39.

readers took the words in either a strictly spiritual/existential or Eucharistic sense, many did not make a distinction at all, allowing the text's indistinctness to remain untamed, so to speak. Apparently, they felt that making a final decision either for or against a sacramental reading of John 6 was both unnecessary and unhelpful.[222] In view of their example, we learn that the decisive hermeneutical question interpreters can and should bring to bear on John 6 is *not* 'Does this refer to the Eucharist?', but 'How does this passage teach us to respond rightly to the Lord of the Eucharist, to participate faithfully as his people at his Table?' Once this move has been made, then the remainder of the discourse is illuminated, and casts new light on contemporary sacramental thought and practice.

'How Can This Be?': (Mis)Understanding Christ

On the heels of Jesus' claim that he is ὁ ἄρτος τῆς ζωῆς (6.48), his promise that 'whoever eats this bread will live forever' (v. 51a),[223] and, more particularly, his explanation that 'the bread' is his 'flesh' (v. 51b),[224] arguments break out: 'how can this man ...' (v. 52). The reader is not surprised by this lack of understanding, because as the Fourth Gospel tells it Jesus' hearers misunderstand him at nearly every turn.[225] To take a few examples, the Samaritan woman misunderstands his words about 'living water' (4.13-15), his disciples misunderstand his claim to 'have food to eat that you do not

---

[222] They would have agreed with the assessment of Dale C. Allison, Jr. ('The Living Water: John 4.10-14; 6.35c; 7.37-39', *SVTQ* 30.2 [1986], p. 145) who observes that attempts to limit the Johannine metaphors to a single, stable meaning are reductionistic, finally distorting the irreducible complexity and variegated character of John's theological code.

[223] This is strikingly similar to Jesus' words about 'living water' to the Samaritan woman (4.10, 13-14); however, *there* he promises her that he *gives* living water, while *here* he claims that he *is* the bread of life. For formal similarities between John 4 and John 6, see Raymond E. Brown, *The Gospel According to John I-XII* (The Anchor Bible; Garden City, NY: Doubleday & Company, 1966), p. 267.

[224] Carson (*The Gospel According to John*, p. 295) is right: the alert reader is sure to think of 1.14.

[225] Some scholars speak of a 'misunderstanding motif' in the Fourth Gospel. For example, see Nicolas Farelly, *The Disciples in the Fourth Gospel: A Narrative Analysis of Their Faith and Understanding* (Tübingen: Mohr Siebeck, 2010); Andreas J. Kostenberger, *A Theology of John's Gospel and Letters: The Word, the Christ, the Son of God* (Grand Rapids: Zondervan, 2009), pp. 141-45; R. Alan Culpepper, *A Study in the Fourth Gospel: A Study in Literary Design* (Minneapolis: Fortress Press, 1987), pp. 152-65; Raymond E. Brown, *The Gospel and Epistles of John: A Concise Commentary* (Collegeville, MN: Liturgical Press, 1988), p. 17.

know about' (4.31-33), the 'Jews' mistake his claim to be 'before' Abraham (8.31-39), and the disciples again misunderstand him when he explains Lazarus has merely 'fallen asleep' (11.11-13). Again and again, a particular question surfaces: *how is it possible* (πῶς δύναται) for Jesus to perform what he has promised? Nicodemus asks it (3.4, 9), as do those interrogating the man whom Jesus has healed of blindness (9.10, 15, 26). Jesus does not answer the question, does not explain himself, or offer any clarification. Instead, he restates and *intensifies* his claim:[226]

> So Jesus said to them, 'Very truly, I tell you, unless you eat the flesh of the Son of Man and drink his blood, you have no life in you. Those who eat my flesh and drink my blood have eternal life, and I will raise them up on the last day; for my flesh is true food and my blood is true drink.[227]

'For the Life of the World': The Scope of Jesus' Sacrifice

Twice in the discourse, once at the beginning and again at the end, Jesus makes clear that he has come from the Father for the sake of 'the world' (τόν κόσμον).

6.33   For the bread of God ... gives life to the world.

6.51   ... the bread that I will give for the life of the world is my flesh.

Needless to say, the entire Gospel resonates with these claims. To take but a few examples, the Gospel identifies Jesus as 'the light of the world', the light that gives light to all in the world (1.9; 8.12; 9.5; 12.46). He is sent from the Father because of the Father's love for

---

[226] As W.H. Kelber ('The Birth of a Beginning: John 1.1-18' in Mark W.G. Stibbe, *The Gospel of John as Literature: an Anthology of Twentieth-Century Perspectives* [Leiden: Brill, 1993], p. 224) explains, 'Far from accommodating the Jews, Jesus proceeds to radicalise [*sic*] the language of his self-identification with the bread ... As if to rub salt in their wounds, Jesus elaborates the metaphor of flesh in starkly realistic, cannibalistic terms'. Carson (*The Gospel According to John*, p. 296) puts it this way: 'The Jews had found Jesus' statement in v. 51c impenetrable at best, blatantly offensive at worst, but in this expansion Jesus in their view is even more offensive'. See also Lincoln, *The Gospel According to Saint John*, p. 231.

[227] Neyrey (*The Gospel of John*, p. 128) notes that the 'unless' of 6.53 parallels other such demands in the Gospel: being born of water and the Spirit (3.3, 5), special belief in Jesus as one who saves from sins (8.24), washing by Jesus (13.8), and abiding in the vine (15.4). Interestingly, three of the four seem to have at least a secondary reference to sacraments of baptism and Eucharist.

the world (3.16); nonetheless, when he comes from the Father into the world, the world does not recognize him as the source of its light and life (1.10), but hates him (15.18). Ironically, it is not Jesus 'own', but the Samaritans who first recognize him as 'the savior of the world' (4.42). Jesus is 'for' the world (*pro mundo*) precisely as the one who brings the world and the world's ruler to *judgment* (3.17-19).[228] In fact, he himself is both judge and judgment (5.22, 27), and the 'hour' to which he is drawn is nothing less than the 'now' of judgment, the time in which world's ruler is 'driven out' (12.31), the moment in which he fulfills his purpose to take away the world's sin (1.29). Because this judgment is oriented to the world's salvation, Jesus can rightly say that he has not come to judge but to save the world (12.47). Jesus, therefore, is known to be the Father's *missionary* Word. In offering his 'flesh' on the cross, Jesus is saving the world, destroying the devil, and carrying away the world's sins.

The theme of judgment touches on the eating and drinking motif through the story of the manna, which God provided not only to sustain Israel in the wilderness, but also to test their faith and to humble them (Deut. 8.16). In the same way, Jesus himself is a gift from the Father who comes as something strange and wonderful ('What is it?'). This judgment-as-salvation motif also works from and back to the image of Moses' brass serpent (Num. 21.4-9), an image John has already used to explicate Jesus' death: like the serpent in the wilderness, the Son of Man must be 'lifted up' (Jn 3.14). It is taken up again in 6.40, where the text pairs 'seeing the Son' (ὁ θεωρῶν τὸν υἱὸν) with *believing* in him.[229] In light of this image, the reader sees that eating and drinking Christ's flesh and blood is a way of receiving and submitting to Christ's saving judgment. Truly to eat Christ is to accept Christ as the Father's loving condemnation of sin, to step into the light and allow the darkness to be driven out of one's life.

---

[228] See Maloney, *The Gospel of John*, pp. 176-84; 354-56. Also, Andreas J. Köstenberger, *The Missions of Jesus and the Disciples According to the Fourth Gospel* (Grand Rapids: Eerdmans, 1998), pp. 121-22;

[229] On the theme of 'lifting up' in John's Gospel, see Benjamin E. Reynolds, *The Apocalyptic Son of Man in the Gospel of John* (Tübingen: Mohr Siebeck, 2008), pp. 117-30.

'Looking to' Jesus and the Promise of Eternal Loyalty

Four times in the Discourse (vv. 39-40, 44, 54), Jesus promises to 'raise up' those who are his. Besides the Son's eschatological action, the passages emphasize the Father's will, and the need for believers' response to the Son.

> 6.39-40 – And this is the will of him who sent me, that I should lose nothing of all that he has given me, but raise it up on the last day. This is indeed the will of my Father, that all who see the Son and believe in him may have eternal life; and I will raise them up on the last day.

> 6.44 – No one can come to me unless drawn by the Father who sent me; and I will raise that person up on the last day.

> 6.54-55 – Those who eat my flesh and drink my blood have eternal life, and I will raise them up on the last day; [55]for my flesh is true food and my blood is true drink.

These promises seem to fit into two pairs, with the claims of v. 40 and v. 54 belonging together, and those of v. 39 and v. 44 belonging in the other set. Each pair has a different theological focus; vv. 39 and 44 plainly emphasizing the Father's sovereignty and the Son's faithfulness, but vv. 40 and 54 focus on the relation of belief in Christ to receiving 'life' (ζωή) in and from him.

> 6.40 – This indeed is the will of my Father, that all who see the Son and believe in him may have eternal life and I will raise them up on the last day.

> 6.54 – Those who eat my flesh and drink my blood have eternal life, and I will raise them up on the last day.

When these verses are read in tandem, and in this way allowed to interpret one another, the reader sees that eating Christ's flesh means, at least in part, to 'see' him believingly, allowing his crucifixion, his death, to be life-bringing.[230] In turn, Christ promises that those who do 'eat' him, who look to him believingly and 'abide' in him truly and completely, will never be orphaned (14.18). This

---

[230] Herman N. Ridderbos, *The Gospel According to John: A Theological Commentary* (Grand Rapids: Eerdmans, 1997), pp. 136-37, 238-43, 430-31.

means, in part, that he will be eternally loyal to them,[231] that he will not only be with them now but also will raise them up in the End, 'on the last day', to an eternal life of abiding love. It also means that this eternal life is *already* at work in them, already energizing and orienting them; even now, short of the *eschaton*, they participate in the life that they are promised to receive in the End.

Nourished for the Journey: The Benefits of Eating Christ

According to the Fourth Evangelist, this believing, this 'eating' and 'drinking' of Christ's 'flesh' and 'blood', produces an excess of blessings. All of these benefits can be summed up in saying that to eat Christ is to receive nothing less than – *abiding intimacy with Christ himself.* 'Those who eat my flesh and drink my blood abide in *me*, and *I* in them' (v. 56).[232] Not only Christ himself, but the believer also receives in him communion with the Father in and through and with the Spirit. 'Just as the living Father sent me, and I live because of the Father, so whoever eats me will live because of me' (v. 57). In John's Gospel, to 'abide' describes both true personal allegiance to Christ and unbreakable intimacy with him,[233] an intimacy that expands out from Christ's intimacy with the Father to embrace, to take in the believer. The 'intra-divine life is mediated to believers through Jesus'.[234] That is to say, '... the believer's union with Jesus not only *parallels* but *participates in* the union between the Father and the Son'.[235] To put it another way, believers take up the same 'space' occupied by the Word who is 'with' (πρὸς) God (1.1), and 'close to the Father's heart' (1.18). In fact, it would not be an exaggeration to say that Christ's flesh and blood are that 'space', or, at least, a 'door' into it.

---

[231] Neyrey, *The Gospel of John*, p. 128. See also Maloney, *The Gospel of John*, pp. 214-25.

[232] This language appears frequently in the Gospel (e.g. in 8.31; 15.4, 6, 9-10). It is first used (in 1.32-33) of the Spirit's relation to Jesus – the Spirit 'remains' on Jesus – and then immediately used of the relation of the disciples to Jesus (1.39). Even more impressively, the majority of uses come in the Farewell Discourse, so that the reader can reasonably conclude that according to John the disciple shares the same relation to Jesus as the Spirit has to Jesus and Jesus has to the Father. For a treatment of this theme in the Gospel, see Jurgen Heise, *Bleiben: Menein in den Johanneischen Schriften* (Tübingen: Mohr Siebeck, 1967).

[233] Lincoln, *The Gospel According to Saint John*, p. 233.

[234] Lincoln, *The Gospel According to Saint John*, p. 233.

[235] Emphasis added.

To be brought into the divine life in this way is also to have one's life shaped into a Christ-like form. Feeding on Christ is to be consumed by him, 'eaten up' with zeal for God (2.17), so that God's will becomes the energy-giving source of one's life. As Jesus says, 'My food is to do the will of him who sent me and to complete his work' (4.34). Also, partaking of Christ is accepting and embodying the way of life he pioneers, models, and perfects – the way of self-emptying service, the way of the cross. 'To eat Jesus' flesh is to take his humanity into our own, identifying with him in lowly service at the cost of life itself'.[236]

Finally, then, we can turn back to the passage and draw out from the text's embedded sacramentality a few implications for a Pentecostal theology of the Lord's Supper.

Toward a Johannine Theology of the Eucharist: Conclusions

First, when read in this way, the discourse, specifically, and the Gospel, more broadly, teach that the Eucharist-event works as one of the definitive signs of the Christian life, and in just this way also serves as a means of 'seeing' and 'following' Christ, and 'abiding' in him.[237] The history of interpretation shows that most readers of John agree that Jesus' teaching has to do first and foremost with life-shaping *belief* in Christ, so that even the metaphors of eating and drinking are – at the first level, anyway – theological code for spiritually receiving Christ and his benefits by faith in his life-giving death for the sake of the world. Nonetheless, because of the church's sacramental experience and the nature of the text of John's

---

[236] Lamar Williamson, *Preaching the Gospel of John: Proclaiming the Living Word* (Louisville: WJKP, 2004), p. 83.

[237] Chauvet (*The Sacraments*, p. 50) notes, 'For John, the Eucharistic act of eating is the great symbolic experience in which we are given, to feel and live, this scandal of the faith until it enters our bodies, that is to say, our life'. James W. Voelz, ('The Discourse on the Bread of Life in John 6: Is It Eucharistic?, *Concordia Journal* 15.1 [Jan 1989], p. 34) makes a similar point: 'I believe that in the discourse on the Bread of Life, our Lord is speaking of heavenly sustenance which He gives for His own, for the people of God. What is that heavenly sustenance? It can properly be thought of, I believe, in specifically Eucharistic (i.e., oral eating) terms: (verse 54) "He who eats my flesh and drinks my blood has eternal life, and I will raise him up on the last day." But it can *not only* be thought of in such specifically Eucharistic terms: (verse 47) "He who believes has eternal life." Yet, the Sacrament of the Altar is one means – and it is the only means of *oral* eating and drinking – for the Body of Christ to be fed with the body of Christ, by the living food of the Lord, her living Savior …'

Gospel, it is entirely fitting to read these same references to eating and drinking as descriptions of the Lord's Supper.

Taken in this way, the discourse teaches that the church's celebration of the Supper is one of the God-given signs of Christ's being 'lifted up'. The blood bears witness, as 1 Jn 5.6-8 says. Because the Eucharist is the sign that it is, believing necessarily entails faithful partaking. Whoever *believes* (v. 40) also *eats* (vv. 47, 54), and to refuse to eat is to be severed from the Vine.[238] While it *is* possible to eat faithlessly – and so without benefit[239] – it is *not* possible to believe and yet refuse to partake of the Eucharist. It is possible to eat the church's bread without eating/'eating' Christ – Judas eats the bread, but still 'lifts up his heel' – but the reverse is *not* true. In light of this reading of John 6, then, we discover that we cannot make a hard-and-fast separation between spiritual 'feeding' on Christ and sacramental participation, even if some distinctions are drawn for the sake of study and explanation. Respecting the theology of the Fourth Gospel requires us to let the spiritual and the sacramental stand in the closest possible connection, each interpreting the other.

Second, for John, sacramental thought and practice must take care never to drift away from identification with Christ and his cross, from suffering with him – or of being his 'witness', in the language of the Apocalypse. The eating and drinking of Communion must draw us into the very life of the Christ who invites us to imitate him, making it possible us to be conformed to his reality, his 'image'.

Third, the Gospel declares that Jesus gives himself 'for the sake of the world', so that the Eucharist is never solely about the church but always also about 'the world', that is, about all of the creation. It follows, then, that Jesus Christ is the Father's *missionary* Word, and that Communion is by definition a missionary meal. To be sure, the Eucharist is for the world a *saving* sign, a life-giving (visible) word

---

[238] In order not to lose sight of the intimate relationship between sacramental practice and believing, it is perhaps helpful to insist on speaking of eating/'eating' and drinking/'drinking' Christ's flesh/'flesh' and his blood/'blood', in this way always holding together the symbolic and the actual, even if this looks inelegant on the page or sounds inelegant to the ear.

[239] As Borchert (*John 1-11*, p. 273) warns, 'These elements can indeed symbolize the eternal and actual bread that came down from heaven, but they must never take the place of the living Lord ...' Therefore, he concludes, 'Inwardly digesting him is the way of life. Eating and drinking elements of physical food, even God-given physical food, does not guarantee life.'

(*verba visibilia*), but this necessarily entails a word of judgment, too. This judgment is enacted on the world, at least in part, through the mysterious nature of the Eucharist, specifically, and of Jesus' teaching, in general; both give occasion for offense. It is not for no reason that for John the Eucharist is prefigured by the manna, given not only to sustain Israel, but also to humble her, and to prove the integrity of her faith.

The Eucharist, like Christ himself, both reveals and conceals, judges and saves; like Jesus' teaching, it is an intelligible word and at the same time an inscrutable word, a word that retains its mystery even in its lucidity; it is as deep as it is clear. Insofar as we *do* grasp the meal's meaning, we find ourselves confronted with the glories of Christ's saving death; he is 'lifted up' before our very eyes, and we see him crucified for us and for the whole world (Gal. 3.1). Insofar as the meaning of the meal exceeds our grasp, we find ourselves humbled, drawn up short by our own inadequacies; seeing nothing, we know that it is our vision that is flawed. In these ways the 'visible word' of the Lord's Supper is for us a judging and so a saving word.

Fifth, because the Gospel teaches us that what happens to us in our (sacramental) encounter with Christ is beyond human understanding, that it is always beyond our capacity to answer how it is possible, it also reminds us that the willingness to remain in Eucharistic communion with Christ even in the face of confusion marks the decisive difference between those who believe in him and those who do not. The mysteriousness of the meal makes possible the articulation of our abiding faith. The narrative of John 6 makes clear that misapprehension of and distaste for Jesus' teaching is decisive for the making of the believing community. That is to say, those who take offense at his words abandon him, and those who remain in Jesus' company do so not because they grasp his teaching completely, or even because they understand it better than those who deserted him, but simply because they continue to cling to their confidence in him in spite of their lack of clarity. Believers need not overcome their perplexity about what it is that happens in Communion, but simply and only continue to lean on Christ as the one who has 'the words of life'; belief in Christ does not elide the questions altogether, but puts them in their (penultimate) place. Besides, believers remain confident that all the understanding they need is sure to come to them as they simply obey. Like the servants who bring the wine to the steward of the wedding feast, the faithful ones come to know what Christ has done (2.9).

Sixth, Johannine sacramentality will not allow a divorcing of Christ from his gifts, the bread that he *is* from the (Eucharistic and spiritual) bread that he *gives*.[240] As a result, we must not think of the Lord's Supper in mechanical, non-personal terms, but always as personal encounter with Christ himself, who in himself brings to us all the gifts entrusted to him by his Father.

Seventh, the Eucharist is life-giving for those who truly turn to Christ believingly, but ineffectual or destructive for those who eat faithlessly. For John the Eucharist works no more or no less than did Moses' serpent: instituted by God, it requires a certain kind of human participation – there must be a 'looking to' Christ, without which nothing graceful happens. This 'looking to' must be, at its heart, a believing in Jesus' *words*, which, as he says, are 'spirit and life'.[241] By themselves, the bread and wine 'profit nothing', but when they are received in faith, they become life-giving[242] because they are instruments of the saving words of Jesus, who himself is the Father's saving Word.

Conclusions: Toward a New Testament Theology of the Eucharist

In this chapter, I have attempted to explore what the New Testament has to say about the Lord's Supper by reading a trio of what I judged to be relevant texts. Now we have to assess our findings. What harmonies emerge when we let the voices of John, Paul, and Luke sing together as a single chorus?[243] What implications have we

---

[240] Eugene LaVerdiere (*The Eucharist in the New Testament and the Early Church* [Collegeville, MN: Liturgical Press, 1996], p. 123) agrees with those scholars who see a division within the discourse, with 6.25-50 constituting the first part in which Jesus declares *himself* as the bread of life and 6.51-58 making the second part in which Jesus proclaims the bread that he *gives*. Still, 'Jesus' teaching on the bread that he gives, his flesh and blood in the Eucharist, must not be separated from the bread of life that he is'.

[241] Jn 6.63: '... τὰ ῥήματα ἃ ἐγὼ λελάληκα ὑμῖν πνεῦμά ἐστιν καὶ ζωή ἐστιν'.

[242] Paul S. Berge, 'John 6.1-71: The Bread Which Gives Life to the World', *Word & World* 5.3 (June 1985), pp. 311-20.

[243] Here I am drawing on John Christopher Thomas' analogy of the black gospel choir; see Thomas, *The Spirit of the New Testament*, p. 24.

discovered that might inform theological reflection on contemporary Pentecostal Eucharistic thought and practice?

First, the testimony of these three witnesses indicates that a variety of early Christian communities regularly celebrated the Lord's Supper, and that this liturgical event was believed by them to have deep significance for the life of the believer and the believing community. It seems clear that Paul, Luke, and John – as well as the communities for whom they spoke – understood the church's celebration of Christ's Supper as in some sense a continuation of Jesus' ministry, re-enacting his life of sweeping, boundary-violating hospitality and his atoning death for the life of the world, while pre-enacting the future messianic feast as well.

Second, we learn that in the Eucharist we come to have fellowship with Christ. In Paul's language, in the sacramental cup and loaf we have 'participation' with Christ, and, in John's language, 'abide' in him, to receive 'eternal life' here and now, and to share in his intimacy with the Father in the Spirit, as well as in the benefits of his victory. Of course, truly to 'abide' in him is to share not only in the benefits but also in his *sufferings*, to be 'lifted up' with him, to be broken and poured out, just as he was. In fact, this sharing in his suffering is necessary because we live in the already-not yet eschatological tension. Nonetheless, we stand assured that because we abide in him, at the end of all things he will raise us up into the eternal and all-encompassing reign of God. The church's communing always is carried out in light of what God has already accomplished in Christ and what God has promised to do at Christ's *parousia* and in the establishing of the eschatological kingdom, so that the Eucharist is always both a remembering of God's faithfulness in the past and an anticipation of God's faithfulness in the final future.

Third, we hear from this chorus of texts a symphony of promises for those who commune faithfully, in particular the promise of deep and (ever)lasting communion with Christ and with his church, the people of God. Although expressed in various ways and with different emphases, these apostolic witnesses agree that in our celebration of the Lord's Supper we are brought up together to participate in the Trinitarian life, a life of always-overflowing love and mutual delight. In Christ, who presents himself to us in this sacrament, we truly receive God and one another.

We also hear warnings of judgment. Both John's and Paul's sacramental theologies make clear that eating and drinking Christ can bring either judgment or salvation, depending on whether or not we 'look to' Christ faithfully and rightly discern his body.

Fourth, we hear from the witness of these texts the call to follow Christ. This *imitatio* is, in one sense, a *liturgical* following of Christ's example. That is to say, in the celebration of the Eucharist, celebrants ritually repeat Jesus' and the apostles' actions and words as host and guests of the last Passover and first Lord's Supper, liturgically re-enacting the taking, blessing, breaking, sharing, and receiving of the bread and the blessing, sharing, and drinking of the cup. In this very imitation, however, celebrants open themselves to the Spirit whose work is continually to transform them into Christ's body. Therefore, because of the Spirit's activity, this imitation always already spills over from the liturgical event into everyday, worldly life, so that through the community's shared Eucharistic experience the truth comes clear: our lives are secured at every turn only by God's hospitality. We live by the Word of God alone and the bread he provides. For Luke, it is in the community's sharing in Communion that believers receive a share in this divine plentitude and generosity that gives shape and energy to their political imagination and economic practices.[244] Because the Spirit makes us one at the Table, we find ourselves compelled to live lives of radical hospitality – feeding the hungry, protecting the widow and the orphan, inviting the weak, poor, and diseased to share with us in the life God gives.

Fifth, we hear the story of cosmic salvation, and know ourselves as narrated into that story – the one story of creation and redemption and consummation, the story of Israel and the church and the world for which they are called as God's ambassadors and collaborators. At each celebration, the Eucharist (re)situates us in this narrative. This means, in part, that the Lord's Supper for us is the 'present tense of Calvary', and in some sense is also the present tense of all the feasts of God's people, past and future, including of course the eternal messianic banquet. It also means that our sharing in the cup and the loaf is a covenant-making affair exactly as the Passover has been for Israel. In sharing this wine and this bread, we not only

---

[244] Not exclusively, of course, but really.

receive Christ and his benefits, but also again and again bind ourselves to one another and devote ourselves anew to God, refusing all other (idolatrous) allegiances. In short, in offering the bread and wine as gifts of our thanksgiving, we echo back to God our promise of covenant faithfulness.

Seventh, these texts teach us that the sharing of a common loaf and cup is truly the *Lord's* Supper for us only as we faithfully respond to the Word of God that comes to us alongside, through, and as the sacred meal. Israel ate the manna in the wilderness and died – both John and Paul are careful to underscore this fact. They, with Luke, make it a point to show that life comes from communing faithfully, taking the cup and the loaf while looking to Christ, by breaking bread with a desire to see the kingdom come and a readiness to take on Christ's sufferings and humiliations for the sake of God and the world God loves so riotously.

Finally, we learn that the Lord's Supper is to be understood as the *church's* meal – but only and always for the sake of the world. The Eucharist is for the church an intimate, even *romantic* encounter with her betrothed, and just in this way remains necessarily 'closed' to those who are not baptized into intimacy with Christ. At the same time, the Eucharist is for the world – that is, all created reality, seen and unseen, heavenly and earthly – a kind of enacted prolepsis of the feast which God intends for all to share in, and so must necessarily be kept 'open' to them. What, then, is the implication for contemporary sacramental thought and practice? The Eucharist must always be experienced and explained as in some sense a *missionary* meal that precisely in its strangeness draws all people to Christ, and precisely in its mysteriousness reveals God truly.

5

TOWARD A PENTECOSTAL THEOLOGY OF THE LORD'S SUPPER: DISCERNMENT AND CONSTRUCTION

Introduction

To this point in the tradition's theological history, there have been few attempts to articulate a distinctly Pentecostal theology of the sacraments. Those attempts that have been made are often brief, engaging many of the more difficult and perhaps most important issues only in passing, if at all. What is more, many if not most of these attempts have been carried out in exclusively baptistic terms, with all of the emphasis falling on the memorialist dimensions of the Supper. It is unsurprising, then, that many contemporary Pentecostals[1] – perhaps even the great majority – consider the sacraments mere ordinances,[2] holding participation in the Eucharist-event as

---

[1] As the survey of literature (Chapter 2) has made clear.

[2] Kärkkäinen ('The Pentecostal View', pp. 118, 121-22) finds that at least at the grass-roots level, most Pentecostals continue to assume a 'nonsacramental Zwinglian and free church view' of the sacraments; he also believes the movement is 'loaded with antisacramental sentiment'. Similarly, the British Pentecostal Richard Bicknell ('In Memory of Christ's Sacrifice', pp. 67, 76) finds that Elim Pentecostals' view of the Lord's Supper is staunchly 'anti-sacramental', and, in his opinion, reduces Zwinglian 'bare commemoration' to something even more memorialistic. In ecumenical discussions with Roman Catholicism, a vocal minority of Pentecostals have insisted that the Lord's Supper is 'more than a reminder of Jesus' death and resurrection', that it is in fact a 'means of grace'; the majority of Pentecostal representatives have held what some have criticized as a 'too-evangelical' (i.e. more or less strictly memorialist) view of the Supper. See William G. Rusch and Jeffrey Gros (eds.), *Deepening Communion: International Ecumenical*

nothing more than 'an outward response to an inward grace that has already been received'.[3] This is, however, all out of sorts with the views and practices of early Pentecostals, as shown in the exploration of early Pentecostal sacramentality (Chapter 3).[4] And more and more Pentecostals have begun taking up the task of developing[5] an authentically Pentecostal sacramentality, one shaped by specifically Pentecostal concerns and resources.[6] My own construction is a species of this kind, and it is characterized by three distinguishing marks. First, my approach takes the fathers and mothers of the Pentecostal movement as major conversation partners, allowing their peculiar emphases and characteristic insights to inform both

---

Documents with Roman Catholic Participation (Washington, DC: USCCB Publishing, 1998), pp. 386-87; Anderson, *An Introduction to Pentecostalism: Global Charismatic Christianity*, p. 253.

[3] Biddy, 'Re-envisioning the Pentecostal Understanding of the Eucharist', p. 229. Biddy spells out the core convictions of this memorialist position: 'It is understood that we undertake these particular actions simply because they are ordinances of dominical institution: Jesus instructed us to carry them out, and so we do, but our obedience in that regard does not create the occasion for a dispensation of grace; the grace – which, in a usage not uncommon to post-Reformation thought, refers almost strictly to the forgiveness of sins – has already come to us before our responsive action, and does not come thereafter or therein'. Obviously, this position has been defended rigorously by many Pentecostals, perhaps especially by those who most closely identify themselves with Evangelicalism. For example, see Pruitt, *Fundamentals of the Faith*, p. 365 and Menzies and Horton, *Bible Doctrine*, p. 111; Hunter, 'Reflections by a Pentecostalist on Aspects of BEM', pp. 317-45; Hunter, 'Ordinances, Pentecostal', pp. 947-49.

[4] This research has dramatically (re)shaped the way I think and feel about the Lord's Supper, and so has determined what I intend to propose in this chapter regarding its meaning and significance for Christian life. Needless to say, my construction would have looked drastically different if I had written it before or without attending to the early Pentecostal material in the way I have done.

[5] Or at least they have been working to lay the groundwork for such a development to take place.

[6] For example, John Christopher Thomas ('Pentecostal Theology in the Twenty-First Century', pp. 3-19) and Ken Archer ('Nourishment for Our Journey', pp. 79-96) have offered descriptions of the sacraments under the rubric of the Five-fold Gospel. Wesley Scott Biddy ('Re-envisioning the Pentecostal Understanding of the Eucharist', pp. 230-31), whose thesis is largely indebted to the pioneering work of Frank Macchia, has proposed a Pentecostal sacramentality that begins with 'an account of sacraments as events of a divine-human encounter that take place through symbols' because he believes that Pentecostals have at their disposal two primary resources for 're-envisioning' the Lord's Supper: first, the belief that 'divine-human encounters take place in, with, and under *signs*' – as in Macchia's claims about *glossolalia* – and, second, the conviction that these moments of encounter are moments in which God 'dispenses *grace*' – albeit not the forgiveness of sins.

the profile and the substance of my construction. Second, the hermeneutical model laid out in the first section of Chapter 4 (and exemplified in the bulk of the rest of the chapter) affords me the ability to 'hear' a wide range of Scriptural texts, which in turn provides me with a rich treasure from which to fund my theological construction. Third, my construction is shaped and sourced by my experience in the local Pentecostal community where I have served as a lead pastor, a community where participation each week in the Lord's Supper is a central and centering act of our worship. Energized and oriented by these resources, this chapter is intended to put forward a constructive and revisionary proposal for a theology of the Lord's Supper that engages discerningly in dialogue with partners inside and outside the Pentecostal tradition while remaining consistent and continuous with Pentecostal spirituality.[7] Informed by the work already done, it is evident that my account must necessarily be a vibrant and full-bodied one if it hopes to remain true to the biblical witness and the Pentecostal tradition.

Finally, I need to offer a couple of clarifying remarks about the methodology I am putting to use in this chapter. First, in the process of working out my account of the Supper's meaning, I engage in critical conversation with dialogue partners selected from the length and breadth of the wider Christian tradition – Protestant, Orthodox, and Catholic, historical and contemporary. In the conversation, I attempt to take seriously their insights, carefully discerning how their work instructs and/or confirms a genuinely Pentecostal theology of the Sacrament. Second, I move through my construction in three primary stages, slowly moving into ever-deeper waters (as in Ezekiel 47), dealing, first, with the fact of the Eucharist's mandated place in the Christian life *coram deo*; second, with the ways in which God has promised to act salvifically in and upon us through the sacrament of Communion, and, third, with discerning reflections on how it is that God fulfills these promises of transformation.

---

[7] In this construction, I am trying to model all-at-once what Rowan Williams calls the three modes of theology: celebratory, communicative, and critical. See Rowan Williams, *On Christian Theology* (Oxford: Blackwell, 2000), p. xiii.

Prescription: What Is Required of Us?

'*Do* This': The Lord's Supper as Divine *Lex*

We begin where most early Pentecostal accounts of the Lord's Supper began – with Jesus' *command*: 'Do this …'[8] We begin here because as Pentecostals we recognize that response to divine command is fundamental to our way of life, to our very being, in fact.[9] This, then, has to be for us the first word: the Eucharist is a *mandated* rite. Christian communities from the first have observed this meal in keeping with Jesus' words and acts at the Last Supper.[10] In keeping with this tradition, early Pentecostals – at least very many of them – observed the Eucharist regularly and with great expectation.[11] For us, then, both as Pentecostals and as Pentecostal Christians, the way is unmistakably clear and straight: the celebration of Holy Communion belongs at the center[12] of our life with one an-

---

[8] See for example Seymour's comments in *AF* 1.10 (Sept 1907), p. 2. Also, Michael Welker, *What Happens in Holy Communion* (Grand Rapids: Eerdmans, 2000), pp. 62-63 and Jenson, *Visible Words*, pp. 62-64.

[9] In Chan's (*Liturgical Theology*, p. 75) words: 'Life, as God originally intended it, is meant to be wholly sacramental, wholly oriented toward thanksgiving (*eucharistia*). Redemption restores the basic Eucharistic nature of life, so that we may once again eat and drink to the glory of God'.

[10] Jenson (*Visible Words*, p. 62) notes that the Eucharist is 'exactly as old as the gospel itself, and its centrality in the church's life is uninterrupted'.

[11] In the words of an early Assemblies of God Sunday School lesson, 'There are two ceremonies the observance of which is obligatory on Christians, because divinely ordained: they are Water Baptism and Communion. Because of their sacred character, distinguishing them from man-devised rites, they are known as "sacraments," which means literally, "sacred things," or "oaths consecrated by holy ceremonies." See *PE* 1098 (May 11, 1935), p. 8.

[12] Richard John Neuhaus ('Passion for the Presence: The Eucharist Today', *Currents in Theology and Mission* 5.1 [Feb 1978], pp. 6-7) explains what it means to use this language: 'I recognize the danger is speaking of "the center" in this way. Theologians have a way of focusing on one theme or aspect of Christian existence and claiming it is the whole. Thus it is said the whole of Christian existence is encompassed in baptism, or in the understanding of faith, or of hope, or of the cross, or of the resurrection, or of whatever. Such monothematic claims, while understandable, are highly problematic. But when one says the eucharist is the center of the Church's life it excludes or shortchanges nothing, for the eucharist is the presence of Christ among his people, and surely Christ must be the center of the Church's life. Nothing that is appropriate to the Christian reality is foreign to the Eucharistic celebration'.

other before God in the world.[13] If we refuse to eat and drink the bread and wine, then we have no right to claim that we believe in him, as John 6 makes clear. We can no more shirk Holy Communion than Israel could have refused Sabbath observance or the celebration of the festivals without in this very refusal betraying her vocation and identity.[14] As A.J. Tomlinson said, those who refuse the ordinances cannot hope to receive God's blessing.[15]

Of course, this command, like all God's commands, is to be heard by us as *invitation*.[16] As people baptized into Christ, we have been filled with the Spirit who himself is the New Law 'written in our hearts', so that we naturally delight in the law of the Lord (Psalm 1). God's *lex* is never for us burdensome or taxing, but is always received as graceful direction toward the richer, ever more joyful life promised to and purposed for us.[17] Besides, in submitting to the mandate we are not merely obeying, but are also *imitating* Christ, following his example, and in the mimetic process are being

---

[13] Simon Chan (*Liturgical Theology*, pp. 63-66) insists that Word and Sacrament belong together, and that we must not think of the Supper as either *optional* or *marginal*; in his words, 'there is no sound basis for relegating it to a once-a-month ritual'.

[14] What of those who refuse to follow the mandate? Can and should Pentecostals believe that disobedience in this matter is fatal? Can and should Pentecostals teach that the sacraments are the (exclusive) ways in which God does God's work? According to M.A. Tomlinson (*Basic Bible Beliefs*, p. 56), 'If such terrible vengeance were pronounced upon those who failed in the observance of the Passover, how much more do we displease God if we fail to commemorate the death of His Son who was wounded for our transgressions...', a commemoration that takes place at the Table. However, John Wesley is reported to have said that he would as soon be a Deist as a Quaker, but he would not accept the claim that the Quakers would be damned for their rejection of the sacraments. Wesley scholar Randy L. Maddox (*Responsible Grace: John Wesley's Practical Theology* [Nashville: Abingdon, 1994], p. 195) explains that Wesley 'refused to confine God's grace in either direction – whether by excluding it from all created means or by restricting it to certain authorized means'. This stance, Maddox points out, arose from Wesley's pnuematologically-shaped soteriology. 'If grace is the uncreated personal Presence of the Holy Spirit, then while it surely can be mediated through created means (for these are products of God's gracious activity in creation), it need not be confined to such means'.

[15] *COGE* 8.39 (Oct 6, 1917), p. 1.

[16] In the words of Robert W. Jenson (*Story and Promise: A Brief Theology of the Gospel about Jesus* [Philadelphia: Fortress Press, 1973] p. 84), 'The morality of the gospel-promise is the morality of what we *may* do because Jesus lives'.

[17] As Sergius Bulgakov (*The Comforter* [Grand Rapids: Eerdmans, 2004], pp. 311-13) makes clear, true obedience is necessarily always also an expression of *freedom*.

made like him. In Ken Archer's words, partaking of the Sacrament is a 'redemptive experience', uniquely providing worshippers with the occasion for the 'ongoing spiritual formation of being conformed to the image of Christ by encountering the Spirit of Christ through the *participatory enactment*[18] of the story of Jesus'.[19]

This is so, first, *liturgically*. As the bread is taken and God's blessing is invoked over it, as the bread is broken for us and as we partake of it, we are re-enacting the Last Supper and the agonizing events of Christ's last days.[20] At the same time, in the very same movements, we also are *pre*-enacting the marriage feast that is the joy of the eschatological kingdom of God. This liturgical practice reminds us that all of our life is meant to be lived *imitatio Christi*: 'As he is so are we in this world' (1 Jn 4.17). Therefore, although it begins liturgically, it can never be *limited* to that. All of our lived lives in their complex and often prosaic entirety are to be offered up to God. Like Christ, we are *always, everywhere* sacrificing ourselves—for God, one another, and the world.

'Do *This*': The Lord's Supper as Great Thanksgiving

Clearly, then, we are bound to observe the Lord's Supper. It remains less clear, however, *what* exactly we are to do in this observance. What is the 'this' that has been mandated? In a word, it is a ritual,[21] communal meal of thanksgiving and *koinonia*.[22] Believers

---

[18] Again, Jenson (*Story and Promise*, p. 171) suggests that '… the Eucharist is the only dramatically developed enactment of the gospel's whole recollection and whole promise. Other churchly performances enact [only] particular functions in the life of the gospel.'

[19] Archer, 'Nourishment for Our Journey', p. 85. Emphasis added. It is difficult to discern exactly what Archer means when he speaks of 'sacramental ordinances'. He appeals to Grenz who affirms the Radical Reformers' reaction against the Scholastic 'overemphasis on the sacraments and the magical understanding of their workings' but denounces the rationalistic impulse that strips the ordinances of any divine effectiveness. Grenz attempts to find a *via media* between medieval sacramentalism on the one hand and rationalistic memorialism on the other. Archer, apparently, occupies that middle ground, too. One wonders if this middle ground is firm enough to build on, however.

[20] Obviously, the one who presides at the Supper plays the role of *Christ*, and the rest of the community, the role of the *apostles*, a fact I will return to in a later section.

[21] Speaking of the Eucharist as a 'ritual meal', I intend to emphasize the pre-established, formalized patterns of speaking ('On the night he was betrayed …') and acting (the actual eating and drinking) that give the meal its recognizable structure in and for the worshipping community. This is in keeping with Albrecht's definition (*Rites in the Spirit*, p. 22): 'ritual connotes those acts, actions,

are required by Christ's mandate 'to share bread and drink together from one cup, as fellowship in the praise of God'.[23] When we do this – and *only* then – 'an event occurs to which eschatological promises "come", to create a sacrament'.[24] As Pannenberg has it, the church gathered at the Table, offering a shared, communal thanksgiving, finds itself there 'at-oned' with Christ: 'Precisely by the celebrating of the Lord's Supper as Eucharist, in the form of thanksgiving, the church thus follows what Jesus himself did and shares in the relation of Jesus to the Father articulated therein'.[25]

But *how* are we to give thanks? As a community in one heart and mind, with words and with the bread and the wine[26] offered and received in conformity with the rubric laid down by Scripture.[27] In this regard, two points need emphasizing. First, our thanksgiving falls to the ground if we are not making every effort to live together as one body, as a genuine covenant-community. Of course, this is *not* to say that only the already-perfected community can rightly celebrate the Supper, for the Eucharist is meant to *make* us one, to incubate and nurture and perfect our unity, as 1 Cor. 10.16-17 makes clear. However, it *is* to say that we cannot hope to discern faithfully the Lord's body in the bread and wine if we are not striving to live at peace with one another both before we come to the Table and after we leave it.[28] Second, in spite of the fact that

---

dramas and performances that a community creates, continues, recognizes and sanctions as ways of behaving that express appropriate attitudes, sensibilities, values and beliefs within a given situation'. See also Cartledge, *Testimony in the Spirit*, pp. 39-45.

[22] Jenson (*Visible Words*, p. 68) observes that 'the [biblical] texts mandate thanksgiving, with sharing of bread and cup'. He is also right that for our thanksgiving to be what Scripture requires it to be, it must include in some way all of these factors: 'doxology, recitation of saving history, and eschatological invocation'.

[23] Jenson, *Visible Words*, p. 69.

[24] Jenson, *Visible Words*, p. 74.

[25] Wolfhart Pannenberg, *Systematic Theology* (3 vols.; London: T&T Clark, 2004), III, p. 305.

[26] Perhaps a word about the bread and the wine themselves is in order at this point. Early Pentecostals discerned that each 'element' symbolizes/signifies different dimensions of the one event of the Supper. The bread, they believed, is the locus of Christ's body broken for our *healing*, while the cup serves as the locus of Christ's blood shed for the *sins* of all.

[27] To speak of '*the* rubric' is not to downplay the diversity of the biblical institutional accounts, but only to emphasize their basic harmony.

[28] Welker (*What Happens in Holy Communion*, pp. 56-59) warns against thinking of the Supper as *only* a thanksgiving meal.

thanksgiving comes 'naturally' to us as Pentecostals, it should be maintained that our praise should remain always anchored to and in harmony with the Communion rite. And this means, in turn, that liturgical exactness is required – not in a legalistic way, of course, but because, as Jenson rightly sees, 'Scripture's sacramental promises are about acts we are bidden to do; if we do not do them, there is nothing for the promises to be about'.[29] More specifically, because of what is at stake (really and symbolically), we, like our early Pentecostal mothers and fathers, can and should insist that a single loaf and a single cup are used and that the congregation are given both broken bread to eat and wine to drink.[30] Contrary to the thought of much popular piety – a piety that afflicted some sectors of early Pentecostalism and continues to trouble the contemporary movement at various points – it *is* necessary to go through the ritual motions of giving and receiving the loaf and cup, following a liturgical rubric. The *actual* eating and drinking are *not* superfluous activities, and talk of eating Christ's flesh and drinking his blood must never be cut off from the rite of receiving the cup and the loaf. 'The eating and drinking are the heart of the Supper as sacrament.'[31] Sharing in the meal, celebrants are 'completing the significance of the signs'.[32] If they do not go through the motions of enjoying the meal, then they do not in fact believe God's promises, for 'the act of faith and the act of taking, chewing, and swallowing are one act'.[33] As a result, the attempt of some Pentecostals to separate the *believing* in the benefits of Christ's passion from the actual *receiving* of the loaf and the cup must be judged as a serious error.[34]

---

[29] Jenson, *Visible Words*, p. 70. He continues (*Visible Words*, p. 74), 'If, of course, we do not do what we are told to, there is nothing more to be said about the Supper, since no Supper occurs'.

[30] That is, we must offer the Supper in 'both kinds', i.e. both the loaf and the cup are to be shared and received, and we are not allowed to substitute other 'elements' for them; e.g. water cannot substitute for the wine. Again, early Pentecostal leaders were quite emphatic on this point, and rightly so. See, for example, *PHA* 3.11 (July 10, 1919), p. 2. For a qualifying position, see Welker, *What Happens in Holy Communion*, pp. 79-82.

[31] Jenson, *Visible Words*, p. 106.

[32] McCabe, 'Eucharistic Change', p. 220.

[33] Jenson, *Visible Words*, p. 107. This means that the effort to say that Christ is really present *only* in the heart or in the gathered community and *not at all* in the bread and wine is misguided.

[34] F.F. Bosworth (*LRE* 6.9 [June 1914], p. 3), to take but one example, made just this separation. This claim appears to be peculiar to the Finished Work tradi-

Now, it perhaps should almost go without saying that healing *may* come through other means than participation in the Lord's Supper, and that healing *may* occur in the context of the Eucharist-event apart from the actual eating and drinking. The point remains, however, that believing in the healer – not the *healing!* – symbolized in the broken bread cannot be sharply separated from the act of actually eating the bread. It is unacceptable that some Pentecostals talk as if the receiving of the loaf and the cup were entirely super-fluous, as if their value is entirely symbolic. Those who have faith to receive healing (or whatever grace comes from God) are those who obey. Those who believe, *eat*.

Of course, liturgy must be S/spirited. The liturgical giving and receiving must remain in every way consonant with the Spirit-fired truth the Eucharist itself signifies and accomplishes, for without doubt apart from the Spirit's intercession all our liturgical efforts, however exact and seemingly inspired, are in the final analysis futile and inane. As Moltmann says, the meal 'becomes a *feast* when this gratitude is expressed not only in official liturgies but in the free utterance of those who meet at the table and their spontaneous joy'.[35] Donald Gee said it well: only a 'fresh Unction' can preserve the weekly Communion celebration from becoming 'mere cus-tom'.[36] Still, spiritual fervor cannot make up for theological or ethi-cal misrepresentation of the gospel embodied in the Eucharist-event. For priests to offer 'strange fire' in God's presence (Lev. 10.1-3) is deadly, now no less than then.[37]

In spite of what many Pentecostals fear,[38] this insistence on li-turgical exactness does not necessarily hamper, much less extin-

---

tion and to have no parallel in the Wesleyan-Holiness literature of the period, presumably because of the differing theological assumptions that underlie the two streams of early Pentecostalism, as Alexander (*Pentecostal Healing*, pp. 230-42) has argued.

[35] Jürgen Moltmann, *The Church in the Power of the Spirit* (Minneapolis: For-tress Press, 1993), p. 257. Emphasis added.

[36] *PE* 894 (April 18, 1931), p. 2.

[37] Some Pentecostals (e.g. Slay, *This We Believe*, p. 98) hold that if believers are truly led by the Spirit there will be no need for any liturgical forms to guide Chris-tian worship. This mindset perhaps arises from a (mis)reading of Acts that leads to the assumption that the Spirit's leading is so clear, so overpowering, that it becomes virtually impossible to err. On this, see the insightful critique of Sergius Bulgakov, *The Comforter* (Grand Rapids: Eerdmans, 2004), pp. 288-89.

[38] See, for example, Amos Yong, *Discerning the Spirits* (JPTSup 20; Sheffield: Sheffield Academic Press, 2000), p. 165; Warrington, *Pentecostal Theology*, p. 169;

guish, spontaneous, Spirit-impelled activity. Against those Pentecostals who believe liturgical order unnecessary and dangerous,[39] we should insist that the proper use of liturgy rightly orients Pentecostal worship and so powerfully invigorates it. Against those who believe the service needs to be *designed* to 'bring the symbols to life',[40] we should maintain that the sacraments live already by virtue of God's word of promise and the Spirit who brings those promises to reality. Given the history of Christian practice, it would appear that without predetermined rites and practices shaped to focus attention on the God of the once-delivered faith, celebrants run the risk of losing themselves in their own world,[41] effectively alienating themselves from the gospel's concreteness and specificity. In fact, as Simon Chan[42] and Jamie Smith have argued,[43] a proper ritual grounding promises to safeguard and reenergize the improvisational quality of Pentecostal spirituality.[44] So long as our praise remains grounded and centered in the mandated ritual words and actions, we are free to 'improvise', to express in any number of ways our thanks to God for God's good works toward us.

Turning, then, to another basic question: What are we giving thanks *for*? In a word, for God's 'mighty acts'.[45] We come to the Table, gathered by the call of Christ and the gospel of the kingdom, and in our sharing of the wine and bread say our thanks in the Spirit to God for Christ – and in Christ for all things in this age and the age to come.[46] These mighty acts for which we praise God include all that God has done both in creating and sustaining creation and in saving it from sin and death and bringing it into its perfection. In

---

Daniel Castelo, 'The Improvisational Quality of Ecclesial Holiness', in John Christopher Thomas (ed.), *Toward a Pentecostal Ecclesiology: The Church and the Fivefold Gospel* (Cleveland, TN: CPT Press, 2010), p. 89; Peter Althouse, *Spirit of the Last Days* (JPTSup 25; London: T&T Clark, 2003), p. 98.

[39] As seen for example in Slay, *This We Believe*, p. 98.

[40] See Yong, *Discerning the Spirits*, p. 165.

[41] What Jenson specifies as 'religious self-concentricity'.

[42] See Chan, *Liturgical Theology*, pp. 41-61.

[43] See Smith, *Desiring the Kingdom*, pp. 131-214.

[44] See Castelo, 'The Improvisational Quality of Ecclesial Holiness', p. 89.

[45] Jenson, *Visible Words*, p. 68.

[46] As we will discuss later, this 'we' includes not only those of us in a particular local congregation, but every member of the church, wherever and whenever the member is in time or space. The Eucharist, however uneventful it might seem to lookers-on, is nothing less than a *cosmic* event.

this connection, it bears pointing out what may seem to some brutally obvious: the bread and wine are gifts of *creation*, both natural and cultural, and by virtue of Christ's and the church's words[47] they come to signify God's atoning act in Christ. Moltmann says it well: 'the feast of Christ's fellowship is the great thanksgiving to the Father for everything he has made in creation and has achieved in the reconciliation of the world, and has promised to accomplish in its redemption'.[48]

Although praise and thanksgiving come easily to Pentecostals, as has been said, the Orthodox tradition has much to teach us about the ontological depth of our praise. As Schmemann insists, the Eucharistic thanksgiving is nothing less than 'the experience of paradise',[49] for in the offering of thanksgiving, we find what we were made for – true knowledge of the God for whom we were made and in whom we 'have our being'. Receiving the bread and the wine thankfully, we rise to heaven, entering the divine presence.[50]

> Thanksgiving is the 'sign', or better still, the presence, joy, fullness, of knowledge of God, i.e. knowledge as meeting, knowledge as communion, knowledge as unity. Just as it is impossible to know God and not give him thanks, so it is impossible to give him thanks without knowing him. Knowing God transforms our life into thanksgiving, and thanksgiving transforms eternity into life everlasting.[51]

---

[47] It also bears pointing out that words belong uniquely to humanity's creatureliness.

[48] Moltmann, *The Church in the Power of the Spirit*, p. 256.

[49] Alexander Schmemann, *The Eucharist: Sacrament of the Kingdom* (New York: SVS, 1987), p. 174.

[50] This may not be the sensual or psychological *experience* of the participants – or the interpretation they give to their experience – but it is in fact what Scripture promises to be true nonetheless. In Christian worship – and this necessarily includes our gathering at the Lord's Table – we have come 'to Mount Zion and to the city of the living God, the heavenly Jerusalem, and to innumerable angels in festal gathering, and to the assembly of the firstborn who are enrolled in heaven, and to God the judge of all, and to the spirits of the righteous made perfect, and to Jesus, the mediator of a new covenant, and to the sprinkled blood that speaks a better word than the blood of Abel' (Heb. 12.22-24).

[51] Schmemann, *The Eucharist*, p. 176. What, for Pentecostals, could be more important than this 'knowledge'? If the Eucharist can initiate us into that knowing – as I, with Schmemann, believe it can – then how could we refuse it a central place in the worship of our community?

It is for this reason that, in the words of Scripture, we enter God's gates with thanksgiving.

Anamnesis: the Eucharist as Locus of Memory-in-Hope

The Lord's Supper is a meal of remembrance. In giving thanks with our bodies and the bodies of the bread and wine, we are in some sense *re-calling* Christ. This is the import of speaking of the Supper as *anamnesis*. But what does it mean to 'remember' Christ thankfully?

In the first, most obvious sense, we are remembering Christ as he *was*.[52] At one level of significance, the Eucharist simply directs our attention to the historical realities of the life of one Jesus of Nazareth, to his subversive table-fellowship and his Last Supper,[53] and to the event of what the church understands as his once-for-all agonizing death for us and for the world.[54] Briefly said, in celebrating the Communion rite we are reminded of those decisive past events experienced by Jesus in Nazareth and Galilee, in Jerusalem's streets, the upper room and outside the city's walls. In the present-day liturgical breaking of the bread and offering of the cup, we 'see' Christ crucified before our very eyes (Gal. 3.1) and 'hear' his death proclaimed (1 Cor. 11.26).[55] As early Pentecostal theologian Myer Pearlman put it, the Supper is 'the most impressive means for continually presenting before our minds and hearts the central fact of

---

[52] This assumes that the Lord's Supper brings Christ to *our* remembrance. However, it is also in some sense a bringing of Jesus to mind *for God* (Jenson, *Visible Words*, pp. 72-73). In Communion, we *petition* God to bring Jesus' victory to bear on our lives and our world. In taking and giving the bread and wine, we *pray* for the kingdom to come, in fact; it is an embodied, dramatically enacted *Marana Tha!* Neuhaus ('Passion for the Presence', p. 15) has it right: 'In that Eucharistic *maranatha* is discovered the fullness of the Church's mission, to sight, signal, support and celebrate the coming of the Kingdom'.

[53] Not this only, however. Given Christian theological convictions, to speak of Jesus' life is also to speak of the life of the eternal Word; therefore, in Communion, believers are remembering not only the so-called 'historical Jesus', but also his work in creation and in the playing out of creation's history. This means, among other things, that *all* of Jesus' table-fellowship – including the theophany meals of the Old Testament – lie at the roots of the church's Eucharistic practice.

[54] In the words of Donald Gee, the Supper 'center[s] the thought upon Christ'. See *PE* 894 (April 18, 1931), p. 2.

[55] Williams (*Renewal Theology*, III, p. 245) maintains that 'The Lord's Supper is the recollection and showing forth of Christ's death ... a perpetual memorial to the sacrificial death of Christ'. It is also an 'affirmation of a historical event', a reminder of and 'reaffirmation of God's new covenant in Jesus Christ'.

His life'.[56] In this way, believers-in-community are narrated into the grand story of creation's salvation, a story whose central characters are the Triune God, Israel, and the Church. As Rowan Williams points out, the practice of Holy Communion 'presupposes a connectedness with the history of the covenant people' and for many reasons it is especially at the Lord's Table that that connectedness makes itself real and (sometimes at least) felt as such.[57]

At another level, this *anamnesis*[58] is never merely memorialistic because we are also remembering Christ as he *is*: the once-dead, now-risen-and-enthroned one.[59] In the words of D.W. Kerr, the early Assemblies of God evangelist, while the Sacrament is rightly understood as a memorial, a proclamation, and an expression of our hope in Christ's *parousia*, it is above all a way of Christ's immediate presence to the church. '*Here* is the present tense of Calvary.'[60] To 'remember' rightly, then, is to receive the meal in such a way that Christ is present to us and the benefits of his victorious death are made effective in our lives.[61] It does this by drawing the believing community into authentic and transformative encounter with the Spirit-mediated presence of the living Christ – the one who is by God's free decision never without the church and creation. In the Eucharistic encounter, believers are bound together not only with Christ, but also with one another and with the whole of created reality, for Christ is κεφαλή of the church as his body (Eph. 1.22; Col. 1.18) and the ἀρχή of the new creation for the church's sake (Eph. 1.21; Col. 1.18).

As just mentioned, for some people (at least some of the time) participation in the Eucharist-event involves the awakening and intensification of sacred affections, the 'passion for the kingdom' in

---

[56] *PE* 1077 (Dec 8, 1934), p. 9. As seen in Chapter 3, this conviction that the Supper points us both to the past and to the future is characteristic of early Pentecostal thought. See, for example, *AF* 1.4 (Dec 1906), p. 2.

[57] Rowan Williams, 'The Bible Today: "Reading" and "Hearing"'. Available online: http://www.archbishopofcanterbury.org/1718. Accessed March 12, 2011.

[58] As Macchia (*Baptized in the Spirit*, p. 252) says, 'Without Jesus as the Spirit Baptizer, there is no clear link between the *anamnesis* and the *epiclesis*. In fact, the *anamnesis* is fulfilled in the *epiclesis* in the light of Jesus' resurrection from death to mediate the Spirit'.

[59] In agreement with, among others, Archer, 'Nourishment for our Journey,' p. 96.

[60] *WE* 162 (Oct 28, 1916), p. 4.

[61] See Biddy, 'Re-envisioning the Pentecostal Understanding of the Eucharist', pp. 234-36.

Land's memorable phrase. Holy Communion – the whole event of churchly participation in the meal, as well as the bread and wine in and of themselves – is a 'visible word' (*verba visibilia*) that brings the gospel of Christ's victory forcefully to bear on the minds and hearts of the participants,[62] awakening in the participants the (re)new(ed) conviction that Jesus is cosmic *kyrios*, head of the church,[63] and archetype of new creation, stirring up in them a (re)new(ed) desire and determination to conform their lives to the reality the gospel reveals.[64]

At still another level, we 'remember' Christ as he *shall be*. 'The anamnesis looks more to the future than to the past, it is an eschatological formula.'[65] As early Pentecostals often pointed out, the church's celebration of the Lord's Supper is always carried out in the light of the eschatological messianic banquet, the promised and expected 'marriage supper of the Lamb'. We remember Christ as the one who in the Eschaton is everything to everyone, the πλήρομα who gives life – *his* life – to all creation. Pannenberg, then, is right to insist that the Lord who is present at the Table is 'the one who died on the cross',[66] but he is wrong to say that Christ is present '*only* by means of recollection of the historical Lord who went to his death'.[67] What happens in the Eucharist-event is not only 'recollection of the earthly story of Jesus and his passion', but also is in some real sense the 'descent' of the enthroned Lord, the coming of Christ to the church in and with the bread and wine given and received in thanksgiving for the one was, is, and is to come.

At his Last Supper, Jesus promised not to eat the meal again 'until it is fulfilled in the kingdom of God' (Lk. 22.16-18). According to the Fourth Gospel, he promised his disciples he would raise up at the last day those who eat his flesh and drink his blood (Jn 6.39-40).

---

[62] In the words of an early Pentecostal minister (*COGE* 1.10 [July 15, 1910], pp. 1-2), the Lord's Supper provides 'a broader view of the Christ and wonderful scheme of redemption than ever before'.

[63] This is in keeping with the instruction of Myer Pearlman: 'The Head of the church will Himself administer the Sacrament, as we receive Him by faith'. See *PE* 1479 (Sept 12, 1942), p. 2.

[64] Of course, this awakening and conviction, this ambition and resolve are never human achievement, but always come as a gift from the divine Spirit that enables authentic response.

[65] Neuhaus, 'Passion for the Presence', p. 15.

[66] Pannenberg, *Systematic Theology*, III, p. 311.

[67] Pannenberg, *Systematic Theology*, III, p. 312.

In the words of the apostle Paul, when the church celebrates Holy Communion faithfully, she proclaims Christ's death 'till he comes' (1 Cor. 11.26). It comes clear, then, that the Eucharist is uniquely the event in which Christ's past, the church's present, and creation's future come together – if only mysteriously and hiddenly.[68] In the very act of remembering in our words and actions the unspeakable horrors of Good Friday, we proclaim the unspeakable good news of the reign of the one whom God 'gave up' for us and for all creation so that through him sin might be finally put away and death utterly destroyed in the End. In remembering this way, we orient ourselves to the promised future. As Jenson says, the Eucharist is not only a restaging of the table fellowship of Christ's pre-Easter ministry, but also an 'acted-out promise of the last fellowship'.[69] When the church enacts the liturgy 'in the right spirit' she enters into 'play with the Trinity', and just so anticipates 'life in the Fulfillment'.[70] Simon Chan agrees: 'In the eucharistic worship of the church, the Spirit actualizes the past through remembrance (*anamnesis*) and anticipates the future (*prolepsis*) when created things are transfigured ...'[71] In the liturgical event, heaven and earth touch,[72] the 'now' of our history opens up to the 'then' of holy week and the Eschaton.[73] What is more, given that this is true – that this 'opening up' of earth to heaven in the Eucharistic moment indeed takes place – then it seems most fitting to say that the bread and wine themselves are also taken up in this event and are made replete with new creation reality, as are the (faithful) participants. They too are

---

[68] See Welker, *What Happens in Holy Communion*, pp. 131-32.

[69] Jenson (*Visible Words*, p. 79). He continues, 'To be brought into the fellowship of this Supper is to anticipate belonging to the fellowship of the kingdom; it is bodily promise of that belonging'.

[70] Jenson, *Story and Promise*, p. 184.

[71] Chan, *Liturgical Theology*, p. 37.

[72] Jenson (*Systematic Theology* [Oxford: OUP, 1999], II, p. 251) defines heaven as 'the place of the future as this is anticipated by God' and then describes it in this way: '... sacramental events make the boundary between our world and heaven, marking it by the "visible" objects they involve. Just as they are the embodied presence to our world of what is in heaven; in the present context, they are the embodied presence of the risen Jesus and the Kingdom he presents to the Father in the Spirit, as these are anticipated for the Father by the Spirit.'

[73] N.T. Wright, *Surprised by Hope: Rethinking Heaven, the Resurrection, and the Mission of the Church* (New York: Harper Collins, 2008), pp. 271-75.

baptized in the glory of new creation[74] – hiddenly to be sure, but really and transformatively.[75] How can we consistently affirm that new creation comes to the celebrants in the Eucharist while denying that it comes to the other creatures they have brought to bear in their thanksgiving?

Even if his account of the Supper is lacking in some respects,[76] what Moltmann says of the relation of the Eucharistic *anamnesis* to the future hope of creation remains instructive. In his view, the Eucharist ultimately takes its shape not from a historical-critical reconstruction of the institution of the Supper at Jesus' last meal with his disciples or even from a theological account of the relationship of the Eucharist to the events of Good Friday, but from the church's hope in the coming kingdom of God and the eschatological banquet – a hope that Christ's resurrection alone engenders and undergirds.[77] 'It is not the historical remembrance as such which provides the foundation for the Lord's supper, but the presence of the crucified one in the Spirit of the resurrection.'[78] The Lord's Supper is first and foremost 'the sign of remembered hope',[79] and the 'eschatological sign of the coming kingdom in history'.[80] In other words, the Supper is the celebration of the hope the kingdom and new cre-

---

[74] Metropolitan John D. Zizioulas (*Lectures in Christian Dogmatics* [London: T&T Clark, 2008], p. xxi) suggests that in the Eucharist-event, 'material creation is able to sing the praises of God and so participate *through us* in the freedom of God'. Emphasis added.

[75] T.F. Torrance (*Atonement: The Person and Work of Christ* [Downers Grove, IL: IVP, 2009], p. 307) suggests that baptism and the Eucharist 'enshrine together the two essential "moments" of our participation in the new creation …' While they can agree that the sacraments do in fact provide this momentary participation, Pentecostals would *not* limit participation to these two sacraments.

[76] Perhaps because it is exaggeratedly more Lukan than it is Pauline or Johannine in its theological emphasis and orientation.

[77] So he says (*The Church in the Power of the Spirit*, p. 251), 'the history of Christ's passion is proclaimed in the Lord's supper … The connection between eating and drinking in the kingdom of God and the gift of his given body and his shed blood becomes clear. At long last we no longer have any need to seek for a historically dated institution for the Lord's supper, nor must we confine its christology to a founder christology. The Lord's supper is, with inner, factual cogency, the expression of the eschatological history of Christ – that is to say, the dawn of the kingdom of God in his self-giving and his resurrection from the dead'.

[78] Moltmann, *The Church in the Power of the Spirit*, p. 250.

[79] Moltmann, *The Church in the Power of the Spirit*, pp. 246-52.

[80] Moltmann, *The Church in the Power of the Spirit*, p. 251.

ation Jesus promised to bring.[81] To be sure, Moltmann believes that it is right to remember the salvific events on Golgotha, but in spite of the fact that the Supper 'points expressly to the one who was crucified', Luther insists that the one who actually is present to the church in Communion is the risen Lord of creation's *future*.[82]

> ... the manifestation of the crucified Jesus in the fellowship of his body and his blood takes place in no other way than through himself, the exalted one ... The fellowship of the table with the one who was crucified for us once and for all, takes place in the presence of the one who is to come; and it is therefore, as fellowship with the crucified Jesus, the anticipation of the coming kingdom. In the one who is to come the one who died for us is present in our midst.[83]

Each Eucharistic celebration, then, is a foretaste of the new creation – God's mercies are new each time (Lam. 3.23). In this light, it is easy to see why Moltmann believes the church's meal should be eaten with joy and 'gladness of heart' – striking a harmony with the Lukan theology of the Eucharist outlined in the previous chapter. 'The feast is a bond with the kingdom',[84] and precisely for this reason, is the feast of gratitude and joy.[85] '[T]his meal is a messianic party "in" the kingdom, in which Jesus joins anew.'[86] As Pentecostals, how could we not join in such a party? The Pentecostal habit of explosive praise is nothing if not an anticipation of the glories of the Eschaton.

---

[81] In much the same way, Schmemann (*The Eucharist*, p. 210) contends that the Eucharistic remembrance is not primarily a remembering of Christ's Last Supper or of the events on Golgotha, but a 'remembrance of the kingdom of God' that Jesus conferred on his apostles (and so on the church throughout history) on the night of his betrayal (Lk. 22.29-30).

[82] In support of these claims, Moltmann works out a rather elaborate theory of eschatological time. See Moltmann, *The Church in the Power of the Spirit*, pp. 253-56. See also Welker, *What Happens in Holy Communion*, p. 97.

[83] Moltmann, *The Church in the Power of the Spirit*, p. 254.

[84] Moltmann, *The Church in the Power of the Spirit*, p. 250.

[85] In Moltmann's (*The Church in the Power of the Spirit*, p. 257) view, 'Just because the fellowship in the supper is a remembrance of Christ's death as the ground of liberation and reconciliation, this remembrance can only be gratitude; and this gratitude will be as wide and as all-embracing as the liberating reconciliation itself. It comprehends the whole of creation in representative thanksgiving and intercession and awaits its coming redemption'.

[86] Jenson, *Visible Words*, p. 78.

At the end, all creation's voices will praise God in chorus, the created historical powers among them. Insofar as we now at the Supper anticipate the end, we anticipate that chorus. But we can do this only as we *let go* of our praises, only as we sing and let our song rule what we say, only as we speak a little bit 'in tongues'.[87]

And yet – is this view not woefully one-sided? Is the Supper not at least sometimes a moment for solemnity, for sorrow even, and contrition?[88] If a *Lukan* theology of the Eucharist emphasizes the ecstatic nature of Christian table fellowship, perhaps a predominantly *Pauline*-informed theology of the Eucharist puts the focus elsewhere, encouraging introspection and careful 'discerning of the Lord's body'? If so, how do we decide between the two views? J. Rodman Williams suggests that one simply follows the other:

> … we initially come to the Lord's Supper with solemn, and indeed penitent, hearts. To be sure, there is the ensuing joy of fellowship with Christ and anticipation of His coming again, but this joy can occur only against the solemn background of knowing that both the broken bread and the cup of wine represent the awesome and terrifying death of Jesus Christ our Savior. We must first share with Christ in His death, partaking of the symbols of that death in order to rejoice in his life.[89]

This strikes me as not quite right, for at least two reasons. First, I would want to say that there need not always be a progression from contrition to joy, from solemnity to elation. Instead, there may be times in which the entire Eucharistic-event is an occasion for deep sorrowing and contrite self-critique, and, at other times, the entire event may be in fact a time of joyous, even raucous celebration.[90] Second, I would insist that the hope-inspired joy of intimacy with God in the future at-one-ment of all things is *never* merely foregrounded against the sufferings of Christ. If anything, the very opposite is true. The sufferings of Christ are what they are on-

---

[87] Jenson, *Visible Words*, p. 97.
[88] Certainly, many early Pentecostal testimonies point up these dimensions of Eucharistic experience.
[89] Williams, *Renewal Theology*, III, p. 246.
[90] For example, J.H. King (*PHA* 2.49 [Apr 3, 1919], p. 6) speaks of 'the thrill of unspeakable ecstasy' occasioned by the Supper.

ly when seen in the light of the news of Christ's resurrection. Good Friday is *good* only because Easter follows and redefines it, and the church's message is good *news* only if the Eschaton vindicates our witness.

If Pentecostals are to receive the Supper rightly, to let it be all that God intends that shared thanksgiving to be, then we must give ourselves to Spirit-led discernment. In and throughout each Eucharist-event, the congregation must carefully follow the Spirit's leading, discerning together what it is Christ intends to do in and for them in that moment. Without doubt, the Eucharist can and should be experienced at times as a feast of joy and at other times as a sobering and even sorrowful event, one that moves celebrants to new dimensions of compassion with God and one another. In truth, however, there is no way to *pre*determine what the event might mean for a particular congregation at a particular moment. God's ways are not our ways and God's work is always more than we can grasp. It follows, then, that some participants may feel *nothing* at the Table while others may be overwhelmed with feeling. Neither experience can be established as the norm. Those who feel only the absence of God's presence have not necessarily received the bread and wine in vain, and those who have been deeply moved by the experience of God's presence nonetheless cannot comprehend the breadth and depth of God's work in them in that moment.[91] Yes, 'To love God is to be shaped by that love so as to share its affections and passions',[92] but the love with which we love and are loved is *divine*, so our affections and passions are ultimately powerless to grasp what it is that has taken us and now holds us fast.

A final word in this regard: insofar as our Eucharist is a faithful thanksgiving, then the event is nothing less than a rite of covenant renewal.[93] As we give thanks for God's covenant-making acts, of-

---

[91] As Macchia (*Baptized in the Spirit*, p. 254) explains, '… the experience of God in the sacrament is deeper than that which I may consciously feel or understand, for God is the one who is able to do "immeasurably more than we ask or imagine" (Eph. 3.20). The Spirit's involvement in the Lord's Supper transcends time but also human rationality and speech. Like art, these rituals bear more meanings than we know'.

[92] Macchia, *Baptized in the Spirit*, p. 264.

[93] Williams (*Renewal Theology*, III, p. 245) sees this as especially signified in the cup: 'Thus the cup at the Lord's Supper is the vivid symbol and continuing reminder of that new covenant, which Christ's death made possible. Hence every celebration of the Lord's Supper is a reaffirmation of God's new covenant in

fering up and receiving these gifts of bread and wine – gifts carried along by and embodying the sacrifice of our praise – we are also promising that we will continually offer *ourselves* to God, as *living sacrifices* (Rom. 12.2). At the Table, 'in the presence of God with our sacrifices of praise and thanksgiving for the Sacrifice of Calvary',[94] we are dialoguing with God, saying our Amen to his promise, our Yes to his graceful command.

Promise: What Does God Do For Us?

'I Am with You': The Lord's Supper and the Church's Communion with God

As witnessed by scores of testimonies,[95] early Pentecostals came to the Lord's Table not only impelled by the desire to obey but also drawn by the hope of blessing[96] in the 'sweetness of the sacred presence',[97] confident that the divine mandate is at its depth always energized by divine promise.[98] They gathered in joyfully expectant worship to 'put His promises to the test'.[99]

But *has* God in fact promised anything to those who celebrate Communion?[100] Yes: God has promised Christ and the Spirit.[101] To

---

Jesus Christ'. See also, Donald L. Gelpi, *Committed Worship: A Sacramental Theology for Converting Christians* (Collegeville, MN: Liturgical Press, 1993), II, p. 233.

[94] Arrington, *Christian Doctrine*, III, p. 212.

[95] As Yong (*Spirit-Word-Community*, pp. 249-50) explains, a theology of the Eucharist must take seriously 'the Church's reflecting on its *actual experience* of the Eucharist throughout history'.

[96] Both the impelling and the compelling forces are the Spirit's work, of course.

[97] *PHA* 2.16 (Aug 15, 1918), p. 7.

[98] They believed, for instance, that Scripture promised bodily healing as well as spiritual nourishment. In holding that no command is without promise, they would have agreed with Dietrich Bonhoeffer (*Sanctorum Communio* [*Dietrich Bonhoeffer Works Vol. 1*; Minneapolis: Fortress Press, 1998], p. 244): 'This free gathering together to eat from the table of the altar is not a self-chosen but rather an obedient symbolism, and *thus it has the warrant that God will act in it*'.

[99] *WE* 131 (Mar 18, 1916), p. 13.

[100] As seen in the examination of the early periodical materials (Chapter 3), the first generation of Pentecostals believed that Christ (and/or the Spirit) was actively present to them in their celebrations of the Supper. This is true of most contemporary Pentecostals, as well, as evidenced in review of literature (Chapter 2). Of course, most Pentecostals then and now would insist (1) that this *would not* happen if the participants came to the Table faithlessly and unprepared; (2) that Christ is present in other ways, apart from the Sacrament; and (3) that Christ's (and/or the Spirit's) presence is never so much *in* the bread and the wine as in

push the question further, we might ask if is there anything *unique* and irreplaceable in the Supper? Again, yes. Nearly half a century ago, A.D. Beacham Sr., then an official in the PH church, put the point clearly and precisely:

> The communion that a person enjoys in the proper observance of this worship is *necessary* to victorious Christian living. As one considers the death of the Lord and becomes a partaker of that death, there is experienced a consecration and submission to God that cannot be found in any other experience.[102]

Of course, communion with Jesus *exceeds* the encounter of the Eucharist-event,[103] but it is never wholly *separate* from it. Partaking of the Sacrament is indispensable to the life of 'feeding on Christ' because it makes possible a partaking in Jesus' death and his life not realizable otherwise.[104]

So, the Eucharist-event occasions, first, the *communion* of God and Human. At the Table, there is experienced a moment of genuine divine-human encounter, an intimate exchange between the Triune God and the *ecclesia* gathered in his name.[105] In the words of E.N. Bell, the Lord's Supper is always more than a memorial because '*Jesus is there in the Spirit* to bless, quicken, uplift and heal' the

---

the 'midst' of the congregation. In other words, while they affirm that Christ (and/or the Spirit) is present to the celebrants, they maintain that Christ can draw near with or without the Sacrament, and that this drawing near is not so much *through* the elements as *alongside* them. Perhaps it is precisely at this point that the most careful but drastic revisioning of the tradition is required.

[101] As the New Testament witnesses, the Father sends the Son by the Spirit and the Spirit by the Son. In other words, Jesus is both the Spirit-bearer *and* the Spirit-baptizer.

[102] *PHA* 49.16 (Aug 14, 1965), p. 9. Emphasis added.

[103] Bulgakov (*The Comforter*, p. 303) contends that while 'the life of grace in the Holy Spirit' comes in the life of the church with its sacraments and prayers, it also comes by 'direct illumination', for 'there is one active Spirit and the grace bestowed in the sacraments continues to operate *beyond the limits* of their immediate celebration'.

[104] Although he does not single out the Lord's Supper specifically, Pentecostal Holiness theologian Noel Brooks (*Scriptural Holiness* [Franklin Springs, GA: Advocate Press, 1967], p. 51) shows how Pentecostals can hold the work of the Spirit in sanctification in tightest possible relationship with the church's public ministries: 'This is the mighty ministry of the Holy Spirit in the Church; and this is its objective and goal, the formation and development of Christ in human personality and character'.

[105] In agreement with, among others, Biddy, 'Re-envisioning the Pentecostal Understanding of the Eucharist', p. 233.

gathered saints. Seen in this light, it comes clear that Jesus' words spoken over the bread of his Last Supper – 'This is my body' – reveal how he keeps his final pre-Ascension promise, 'I am with you always, till the end of the age' (Mt. 28.20), a promise that depends upon Pentecost and the Father's and Son's sending of the Spirit, the ἄλλον παράκλητον. In the Eucharist-event, the church encounters the risen and enthroned Christ who is present by the agency of the Spirit.[106] At the Table, believers come face-to-face with 'the spiritually present living Christ'.[107]

If at first this seems overstated, remember that Holy Communion, as a 'visible word' spoken to God from the church and to the church from God serves as genuine *conversation* between God and God's people, a divine-human dialogue of heaven and earth. In their celebration, believers speak to God[108] a 'visible word' embodied in the offering and receiving of the bread and wine. As Paul says, in rightly celebrating the Supper the church 'proclaims' Christ crucified. Moreover, God speaks to the church in and by the same bread-and-wine-embodied 'word', and in this way re-minds the *ecclesia* of Christ's victorious sacrifice.

The decisive question, then, is this: What *is* this 'word' spoken and heard, given and received? At one level, it is merely the semiotic import of the elements themselves. In other words, the 'word' is what the meal means for the participants. At another level, however, this word is – Christ himself![109] He is the meal's meaning, the

---

[106] As seen in the previous chapter, G.F. Taylor, editor of the PH *Advocate*, explains the relation of Christ and Spirit in the Eucharist in these terms: 'as we partake of the bread and wine, our souls feed on the flesh and blood of Jesus Christ, brought to us through the Holy Ghost'. See *PHA* 3.11 (July 10, 1919), p. 2. A.S. Copley, speaking more broadly of the Christian spiritual experience, expresses a similar conviction: 'Jesus is the food, the Holy Ghost the feeder'. See *The Pentecost* 1.2 (Sept, 1908), p. 7.

[107] *WE* 146 (July 1, 1916), p. 8.

[108] They also speak to one another, to those outside the church, and to the powers (both seen and unseen).

[109] What is the justification for claiming this other 'level' of meaning? (1) The words of Jesus himself; (2) the witness of the church's theological traditions, and especially the Patristics; (3) the testimony of early Pentecostal experience, and (4) the theological fittingness of the claim. The sacrament is a means of salvation precisely because it perfectly signifies what salvation is: the consuming and being consumed by Christ. It would be nothing less than a cheapening of God's wisdom and power to say otherwise.

significance of the signifier.[110] As he said, 'This is my body ... my blood'.[111]

To keep the focus on this *communio* with and in God realized through the church's celebration of the Lord's Supper, one must be careful to speak of Jesus' personal presence in the Eucharist-event.[112] It cannot be overstated: *Christ* is present – and not merely 'grace' as abstracted, impersonal 'essence'.[113] In the words of Nicholas Cabasilas, 'That of which we partake is not something of His, but Himself'.[114] 'The gift is the giver; the giver is the gift.'[115] Also, because Jesus Christ is eternally the one whom God raised from the dead, he is *bodily* present[116] – he could not be present otherwise and remain himself.[117] Bonhoeffer, drawing on the resources of his Lutheran sacramental tradition, presses this very point home, insisting that Jesus Christ is '*completely* present in the Sacrament, neither his

---

[110] In this, I am drawing on the Lutheran tradition that holds preaching and the Eucharist in the closest possible connection. The one Word of God – Jesus – comes both to preaching and to the Sacrament. See especially Dietrich Bonhoeffer, *Christ the Center* (New York: Harper & Row, 1978), pp. 49-58 and Jenson, *Visible Words*, pp. 3-25. At least two provisos are required. First, for Pentecostals, 'Word' includes more than preaching and 'preaching' includes more than the sermon; second, the whole of Christian worship cannot be reduced to Word (even in this expanded sense) and observance of the Sacrament; the Spirit cannot be proscribed in these ways. Given the infinite creativity of the Spirit, there are potentially a *limitless* number of 'means of grace'. That said, any means the Spirit might use would of course be used in ways consonant with the dynamics of the Lord's Supper.

[111] Chan (*Liturgical Theology*, p. 141) avows that 'The rite of Holy Communion that the church observes is not a result of some historical event that eventually produces a commemorative event. It is not the creation of the community but the creation of Jesus Christ himself. He instituted it because he actualized or fulfilled the reality that the bread and wine symbolize.'

[112] See Biddy, 'Re-envisioning the Pentecostal Understanding of the Eucharist', p. 230.

[113] In a *PHA* article, E.L Boyce, a PH pastor, affirms the Calvinist view as the one best fitted to Pentecostals: '... the communicant, through the operation of the Holy Spirit, comes into spiritual contact with *the entire person of Christ* and he is thus fed unto life eternal'. See *PHA* 46.46 (Mar 23, 1963), p. 15.

[114] Nicholas *The Life in Christ* IV.1 ([Crestwood, NY: SVS Press, 1998], p. 115).

[115] Welker, *What Happens in Holy Communion*, p. 93.

[116] This is an ecumenically agreed-upon claim. See Welker, *What Happens in Holy Communion*, pp. 95-99; Herbert McCabe, 'Eucharistic Change', *Priests and People* 8.6 (June 1994), pp. 217-21, and Pannenberg, *Systematic Theology*, III, pp. 311-26.

[117] See Welker, *What Happens in Holy Communion*, pp. 93-99.

Godhead alone, nor only his humanity'.[118] For Bonhoeffer, the critical question is not *how* but *who*, and there can be no doubt of Christ's identity: 'The complete person of the God-Man is present, in his exaltation and humiliation'.[119]

At the Table, therefore, believers personally and corporeally encounter the once-dead, now bodily-risen, wounded-but-glorified eternal Word 'so very real and near'.[120] Leaving aside (for now) questions of *how* Christ is so present and what this presence means for the bread and the wine in themselves, we can confidently affirm with early Pentecostals that Christ is really and effectively present in and at the Supper[121] to commune with us – to touch us, and to be touched by us.[122] As Amos Yong has argued, the event of Communion brings into focus the 'inter-subjective mutuality' Christ shares with his church, so that through the agency of the Spirit the Eucharist 'becomes a mysterious interpersonal encounter wherein Christ and his body are brought into real relationship' with each other.[123] We can and should affirm, then, that by the power of the Holy Spirit the church's sacramental participation is nothing less than 'the gate of heaven' (Ps. 118.20)[124] through which believers

---

[118] Bonhoeffer, *Christ the Center*, p. 53. Emphasis added.

[119] Bonhoeffer, *Christ the Center*, p. 57.

[120] *PHA* 7.31 (Nov 29, 1923), p. 7.

[121] Of course, Christ is present everywhere – this is what it means for him to be 'seated at the right hand of God the Father Almighty'. However, Christ is *uniquely* present at and in the Eucharist. He is not exclusively present there, of course; he is present in other sacraments, too including preaching, as well in ways beyond the sacramental. As Macchia (*Baptized in the Spirit*, p. 255) phrases it, 'the Eucharistic mode of God's presence, though special, is continuous with all other modes' of God's presence. It is this *continuity* that must be emphasized. Early Pentecostals talked often of the 'continual feast' they enjoyed, and contemporary Pentecostals are right to maintain this emphasis. However, we must be careful always to ground that talk in actual, regular Eucharistic participation. For by participation in the concreteness and specificity of the Eucharist-event the Spirit inscribes in us the very character of Christ, and so sensitizes us to the ways of God.

[122] Yong (*Spirit-Word-Community*, p. 258) notes: '... the community of faith gathers around the Lord's Table to celebrate Jesus as the object of faith on the one hand, and fellowship with him in an interpersonally subjective manner on the other. It is this Jesus who is preached, and in that proclamation draws near to us'.

[123] Yong, *The Spirit Poured Out on All Flesh*, p. 164. Whether Yong intends it or not, it is perhaps always best to hear talk about to 'the body of Christ' as having multiple references, as it apparently does in 1 Cor. 11.27-34. On this, see Thomas, *Devil, Disease and Deliverance*, pp. 47-50.

[124] Early Pentecostals often spoke of heaven 'coming down' to them in their celebration of Communion. See *AF* 1.2 (Oct 1906), p. 4; *TBM* 3.51 (Dec 1,

enter boldly into Christ's presence and Christ enters humbly into theirs.

But because the Supper is Christ's, it occasions not only believers' communion with God but also believers' communion with one another. Indeed, this is one communion in Christ, for, as David Coffey rightly sees,

> ... the sending of the Holy Spirit upon the Church by Christ, begun at Pentecost and continued over the centuries through the Church's ministry of word and sacrament, is *nothing other than Jesus' love for his brethren*, an essential dimension of his love of the Father.[125]

It is that love, that very Spirit, whom celebrants receive, are again and again newly filled with, as they faithfully receive the gifts of the Altar. This is the very reason Paul found the Corinthians' failure to live in just harmony with one another so troubling: their schisms were an egregious violation of the very reality the Supper embodies and effects.

'Sharing in the Body and Blood': The Lord's Supper and Our Salvation

To be in Christ's presence is to be *transformed*, for he is always present in transformative power.[126] Accordingly, the church's celebration of the Supper occasions nothing less than an atoning, *taboric* communion with Christ who in himself by the Spirit is both redeemer and redemption, sanctifier and sanctification itself. In the

---

1909), p. 4; *PHA* 2.27 (Oct 31, 1918), p. 12. This language recalls Luther's theology of the church and sacraments. Reflecting on Gen. 28.17, he insists, 'Direct your step to the place where the word resounds and the sacraments are administered, and there write the title THE GATE OF GOD'. Quoted in Jonathan D. Trigg, *Baptism in the Theology of Martin Luther* (Leiden: Brill, 1994), p. 20. As Trigg explains, Luther affirmed the rite of washing as 'one of those places where God wills to be found, a divinely appointed "trysting place" for the encounter of God and man'. By all accounts, early Pentecostals availed themselves of this gate, and found God to be exactly where the Scriptures promise God will be.

[125] David Coffey, 'The "Incarnation" of the Holy Spirit in Christ', *Theological Studies* 45 (1984), p. 478.

[126] This is another way of saying he is present in the *Spirit*. Also, as seen in Chapter 3, this was a characteristic emphasis of early Pentecostal theological reflection on the meaning of the Supper. Mary Boddy, for example, speaks of the 'wonderful power of His precious Body being given for us'. See *Confidence* 7.8 (Aug 1914), p. 150. See also *COGE* 5.31 (Aug 1, 1914), p. 6; *PHA* 1.45 (Mar 7, 1918), p. 16; *PHA* 5.30 (Nov 23, 1921), p. 4.

Eucharist-event, the presence of Christ affects us at the depths of our humanity[127] so that we in fact become partakers of the divine nature (2 Pet. 1.4).[128] Through Holy Communion,[129] we are assimilated to the divine life.[130] By the δύναμις of the Spirit, Christ's grace 'penetrates our very being, unites us to one another and transforms us into him'.[131] That is to say, Christ *both* humanizes us *and* deifies us.[132] So we can ask: What is the Eucharist for? And answer: To make us holy with Christ's own divinely human holiness.[133]

---

[127] Many, perhaps most, early Pentecostals believed that the Lord's Supper was a means of healing. When taken in faith, the bread, which signifies 'his body broken for our bodies', effects physical healing. Less often, they talked of the Supper as a means of sanctification as well. To be clear, by 'sanctification' I mean to name the entire process of being saved, of being conformed to the image of Christ by being drawn into the life of the Triune God.

[128] Myer Pearlman makes just this connection. See *PE* 1077 (Dec 8, 1934), p. 9; *WE* 170 (Dec 23, 1916), p. 8. In this, Pearlman sounds very much like John of Damascus (*Exact Exposition of the Orthodox Faith* 4.13) and Cabasilas (p. 113), who says: 'But when He has led the initiate to the table and has given him His Body to eat He entirely changes him, and transforms him into His own state'. In similar fashion, C.E. Bowen, Church of God (Cleveland, TN) minister in the 1950's, could speak of the need for communicants to 'realize while we eat the bread we are being partakers of divine life' and the 1916 Assemblies of God Statement of Fundamental Truth includes this statement: 'The Lord's Supper … is the symbol expressing our sharing the divine nature of our Lord Jesus Christ, 2 Pet 1.4; a memorial of his suffering and death, 1 Cor. 11.26; and a prophecy of His second coming, 1 Cor. 11.26; and is enjoined on all believers "until he comes"'. At times, for some at least, this talk could move away from explicit connection to the Communion. For example, a contributor to *PE* (964 [Sept 3, 1932], p. 3), reflecting on Jn 6.35, boasts that 'The Holy Ghost would lead us to gather around this Lamb in fellowship and communion, feeding upon Him, being partakers of His divine nature'.

[129] Again, not *only* through Communion. Central as it is to Christian life, the Lord's Supper is one among other 'means of grace'.

[130] See Elena Vishnevskaya, 'Divinization as Perichoretic Embrace in Maximus the Confessor', in Michael J. Christensen and Jeffery A. Wittung (eds.), *Partakers of the Divine Nature: The History and Development of Deification in the Christian Traditions* (Grand Rapids: Baker Academic, 2007), p. 139.

[131] Bonaventure, *Breviloquium*, VI.9.3 (Works of St Bonaventure Vol. IX; Saint Bonaventure, NY: Franciscan Institute Publications, 2005, p. 241). Similarly, Jenson (*Systematic Theology*, II, p. 299) explains that in the event of justification '… Christ himself becomes the subject by whose liveliness I am what I am', so that, through the mediation of the Spirit, 'the Christ who is *what* I am is the Christ who is *who* I am'.

[132] In other words, Christ makes us like he is without in any way obliterating the creator-creature distinction. As Macchia (*Justified in the Spirit*, p. 31) sees, 'Jesus as the man of the Spirit in communion with the Father thus reveals both God and ideal humanity at the same time'. This confirms both the word of Athanasius (*On the Incarnation* 54.3) – God became human so that the human might become

Of course, having made such a claim we are then left to ask *how* exactly participation in the Eucharist-event accomplishes the Christification of the church and its members. First, it does so by enflaming believers' passions for God and the kingdom. By awakening this desire for full and immediate communion with God, the Spirit begins to conform believers to the *imago dei*.[134] On this score, Bonaventure provides a key insight. He identifies the Eucharist as 'the sacrament of communion and love' that 'enkindles us toward mutual love' of God and one another.[135] In his explanation, the saving transformation that takes place in and among us is nothing less or other than the outcome of the 'burning love'[136] that Christ imparts to us in Communion. The bread and wine are like the burning coal put to the prophet's lips (Isaiah 6)[137] or the lover's kiss (Song 1.1) that draws the believer into the embracing bliss of intimacy with God.[138] Obviously, this resonates nicely with the tenor of Pentecostal spirituality, which is characterized by this very passion for

---

a god – and Bonhoeffer – God became human in order than the human might become human.

[133] Rowan Williams (*On Christian Theology*, p. 197) notes that '… what makes sacraments distinct is what they are for, the activity in which they are caught up, which is making human beings holy'.

[134] In Macchia's words (*Baptized in the Spirit*, p. 281), 'God as a self-giving fountain of love poured out abundantly begins to shape us into something similar. Jesus pours out the Spirit so that the Spirit may pour forth in our empowered love for others. We become "Spirit-baptized personalities"'.

[135] Bonaventure, *Breviloquim* VI.9.3 (p. 241).

[136] Bonaventure, *Breviloquim* VI.9.3 (p. 241). Also, Bonaventure (*Breviloquim* VI.9.6-7) believes that Paul's warning against partaking unworthily (1 Corinthians 11) is a caution against eating and drinking 'with lukewarm, irreverent, and unthinking hearts'.

[137] John of Damascus uses this very image: 'Let us draw near to [the Eucharist] with an ardent desire, and with our hands held in the form of the cross let us receive the body of the Crucified One: and let us apply our eyes and lips and brows and partake of the divine coal, in order that the fire of the longing, that is in us, with the additional heat derived from the coal may utterly consume our sins and illumine our hearts, and that we may be inflamed and deified by the participation in the divine fire'. See *Exact Exposition of the Orthodox Faith* 4.13 in *NPNF*, 2nd series, vol. 9 (Grand Rapids: Eerdmans, 1983), p. 83.

[138] Many ancient and medieval writers took up this image, including, for example, Ambrose, Bishop of Milan, and William of St. Thierry. See Owen F. Cummings, *Eucharistic Doctors: A Theological History* (Mahwah, NJ: Paulist Press, 2005), p. 69; Elizabeth Saxon, *The Eucharist in Romanesque France: Iconography and Theology* (Woodbridge, Suffolk, UK: Boydell Press, 2006), pp. 105, 202.

God's presence and by the fervent love for neighbor and enemy engendered by the genuine encounter with God.

Somewhat paradoxically, however, this sanctifying work also happens by the quenching of the 'fleshly' appetite for God's presence and blessings. In this way, the Eucharist is for Christian pilgrims what the manna was for the wilderness-bound Israelites. Although real and effective, Christ's presence in Communion is and remains *hidden* – in a sense, unexperiencable. Not from any lack of divine power or due to anything like divine capriciousness, but just so that we may act in faith, and in so acting, develop the character of Christ.[139] Christ's hiddenness is a gift that opens up for us the possibility of transformative, deifying faith-acts. As John 6 teaches, Christ's Eucharistic promise is purposefully *scandalous*, and to accept his words as true, believers must humble themselves, throw off everything except trust in and fidelity to Jesus as the Word. Glorious as it may be, the Eucharist is a form of Jesus' ongoing humiliation in this time before the ἔσχατον.[140] In Bonhoeffer's words, Christ humbles himself as creature in the Sacrament and in so doing makes it so that only those who humble themselves in response may receive him and his life.[141] This comes right to the heart of what the Eucharist is for. As G.F. Taylor puts it, the Communion rite is designed 'to humiliate us, to teach us the spirit of Jesus, and to unite us as a church in the spirit of fellowship'.[142] The second and third of these transformations simply *cannot* happen without the first.

How can it be that God transforms us both by enflaming our passions *and* by simultaneously humbling us? How can both be true at the same time? Because the Jesus who is present in humiliation is none other than the Christ of new creation,[143] and the Spirit who makes Jesus' presence possible and effective is none other than the eschatological Spirit, the Spirit of Jesus' resurrection and the restitu-

---

[139] See Bonaventure, *Breviloquim* VI.9.4-5.

[140] In Bonhoeffer's own words (*Christ the Center*, p. 54), 'The sacrament is not God becoming Man, but the humiliation of the God-Man'.

[141] Bonhoeffer, *Christ the Center*, p. 58.

[142] *PHA* 3.11 (July 10, 1919), p. 2.

[143] As Bonhoeffer, (*Christ the Center*, p. 58) explains, 'The Christ present in the sacrament is the creator of this new creation and at the same time a creature. He is present as our creator, who makes us into new creatures. But he is also present as the humiliated creature in the sacrament and in no other way. Thus is he present'.

tion of all things.[144] The Eucharist itself, then, is a new creation event, a sign and foretaste of the Eschaton, and to take the loaf and cup in faith is to receive an ontologically-transforming proleptic share in the metaphysics of the life everlasting.[145] 'God brings the future down to the present tense'[146] and in this way *eschatologizes* us, just as he does the bread and the wine.[147] We partake of a 'sacramental oneness' that speaks of the not-yet realized 'unity of heaven and earth and all humanity in Christ as the *omega* of all existence (Rev. 1.8)'.[148] At the Lord's Table, we share in the Spirit and just in this way taste the heavenly gift and the powers of the world to come (Heb. 6.4-5).[149] For this reason, the church can avow with Irenaeus that in partaking of the Eucharistic 'bread of heaven', believers' *bodies* are already being transformed by the sacramental reality and readied for the Resurrection, at the end of all things.[150]

We must be careful, however, not to adopt a hypertrophic *theologia gloriae* that causes us to forget that the triumphant Christ who comes from the new creation in the Spirit to us at the table is even yet the *crucified* one, and that partaking faithfully of the Eucharist, believers therefore are filled again and again with the Spirit of the

---

[144] 'In the Spirit we participate in the righteousness yet to come in the new creation and in ultimate communion because of our participation in the crucified and risen Christ' (Macchia, *Justified in the Spirit*, p. 294).

[145] Welker (*What Happens in Holy Communion*, p. 122-23) suggests that 'Inasmuch as the Supper is a foretaste, inasmuch as the shadow of the proclamation of Christ's death still lies over it, the Supper points to the path and the distance which lie between us and the fulfillment of God's rule … The celebration of the Supper proclaims Christ's death as long as the fullness of creatures, the fullness of times and worlds cannot join in the heavenly doxology before the face of God.'

[146] Archer ('Nourishment for Our Journey', p. 86) explains, 'During worship "time and space [are] fused and transcended in the Spirit" through proleptic foretastes of the coming promise and through the recapitulation of past biblical experiences'. He also cites Land (*Pentecostal Spirituality*, p. 55) approvingly: 'Pentecostals [travel] in the Spirit forward or backward in time – back to Sinai, back to Calvary, back to Pentecost – forward to Armageddon, the Great White Throne Judgment, the Marriage Supper of the Lamb'.

[147] As Bonhoeffer (*Christ the Center*, p. 65) says, in the Sacrament 'elements of the old creation … become elements of the new' and by the Spirit are 'set free from their dumbness and proclaim directly to the believer the new creative Word of God'.

[148] Augustine, 'Empowered Community', p. 175.

[149] On the traces of Eucharistic theology in the Letter to the Hebrews, see Arthur A. Just, Jr. 'Entering Holiness: Christology and Eucharist in Hebrews', *Concordia Theological Quarterly* 69.1 (Jan 2005), pp. 75-95.

[150] *Against Heresies* 5.2.3.

Crucified and become more and more gifted and empowered to think, feel, and live *sub specie crucis*.[151] As the worshipping community begins to live cruciform lives, it 'puts on' its identity as a missionary people, as the *soma Christou*: the body broken and the oblation poured out for the world's salvation. Participants come to share in Christ's glory (now and in the End) precisely as they take up their cross and allow the Spirit to lead them where they do not want to go (cf. Jn 21.18-19). Disciples come to learn that precisely in humbling themselves, they are availing themselves of the glorifying mercies of God.[152]

Christ the Coming King

Talking in this way of our salvation makes possible a revisioning of the 5-fold gospel as traditionally understood. First, it makes possible a reimagining of Christ's *parousia* as not only a singular event that lies in our future – i.e. the 'second coming' that brings human history to its climax – but also as Christ's continual coming to the church in the *charismata*, in the preaching of the Word, and in the giving/receiving of the sacraments. As already described, the Christ who is present at the Table is the whole Christ, identical with the man Christ Jesus whom the Scriptures and creeds together identify as God's eternal Son, head of the church, and judging savior of the creation. This Christ, by the Spirit, comes to us over the eschatological horizon, bringing in his train all the gifts of the Day of justice and peace that are promised to us in the final establishment of the divine kingdom. In other words, Jesus is 'coming king' in the church's sacramental experience, just as he was in the incarnation and shall be in the *parousia* – with this difference only: in the End, his kingdom shall be finally and fully established beyond dispute. Hence, in the Eucharist-event believers are given a foretaste of the

---

[151] Not without reason, Cartledge (*Testimony in the Spirit*, p. 46) has suggested that 'A greater focus on the sacrament of Holy Communion' would be one way of 'renewing and reorienting Pentecostal worship and ministry, especially if this sacramental theology and practice were linked to a theology of the cross and an awareness of divine sovereignty'.

[152] This language of humbling oneself at the Lord's Table recurs throughout the early Pentecostal periodical literature. For just a couple of examples, see *PHA* 2.33-34 (Dec 19-26, 1918), p. 6 and *Confidence* 7.1 (Jan 1914), p. 11.

kingdom owing to the fact that they are being filled with the Spirit, the *arrabon* of the restitution of all things.[153]

Christ the Savior-Sanctifier

This eschatological and sacramental reimagining of the 5-fold gospel also suggests that to speak of Jesus as Savior is to say he is the one who saves by sanctifying through the deifying power of the church's sacramental life in God. In other words, sanctification names the way in which God justifies us,[154] for salvation comes not at the beginning but as the end of the process of being drawn into ontically-transformative communion with Christ. Believers are not saved (in full) until the End, when in coming face-to-face with Christ, they are made like him, finally fully conformed to his divine-human image and likeness. Now, they are *being* saved as they are being Christified, a process that comes only through the healing presence of the risen, ascended Jesus, the Spirit-baptized and Spirit-baptizing one. This, then, is the heart of Pentecostal convictions about the Lord's Supper: 'Jesus is present through the Holy Spirit during the Eucharistic meal to commune with believers, to transform them toward greater love and holiness, and to heal them in body and mind'.[155]

As Pentecostals, we have always emphasized Christ's saving work. But a renewed emphasis on the Eucharist can help us remember, in the first place, that God's salvation is not merely juridical or 'positional' but truly *transformational* and, in the second place, that this transformation necessarily comes in and through the *body* of Christ.[156] In the words of an *AF* contributor:

---

[153] Because the Spirit is the divinely-personal instantiation of the fulfillment of all God's purposes for creation. Jenson (*Systematic Theology*, II, p. 222) explains it in these terms: 'The church, we have said, exists in anticipation. What she anticipates is inclusion in the triune communion. In the End, the *koinonia* that the risen Christ and his Father now live in their Spirit will become the mutual love in which believers will limitlessly find one another. The church exists to become that fellowship; the church's own communal Spirit is sheer *arrabon* of that Community'.

[154] In this, I am drawing especially on Macchia's *Justified in the Spirit* and Jenson, *Systematic Theology*, II, pp. 289-305 in agreement with Macchia's vision of 'a Trinitarian understanding of salvation that gathers up and integrates all soteriological categories' (see *Justified in the Spirit*, p. 4).

[155] Macchia, 'Eucharist: Pentecostal', p. 189.

[156] Zizioulas (*Lectures in Christian Dogmatics*, p. 118) notes, 'There is no distance between Christ and his body in the Eucharist'.

If His flesh had seen corruption, then we could not have healing for the body nor look for another immortal body from heaven. So, dear beloved, we get healing for our body, soul, and spirit and an immortal body from heaven at His coming, through the perfect body of Jesus. Praise God![157]

Recognizing that Christ's 'perfect body' is 'the Bread of Life', the contributor declares that only by eating and drinking Christ can believers receive a share in eternal life (Jn 6.51). Thus, the believers' prayer becomes: 'May we drink His Blood daily and eat His flesh, through faith in His word, for salvation, health, and healing'.[158]

To say God saves us through the body of Christ is to acknowledge not only the centrality of the rite of the Sacrament but also that salvation is primarily and ultimately *ecclesial*.[159] The pneumatiochristic *pro me* radiates out from the *pro nobis*, and not the other way around. Personal salvation comes always in and through community, through participation in the churchly, sacramental, and missional life.[160] Apart from the church, there *is* no salvation.[161] After all, communion draws worshippers into fellowship not only with the Triune God but also with the church, and never one without the other. Jenson suggests 'churchly and Eucharistic communion are one, in that both are communion in the body of Christ'.[162] In this connection, he quotes John Damascene:

> [The Eucharist] is called 'communion' and truly it is. For through it we both commune with Christ, and share in his body as well as in his deity, and commune and are united with one an-

---

[157] *AF* 1.6 (Feb-Mar 1907), p. 2.

[158] *AF* 1.6 (Feb-Mar 1907), p. 2.

[159] As is the faith that receives and embodies this salvation; that means that the church's (collective) faith is basic to the believer's.

[160] Matthias Wenk ('The Church as Sanctified Community', in Thomas [ed.], *Toward a Pentecostal Ecclesiology*, pp. 124-26) suggests that when rightly observed the Eucharist and/or 'ecclesial meals' (along with baptism and foot-washing) are enactments of the divine acceptance that assures the genuine holiness of the community and its members, the holiness that is their (personal) salvation.

[161] George Florovsky (*Bible, Church, Tradition: An Eastern Orthodox View* [Belmont, MA: Nordland Publishers, 1972], pp. 37-38) claims that 'In the Church our salvation is perfected; the sanctification and transfiguration, the *theosis* of the human race is accomplished'. Of the ancient claim, *extra ecclesiam nulla salus*, he says, 'All the categorical strength and point of this aphorism lies in its tautology. Outside the Church there is no salvation, because salvation is the Church.'

[162] Jenson, *Systematic Theology*, II, p. 212.

other. For as we all eat of one loaf we become one body and one blood of Christ and members of one another. Thus we may be called co-embodiments of Christ.[163]

Christ the Healer and Spirit-Baptizer

If we think of sanctification (*theosis*) as the aim of all Christ's new-creation ministry to us, and of the Supper as mediating this sanctifying work, then we position ourselves also to revision the doctrines of divine healing[164] and Spirit baptism along soteriological and sacramental lines. Briefly put, we see that Jesus – the one who has come, shall come, and is coming[165] – is Savior as the one who sanctifies us by healing us and baptizing us in the Spirit in and through the Eucharist-event.[166]

To say that God saves *via* the church's Eucharistic participation is also to say that the Sacrament is rightly understood as *pharmakon*. Ignatius famously – and aptly – identified the Eucharistic grace as the 'medicine of immortality' (Eph. 20.2), and for good reason early Pentecostals insisted on the convergence between the celebration of the Supper, the work of salvation/sanctification, and the healing of the sick and diseased:[167] 'Let us take the Lamb's body, through faith in our Lord, for salvation and healing of these bodies, as we honor His blood for saving and sanctifying our soul and spirit. Amen'.[168] Of course, short of the kingdom healing remains incomplete; but it is really, already begun. Already, believers enjoy in fragmentary but real ways the restoration, newness, and wholeness promised in the

---

[163] John of Damascus, *Exact Exposition of the Orthodox Faith* 4.13; cited according to Jenson, *Systematic Theology*, II, p. 212.

[164] Cartledge (*Testimony in the Spirit*, p. 51) finds that healing is for Pentecostals perhaps *the* dominant soteriological metaphor.

[165] In other words, Jesus is 'coming king' no less in the church's sacramental experience than he was in the incarnation or shall be in the *parousia*, although at the End, of course, his kingdom shall be finally and fully established beyond dispute.

[166] Once again, let me make clear that this is not to suggest that the Eucharist-event is the *only* 'place' in which Christ meets us gracefully. It is to suggest, however, that it is unique and paradigmatic event, and in some sense the most fitting moment for transformative encounter with God. In the words of Bulgakov (*The Comforter*, p. 303), 'there is one active Spirit and the grace bestowed in the sacraments continues to operate beyond the limits of their immediate celebration'.

[167] Macchia (*Baptized in the Spirit*, p. 276) notes that William Seymour more than once speaks of divine healing as the 'sanctification' of the body.

[168] *AF* 1.4 (Dec 1906), p. 2.

Eschaton.[169] Holy Communion is one of several 'theophanic signs of glory' and as such is an 'eschatological foretaste of [the] healing and unity in the heavenly banquet'.[170]

Healing of the *body* is one manifestation of this coming fullness of life, and in this way divine healing serves uniquely as a proleptic *signum* of the Christification[171] already at work in the believer and yet to come with the full arrival of the eschatological kingdom.[172] Noel Brooks describes it in this way:

> When Jesus healed the sick He was giving to them a 'firstfruits' of 'the redemption of the body' which He was to make possible by His death. So with the healing ministry of the Apostles and their helpers: it was an 'earnest' and 'firstfruits' of final physical salvation. Every miracle of healing that the risen Lord has given through His Church on earth is a deposit and pledge of that 're-demption of the body' which He has purchased by His death upon the Cross.[173]

As seen throughout the early Pentecostal periodical literature, this healing was believed to have come through participation in the Supper. It almost goes without saying that this does not imply all those who eat in faith will be healed, and obviously Pentecostals should vigilantly guard against formulaic doctrines of the Supper that guarantee healing as a predictable, always-repeatable effect triggered by some mechanistic control. After all, it is Christ the heal*er* – not healing itself – who is present in the Eucharist-event, and he is

---

[169] Eschatological healing is *cosmic* in scope; 'all things' shall be put right, restored and perfected. 'The goal is the final new creation where righteousness dwells as well as the communion of saints at the messianic banquet where the favor and covenant faithfulness of God find fulfillment. Together as dwelling places of God, we will commune face to face with Christ and receive the vindication of our hope' (Macchia, *Justified in the Spirit*, p. 292). In the words of Elizabeth Sexton (*TBM* 3.54 [Jan 1910], p. 1), 'This final making new of all things is the end of the whole plan of the new covenant worked out'.

[170] Cartledge, *Testimony in the Spirit*, p. 185; see also Yong, *The Spirit Poured Out on All Flesh*, p. 163.

[171] This is in keeping with the early Pentecostal habit of holding healing and sanctification in the closest possible connection. See for example *AF* 1.6 (Jan-Feb 1907), p. 6.

[172] It must be said that healing is not *only* a sign. For someone to be healed now is both a fulfillment of an already-given promise and at the same time a reaffirmation of another, larger promise to heal all things in the End.

[173] Noel Brooks, *Let There Be Life* (Franklin Springs, GA: Advocate Press, 1975), p. 88.

of course there in the fullness of his freedom, wisdom, and compassion.[174] This is not only a word of caution, but also a word of reassurance and promise. Celebrants can and should come to the Table confident that the one present to them is the one who comes in the power of the Spirit to heal the sick and to deliver the oppressed.[175] Indeed, if they receive Christ's body and blood in faith, they can be sure that healing *is* taking place at the ontic depths of their being. Taking seriously the witness of Scripture and the testimony of early Pentecostal sacramental experience means believing also that this healing will sometimes 'break out' in the miraculous restoration of the ailing and diseased. In the theology of the Lord's Supper here envisioned, Pentecostal communities can and should anticipate these kinds of healings in and through the Sacrament, as well as in the broader context of the celebration.[176]

The sanctifying Christ who is present to heal is also present to baptize in the Spirit;[177] that is, to fill beyond measure the ecclesial community and its members with the inexhaustible goodness of the divine nature.[178] In Holy Communion, as believers encounter the sanctifying Christ, eating and drinking his body and blood, they par-

---

[174] As Alexander (*Pentecostal Healing*, pp. 233-34) notes, it is critical not to lose touch with the fact of God's *transcendence*. In her engagement with early Pentecostal literature, she found that Finished Work models of healing overemphasized the already-accomplished victory of Christ on the cross at the expense of the still-to-come eschatological kingdom. For obvious reasons, this way of thinking led in many cases to an exaggerated sense of the Spirit's immanence and so to a mechanistic model of healing. In the light of Alexander's arguments, it seems to me best to follow the Wesleyan-Holiness Pentecostals in thinking of healing as a sign of 'the inbreaking of the Kingdom to come' that awakens faith in the Christ whose salvation is both already and not yet come.

[175] Alexander (*Pentecostal Healing*, p. 229) explains that many early Pentecostals learned to live wisely in 'the tension between trusting Jesus as healer and knowing that not all will be healed'.

[176] If this kind of healing is *not* taking place in the context of the Supper, perhaps reflection is needed to identify why it is that the promised signs are not 'following'. See Thomas, *The Devil, Disease and Deliverance*, pp. 311-19.

[177] Chan ('Jesus as Spirit-Baptizer: Its Significance for Pentecostal Ecclesiology', in Thomas [ed.], *Toward a Pentecostal Ecclesiology*, pp. 140-41) reminds us that of all the New Testament descriptions of Jesus' identity, his identity as Spirit-baptizer is the most widely attested (Mt. 3.11-12; Mk 1.8; Lk. 3.6; Jn 1.26-27, 33; Acts 1.4; 11.16).

[178] In Macchia's (*Baptized in the Spirit*, p. 87) judgment, 'The Pentecostal belief in the connection between Spirit baptism and sanctification, on the one hand, and between Spirit baptism and the latter rain of the Spirit to end the age, on the other, can nourish an ecumenical doctrine of Spirit baptism in which many voices can have a significant role to play'.

take of the divine Spirit[179] and are baptized into the divine love[180] that God the Holy Spirit personally is.[181] It is no exaggeration to claim that all of Christ's ministries are summed up in his work as Spirit baptizer, for all that Christ does for us, he does by providing a share in the divine *energia* and in this way deifying and humanizing us.[182] Like healing, Spirit baptism names the entire complex of Christ's sanctifying ministries.[183] And because he is present in the bread and wine, so are all of his works. The Eucharist-event is the locus of all that Christ and the Spirit are and do for us.

What do these proposals mean for the distinct(ive) experience of *Spirit baptism* as traditionally understood by Pentecostals? They contextualize that experience in the larger work of Christ in the

---

[179] Irenaeus (e.g. *Against Heresies* 3.24.1 [*ANF*, I, p. 458) makes this point forcefully: communion with Christ is possible only in and with and through the Spirit. The inverse also holds true: to be filled with the Spirit is to share in Christ's life (and death), to be drawn into mutuality with Christ and so with the Triune God. Along the same lines, John Wesley spoke of drinking 'larger Draughts [*sic*] of God' and of being filled with God's own life through participation in the sacraments; see Ole E. Borgen, *John Wesley on the Sacraments* (Grand Rapids: Francis Asbury Press, 1972), pp. 208-11. This is very much in keeping with the many early Pentecostals who understood salvation as the 'increasing acquisition of God's triune life'. See Dale Coulter, '"Delivered by the Power of God": Toward a Pentecostal Understanding of Salvation', *IJST* 10.4 (Oct 2008), p. 466.

[180] See Macchia, *Baptized in the Spirit*, pp. 257-82.

[181] Jenson (*Systematic Theology*, II, p. 298) draws on and highlights a characteristic Augustinian insight: 'as the Spirit [is] the bond of love in the Trinity, so he [is] himself believers' bond of love with God and one another'. Because the Spirit is the Spirit of Christ, 'the bond of love he creates is participation with and in Christ'. Bulgakov (*The Comforter*, p. 154) makes a similar move: 'The Holy Spirit exists by virtue of the Father and the Son, as Their mutual love and as very Love for Them. In this sense, the Holy Spirit does not belong to Himself, is not His own, but is the Spirit of the Father and the Son ... But at the same time, as a hypostasis, the Holy Spirit is personal, that is, He is the Spirit contained within Himself, the Third hypostasis'. Macchia (*Justified in the Spirit*, pp. 301-303) warns that this notion needs to be carefully nuanced lest the Spirit seem to be less personal than the Father and the Son. See also David Coffey, 'The Holy Spirit as the Mutual Love of the Father and the Son', *Theological Studies* 51 (1990), pp. 193-229.

[182] Macchia (*Justified in the Spirit*, p. 74) describes it exactly: 'The Spirit-indwelt Christ baptizes us in the Spirit so that we can be taken up in him into the embrace of the divine communion'.

[183] In Macchia's words (*Baptized in the Spirit*, pp. 255-56), 'Spirit baptism is not a once-and-for-all event but an ongoing, dynamic reality that is shared in *koinonia* ...'

church[184] and in the cosmos, identifying the experience of Spirit baptism as an epiphanic manifestation of the reality of the promised kingdom and so as an eschatological sign. In the same way as those who receive bodily healing, believers who are filled with the Spirit are taken up as *signa* of the divine future in which all of creation will be enlivened by the very life of God's own Spirit.[185] The upshot is this: Spirit baptism should be understood not only as one experience alongside others – one event of the Pentecostal *via salutis* – but also as a reality that always already 'spills out' to encompass all other 'charismatic and missionary experiences that relate us to others in the church and to people in the world'.[186] On this view, Pentecostals can and should expect the Spirit to 'fall' on the worshiping community, freeing particular members to exercise the *charismata* exactly as 1 Corinthians 11 indicates. But these phenomena should be understood as witnessing to a reality that is not yet arrived in its

---

[184] Killian McDonnell, O.S.B. and George T. Montague (*Christian Initiation and Baptism in the Spirit: Evidence from the First Eight Centuries* [2nd rev. ed.; Collegeville, MN: Liturgical Press, 1994], p. 370) suggest that 'If the baptism in the Holy Spirit is integral to Christian initiation, to the constitutive sacraments, then it belongs not to private piety but to public liturgy, to the official worship of the church'.

[185] Given that Spirit baptism/infilling is an *eschatological* reality, a foretaste of the End, it is fitting that such a tight interplay exists between the infilling of the Spirit and *glossalalia*, as seen not only in the text of Acts but also in the experience of the Pentecostal communities. The phenomenon of 'speaking in unknown tongues' points to realities that 'transcend our rational or linguistic abilities', as Macchia (*Baptized in the Spirit*, p. 281) says, and in this way witnesses in its very obliqueness to the ineffable glories of the End. For these reasons, Macchia emphasizes the 'brokenness' of tongues-speech, identifying it with what Paul describes as the 'unutterable groaning' for eschatological redemption (Romans 8). Macchia ('Baptized in the Spirit: Toward a Global Theology of Spirit Baptism' in Veli-Matti Kärkkäinen (ed.) *The Spirit in the World: Emerging Pentecostal Theologies in Global Context* [Grand Rapids: Eerdmans, 2009], p. 10) also speaks of *glossolalia* as an 'ecumenical language' that shows up the shortcomings of all other languages, and 'calls into question the adequacy of human speech to capture divine mystery and lodges an implicit protest against any effort to make one language or cultural expression determinative for how the gospel is to be understood or witnessed to in the world'. Especially in light of the events described in Acts 2, one might also agree with Murray Dempster ('The Church's Moral Witness: A Study in Glossolalia in Luke's Theology of Acts', *Paraclete* 23 [1989], pp. 1-7) that *glossolalia* is the sign par excellence of God's renewal of humanity (in terms of both culture and society) in Christ.

[186] Macchia, *Baptized in the Spirit*, p. 249.

fullness but is already at work powerfully in other, hidden ways in the lives of the *ecclesia*.[187]

Claims as bold as the ones in this and the preceding sections require some attempted articulation of *how* this might be so. The next section provides just such an attempt.

Presence: How Does God Do What God Does?

Orientation

For now, Christ is in heaven, at the Father's 'right hand', as Scripture and the creeds proclaim. What sense does it make, then, to say he is bodily present in the Eucharist-event? This question lies at the heart of the controversies that long have troubled Christian thinking about the Eucharist.[188] *How* can it be true that Christ can be present in such a way in the Supper? Attempting to answer this takes one into deep, deep water; but it is a dive one can and should make.

Before offering any constructive proposals, however, a few qualifications need to be made. First, in the words of Herbert McCabe, 'anything that takes the mystery or scandal out of the Eucharist *must* be wrong',[189] because the mystery and the scandal are properly basic to the Eucharist's meaning and purpose.[190] Second, the *how* question, while important, is never as important as the question of *who* is present.[191] Even if one cannot find a satisfactory explanation[192] for the way in which the Spirit makes Christ present in

---

187 Nonetheless, if these *charismata* are not in evidence, then the community should consider seriously the possibility that their worship is somehow restraining the Spirit's grace, discerning what if anything needs to be changed in other to remain in step with the Spirit.

188 This is the question, of course, that divided the Reformers in particular.

189 McCabe, 'Eucharistic Change', p. 219.

190 Also, this mystery and scandal point to its identification with Christ himself, who as the mysterious revealer of the revealing God is the *scandalon* that brings the world into judgment.

191 As already mentioned, Bonhoeffer warns against dealing with the *how* question at all. But I will disregard that warning for now.

192 John Wesley seems to have thought that such an explanation was not only impossible but even unnecessary. According to Borgen (*John Wesley on the Sacraments*, pp. 185-86), 'Wesley needs neither a doctrine of ubiquity nor a philosophy of "substance" and "accidents" to explain this mystery' and any attempt to overcome by explanation the mystery of the Supper would necessarily prove both 'futile and purposeless'; instead, all that was necessary was the graceful experience

Communion *pro nobis*, one must be able to say that the Christ who is present is the 'whole Christ', the bodily-risen Christ who is present in his divine-human fullness as the *kyrios* of all things, the first-born of new creation, and the head of the church. Third, we must be careful not to suppose that there is an already-existing metaphysical system that can be used to once-for-all explain Christ's Eucharistic presence. If what is claimed in this chapter about the Real Presence in the church's Eucharist is true, then it is fundamentally true; and it follows, then, that 'our grasp of the Son's real body and blood is the *criterion* of all our other attempts to grasp something real'.[193] Fourth, and finally, the truth of the fact *that* Christ is present is not threatened by the shortcomings of our attempts to explain how such a thing might be true. In the end, believers simply have to step back from their books, stand or fall in believing awe – then rise and eat![194] In the wisdom of John Damascene, while we can and should affirm that the bread and wine really are 'changed into God's body and blood', we can not discover some fully-satisfying *explanation* of this change.

> But if you inquire how this happens, it is enough for you to learn that it was through the Holy Spirit, just as the Lord took on Himself flesh that subsisted in Him and was born of the holy Mother of God through the Spirit. And we know nothing further save that the Word of God is true and energizes and is omnipotent, but the manner of this cannot be searched out.[195]

---

of the celebrants: 'For him it is enough when experience proves that grace has actually been received through this means, thus proving God's promises to be true …'

[193] Robert W. Jenson, *On Thinking the Human: Resolutions of Difficult Notions* (Grand Rapids: Eerdmans, 2003), p. 57. See also Wolfgang Vondey and Chris W. Green, 'Between This and That: Reality and Sacramentality in the Pentecostal Worldview', *JPT* 19.2 (Fall 2010), pp. 243-64.

[194] Pannenberg (*Systematic Theology*, III, p. 331) insists, 'True, theological understanding, even if incomplete, is important for what the church proclaims and teaches about the Lord's Supper. Yet it is not a prerequisite of receiving it'.

[195] John of Damascus, *The Exact Exposition of the Orthodox Faith* 4.13 (*NPNF*, 2nd ser., vol. 9, p. 83). On John's theology of the Eucharist, see Geoffrey W. Bromiley, *Historical Theology: An Introduction* (Grand Rapids: Eerdmans, 1978), pp. 152-53. Similarly, John Wesley could sing: 'Who shall say how Bread and Wine/GOD into Man conveys?'

With these caveats in mind, the following construction, then, is not an attempt to 'search out' the nature of Eucharistic presence in such a way as to dispel the mystery or take the edge off the scandal. Instead, it is an attempt to gesture toward the Beauty-Holiness[196] embodied in the Supper, to provoke believing awe in those who know themselves called to the Table.

Toward a Metaphysics of Communion

This is the heart of the matter: Christ is really, personally, and *bodily* present in Communion because the Father wills it and the Spirit makes it so for the sanctification of the church on mission in the world.[197] In the Eucharist-event, the Spirit 'broods over' the cosmically-enthroned Christ, the celebrating congregation, and the elements on the Table,[198] opening the celebrants to the presence of the risen Jesus who the Spirit makes in that moment bodily present for them with, in, and through the thereby-transfigured bread and wine.

Christ is capable of this kind of presence because of the power of the eschatological Spirit and the nature of Christ's own new-creation body, which is both like and *un*like our bodies.[199] Whatever some have imagined resurrection to mean, it is not just that Jesus' once-dead body was *revived* on Easter. He received from the Father through the Spirit an entirely new form of embodiment, a σῶμα πνευματικόν that perfectly befits him in his identity as *Pantokrator*.[200] Therefore, in the End his body shall include *all things*, and in

---

[196] Bulgakov, *The Comforter*, p. 280.

[197] Obviously, to say that Christ is present by the Spirit in the rite of Holy Communion is to make a starkly *metaphysical* claim, an assertion about the nature of creaturely reality. As Williams (*On Christian Theology*, p. 209) says, Christian talk of the sacraments is 'at odds with other sorts of description' because 'the sacramental action itself traces a transition from one sort of reality to another'.

[198] In the Wesleyan tradition, there is no need to decide whether the *epiclesis* invokes the Spirit to 'fall' upon the bread and the wine or upon the celebrants themselves. For example, the Wesley brothers' *Hymns on the Lord's Supper* included a number of hymns of invocation for the Spirit upon the elements and the community alike. See Maddox, *Responsible Grace*, pp. 197-200.

[199] Whatever we mean by 'body' must include the notion of material substantiality, even – *especially*! – when we are talking of Christ's resurrected body.

[200] As Paul says, God gives bodies that fit the identity of the embodied ones (1 Cor. 15.38). Christ, as the one in whom all things hold together (Col. 1.17-18), necessarily receives a body that gives all other bodies their sanctity and eternal viability. Christ's body is inseparable from the Spirit's eschatological work of giving all other bodies their share in resurrection life. This is why the bodily-resurrected Christ is spoken of the life-giving spirit (1 Cor. 15.45). In the words

the beatific vision Christ shall be seen not only as one object among others but also as *the* object through which all other objects – and the Father and the Spirit – are somehow truly revealed. Then it shall be clear that the βασιλεία τοῦ θεοῦ simply *is* the body of the 'whole Christ'.[201] But for now, his embodiment is heavenly, sacramental, and ecclesial;[202] that is to say, his embodiment at the Father's right hand[203] *includes* the Eucharistic bread and wine, the preached Gospel, and the *sanctorum communio*,[204] and these last serve as sacraments – effective signs in the present of the future eschatological state of things.

But how can this be? One of the oldest problems in sacramental thought concerns the nature of Christ's post-resurrection embodiment. Jenson puts the question with characteristic dash:

> What does the body of the risen Christ look like? For if it 'really' is a body, it must look like *something*. Is there extant somewhere a human organism which looks like a first-century Galilean Jew, and which is somehow identifiable as the one named Jesus? Or what?[205]

It seems possible to answer along these lines: Yes, there *is* with God a 'human organism' that bears even now in itself the marks of slaughter and that in the beatific vision shall be seen and touched. However, the resurrected and enthroned Christ, who is the beginning and end of the *novum ultimum,* is uniquely embodied, so that his body is capable of being 'here' without failing to be 'there'. This 'miracle' is not generated by or dependent upon the priestly consecratory acts, but belongs to the nature of Christ's eschatological

---

of John Damascene, 'The Lord's flesh is life-giving spirit because it was conceived of the life-giving Spirit. For what is born of the Spirit is Spirit' (*Exposition of the Orthodox Faith* 4.13 [*NPNF*, p. 83].

[201] As McCabe ('Eucharistic Change', p. 221) phrases it, 'What the bread has become is the body of Christ, which is to say the Kingdom itself – for Christ does not inhabit the Kingdom, he, his body, his human way of communicating with other humans, is the Kingdom of God'.

[202] This is the same interreality spoken of in 1 Corinthians 11, which Thomas (*Devil, Disease and Deliverance*, p. 49) identifies as the 'extremely tight interplay in this entire section between the bread and cup, the body and blood of Jesus, and the church as the body of Christ'.

[203] That is, in 'heaven'.

[204] In agreement with Bonhoeffer, *Christ the Center*, pp. 43-65.

[205] Robert W. Jenson, *Lutheran Slogans: Use and Abuse* (Delhi, NY: American Lutheran Publication Bureau, 2011), p. 47.

embodiment and to the divine relations of Father to Son in their Spirit.

In the light of these assumptions, then, it would perhaps not be going too far to suggest that the bread and wine are miraculously transfigured so they become for us not merely figures of Christ and his sufferings but in fact the form of 'the deified body of the Lord'.[206] As already said, Christ's presence is never limited to the elements as if he were somehow imprisoned in the bread and wine; he is always present also alongside them as well as in and through them.[207] Nevertheless, if, as the biblical texts and witness of Christian tradition suggest, the elements are in some special way Christ's body and blood for us, then in playing this role they must partake of the ontology of the Eschaton – which they can do without ceasing to be the natural objects they are.[208] In eating the sacramental bread, then, are we not in fact tasting 'the future bread which is ἐπιούσιον, that is, necessary for existence'?[209] As McCabe explains, the bread, by the miraculous power of the Creator, does *not* need to become a new kind of thing in this world;[210] it becomes only what it already is in the new world, the world of the Eschaton.[211]

As far as this world is concerned, nothing seems to have happened, but in fact what we have is not part of this world, it is the

---

206 John of Damascus, *The Exact Exposition of the Orthodox Faith* 4.13 (NPNF 2nd ser., IX, p. 83).

207 Cullmann (*Essays on the Lord's Supper*, p. 14) claims to know that 'the early Christians, when they prayed *Maranatha*, did not think at all of a coming of Christ *in* the species of bread and wine', a judgment he makes on the basis of, among other things, a reading of prayers of the *Didache*. But Cullmann's description of Jesus' presence in my opinion is hyper-spiritualized, and assumes a (unnecessary and destructive) break between heaven and earth, between the risen Christ and the liturgical realities of the church's life.

208 I am attempting to get beyond the virtualism, instrumentalism, and receptionism that characterizes John Wesley's reflections on the Supper – reflections which were shaped to a great extent by the sacramental theologies of Thomas Cranmer and Richard Hooker – without landing squarely in the (Thomistic) transubstantiationist camp. On Wesley's view, see Biddy, 'Re-envisioning the Pentecostal Understanding of the Eucharist', pp. 241-43.

209 John of Damascus, *The Exact Exposition of the Orthodox Faith* 4.13 (NPNF 2nd ser., IX, p. 84).

210 Unlike McCabe, however, I am holding that the bread and wine remain natural objects *and* eschatological objects, *both-at-once*.

211 McCabe, 'Eucharistic Change', p. 220.

Kingdom impinging on our history and showing itself not by appearing in the world but by signs speaking to this world.[212]

Contra McCabe, however, I am holding that the bread and wine are natural objects and eschatological objects, *both-at-once*. Or, put another way, they remain natural objects that have been eschatologized. As Bulgakov says, Eucharistic presence comes not by a physical but a *metaphysical* event.[213] The wine and bread are transfigured not by virtue of some change in the chemical make-up of the elements, but by a creation *ex nihilo* that takes up the bread and wine and imbues them with an *ousia* that perfects them with the perfection all natural objects shall enjoy in the End.[214] Therefore, inasmuch as each Eucharist-event is new creation writ small, when the church gathers to the Lord's Supper it is confronted by a sign of the *novum ultimum* and just in this way experiences the grace of the soon to-be-established reign of God in the mystery of Christ's sacramental presence, a presence that comes in and with and by the transfigured elements, as well as the (proleptically, anticipatorily) transformed hearts and minds and bodies of the worshippers.

Before moving on, a couple other clarifying remarks are in order. One, the reality of Christ's and the Spirit's shared presence in the Supper does not wait on our believing (in) it. Christ is *there* by the Spirit, whether we believe it or not.[215] Still, the Eucharist-event is divinely designed to speak the gospel to our faith, to provoke us to believe wholeheartedly and whole-bodily. Two, this reality does not wait on the power of some consecratory priestly-liturgical act. To be sure, the liturgy is there by God's purpose to draw celebrants' attention to the Christ who directed the church to 'do this' and to a relation to him that exists in any case. The acting out of liturgical rubrics remains necessary because that is the divinely-given way to show us the Lord who is really present just at that moment. Nonetheless, the Lord is *not* under sway of liturgical rubrics.[216]

---

212 McCabe, 'Eucharistic Change', p. 220.

213 Sergius Bulgakov, *The Holy Grail and the Eucharist* (Hudson, NY: Lindisfarne, 1997), p. 63.

214 See McCabe, 'Eucharistic Change', pp. 217-22.

215 Jenson (*Visible Words*, p. 108) puts it this way: 'The sacramental identity is not given because we believe it is, but by the structure of the word we here believe'.

216 Welker (*What Happens in Holy Communion*, p. 97) argues that 'the so-called elements and the performance of the rite are not self-sufficient. As "elements"

Pentecostal Sacramentality and the (Im)Mediacy of Divine Presence

It is universally agreed that Pentecostals expect to experience God directly, immediately, 'face-to-face'. Indeed, it is regarded by many scholars as one of the defining characteristics of Pentecostal spirituality.[217] Furthermore, nearly everyone seemingly agrees that there exists a kind of 'fundamental tension' or 'basic antinomy' between the 'immediacy of direct religious experience' and the forces of institutional *media* and liturgical structures, which effect encounter with God only *in*directly.[218] Does this not *ipso facto* abolish the very possibility of a strong Pentecostal sacramentality before the attempt to construct one has even begun? No, but a reimagined metaphysics is needed, a new understanding of reality that is informed by what Graham Ward names as an 'analogical world-view'[219] and grounded in trinitarian/christological presuppositions that in turn enable us to think the nature of divine and human being in ways that make Eucharistic – and so *gospel* – sense.

To that end, we have to address, first, a widely held but nonetheless mistaken notion about human relationality. Because of the nature of our unique embodiment and the peculiar form of our rationality, all human experiences – whether of God or of our fellow creatures – are always already necessarily mediated. All knowing is for human beings a *knowing-through* and *knowing-with*. We do not know as God knows or as the angels know. Therefore, if *we* are to see God, we *must* see God in, say, the burning bush or the mutilated flesh of Jesus Christ.

---

and as a cultic performance they depend upon the gathered community, the word of proclamation, the explicit remembrance of Christ, and the clarification of this process.'

[217] See, for example, Chan, *Pentecostal Theology and the Christian Theology*, pp. 54-55; Anderson, *An Introduction to Pentecostalism*, pp. 9, 36, 226-36; Alister E. McGrath, *Christianity's Dangerous Idea: The Protestant Revolution – A History from the Sixteenth Century to the Twenty-First* (New York: Harper Collins, 2007), pp. 429-33.

[218] Margaret M. Poloma, 'The Symbolic Dilemma and the Future of Pentecostalism: Mysticism, Ritual, and Revival', in Eric Patterson and Edmund John Rybarcyck (eds.), *The Future of Pentecostalism in the United States* (Lanham, MD: Lexington Books, 2007), p. 105. In this vision, the mystic or charismatic experiences God first-hand, while the pious and religious experience God at some remove.

[219] Graham Ward, *Cities of God* (London: Routledge, 2000) p. 137.

Second, we have to continue to sharpen and strengthen our understanding of the nature of God's way with God and with creation. In my opinion, this then should be(come) axiomatic for us: because Christ and the Spirit are who they are to and for one another as sharers in one *ousia*, separate but not distinct *hypostases* and because creation in its heavenly and earthly realities is peculiarly apt for God (since made by this God for this end), then God's immediacy does not obviate the means of grace or render them redundant.[220] In fact, God's immediacy in Christ by the Spirit is the very reality that makes room for the means of grace and holds them in being, as it does all created things. Because Christ is the Spirit-bearing, Spirit-baptizing one and the Spirit is the one who 'testifies' of Christ and just so makes Christ available to the Father and to us, God's nearness does not edge out but includes, takes up, the various 'media' that bear the divine presence to us.[221] Think, for instance, of the Shekinah dwelling upon the Ark and the vizierial ministry of the Angel of the Lord. Think of Scripture and preaching. Think, most of all, of Christ's Spirit-baptized, human nature.

Third, we have to make clearer that God's revelation and our salvation are inseparably bound up with the God-given and God-giving *mediation* – via Jesus Christ, the church, the angels, the Scriptures, and the sacraments – that brings this revelation to bear on us in such a way that in time all creation is redeemed and we are renewed in the image and likeness of God.[222]

---

[220] At least, insofar as it is proleptically known as eschatologically healed and set to rights.

[221] Adrienne Denerink Chaplin ('The Invisible and the Sublime: From Participation to Reconcilation', in James K.A. Smith and James H. Olthius [eds.], *Introducing Radical Orthodoxy: Mapping a Post-Secular Theology* [Grand Rapids: Baker Academic, 2005], p. 91) insists, contra Milbank and Radical Orthodoxy, that 'participation and mediation' are necessary not because of creation's *finitude*, but solely because of its *falleness*. In characteristically Reformed fashion, Chaplin seeks at every turn to downplay the notion of creation's divinizing participation in God's glory for fear of collapsing God into the creature(ly). She fundamentally misunderstands (in my judgment) what it is that Radical Orthodoxy – and, more importantly, the Patristics – believe(s) about the relation of 'heaven' and 'earth', and so posits what I take to be a false choice between 'reconciliation' and 'participation'. That said, she is correct to insist that Reformed theology has no room for mediation, or the analogical.

[222] See Graham Ward, *Christ and Culture* (Malden, MA: Blackwell, 2005), p. 31.

That done, it becomes clear enough that sacramental means do not interfere or come between God and the worshipper but exists as the very stuff (*ousia*), the raw material of the direct encounter. Plainly put, the church's Eucharist-event *is* an experience of Christ's personal presence, by the power of the Spirit immediately mediated and mediately immediate.[223] The Eucharist is not a *replacement* for the words and works of an absent, far-removed Christ. No, through sacramental bread and wine 'the sign transmits the signified' so that Jesus is thereby and therein transformatively *present*. 'What takes place in the sacraments is the immediate encounter in mutual availability between the living *Kyrios* and ourselves. The sacraments *are* this encounter.'[224] A.B. Simpson had it exactly right: the Lord's Supper is 'a direct personal touch of God'.[225]

In sum, then: to speak of 'immediate' encounter is *not* necessarily to refer to *unmediated* experience.[226] All human experiences, whether of God or of our fellow creatures, are always already necessarily mediated sensibly, affectively, and/or conceptually – through *logos*, *pathos*, or *soma* of one kind or another – because of the very structure of our nature, the character of human being-in-the-world. It follows, then, that sacramental 'means of grace' do not interfere or come between God and the worshipper, but are themselves the very stuff, the raw material of the direct encounter. The Eucharist-event simply *is* an experience of Christ's personal presence. The eating and drinking of the Eucharistic bread and wine, the giving of thanks, the remembering of the paschal mystery are not means-to-an-end, but, like lovers' kisses, belong ineluctably to the thing itself.

---

[223] Contra Chauvet's Heideggerian claims that Christians must 'consent to the presence of the absence', to resign themselves to the fact that the church and the Eucharist 'radicalize the vacancy of the place of God', I am arguing that the Sacrament in fact *focalizes* the presence of the risen Christ. See Chauvet, *Symbol and Sacrament: a Sacramental Reinterpretation of Christian Existence* (Collegeville, MN: Liturgical Press, 1995), pp. 170-80.

[224] Edward Schillebeeckx, *Christ the Sacrament of the Encounter with God* (Lanham, MD: Sheed & Ward, 1963), p. 62.

[225] *Christian and Missionary Alliance* 26.20 (May 18, 1901), p. 4.

[226] Edward Schillebeeckx (*On Christian Faith* [New York: Crossroad, 1987], p. 66) explains, 'From God's side this absolute nearness is immediate; for us this immediacy is mediated, while it remains immediacy …' For further exploration of the notion of mediated immediacy, see William L. Power, 'Religious Experience and the Christian Experience of God', *International Journal for Philosophy of Religion* 31.2-3 (Apr-June 1992), pp. 177-86.

This is the form that human, ecclesial encounter with God necessarily takes.[227]

The Trinity and the Sacrament

Pentecostal spirituality is nothing if not a *personal* engagement with Christ and the Spirit.[228] To this point, however, the experience of God's 'personal presence' has not been satisfactorily worked out in theological terms. In spite of the fact that they have 'a deep familiarity with the persons of Jesus and the Spirit',[229] Pentecostals have yet to articulate an adequately clear explanation of how Christ's presence and work in the Sacrament is related to the Spirit's work and presence,[230] and how their personal contributions relate to the will and purposes of *'our Father* in heaven'.[231] This is so, at least in part, because the desire for *personal* relationship leads believers to focus on the unitary presence of God.[232] Tellingly, one finds a functional interchangeability of the names 'God', 'Jesus', 'heaven', and 'Spirit' in early Pentecostal testimonies of sacramental experience.[233]

---

[227] This is in keeping with the Wesleyan sacramental tradition. Maddox (*Responsible Grace*, p. 193) explains that Wesley himself 'explicitly rejected attempts to substitute a purely spiritual or unmediated communion with Christ for the mediated communion of the Lord's Supper. He insisted that while Christ is the meritorious cause of grace being provided to humanity he is not the efficient cause by which it is conveyed. This efficient cause (or power), in the most proper sense, is the Holy Spirit's Presence. Precisely because of its "uncreated" nature, this Presence is *im*mediately effective even when mediated through means'.

[228] Chan, 'Jesus as Spirit-Baptizer', pp. 149-50.

[229] Chan, 'Jesus as Spirit-Baptizer', p. 152.

[230] This was a characteristic emphasis in John Wesley's theological reflections on the sacraments; see Borgen, *John Wesley on the Sacraments*, pp. 82-85.

[231] Zizioulas (*Lectures in Christian Dogmatics*, p. 118) declares, 'The Father accepts the Eucharist in the presence of the Son and the Spirit, so the Holy Trinity as a whole is involved in the Eucharistic event'.

[232] Chan ('Jesus as Spirit-Baptizer', p. 153) sees that this usually leads to either Christomonism or pneumatomonism.

[233] While Pentecostals (rightly) allow their sacramental experience to inform their theological reflection, it is impossible in experience to differentiate the divine persons in their distinct activities. Therefore, unless the experience is intentionally interpreted through the lens of a Trinitarian theology, it becomes impossible to 'read' the experience Christianly, that is, in keeping with the Scriptural and dogmatic tradition. When the ways of the Trinity's presence in the Sacrament are not kept distinct, the collapse or divergence into Unitarian thinking is inevitable. Surely this failure to talk carefully about God's presence(s) and work(s) in the Eucharist did not help when the Oneness controversy arose in the early days of the Pentecostal movement.

Contra Simon Chan, who finds early Pentecostals guilty of a misappropriating the doctrine of divine personhood and of holding to a 'crude conception of the Trinity bordering on tritheism',[234] it could be argued on the strength of the early periodical material provided in Chapter 3 that Pentecostals were attempting to discern their way forward in an effort to construct a theology that justly described both the reality of personal encounter with God and the distinctiveness of the Spirit's and the Son's ministries. As Macchia explains, 'By bearing witness to both Christ and the reality of the Spirit's presence imparted through him, [early] Pentecostals were able to emphasize pneumatology as much as Christology'.[235] That work needs to be carried on.

Of course, the Spirit's work is never *separate* from the Son's, but the Spirit's work remains always *distinct* from Christ's.[236] The Spirit's unique work is to effect the Father's promises that are embodied, revealed, and accomplished in Christ.[237] Christ is God's objectivity in a unique sense: the Son alone of the divine Three is *embodied*. The Spirit is the one who makes possible real and transformative communion with Christ – as *soma theou* – and so with God and God's creation. According to Zizioulas, 'The contribution of the Holy Spirit is therefore to allow each agent to act as a person, unconstrained by all limits and pressures'. Just as Christ through the Spirit 'is able to surmount the bounds of biology and history, and act in freedom,'[238] so, in communion with Christ, believers enjoy this same freedom and bear this same anointing. The Spirit is able to do this because he is the Freedom[239] who liberates Christ, the church, and their shared ministry from the contingencies of history – and so

---

234 Chan, 'Jesus as Spirit-Baptizer', p. 153.

235 Macchia, *Justified in the Spirit*, p. 79.

236 As Yong (*The Spirit Poured Out on All Flesh*, pp. 162-63) says, we must champion the centrality of the Spirit's work in the Meal.

237 Somewhat against the flow of typical contemporary theological reflection on the role of the Spirit, McDonnell and Montague (*Christian Initiation and Baptism in the Spirit*, p. 354) contend that 'However much one has reason to speak of the neglect of the Spirit, neither the New Testament nor the theological tradition makes the Holy Spirit the central content of the gospel or the principal focus of Jesus Christ, crucified and risen from the dead'.

238 Zizioulas, *Lectures in Christian Dogmatics*, p. 107.

239 Jenson, *Systematic Theology*, I, pp. 160-61.

allows them to be participants in that history in a new-creation way.[240]

In terms of the Sacrament, the Spirit is the 'remembrancer divine', the one who brings the historical realities of Christ's life and the eschatological realities of the not yet realized kingdom to bear on the celebrants and their shared meal. He is the *subject* of our receiving Christ in the Meal. However, because Christ is the Spirit baptizer, the Spirit is in a sense also an *object* of our sacramental experience. Of course, as was just said, the Holy Spirit is not incarnate and so he cannot be experienced *in the same way* that Christ can. Nonetheless, the Spirit is personal and personally present, in and with Christ. 'Both Jesus and the Spirit occupy the center but in different ways.'[241] We can, therefore, talk of being moved and touched by the Spirit as something distinct from what Christ does to and for us in the Supper.[242] We can even say, as Paul does, that we 'drink the Spirit' (1 Cor. 12.13).[243] This is because the Spirit is personally present as the agency who makes possible Christ's transformative presence to us, sacramentally and otherwise. Of course, the Spirit's is not a second, discrete presence alongside Christ's but the very vitality and effectiveness of Christ's own presence.[244] 'The hypostat-

---

[240] Jenson, *Systematic Theology*, II, p. 179.

[241] McDonnell and Montague, *Christian Initiation and Baptism in the Holy Spirit*, p. 354.

[242] Bulgakov (*The Comforter*, pp. 276-77) describes it in this way:

The presence of the Holy Spirit is invisible and mysterious; it is like the breath of the wind, about which one cannot tell 'whence it cometh, and whither it goeth.' His presence cannot be held on to, just as it cannot be attracted by the mere force of one's will. Sometimes His presence flees us, but sometimes it is the most intimate, gentle, personal, and genuine thing in our lives. It is as if gentle transparent fingers touch our hardened heart, burning and melting it, so that it is 'illuminated with sacred mystery' (as it is said in the Matins service) ... But the Holy Spirit comes, and you become other than yourself. You feel fullness in partiality, abundance in meagerness, eternal joy in the pain of semi-being, catharsis in tragedy, the triumph of eternal life in dying, resurrection in death.

[243] Of course, this is not limited to Communion, but surely includes it. John Wesley certainly understood it in this way; commenting on 1 Cor. 12.13, he writes: '*We have all drunk of one Spirit* – In that cup, received by faith, we all imbibed *one Spirit*, who first inspired, and still preserves the life of God in our souls'. See Borgen, *John Wesley on the Sacraments*, p. 208.

[244] This is why Zizioulas (*Lectures in Christian Dogmatics*, p. 107) suggests that 'The Holy Spirit never makes the creature aware of his presence, so the creature is not overawed, but simply aware that all other pressures are taken off, so that

ic life of the Holy Spirit therefore consists in manifesting Christ, Christ's power, Christ's life.'[245] Perichoretically, the Holy Spirit gives Christ to us and, as we are receiving him, Christ gives us the Holy Spirit. At the Table,[246] believers personally and corporately encounter Christ-in-the-Spirit and the Spirit-through-Christ.[247]

Perhaps no one has said this better than T.F. Torrance. In his description, the Spirit comes as 'the other Paraclete answering to the Paraclete above'. And in this way, 'when the Holy Spirit comes to us as the Agent of our renewal he comes not only as the Holy Spirit of the one eternal God but as the Spirit mediated through Christ Jesus and charged with his divine-human holiness'.[248]

> ... the Holy Spirit so unites earth to heaven and heaven to earth that in his coming Christ himself returns to take up his dwelling in the Church, and he it is who intercedes in its midst, who stands among us as our prayer and worship and praise, offering and presenting himself in our place to the Father, so that is in him and through and by him, in his name alone, that we appear before the Face of God with the one offering of his beloved Son in whom he is well pleased.[249]

What does this mean for the church's Communion? Simply this: the Eucharist-event is possible only by virtue of and as an extension of the eternally ongoing Pentecost-event.[250] If Pentecost is possible only because of the incarnate work of Christ, so the post-ascension ministry of Christ – including his *sacramental* ministry – is possible

---

they are able to make a decision that is entirely free'. Similarly, Bulgakov (*The Comforter*, p. 276) maintains that the Spirit makes himself known only through the very act of making Christ known: 'His presence is recognized according to a certain state of life, of inspiration, not according to a personal apprehension of Him Himself; and the subject or content of the inspiration is Christ'.

[245] Bulgakov, *The Comforter*, p. 274.

[246] But not there *only*.

[247] This is in keeping with Kilian McDonnell's ('Spirit and Experience in Bernard of Clairvaux', *Theological Studies 58* [1997], p. 11) characterization of Bernard of Clairvaux's trinitarian theology of experience: '... interior to the experience of Christ is the experience of the Spirit, and the experience of the Spirit is through the experience of Christ'.

[248] T.F. Torrance, *Theology in Reconstruction* (Grand Rapids: Eerdmans, 1965), pp. 249-50.

[249] Torrance, *Theology in Reconstruction*, p. 250.

[250] Bulgakov, *The Comforter*, p. 287.

only because of Pentecost. Christ cannot[251] act in the Eucharist apart from the Spirit and believers cannot partake of Christ in the Eucharist without receiving the Spirit. So Ephraem the Syrian hymns:

> In your Bread there is hidden the Spirit who is not consumed,
> In your Wine there dwells the Fire that is not drunk;
> the Spirit is in your Bread, the Fire in your Wine –
> a manifest wonder, that our lips have received.[252]

Praxis: What Does This Mean for Pentecostal Thought and Practice?

Introduction

If Christ indeed is sacramentally present by and with the Spirit in the Eucharist-event to effect transformation into his divine-human likeness, then what does this reality mean for Pentecostal spiritual life, ministry, and worship now and in the future? In this section, I will sketch the broad contours of some constructive proposals for Pentecostal theology and practice in the light of the constructive work of the previous chapter, allowing some the major notes struck there to resolve. Attention will focus on three interrelated and mutually-instructive dimensions of Pentecostal praxis: hermeneutics and theological method, mission, and worship.

---

[251] For the same reason that God cannot lie.

[252] The Orthodox Patriarch Ignatius, one-time Metropolitan of Latakia, echoed these same sentiments:

> *Without* the Holy Spirit: God is far away, Christ stays in the past, the Gospel is a dead letter, the church is simply an organization, authority a matter of domination, mission a matter of propaganda, liturgy no more than a evocation, Christian living a slave morality. But *with* the Holy Spirit: the cosmos is resurrected and grows with the birth-pangs of the Kingdom, the Risen Christ is there, the Gospel is the power of life, the Church shows forth the life of the Trinity, authority is a liberating service, mission is a Pentecost, liturgy is both memorial and anticipation, and human action is deified.

Quoted in Raniero Cantalamessa, *Come, Creator Spirit* (Collegeville, MN: Liturgical Press, 2003), pp. 59-60. On Ephraem's theology of the Eucharist, see Sidney H. Griffith, '"Spirit in the Bread; Fire in the Wine": The Eucharist as "Living Medicine" in the Thought of Ephraem the Syrian', *Modern Theology* 15.2 (Apr 1999), pp. 225-46.

Hermeneutics and Theological Method

Hermeneutics

As seen in Chapter 4, a firm consensus is forming among Pentecostals: theology must arise from a deep, authentic spirituality and be done in, with, and for the worshipping community.[253] While in agreement with that consensus, I want to suggest additionally that the church's observance of the Lord's Supper and reflection on the theological significance of this event belongs at the center of this proposed theological method. Land's call for a people 'formed in the Spirit by the whole counsel of God'[254] cannot be answered apart from the community's unique experience of God in the Eucharist and the theological reflection to which this experience gives rise.

Interpreters are transformed in and through the encounter with Christ in the Eucharist-event, a conversion that sensitizes interpreters to the mysterious depth, vitality, and infinite intricacy of reality-in-Christ – and thereby fundamentally alters the hermeneutical vision.[255] Through faithful participation in the Sacrament, the imagination is sanctified, healed, and baptized in the Spirit, an event that is parabolically unfolded in the account of the Emmaus disciples' dramatic encounter with the risen, strangely present and suddenly invisible Christ (Lk. 24.13-35).[256]

For those whose imaginations have been altered in these ways, Scripture takes on a distinct, illuminated character.[257] Their own Spirit-impelled transformation into Christ makes possible a vision of the Christological depth and breadth of the biblical witness. Minds renewed, they discern that Holy Scripture's 'treasures are deep and lie hidden except to the mind of the Spirit who reveals

---

[253] See, for instance, Christopher A. Stephenson, 'The Rule of Spirituality and the Rule of Doctrine: A Necessary Relationship in Theological Method', *JPT* 15 (Oct 2006), pp. 83-105.

[254] Land, *Pentecostal Spirituality*, p. 100.

[255] There are of course a variety of churchly ministries through which God acts on the community. The Eucharist-event – when rightly celebrated – does not edge out other ministries but makes room for the Spirit to do as the Spirit wills.

[256] For an exploration of this story as a parable for the relationship of the Eucharist to Scripture, see Chris E. Green, '"Then Their Eyes Were Opened": Reflections on the Pentecostal's Bible and the Lord's Supper', a paper presented at the 39th annual meeting of the Society for Pentecostal Studies (Memphis, TN; 2010).

[257] Perhaps it is also the case that those who regard Scripture as endlessly and multiformly meaningful come to see the Lord's Supper in much the same way.

them …'[258] As a result, Scripture's references to the rite of Communion, whether explicit (e.g. 1 Cor. 10.16-17; Acts 2.42) or implicit (e.g. Gal. 3.1; Jn 6.25-59), as well as many other echoes of or allusions to the Eucharist (e.g. Heb. 6.4-5; 1 Jn 5.8) take on a much richer texture and deeper significance than would have been possible otherwise. What is more, many texts that at least at the primary level have no reference whatsoever to the Supper nevertheless are heard – if only in whispers – to speak to its meaning. For example, the account in Exodus 24 of Moses and Israel's rulers coming up the mountain into the divine presence is clearly not a passage that speaks *of* the Eucharist in any direct sense; however, it just as clearly can and does speak *to* the church's Eucharistic thought and practice.[259] Hence, from this Scripture interpreters come to understand that at the Table where Christ is present by the Spirit both as host and meal, priest and sacrifice, believers are 'coming up' into the presence of a God who is 'coming down' to meet them. They recognize the truth that in the Eucharist-event, they – like (and of course in some ways also *un*like) Moses and Aaron – 'see the God of Israel'; they, (again, like and unlike) the ancients, eat and drink in God's presence. But not only *in* God's presence – they in fact eat and drink *Christ* and so receive into their very being the Spirit of God and in this way partake of the divine nature. A genuinely Pentecostal Eucharistic theology, at least insofar as it intends to remain true to the Pentecostal tradition's practices, comes to the Scriptural texts – Old Testament[260] as well as New Testament – in these ways.[261]

---

[258] *LRE* 2.1 (Oct 1909), p. 17. This is remarkably similar to medieval descriptions of Scripture. See Henri de Lubac, *Medieval Exegesis Vol. 3: The Four Senses of Scripture* (Grand Rapids, Eerdmans, 1998), p. 75. See also McKay, 'When the Veil is Taken Away', pp. 17-40.

[259] Commenting on Exod. 24.12-13, Brevard Childs (*The Book of Exodus: A Critical, Theological Commentary* [Louisville: WJKP, 1974], p. 507) notes that 'these verses in their present position in the biblical narrative function as a Eucharistic festival'.

[260] After all, the entirety of Scripture is apt for the Spirit's use. What Robert Jenson ('A Second Thought About Inspiration', *Pro Ecclesia* 13.4 [Fall 2004], p. 396) says of Christian dogma applies to the sacraments as well, and for the same reason: 'The doctrine of Trinity and Chalcedonian – in fact Neo-Chalcedonian – Christology are, in the appropriate fashion, indeed in the Bible, and most especially in the Old Testament' because the canonical texts in their entirety hang together as God's word for the 'whole diachronic people of God'. See also Rob-

If it is true that the Scripture and the Eucharist are bound together divinely in a mutually-informing relation, then numerous implications follow for Pentecostal engagements with Scripture. It implies, first and foremost, that the liturgical reading and performance of Scripture in the context of the community's Eucharist worship – where the biblical text and the rite of the Sacrament are allowed 'mutually [to] inform each other'[262] as the Spirit sovereignly guides the community's interpretation through the ecclesial offices and the exercise of the *charismata* – serves as the paradigmatic use of Scripture. Put differently, the charismatic and Eucharistic community as it communes in the Spirit with the *totus Christus* is the authoritative interpreter of Scripture. As a result, it is in the context of the community's Spirit-baptized and Spirit-led Eucharistic worship that believers learn best what Scripture is and is for, and over time learns the habits necessary for reading faithfully, with an ever-deepening appreciation for Scripture's 'fuller sense'.[263] All the many other faithful uses of Scripture, whether scholarly or devotional, pastoral or evangelistic, should be judged in this light.

Theological Method

If Scripture and the Lord's Supper indeed are bound together in mutuality, then the Supper – with and like Holy Scripture – would appear to be a *norming norm* for theological reflection and formulation. In the words of Anglican canon theologian Ralph McMichael, 'The nature and method of theology is derived from the Eucharist', and this means that theology is 'called to be ultimately and account-

---

ert W. Jenson, 'The Bible and the Trinity', *Pro Ecclesia* 11.3 (Summer 2002), p. 329.

[261] For a striking example of this hermeneutic in use, see Ephraim Radner's (*Leviticus* [BTC; Grand Rapids: Brazos, 2008], pp. 172-85) Eucharistic reading of Leviticus 17.

[262] Cartledge, *Testimony in the Spirit*, p. 51.

[263] For an exploration of how this hermeneutic differs from the model provided by and used in modern historical-critical studies, see David C. Steinmetz, 'The Superiority of Pre-Critical Exegesis', in Stephen E. Fowl (ed.), *The Theological Interpretation of Scripture: Classic and Contemporary Readings* (Malden, MA: Blackwell Publishing, 1997) and R.R. Reno, 'Biblical Theology and Theological Exegesis', in Craig Bartholomew, Mary Healy, Karl Moller, and Robin Parry (eds.) *Out of Egypt: Biblical Theology and Biblical Interpretation* (Grand Rapids: Zondervan, 2004).

ably Eucharistic'.[264] Methodist liturgist and systematician Geoffrey Wainwright makes a similar claim, holding that '[d]octrinal appeal can be made to the eucharist because in the eucharist the faith comes to focal expression'.[265] He offers two examples: Ignatius of Antioch, who made use of the churches' Eucharistic experience in his attempts to expose the absurdities of the docetists' teachings,[266] and Irenaeus of Lyons, who did the same in his refutation of the emerging gnostic theologies. Irenaeus' famous statement, then, serves as a kind of *lex credendi*: 'Our teaching is in harmony with the Eucharist, and the Eucharist confirms our teaching'.[267] Put negatively, what does not square with the Eucharist does not square with the gospel and therefore invalidates itself.[268]

But can Pentecostals – *as Pentecostals* – accept the methodological basicality of the Eucharist? If so, what differences would follow from it for Pentecostal theology and practice? The answer to the first question is a brief and decisive Yes.[269] The groundwork has already been laid by Pentecostals like Christopher Stephenson, who suggests that Pentecostals' experience of the Lord's Supper should serve as a key facet of theological method,[270] Frank Macchia, who calls for a 'polycentric' worship and theological method[271] in which

---

[264] Ralph N. McMichael, *Eucharist: A Guide for the Perplexed* (London: T&T Clark, 2010), p. 156.

[265] Geoffrey Wainwright, *Doxology: The Praise of God in Worship, Doctrine, and Life: A Systematic Theology* (New York: OUP, 1980), p. 234.

[266] *Smyrneans* 7.1.

[267] *Against Heresies* 4.18.5 in *ANF* (Grand Rapids: Eerdmans, 1973), I, p. 486.

[268] Of course, Paul the apostle had already established this paradigm in his diatribe against the Corinthians' flirtation with idols (1 Cor. 10.14-22).

[269] Of course, much depends on the shape of the theology put forward. Stephenson's Eucharistic model differs significantly from Macchia's, and Macchia's in turn differs from Chan's. These differences have real and far-reaching consequences, of course, but at least in some cases they are not decisive. Even when conceived as a merely symbolic rite, regular participation in the sacrament of Holy Communion may serve, in Stephenson's ('The Rule of Spirituality and the Rule of Doctrine', pp. 101-102) words, as 'a constant reminder that [believers] must actively engage the brokenness and suffering of the world in which they live' and may prove to be an event through which 'the Spirit turns our attention to others and empowers believers for [Christ-like] self-giving'.

[270] Stephenson, 'The Rule of Spirituality and the Rule of Doctrine', pp. 83-105.

[271] The importance of this connection between worship and theological method can hardly be overstated.

preaching, spiritual gifts, and the sacraments share priority,[272] and Simon Chan, who asserts even more directly that Pentecostals[273] must recover the Reformers' pairing of Word and Sacrament, even if they continue to follow Calvin in finally subjecting the sacraments to the Word.[274] In Chan's own view, 'Not only is the sacrament more than the visible form of the Word, but each is indispensable to the other'. As he sees it, 'Sacrament brings the proclaimed Word to its fulfillment', so that 'Word without sacrament remains incomplete, and sacrament without Word becomes an empty sign'.[275] It follows, then, that Pentecostal theologoumena would need to be tested not only against the canonical Scriptures and in the context of the worshipping community, but also in the light of the Eucharistic doctrine and experience.[276] In fact, Wolfgang Vondey goes so far as to suggest that apart from the Eucharist-event, valid discernment simply *cannot* take place,[277] either in the local church or in the academy. Wainwright holds a similar position; in his words, the 'Eucharistic paradigm'

> points us in the right direction: it sets the vector within which the difficult concrete decisions and actions of everyday life have to be taken and performed if they are to be authentically Christian; it excludes the choices which would fall out of the range indicated by the values of the kingdom there expressed in symbolic form.[278]

On balance of what has been said in this and the previous chapter, Pentecostal theology would appear not to be complete or whole without this 'Eucharistic paradigm' and the 'Eucharistic discern-

---

[272] Macchia, *Baptized in the Spirit*, p. 225. In Macchia's vision (*Baptized in the Spirit*, p. 242), the *charismata* 'expand our capacities to receive and further impart the grace that comes to us through preaching and sacrament'.

[273] Chan actually addresses himself to the broader Evangelicalism, but obviously he includes Pentecostals in his audience as well.

[274] Chan, *Spiritual Theology*, p. 111.

[275] Chan, *Liturgical Theology*, p. 66.

[276] Macchia's reflections on footwashing (in conversation with the seminal work of John Christopher Thomas) and his speculative exploration of the sacramental quality of glossolalia provide helpful examples of what it means to bring a sacramental imagination to bear on Pentecostal theology and practice.

[277] Wolfgang Vondey, 'Pentecostal Ecclesiology and Eucharistic Hospitality: Toward a Systematic and Ecumenical Account of the Church', *Pneuma* 32.1 (2010), p. 48.

[278] Wainwright, 'Eucharist and/as Ethics', p. 136.

ment' it makes possible. As Schmemann says, '[e]verything pertaining to the eucharist pertains to the Church, and everything pertaining to the Church pertains to the eucharist and is *tested* by this interdependence'.[279]

Finally, in order to make clear the methodological implications of this proposed methodology, a comparison with other Pentecostal methodologies may prove helpful. To that end, I will take up two such models that not only have been developed and articulated by leading Pentecostal thinkers, but also have been tested and put to use by other Pentecostal scholars in various contexts. The two models I engage – Ken Archer's narrativistic methodology and Amos Yong's 'foundational pneumatology' – differ significantly both from one another and from mine, and the many differences should help to cast my own view into relief. Therefore, having first sketched the outline of their respective theological models, I will bring them into dialogue with my proposed method, identifying key similarities and differences, and finally gesturing toward what these differences might mean for the future of the Pentecostal theological and spiritual tradition.

Archer is concerned above all with faithfulness to the Pentecostal tradition.[280] For him, 'Pentecostal' is not only an *adjective* (as if for example one could only be a Pentecostal Evangelical or a Pentecostal Catholic) but also a *noun* (so that to identify oneself as a Pentecostal is to claim membership in a 'distinctly identifiable community embodying its own Christian spirituality').[281] On his view, the emergence of Pentecostalism is nothing less than 'the creation of a distinctly new and yet still authentically Christian mold' of spirituality.[282] Hence, he calls for and attempts to articulate a theological methodology that does justice to the Pentecostal tradition(s) as he understands it/them. Such a methodology, Archer believes, must be integrative and holistic, bringing ortho-praxis and ortho-pistis into dialogical contact with ortho-pathos,[283] which effects the

---

[279] Schmemann, *The Eucharist*, p. 215. Emphasis original.

[280] For a brief description of the basic shape of Archer's methodological model, see Mark Cartledge, 'Pentecostal Theological Method and Intercultural Theology', *Transformation* 25.2-3 (Apr-July 2008), pp. 92-102.

[281] Kenneth J. Archer, 'A Pentecostal Way of Doing Theology: Method and Manner', *IJST* 9.3 (July 2007), pp. 301-14 (305).

[282] Archer, 'A Pentecostal Way of Doing Theology', p. 305.

[283] Archer, 'A Pentecostal Way of Doing Theology', p. 309.

integration of doing and knowing in a perfectly mutual relationship. Archer insists that this integrative methodology must also be *narrativistic*, by which he means (a) that all theological reflection and discussion must come back to Jesus,[284] who personally is the 'heart of the story' of salvation;[285] (b) that all theological claims should be cast in narrativistic terms. For obvious reasons, then, Archer holds the 5-fold gospel as a distillation of the 'central narrative convictions' of Pentecostalism; it functions for him – and he believes for the whole of the movement – as the decisive feature of an authentically Pentecostal theological methodology. In his words, Pentecostal theology should be 'structured around the Five-fold Gospel and centered upon Jesus Christ', and he provides an image that captures the essence of his proposed model: 'The theological center is the person Jesus Christ, and protruding out of the center are the five spokes which serve to explain the significance of the story of Jesus Christ for the community and the world'.[286] He qualifies these claims by saying that the articulation of the 5-fold gospel must be done so that the 'necessary role and missional activity' of the Holy Spirit is neither eclipsed by nor subsumed in Christ; in effect, this means that all talk of Jesus must work 'out' through recognition of the Spirit to the 'missional story of the Social Trinity' and then back again to Jesus and his story.[287]

As Archer sees it, theology emerges for Pentecostals from 're-demptive encounter with the living Word, Jesus Christ' who is present 'through the powerful presence of the Holy Spirit' in a worshipping community in which the distinctive Pentecostal oral/aural and affective spirituality finds expression in, among other things, 'testimonies, songs, trances, inspired preaching and dance'.[288] Hence, on Archer's view, an authentically Pentecostal theological method-

---

[284] Archer, 'A Pentecostal Way of Doing Theology', p. 311-12. Later in the essay (p. 312), Archer suggests that Jesus *and the Spirit* are at the center of 'God's dramatic redemptive story', and in the conclusion of the article (p. 314), calls for the development of a 'Spirit-Christology' that would remain clear of the 'Christomonistic tendency of Reformation theology of the Word' and make possible a 'fully orbed Pentecostal theology that adequately addresses the various theological themes arising out of the scriptural witness and fleshes out the dynamic interactions of the Spirit and Word'.

[285] Archer, 'A Pentecostal Way of Doing Theology', p. 311.

[286] Archer, 'A Pentecostal Way of Doing Theology', p. 313.

[287] Archer, 'A Pentecostal Way of Doing Theology', pp. 313-14.

[288] Archer, 'A Pentecostal Way of Doing Theology', p. 306.

ology arises from and in the context of Pentecostal worship and privileges the experiences and testimonies of those who are moved by the Spirit and the Word. In these ways, theology becomes a 'personal confessional extension of one's intimate yet communal relationship with the living God'.[289] The 'doxological testimonies' embedded in the claims of the 5-fold gospel are nothing other than 'affectionate affirmations' of the transformative work of God and provide the Pentecostal community with the meta-narrative necessary for making sense of its identity.[290] When such a methodology is put into action, Archer believes it will bear fruit in the development of a 'critical theology' that serves present-day communities while remaining 'in continuity with the manner of the earliest Christians and early Pentecostals'.[291] In spite of Frank Macchia's claims to the contrary, Archer believes that the post-critical narrativistic model he proposes *can* address 'traditional theological *loci*', although of course it will do so in non-traditional ways. His final word is a word of humility: convinced as he is that the methodology he proposes is a legitimate and viable one, he does *not* believe that it is 'necessarily the definitive contribution', for 'surely the Spirit has more to say and ways to say it!'[292]

Amos Yong develops his theological method in conversation with the history of Christian theology. Pentecostalism – which for Yong is not limited to classical Pentecostalism – does not map neatly on any of the post-Reformation models for doing theology,[293] in spite of the fact that most Pentecostals[294] would profess to hold to some version of *sola scriptura*.[295] Accordingly, he is much less confident than Archer that first-generation Pentecostalism can provide an objective standard, a plumb-line, for Pentecostal theology.[296]

---

[289] Archer, 'A Pentecostal Way of Doing Theology', pp. 311-12.

[290] Archer, 'A Pentecostal Way of Doing Theology', p. 312.

[291] Archer, 'A Pentecostal Way of Doing Theology', p. 314.

[292] Archer, 'A Pentecostal Way of Doing Theology', p. 314.

[293] Amos Yong (*In the Days of Caesar: Pentecostalism and Political Theology* [Grand Rapids: Eerdmans, 2010], p. 88) identifies three major methods: 'the Reformation and post-Reformation *sola scriptura*, the liberal Protestant turn to experience, and the Orthodox and Catholic approach that sees Scripture as the book of the church and therefore in continuity with the church's teachings and traditions'.

[294] Yong sometimes uses the lower case to indicate that he refers broadly to classical Pentecostals, neo-Pentecostals, and charismatics.

[295] Yong, *In the Days of Caesar*, p. 91.

[296] Yong, *In the Days of Caesar*, p. 91.

There is, he insists, 'no one Pentecostal story',[297] and he points out that there is 'no monolithic ecumenical tradition with which to engage' owing to fact that 'the Oneness [Pentecostal] position raises questions even about Nicene orthodoxy'.[298] Asserting his commitment to engage the Christian theological tradition as a Pentecostal theologian, Yong nonetheless remains determined not to let the tradition 'dictate the conversation'.[299] Therefore, as an alternative to the hope of a Pentecostal theology fitted to the larger Christian tradition, he proposes that Pentecostals accept the pluralism of experience and begin the theological task with the assumption that the Spirit is 'present and active today'. In his judgment, theology is a 'second-order activity of reflecting on experience' of and in the Spirit.[300] What is more, given the incredible variety of Christian experience, it is inescapably, absolutely *pluralistic*.[301] Informed by his reading of Acts 2 and 1 Corinthians 12, Yong contends that this plurality of experience – and so of theology – is warranted, not only on the individual but also on the corporate level. And as with personal and corporate experience, so with Scripture: the Spirit guarantees that both the biblical texts themselves and the interpretation of these texts are multiple and pluriform.[302] All this to say, no ecclesial or dogmatic meta-narrative can credibly be accepted, and 'no monolithic ecumenical tradition [exists] with which to engage'.[303] Committed as he is to ecumenical discussion, Yong is 'wary' about allowing the theological traditions of the church to dictate the discussion or set the parameters by imposing from outside and above a 'categorical framework'.[304] He is quick to admit, however, that de-

---

[297] Amos Yong, 'Performing Global Pentecostal Theology: A Response to Wolfgang Vondey', *Pneuma* 28.2 (Fall 2006), p. 314.

[298] Yong, 'Performing Global Pentecostal Theology', p 314.

[299] He ('Performing Global Pentecostal Theology', p. 315) believes that 'the tension for Pentecostal theology in our time is to find a way to engage the theological and ecumenical traditions of the church with respect ... but not to kowtow to the tradition in ways that would mute the Pentecostal difference'.

[300] Yong, *In the Days of Caesar*, p. 91.

[301] Yong, *In the Days of Caesar*, p. 93.

[302] Yong, *In the Days of Caesar*, p. 94. Yong finds support in the fact that the Christian canon includes four gospels and not only one, and that readers can find many ecclesial/communal traditions witnessed to in the sacred texts (e.g. Matthean, Lukan, Johannine, and Pauline). To make this point, he also draws on a Pentecostal *textus classicus*: 'it seemed good to the Holy Spirit and to us' (Acts 15.28).

[303] Yong, 'Performing Global Pentecostal Theology', p. 314.

[304] Yong, 'Performing Global Pentecostal Theology', p. 314.

spite the fact that Pentecostals are 'comfortable with the cacophony of many tongues' it is not enough merely to *assert* pluralism as a work of the Spirit or to accept the differences that mark the separate traditions as normative. Instead, an apology is required; 'some indication of how there can be coherence amidst the many'.[305] Pentecostals must be able to discern the truth of the Holy Spirit from the falsity of other spirits? Like Archer, Yong has come to believe that the 5-fold gospel provides the best structure for doing this work.[306]

How do Yong's and Archer's models compare/contrast with the methodology proposed in this chapter and the previous one? Clearly, the three methods overlap in many areas, especially in their attempt to do justice to the distinctives of the Pentecostal tradition(s), and without question much of my own work remains indebted to theirs. Real differences remain, however, mostly having to do with diverging (if not conflicting) assumptions about ecclesiology. Although they express themselves differently and have unique points of emphasis, both Archer and Yong stress the importance of *community* for theological method; nevertheless, their convictions about the nature of the *church* seemingly differ widely from those that underlie the view I have proposed. In the final analysis, the heart of the issue apparently lies in the question of the relation of Christ and the Spirit to the church as Christ's body and the temple of the Spirit. The method I have in view sees the Spirit baptized and Spirit baptizing *totus Christus* – and not Jesus alone or the Social Trinity alone – as the central character in the drama of the Triune God's romance with creation. Also, I assume that one cannot faithfully tell the story of the God of Scripture without also telling the story of the *ecclesia theou*, which means that the church's story must have the same *unity* as does Christ's, for they share one history.

---

[305] Yong, *In the Days of Caesar*, p. 95.

[306] This marks a development in Yong's theological method; since the publication of his *The Spirit Poured Out On All Flesh* (2005), two changes seem to have taken place: first, he has moved from talking of the 4-fold gospel to the 5-fold, and, second, he gives this rubric a much more prominent place in his methodology. It should be noted, however, that he does not regard the 5-fold as distilling an 'essence' of Pentecostal theology – he stands convinced that such an 'essence' simply does not exist; also, he remains doubtful that early Pentecostalism in fact is the 'heart' of the movement in the way that Archer and others have proposed.

It would seem that Archer and Yong would not accept this last claim as true – at least not without major qualifications. In a certain sense, they stand not 'under' but 'beside' the church's liturgico-dogmatic tradition, although each stands at a different distance from that tradition than the other. Given the strength of their claims about the Trinity, about the full divinity and humanity of Christ, and about the deity of the Spirit, this distance from the tradition is puzzling, especially in Yong's case, given that he is suspicious of even the Nicene tradition. Archer is not so wary of the church's dogma; in fact, he claims that Pentecostalism is a genuinely *Christian* movement, and for all that he says about the adequacy of the 'Bible Reading Method' he nonetheless acknowledges that the Pentecostal hermeneutical movement must 'extend past the canon to the Church's understanding of Scripture through time'. In fact, he goes so far as to claim that the interpreting community 'must take into consideration the wider church body and the history of doctrinal development'.[307] Still, he leaves unexplored how this might be done. So, while I affirm his and Yong's relatively strong sacramentality, their high pneumatic christologies, their robust trinitarianism, and their emphasis on the authority of the community, it is difficult for me to see how their respective methodologies in and of themselves provide the necessary grounding for such claims. In a sense, then, my proposals can be understood as an attempt to provide just such a grounding. Insofar as I am successful, I am showing how it might be possible to develop an authentically Pentecostal theological method that remains at every point in discerning conversation with 'the wider church body and the history of doctrinal development', exactly as Archer suggests needs to be done.[308]

This of course forces the question: is it possible for Pentecostals as Pentecostals to establish such a ground for their theological claims? Whatever answer one might give, it is indisputable that throughout the history of the Pentecostal movement at least a vocal minority have recognized the authority of the church's 'living tradition' and attempted to explicate Pentecostal experience in the light

---

[307] Archer, *A Pentecostal Hermeneutic*, p. 257.
[308] See also Simon Chan, 'The Church and the Development of Doctrine', *JPT* 13.1 [2004], pp. 57-77.

of it. Although they were not alone,[309] members of the PH church seem to have taken the lead on this front. G.F. Taylor, for one, held that the early conciliar dogmatic tradition developed under the Spirit's guidance so that throughout subsequent centuries these creeds might serve as divinely-given 'signboards to point to the proper interpretation of Scripture'.[310] Similarly, the trinitarian dogma of the Nicene tradition determined the shape of J.H. King's hermeneutic and theological method.[311] On the strength of the evidence of the early periodical literature, it is possible to say that the ambition to show how Pentecostal theology and spirituality fit within the larger narrative of Christian doctrine was engrained in the culture of the PH church.[312] For instance, in his introduction to G.F. Taylor's *The Spirit and the Bride*, King offers a progressive view of Christian doctrine that suggests he understands Taylor's innovations as an 'unfoldment' that even in their newness remain essentially at one with

---

[309] Some first-generation Pentecostals regarded the teaching and moral example of the ante-Nicene church as particularly authoritative, apparently at least in part because of the witness of the martyrs and the development of the crucial christological and trinitarian dogma. Elizabeth Sexton (*TBM* 3.24 [Jan 1910], p. 1), for example, appeals to the witness of, among others, Justin Martyr, Origen, and Clement of Alexandria to prove the importance of worship on the Lord's Day. She insists that Scripture alone is enough to refute those who say that worship on Sunday is not biblical but a practice imposed by the Roman Catholic Church; however, she agrees with those who hold that the witness of the Ante-Nicene church fathers serves as an 'additional proof'. Similarly, William Schell (*LRE* 7.4 [Jan 1915], p. 11) argues that the church government modeled by the Ante-Nicene fathers – a single congregation-leading bishop flanked by a team of elders and deacons – is in fact a viable New Testament model, and that Pentecostal churches would benefit from 'following after the example of the early Church, the men who lived on the other side of the apostasy'. He predicts that those who organize their church in this way will find that they 'win souls faster and become better saints than any other way, and God will confirm the word with signs following'.

[310] *PHA* 1.25 (Oct 18, 1917), p. 2. See also Elisabeth Sisson's comments on the two natures of Christ in *LRE* 3.10 (July 1911), p. 19.

[311] For a particularly salient example, see his reading of Prov. 8.22-31 in *PHA* 20.13 (July 30, 1936), pp. 3, 9.

[312] In particular, it appears they were concerned to show their theology was in keeping with the Wesleyan/Methodist tradition and the Ante-Nicene church. This does not mean, however, that PH theological reflection was entirely free of strong forms of biblicism. A clear example of this comes in O.T. Spence's *The Quest for Christian Purity* (Richmond, VA: Whittet and Shepperson, 1964), and there are traces of it throughout the early periodical literature, even in the writings of King, Taylor, Brooks, and others who at other times in different contexts appear to hold to a more nuanced hermeneutic.

the *depositum fidei*.[313] Decades later, Noel Brooks worked to reimagine the doctrine of 'healing as in the atonement'[314] by drawing on the history of Christian belief, as well as by extensive Scriptural exegesis and analysis.[315] In much the same way, he asserted in another context the church's role in authoritative interpretation, maintaining that the individual's interpretation of Scripture is neither infallible nor 'the last word'; in fact, even the Spirit-led interpretation must be subject 'to the authority of the Holy Spirit in the Holy Scripture and guided by wisdom of the Holy Spirit in the church today'.[316] In the same spirit, William Bittler, a PH pastor from Harrisonburg, VA, reminds *PHA* readers of the 'divine gifts' of the Church, the Scripture, the ordained ministry, and the sacraments.[317] R.O. Corvin, then dean of the Graduate School at Oral Roberts University, insisted that the claims of the ecumenical creeds (by which he meant Apostles', Nicene, and Athanasian) grew from the 'seed' of Peter's confession (Mt. 16.16), and even while the Apostles' Creed is not divinely inspired in the way that Scripture is, it nonetheless is in 'full harmony with the spirit and letter of the New Testament'.[318]

Whatever else they might be taken to mean, these testimonies suggest that it is possible to imagine an authentically Pentecostal theological method that takes seriously the larger Christian tradition. Perhaps a robust sacramentality is the best means for pointing the way forward along these lines, for as the ecumenist Robert Jenson says the sacraments, conciliar dogma, and theological hermeneutics

---

[313] Similarly, W.H. Turner (*The Finished Work of Calvary or The Second Blessing – Which?* [Franklin Springs, GA: PHC Publishing, 1947], p. 26), a long-time PH missionary in China, argued that the doctrine of sanctification as second blessing 'is a view shared by the Church Universal', whereas the Finished Work doctrine is aberrational, thereby implying that he agreed with Taylor who had said that any doctrine believed by all Christians throughout time was therefore trustworthy.

[314] This in spite of the fact that the Pentecostal Holiness *Discipline* used this language.

[315] Brooks, *Let There Be Life*, p. 65.

[316] Noel Brooks, *Charismatic Ministries in the New Testament* (Greenville, SC: Holmes Memorial Church, 1988), p. 51.

[317] *PHA* 48.6 (June 6, 1964), p. 6.

[318] *PHA* 51.22 (Mar 2, 1968), p. 14. Corvin also says that even though the Athanasian Creed is of medieval provenance and is not included in the Manual of the PH church, members of the church 'hold it as scripturally true with the exception of the condemnatory statements'.

make 'one interlocked complex'.[319] If Pentecostals are to develop a theological methodology that grounds Pentecostal thought and practice in the Nicene tradition as suggested by J.H. King, G.F. Taylor, and other early Pentecostals then it would be helpful if not in fact necessary to develop a sacramentality in keeping with that of the churches that gave rise to that tradition, which is inextricably liturgical as well as dogmatic.[320] Insofar as it achieves my aims, the view of the Eucharist laid out in this thesis is a contribution to that end.

Mission

How does the Eucharist-event and the praxis it entails relate to Pentecostal mission? Clearly, on the view proposed in this and the previous chapter, the Lord's Supper is central to Pentecostal spirituality. In fact, it belongs to every domain of Pentecostal thought and practice. Therefore, a genuinely Pentecostal account of mission needs to be rooted in the realities the Supper embodies and mediates. It remains to be seen, however, what it would mean to work this out in detail.

First, it needs to be clear that the Lord's Supper is – and so must be recognized and enacted as – a *missionary* meal, a meal for the world. Some are sure to think it passing strange to speak of Communion as a meal for the world given that it is so plainly a meal for the *church* and the church's order and unity, as seen for example in the letters of Ignatius, bishop of Antioch.[321] Nevertheless, after some reflection it becomes clear that the Eucharist must be missional principally because the Christ whom the Eucharist gives and praises is himself the embodiment of the *missio dei*, and also because

---

[319] Robert W. Jenson, 'A Lutheran Among Friendly Pentecostals', *JPT* 20.1 (2011), p. 50.

[320] Perhaps it would be helpful for Pentecostals to engage – or to continue to engage, as the case might be – in discerning, critical conversation with theologians (e.g. Lutheran systematician Robert Jenson and Baptist ecumenist Stephen R. Harmon) and movements (e.g. Nouvelle Théologie, Radical Orthodoxy, and Canonical Theism) that seek to 'rethink tradition as the very condition of possibility for theological reflection', as James K.A. Smith ('What Hath Cambridge To Do With Azusa Street? Radical Orthodoxy and Pentecostal Theology in Conversation', *Pneuma* 25.1 [Spring 2003], p. 100) suggests. See also Daniel Castelo, 'Canonical Theism as Ecclesial and Ecumenical Response', *Pneuma* 33.3 (2011), pp. 370-89.

[321] See John E. Lawyer, 'Eucharist and Martyrdom in the Letters of Ignatius of Antioch', *Anglican Theological Review* 73.3 (Summer 1991), pp. 280-97.

the church that receives and celebrates the Eucharist is made by the Spirit of God to be 'an ongoing Pentecost',[322] a prolongation of Christ's incarnational ministry *pro mundo*.[323] In other words, the Lord's Supper brings into focus the community's vocation as the missional *soma Christou*; the call to be one with Christ as his body[324] is both signified and effected in the church's giving and receiving of Christ's sacramental body and blood.[325] Bruce Marshall puts it precisely: 'Eucharistic fellowship is thus essential to the reality of the church, and, more than any other public practice, it gives the church that specific character by which the world comes to faith in the gospel, namely that of a visibly united body'.[326] In the Eucharist-event

> all the facets of the *Missio Dei* find expression: God's continuing love for the world that He created; His self-identification with the fallen world by the incarnation; His redemption of the world through Christ's death and resurrection; His gift of new life in the Holy Spirit; His promise of the new creation at the end of time. Thus the Eucharist shows forth and anticipates that unity of God with all creation, which is the goal of the mission of God.[327]

In one sense, the Eucharist is a gift to the world precisely in its structure as a meal for the church. If this seems absurd, it has only to be remembered that the church's mission to and for the world depends on the integrity of the gospel-message, an integrity that

---

[322] Paul Evdokimov, *The Sacrament of Love* (Crestwood, NY: SVS Press, 1985), p. 124.

[323] Augustine, 'The Empowered Church', p. 161.

[324] See Chan, *Liturgical Theology*, p. 39.

[325] As readers of the Gospels know, many of the post-resurrection stories of Jesus' appearances include an account of his eating and drinking with the disciples, and perhaps these stories are given by the evangelists not only to convince readers/hearers of the reality of Christ's resurrection but also to establish the connection between Christ's pre- and post-Easter ministry in the context of the church's sharing a meal? Thorwald Lorenzen (*Resurrection, Discipleship, Justice: Affirming the Resurrection of Jesus Today* [Macon, GA: Smyth and Helwys, 2003], p. 149) makes a similar suggestion.

[326] Bruce D. Marshall, 'The Disunity of the Church and the Credibility of the Gospel', *Theology Today* 50.1 (Apr 1993), p. 79.

[327] Maynard Dorow, 'Worship is Mission: Seeing the Eucharist as the Drama of God's Mission to the World', *Missio Apostolica* 9.2 (Nov 2001), p. 83.

must be *maintained*.[328] Therefore, mission always already necessarily entails the upholding of the purity of the church's theology (*dogma*) and gospel-proclamation (*kerygma*) to God and God's creation and the striving for and – insofar as it is achieved – the maintenance of the church's visible unity[329] both locally and universally. Only in this way can the work of mission – including churchly discipline, evangelism, diaconal care for widows and orphans, discipleship, pastoral care, and catechesis – be done faithfully. All this notwithstanding, as Pentecostals have always known, there is another sense in which mission requires a turning out to 'the world', to those who do not believe in Christ, who do not know the Triune God. *Synaxis* finds its life in *missio* – 'mission is the mother of the church'[330] – and vice versa. As a result, there is a kind of rhythm to the rightly-ordered churchly life, a Mobius strip-like continuity of going out in mission and coming in, in worship. Or, to change the metaphor once again, the healthy church not only 'inhales', but also must 'exhale'.[331]

This dynamic interchange of worship and mission reveals itself beautifully in the Lukan narrative, especially at the end of the Third Gospel and the opening of Acts. At the conclusion of the Emmaus road story, immediately after the disciples have had their eyes suddenly opened to the reality of the resurrected Christ, they return to Jerusalem to share their story with the eleven apostles and the other disciples (Lk. 24.31-35). Christ meets them there, shows them his wounds and again eats with them, 'opening' their minds to understand the Scripture. Then, he leads them out of the city, blesses them, and 'ascends'. They return overjoyed to Jerusalem to the Temple in worship (Lk. 24.36-53) where they remain until the Spirit falls upon them and propels them, once again, into mission (Acts 1 and 2). In these stories, a basic pattern shows itself: worship fires the disciples into mission, and as they engage in mission, in the tell-

---

[328] See Chan, *Liturgical Theology*, pp. 39-40. The reverse is also true, of course. If the church collapses on itself, concerned only for its own 'purity' or integrity, it just in this way loses touch with Christ, its head (Col. 2.19).

[329] On the relation of the unity and the church and the proclamation and maintenance of the gospel, see Marshall, 'The Disunity of the Church and the Credibility of the Gospel', pp. 78-89.

[330] Richard H. Bliese, 'Speaking in Tongues and the Mission of God *Ad Gentes*', *JPT* 20.1 (2011), pp. 47.

[331] Eberhard Jüngel, 'Texte zum Schwerpunktthema: Mission'. Available online: http://www.ekd.de/print.php?file=/synode99/referate_juengel.html. Accessed July 10, 2011.

ing of the good news, they encounter Christ by the Spirit and worship ensues.

Because early Pentecostalism understood itself as in some sense re-living the story of the Lukan Pentecostal community, it is unsurprising that the tight interplay of worship and mission was a vital aspect of the movement's *ethos*. This distinguished the Pentecostal movement from most of the Protestant movements and denominations of the time. At the turn of the 20th century, missionary activity for many Protestant denominations in Europe and the United States was not conceived as constitutive of churchly identity; instead, 'volunteer parachurch agencies bore the main missionary responsibility within Protestant denominations'.[332] The Pentecostals would have agreed with – and by force of their missionary efforts, arguably contributed to – what is now an ecumenical consensus: 'mission is the *raison d'être* of the church's existence and function in the world'.[333]

For first-generation Pentecostals, the interplay of worship and mission was so tight that at certain points the two became virtually indistinguishable. This is nowhere clearer than in their fellowship meals. What one *Pentecostal Evangel* contributor says of the early Christian habit of 'breaking bread' (as in Acts 2), applies to the experience of early Pentecostals well:

> Do these words describe an ordinary meal or the Communion? Perhaps both. This is what may have occurred: at first the disciples may have taken their meals in common; as they surrounded the tables to ask the divine blessing upon the bread and wine, the memory of their Lord's last meal would come to their minds, and the blessing upon the food would spontaneously enlarge itself into a service of worship, so that in many cases it would have been difficult to determine whether they were having a common meal or partaking of the Sacrament. So real was God's presence to these early disciples that life and worship were

---

[332] John G. Flett, *The Witness of God: The Trinity, Missio Dei, Karl Barth, and the Nature of Christian Community* (Grand Rapids: Eerdmans, 2010), pp. 61-62.

[333] V.C. Samuel, 'The Mission Implications of Baptism, Eucharist, and Ministry', *International Review of Mission* 72.286 (Apr 1983), p. 207.

blended; for them to live was to worship, and to worship was to live.[334]

These times of intimate fellowship at a common table – an adaptation of Wesleyan 'love feasts' and the *agape* meals of the ancient church[335] – served as a unique and uniquely effective vehicle for bearing the reality encountered in worship into 'real life'.

This capacity for flowing in and out of worship, for integrating 'real life' with the doxological realities of corporate communion, is in many ways the most basic skill required in the Christian life. As the Methodist theologian Wainwright says,

> ... what is there [i.e. in worship] received and enjoyed in reality-filled symbols has to be discerned and enacted in everyday life, both among Christian believers and, so far as they are able, in the affairs of society at large. Christians come from the world, bearing (as it were) the raw materials for the eucharist, which is then celebrated in the assembled church. From the liturgical gathering they return to recognize and translate the eschatological reality – there experienced under signs – in quite mundane decisions and deeds which are part of the history of a human race that is an object of God's loving purpose.[336]

The call for discernment/recognition and enactment/translation strikes distinctly Pentecostal notes, for Pentecostals are people who believe that the Christian life depends at every moment on the Spirit's 'leading', on the Spirit's sovereignly wise and infinitely creative guidance through life. As the Spirit enables believers to 'translate'[337] the sacramentally-given realities of the kingdom concretely through the 'mundane decisions and deeds' of normal, everyday life, believ-

---

[334] *PE* 1073 (Nov 10, 1934), p. 21.

[335] In keeping this custom, Pentecostals were carrying on a long tradition that extended back through the Wesleyan 'love feasts' to the 'agape meals' of the ancient church. See Rebecca P. Skaggs, *The Pentecostal Commentary on 1 Peter, 2 Peter, and Jude* (London: T&T Clark, 2004), pp. 123-24, 165.

[336] Geoffrey Wainwright, 'Eucharist and/as Ethics', *Worship* 62.2 (Mar 1988), p. 131.

[337] Undeniably, this work of 'translation' is always a wildly complex, radically context-specific business. However one might wish it to be, simple one-to-one translation of the Eucharistic reality into the dialect of 'real life' is simply not possible. What is needed, then, is a kind of *fluency* – a capacity for creative adaptation – that makes possible the emergence of an *equivalency* of the kingdom in the believer's life.

ers are sacramentalized, so to speak, so that for them 'all occasions of human contact ... become the medium of that communion with God and among human beings which is marked by justice, peace, and joy in the Holy Spirit, and in which the kingdom of God consists'.[338] Now, as then, the Eucharistic reality has to be inscribed in the being of the celebrants so that they come to embody the Word of the Sacrament. Or, to say the same thing another way, the celebrants must become Christified. This is what it would mean for 'all occasions of human contact to become the *medium* of that communion with God'. The Spirit has his 'perfect work' (Jas 1.4) in believers' lives as they take a Eucharistic shape; as they, like Christ and the meal that he identifies himself with, are taken, blessed, broken, and given for the hungry.[339]

Deep moral formation can and should take place in and through the celebration of the Lord's Supper,[340] for to take the bread and the cup is willingly, even delightedly, to receive the obligation to live out the reality signified in the Supper. So much so that the Eucharist simply is not complete, is not truly itself, until it reaches fulfillment in the lived faithfulness of the community and its members.[341] At the Table, Christians offer themselves and their corporate worship in full confidence that precisely in giving to God they are themselves transformed into Christ who himself is both the divinely-pleasing gift and giver. Precisely because the Eucharist-event is *donum*, a sacrifice of thanksgiving and adoration to the God of Jesus Christ, it is an effective sign of transformation. The love *for* God that the church professes in its Eucharistic celebration has at its depth the transforming love *of* God that the Spirit is and effects in the community.

---

[338] Wainwright, 'Eucharist and/as Ethics', p. 131.

[339] LaVerdiere (*The Eucharist in the New Testament and the Early Church*, pp. 54-58) draws attention to the Second Gospel's 'Eucharistic teaching on mission' in the two stories of breaking bread (6.34-44 and 8.1-10) which together show that 'the Eucharist is a sharing in the Messiah's passion, death, and resurrection'.

[340] As Cheryl Bridges Johns, *Pentecostal Formation: A Pedagogy among the Oppressed* (JPTSup 2; Sheffield: Sheffield Academic Press, 1993), p. 124, explains, corporate worship is a primary context for spiritual and moral formation because it is then and there that 'the community becomes the place where affective and cognitive aspects are joined together in a powerful manner'.

[341] See Bernard Häring, 'Liturgical Piety and Christian Perfection', *Worship* 34.9 (Oct 1, 1960), pp. 523-35.

This formation of a Christ-like 'second nature' in the celebrants – that is, the attainment of true holiness – comes as believers
find themselves being narrated into the story of creation's redemption in Christ, the beloved Son.[342] The sacraments, and particularly
the Eucharist, convey this story with unique power and so make
possible a character-forming narration of the community's life as a
life of co-participation in Christ's storied existence as eternally-
beloved Son and 'firstborn of all creation' (Col. 1.15). Hauerwas
provides a dictum that underscores the point: 'In the sacraments we
enact the story of Jesus and in so doing form a community in his
image'.[343] As has been previously argued, this enactment of Jesus'
story has both recapitulative and proleptic dimensions. The
church's celebration of Christ's meal is both a *re*-enactment of Jesus' history and a *pre*-enactment of the eternal messianic banquet
that is the beatific vision, the endless event that makes all angels
'angels of the face', all humans lively members of Christ's mystical
body, and all things effective signs of his victorious passion. As a
matter of practice, then, celebrants should have impressed on their
minds and hearts the full sweep of the gospel narrative in preparation for the giving and receiving of the sacramental loaf and the
cup; in this way, as they experience Lord's Supper in the taboric
light of the eschatological feast and in the shadows of the agonistic
events of Christ's last week, believers are positioned to be led by
the Spirit into the form of life symbolized and signified in the sacred meal.

For good reason, the Christian imagination holds in closest possible connection the Eucharist and martyrdom on one hand and

---

[342] Orthodox ethicist Vigen Guroian ('Liturgy and the Lost Eschatological Vision of Christian Ethics', *Annual of the Society of Christian Ethics* 20 [2000], p. 229)
contends, 'The final decisive Christian distinction is not between the sacred and
the profane, the cult and the world, the just or unjust, or even between good and
evil. The decisive distinction is between the *old* and the *new* ... From this perspective, it may be seen that Christian liberty and virtue arise from the deep, rich
soil of the church's memory of the central salvific events of the faith, soil sown
with a vital vision of the eschaton wherein the ethical is transfigured into the
holiness of God'.

[343] Hauerwas, 'The Servant Community: Christian Social Ethics', in Berkman
and Cartwright (eds.), *The Hauerwas Reader*, p. 383. For a comparison of Hauerwas' moral theology with that of Bernard Häring, see Kathleen A. Cahalan,
*Formed in the Image of Christ: The Sacramental-Moral Theology of Bernard Häring,
C.Ss.R.* (Collegeville, MN: Liturgical Press, 2004), pp. 217-30.

martyrdom and mission on the other hand.[344] This is because mission, like both the Eucharist and martyrdom, is the offering up of the body in and as sacrifice.[345] In giving their bodies to be burned or consumed by wild beasts, the martyrs were in fact imitating Christ in his immolation, and were just in this way becoming embodied, effective signs not only of the kingdom that Christ is, but also of the church as the worshipping missionary people of God. Accordingly, this is what it means to be a witness to Jesus Christ (μαρτύρων Ἰησοῦ):[346] to give oneself in love to God and neighbor and enemy in a life of 'protracted martyrdom'[347] that is perfectly signified in the Eucharist.[348] 'In the Eucharistic celebration, there-

---

[344] For example, in his letter to the Romans, Ignatius proclaims that he does not want to be delivered from martyrdom because he desires above all things to become 'God's wheat' crushed in the mouths of the lions so that, like the Eucharist, he might become 'Christ's pure bread' and the ancient account of the martyrdom of Polycarp, bishop of Smyrna is described in explicitly liturgical terms with Polycarp himself becoming the Eucharist as in the fire he was 'like bread being baked'. See Pope Benedict XVI, *The Sacrament of Charity* (Washington, DC: USCCB Publishing, 2007), p. 72.

[345] As the astute reader recognizes, these claims entail the assumption that the Eucharist is a sacrifice – although plainly it is *not* a re-crucifixion of Christ, or some *superadditum* to Christ's atoning death. On *our* part, the Lord's Supper involves the offering up of thanksgiving to God for Christ with the bread and the wine and the reaffirmation of our promise to give ourselves fully to God and God's will. On *God's* part, the Eucharist is a giving anew of Christ to us in the Spirit (and the Spirit in Christ) and the reenactment and reaffirmation of God's once-for-all offering up of Christ for us on the cross. In these ways, the Supper serves as an act of covenant renewal, a divine-human embodied exchange of the promise to surrender all for the other. Or, to put it another way, in the Eucharist Christ reveals himself as the divinely-human mediator who speaks to us God's word of unconditional promise and just in this way enables us to echo back to God through him our joyfully responsive *Yes* and *Amen*.

[346] See Rev. 17.6 and Acts 1.8.

[347] *LRE* 1.8 (May 1909), p. 23.

[348] Early Pentecostals emphasized this call to living martyrdom; in fact, many of them believed that to be baptized in the Spirit was to receive the 'martyr spirit' (*The Pentecost* 1.2 [Sept 1908], p. 3) and to be initiated into the 'secret of the endurance of the martyrs' (*AF* 1.11 [Oct-Jan 1908], p. 3). G.F. Taylor argued that 'every doctrine of our holy religion has been baptized with the blood of millions of martyrs', insisting that the Pentecostal doctrine and spirituality was made possible through the sufferings of the saints of previous generations. Pentecostals have only what 'the martyred saints bequeathed to us'. See *PHA* 9.27 (Nov 5, 1925), p. 1. Again and again, one finds in the early periodical literature an emphasis on the baptism of the Spirit as a baptism into Christ's suffering. For example (*LRE* 1.8 [May 1909], p. 23): 'Ah the baptism in the Holy Spirit means something more than glory and ecstasy; it is more than physical or psychical manifesta-

fore, we announce not only the death of Christ, but also our own death.'[349] Those who consume the bread of Christ's body are themselves apt to be broken and devoured, ground in the teeth of God's enemies, as Ignatius desired to be and was. Those who drink the one, inebriating Spirit (Ps. 23.5; 1 Cor. 11.13)[350] know themselves as the people who bless the cup of blessing (1 Cor. 10.16) and therefore as the people prepared also to drink the cup of Christ's suffering (Mt. 20.23) for the sake of the world.

In his *Baptized in the Spirit*, Macchia plays on Christoph Blumhardt's description of the Christian life as involving two conversions – 'from the world to God and from God to the world'. Macchia asks his readers to think of Spirit baptism as both 'a prophetic call that draws one close to the heart of God in praise *and* prophetic empathy for the world', but to allow the accent to fall on the 'second conversion', so that Spirit baptism is understood as the needed empowerment for 'witness in the world'.[351] He believes this 'second conversion', this reorientation to the world, comes as the Spirit 'fills us with the love of God so that we transcend ourselves and cross boundaries'.[352] In conversation with Macchia, I would propose two modifications. First, one need never convert 'from God' (or from the church), since God is God always in and for the world as well as in and for the church. In fact, God makes the church to be for the world and the world to be for the church. As Ephesians teaches, God has made Christ head over all things 'for the church' (Eph. 1.22) *so that* 'through the church' God might make the 'mystery' known (Eph. 3.1-10).[353] Second, it might be helpful to think not of a 'second' but of a *series* of conversions, so that the believing

---

tions; it is fellowship with Christ in His humiliation and in His suffering as well as in His glory'.

[349] Karl Rahner, *Spiritual Exercises* (New York: Herder and Herder, 1965), p. 212.

[350] Ephraim Radner (*The End of the Church: A Pneumatology of Christian Division in the West* [Grand Rapids: Eerdmans, 1998], pp. 270-72), drawing on the insights of the twelfth-century Archbishop of Canterbury, Baldwin of Ford, insists: 'The Eucharistic cup itself, then, becomes a place where "mercy and judgment" are manifested and received ...' Therefore, the Eucharistic cup 'is both a "shining" cup of "inebriating mercy" and one of "intoxicating torpor" given in divine anger' all-at-once.

[351] Macchia, *Baptized in the Spirit*, pp. 76-77.

[352] Macchia, *Baptized in the Spirit*, p. 281.

[353] Of course, in a sense, the inverse is true as well: God makes the world exist for the sake of the church.

community and its members are always 'caught' between church and the world, 'hard pressed between the two' (Phil. 1.23). Perhaps that tension is the very dynamic of a genuinely cruciform life.

Worship

At this juncture in the movement's history, the Communion rite does not hold a pre-eminent place in most Pentecostal worship services. Contemporary Pentecostal congregations typically[354] celebrate the Supper infrequently (at most on a monthly or quarterly basis), so that the vast majority of Pentecostal worship services are centered in singing, prayer, and preaching, rather than in the Eucharist.[355] It will come as no surprise for those who have read this chapter and the previous one that I find this troubling and problematic; for, as I have argued, I believe the Lord's Supper belongs at the heart of the Christian life and so at the center of Pentecostal worship. To put it prescriptively, the Eucharist-event should be recognized as the hub of the worship service.[356] Or, to use another image, it should be seen as the hearth around which all the other liturgical furniture is arranged.[357] In the event of the church's corporate worship the whole of the Christian life comes to liturgical focus,[358] and this focus is sharpest in the (rightly spirited and faithful)

---

[354] It would appear that this was less true in the early decades of the Pentecostal movement than it is now. Of course, in those days too one could find a range of practices. However, there is good evidence that many Pentecostals celebrated the Lord's Supper frequently – even weekly. For example, the 1922 Church of God (Cleveland, TN) *Book of Doctrines*, while acknowledging that Scripture lays down no mandate and maintaining the right of the local congregation to decide when to celebrate the Sacrament, nonetheless indicates that most congregations celebrate the Lord's Supper once a month, with a 'very few' congregations celebrating the Lord's Supper every week.

[355] For a description of the basic shape of characteristic Pentecostal worship, see Telford Work, 'Pentecostal and Charismatic Worship', in Geoffrey Wainwright and Karen Westerfield Tucker (eds.), *Oxford History of Christian Worship* (New York: OUP, 2006), pp. 574-80. See also Albrecht, *Rites in the Spirit*; Cartledge; *Testimony in the Spirit*, and Bridges Johns, *Pentecostal Formation*.

[356] This is evident from the fact that the Eucharist embodies in its own way every other act of worship. It is *preaching* (in the form of a visible word), *praise* and *thanksgiving* (in the embodied expression of gratitude and awe), *prayer* (an embodied dialogue with God), *testimony* (witness to God's goodness and the exhortation of other celebrants), and *offering* (in the giving and receiving of gifts).

[357] Simon Chan (*Spiritual Theology*, p. 116) identifies three acts as the 'basic building blocks of corporate worship in all of the traditions', i.e. corporate prayer, public reading of Scripture, and corporate singing. Chan believes the church's celebration of the Eucharist can serve and be served by this practices.

[358] Wainwright, *Doxology*, p. 8.

Eucharistic celebration.[359] At the Lord's Table, the Spirit reminds worshippers that the whole of created life centers in the story of Jesus Christ, who has brought, shall bring, and is bringing all reality into communion with God.[360]

I am not unsympathetic with those who worry that frequent Communion would produce an overemphasis on the Sacrament, drawing attention away from the personal, 'immediate' encounter with God, edging out those practices that have long characterized Pentecostal worship and spirituality, and ultimately collapsing in a 'dead ritualism'[361] that stifles the freedom of the charismatic Spirit. History makes clear that it is possible for the very (Eucharistic) altars that are meant to 'expiate sin' to become 'altars for sinning' (Hos. 8.11). The bread and wine can be given and shared without the *Lord's* Supper taking place (1 Cor. 11.20), for when the rite of Communion is observed in ways that quench the very Spirit who makes the meal to be the sacrament of the coming victory of God and the church's unity ἐν χριστῷ Ἰησοῦ, then it is a sacrifice that *defiles* rather than sanctifies (Hos. 9.4). All these reservations and concerns notwithstanding, I remain convinced that it is possible to revision and reform Pentecostal worship around the Eucharist-event in such a way that the believing community becomes more and more apt for Christ's transformative presence in the Spirit – so long as the revisioning and reformation are done discerningly.[362] To that end, it is crucial that the Eucharist-event be framed and under-girded by characteristic Pentecostal practices, such as the altar call, 'tarrying',[363] prayers for healing,[364] testimonies,[365] and footwashing.[366]

---

[359] Chan, *Spiritual Theology*, p. 115.

[360] And this need not come by suppressing preaching, testimony, song and dance, or anointing with oil, etc.

[361] Work, 'Pentecostal and Charismatic Worship', p. 576.

[362] In broadest terms, the needed reformed Pentecostal liturgies would be lively enough for worshippers to sense the vitality of the divine life; theologically dense enough for the weight and solidity of God's mandates and promises to be felt; structurally expansive and complex enough for worshippers to be awed, and conceptually and practically transparent enough for the radiating beauty of the story of the Gospel to shine through.

[363] Daniel Castelo ('Tarrying on the Lord: Affections, Virtues, and Theological Ethics in Pentecostal Perspective', *JPT* 13.1 [Oct 2004], pp. 50-51) describes this practice as entailing 'travailing, waiting, prostrating, and submitting oneself before the presence of God in the hope that God's presence might break forth in the mundane and profane circumstances of life. Tarrying is an embodiment and demonstration of human desire in search of being ordered by God's very pres-

This is necessary for many reasons. First, these practices keep attention on the God who is present to and for the community so that the church's celebration of the Lord's Supper is understood and experienced as an act of *worship*, an eruption of 'loving adoration'[367] for the God revealed in the narrative of Jesus Christ, and in precisely in that way as a salutary means of blessing. For good reason, from very early in the Christian liturgical tradition the Lord's Supper has been recognized as 'the pre-eminent sacrifice of praise'.[368] In the faithful act of eating and drinking the sacramental body and blood, believers understand themselves as obediently offering up thanksgiving to the triune God who makes them who they are and the event what it is. In this way, celebrants avoid instrumentalizing the Eucharist, resisting the temptation to make of the Supper a *mechanical* 'means of grace'.[369] Second, these practices help to underscore the *communal* reality of Communion.[370] After all, this is at the heart of the matter: the liturgy of the Eucharist-event should (in fact and not merely in word) occasion 'the work of the people'

---

ence'. In these ways, this act of tarrying is 'anticipatory and so eschatological in form because it is a practice that expects encounter; it beckons eschatological time and in doing so focuses one's life on the in-breaking presence of the Spirit of God, thereby anticipating the coming reign of Christ'. Castelo concludes that 'while tarrying on the Lord, one is led by the Spirit to wait actively for the transforming presence of God that makes possible one's faithful existence in the world'.

[364] As seen in Chapter 3, many early Pentecostals were convinced that the Lord's Supper was above all a means of bodily healing. See, for example, *AF* 1.10 (Sept 1907), p. 2; *WE* 104 (Aug 21, 1915), p. 3; *PHA* 5.5 (July 2, 1921), p. 10.

[365] James K.A. Smith (*Thinking in Tongues*, p. 62) describes storytelling – testimony – as 'the oxygen of pentecostal worship'. See also Mark J. Cartledge, *Testimony: Its Importance, Place and Potential* (Renewal Series 9; Cambridge: Grove Books, 2002), and Scott A. Ellington, 'The Costly Loss of Testimony', *JPT* 16 (2000), pp. 48-59.

[366] Not that all of these practices have to take place in every Eucharistic celebration.

[367] Häring, 'Liturgical Piety and Christian Perfection', p. 524.

[368] Paul F. Bradshaw, *Early Christian Worship: A Basic Introduction to Ideas and Practice* (2nd ed.; Collegeville, MN: Liturgical Press, 2010), p. 63.

[369] Chauvet (*The Sacraments*, pp. xiii-xxi) warns against both objectivist and subjectivist forms of this abuse, the latter of which I suspect is more likely for Pentecostals.

[370] Hollenweger (*The Pentecostals*, p. 389) argues that the early Pentecostals' understanding of the meal as a community event served as an incisive prophetic critique of those churches whose Eucharistic devotion focuses on the words and acts of the priests rather than the congregation.

(λειτουργία).[371] Third, these practices make room for the Spirit to act through the charismatically-endowed members of the community for the 'upbuilding of the body' (1 Cor. 14.12). On the one hand, this guarantees that the *charismata* are intimately related to the gospel-story as it is sacramentally enacted,[372] with preaching and other ministries always 'point[ing] to and confirm[ing]' the reality embodied in the sacred meal at the center of the church's liturgical life and in this way opening up the believing celebrants to the pneumatic and eschatological realities of ecclesial life and the cosmic scope of salvation in Christ.[373] On the other hand, it serves to guard against the flattening and hardening of the sacramental celebration into mere ritual.[374]

Some corners of the early Pentecostal movement – and especially the leaders of the Pentecostal Holiness Church – went so far as to develop or at least make use of already existing liturgical rubrics in the attempt to give a faithful shape to the celebration of Communion, rubrics that because they exist as testimonies to the sacramentality that characterized early Pentecostalism may well open the way for contemporary Pentecostal liturgical reforms.[375] In the pro-

---

[371] However central and basic Communion is taken to be, regular participation in the rite must not give rise to a priestly caste.

[372] Wainwright (*Doxology*, pp. 115-16) argues that if 'public glossolalia is to pass the Pauline test of communal edification, it will best be set within the tried structures of the liturgy where the familiar witness to Christ will itself provide a context of interpretation'. Wainwright affirms that 'a literal witness to Christ remains dead without the enlivening Spirit, and that presence of the Spirit brings 'freedom' (2 Cor. 3.17), but he also holds that this 'liberty is defined by the character of Christ'.

[373] Chan, *Spiritual Theology*, pp. 111-12.

[374] Roman Catholic charismatic systematician and ethicist Ralph Del Colle ('Pentecostal/Catholic Dialogue: Theological Suggestions for Consideration', *Pneuma* 25.1 [Spring 2003], pp. 93-96 [96]) believes that in dialogue with Pentecostals, the Catholic Church is reminded that 'sacramental signs beckon for further signification in charismatic manifestation'.

[375] For example, the 1908 *Constitution and General Rules of the Fire-Baptized Church* provides instructions for the observance of 'the sacrament of the Lord's Supper'. To begin, the officiating minister 'read[s] a lesson from the Word, either from the Gospels or Epistles, as he may deem appropriate'. After that, he addresses the congregation, calling them to assume the right attitude to receive the Supper. His exhortations follow this basic pattern:

Beloved in Christ: This precious sacrament commemorates the suffering and death of our Lord whereby He offered Himself a ransom for our souls, making atonement for our sins in His own blood, and thus satisfying the claims of

cess of developing these liturgies, a few basic guidelines must be kept it mind. First, it would seem necessary that the Supper be celebrated in such a way that before, during, and after the receiving of the cup and the loaf 'inspired spontaneity' and 'skilled improvisation'[376] remain possible.[377] Similarly, it seems appropriate that space should be given in the service for discerning reflection in preparation for receiving the meal; celebrants should 'examine themselves' (1 Cor. 11.28) to see if they are living rightly in relation to other members of the community. Also, while the mysteriousness of the event should not be compromised by sentimentality or over-neat explanation,[378] participants – even the young and newly baptized – should have an appropriate grasp of the meaning and purpose of the Supper. To ensure this, it is essential that the minister who presides at the Table take time to explain spiritedly and in instructive detail why it is that the church gathers for this meal and how it is

---

Divine justice against us. It also points to His return to earth, when He shall partake of it anew with us in the kingdom of the Father. Let us draw near in deep humility and take this sacrament to our comfort, and, devoutly kneeling, render our sincere thanks to Almighty God.

Then, the minister offers an extemporary prayer for the purpose of 'consecrating the elements to their sacred use' and gives an invitation for 'all true Christians, all who have fellowship with the Father and with His Son Jesus Christ, and who sincerely love the appearing of our Lord' to come to receive the Sacrament. When all have received, a hymn is sung, and while the congregation kneels, the minister prays over them. Finally, before everyone is dismissed, the doxology is sung. The 1908 *Discipline of the Pentecostal Holiness Church* includes a similar rubric, but it is makes a much sharper difference between the ministers and the communicants. In 1911, the Fire Baptized Church merged with J.H. King's Pentecostal Holiness Church, and the new *Discipline* included the rubric that had been written (by King?) for the pre-merger Pentecostal Holiness Church. For an account of how the merge of these churches came about, see Synan, *The Holiness-Pentecostal Tradition*, p. 121-22. See also R.G. Robins, *Pentecostalism in America* (Santa Barbara, CA: ABCCLIO, 2010), pp. 43-44.

376 Wainwright, 'Eucharist and/as Ethics', p. 137.

377 This is necessary for many reasons, including the fact the liturgy is in part a 'training ground' for the 'real life' situations that require improvisational skill, the ability to discern what it is God requires in a given moment.

378 Relatedly, there is no need to remove the celebration of the Supper from the worship service in the name of making worship more accessible to non-believers and the newly converted. The Sacrament is by its very nature mysterious, scandalous, and even divisive, but these are in fact essential features of its structure as a missional meal. The Eucharistic invitation depends in part upon the awkwardness of the event, its alienating and disenchanting character; this is so because Christ, the desire of all nations (Hag. 2.6-9), is himself strange and estranging, the missionary Word who draws all people to himself even though he comes as one without beauty that he should be desired (Isa. 53.2).

that the meal may be received in good faith. Second, following the example of the early Pentecostal communities,[379] the rite of Communion should require sharing in a single cup and loaf,[380] for the Spirit's work through the meal is inseparable from – although not constrained by – the meal's *signature*, its symbolic power of meaning. Third, contemporary Pentecostals should maintain the traditional Pentecostal (and Wesleyan) practice of keeping an 'open' Table, so that all believers who remain in good standing with their communities, including believing children,[381] are allowed to participate, receiving of course both the loaf and the cup. Some are sure to be uncomfortable with talk of communing children, but so long as the community accepts a child as its own, then the child has every right to receive the Supper.[382] The same applies for those with mental challenges, and for the same reasons.[383] Pentecostals agree with the sentiments of the ecumenical theologian Robert Jenson, who puts the point forcefully: 'Christ's presence as the bread and cup is not separable from the unity it creates of those who share the meal'. Consequently, in spite of the many proposed rationalizations to the contrary, the case for an open table is simple and straightforward:

> if I and my group celebrate the Supper, and do not admit you, this is excommunication; and if we indeed belong to the body of Christ, as we claim merely by our celebration, it is excommuni-

---

[379] G.F. Taylor, for example, insists that Communion be observed using a single cup and that all celebrants drink from it because only in this way can the basic truths of the rite be made plain; in his judgment, when individual cups are used the symbol of the church's fellowship is distorted. As with the one cup, so with the bread. See *PHA* 3.11 (July 10, 1919), p. 2. See also *COGE* (June 18, 1921), p. 4; *Confidence* 10.5 (Sept-Oct 1917), p. 67.

[380] For example, does it not seem obvious that the use of individual cups and wafers only encourages the notion that the Lord's Supper is first and foremost an *individual* experience of blessing?

[381] Pannenberg (*Systematic Theology*, III, p. 332) notes that there can be 'nothing against [giving communion to children] once a child can grasp the thought that Jesus is present at the Supper, mysterious though the thought may still be'. It would appear that a Pentecostal understanding, however, would not bind receiving Communion even this closely to a child's understanding.

[382] This is in keeping with the ethos of the earliest days of the Pentecostal movement, as evidenced by testimonies of children being baptized and receiving Communion and the fact that children were encouraged to seek Spirit baptism. See for example *PHA* 2.14 (Aug 1, 1918), p. 7; *CE* 2.13 (Mar 28, 1914), p. 8; Confidence 1.2 (May 1908), p. 8.

[383] See Yong, *Theology and Down Syndrome*, pp. 209-12.

cation from the body of Christ … There is no middle ground. If you acknowledge that I belong to the church, you must admit me to your Supper. If you will not admit me to your Supper, you should not then talk about my nevertheless being your 'fellow in Christ'.[384]

In this practice of the open Table, Pentecostals bear witness to the generous oneness of the church and the radical hospitality of the church's Lord.

When all has been said, however, a basic and deeply troubling problem remains. If the Eucharist is what it is claimed to be, then how can the church be divided? Anglican priest and theological historian Ephraim Radner raises just this concern, suggesting that most theories of the Eucharist in fact abstract Eucharistic doctrine from the concreteness of the church's brokenness so that the 'whole question of how in fact the Eucharist "tastes" in a contemporaneously divided church can be avoided in this framework, since its savor – "foretaste" – derives from something whose substance lies beyond the "bitter root" of the present'.[385] Radner concludes that 'the Eucharist in this way has been bequeathed to an ahistorical Spirit, whose life, whose sensibilities, are granted immunity from the prophecies that touch the Church's form'. Churchly decisions have in fact dismembered the body of Christ so that the church now exists in 'pneumatic abandonment', in the absence of the Spirit. As a result, the character of the church's sacraments is compromised. 'Until unity is reestablished, the character of any sacrament is emptied of any practical divine effect, and turns into an instrument of increased defilement and alienation.'[386]

Radner is surely right to call attention to the dividedness of the church, and to call into question claims about the Eucharist that for all their intellectual coherence do not touch the realities of churchly life. He wisely raises concerns about whether talking of the Eucharist as a sign of the kingdom does not in fact cut off the Spirit from the church's immediate state. Nonetheless, he misses an all-important point.[387] The Eucharist is not only an effective *sign* of the

---

[384] Jenson, *Visible Words*, p. 113.
[385] Radner, *The End of the Church*, p. 204.
[386] Radner, *The End of the Church*, p. 189.
[387] For an insightful critique of Radner's thesis (and attending methodology), see David S. Cunningham, 'A Response to Ephraim Radner's *The End of the*

heavenly banquet, but it is also the *grammar* of the kingdom's language, a 'visible word' that can be 'translated' into churchly life on mission in the world – if communities and their heads are willing to do that hard work. In this connection, it seems significant that the fellowship meals of primitive Pentecostal communities often turned out to be moments of intra-communal *koinonia*, of a shared experience of the peace of the kingdom of God. For example, in the words of one testimony, 'We had a precious old-fashioned "love-feast" during the meeting which brought together Christians of all denominations, and as we broke bread together all differences of opinion were forgotten'.[388] Perhaps Pentecostals' willingness to 'break bread' together *alongside* the Eucharist points a way toward the fullness of the Eucharistic promise. These meals should not re-place (in the sense of eliminate) the celebration of the sacrament of Communion, but they can help *re-place* it, in the sense of helping the church rediscover what the sacred meal-of-meals is and is for. It would seem, then, that Pentecostal communities should give themselves to the practice of eating and drinking together beyond the bounds of Eucharistic worship, for if communities hope to develop the skills of discerning/recognizing and translating/enacting kingdom realities into everyday life, there must be means of grace to train them for this work, practically inculcating these skills in them. The fellowship meal – when faithfully observed – does this as well if not better than anything else.[389]

Conclusions

Interpreters and theologians agree that all attempts at revisioning and reforming Pentecostal sacramental thought and practice are doomed to fall to the ground if the Holy Spirit does not in fact intercede and make them alive with God's own life. The Eucharist-event must be a liturgy of the Spirit. If it is to be all it is meant to

---

Church: A Pneumatology of Christian Division in the West, *Anglican Theological Review* 83.1 (Winter 2001), pp. 89-100.

[388] See *PE* 964 (Sept 3, 1932), p. 12.

[389] Rick Bliese ('Life on the Edge: A Small Church Redefines Its Mission', *Christian Century* 120.14 [July 12, 2003], p. 27), drawing on the research of Nancy Ammerman and his own pastoral experience, suggests that 'Meaningful worship and meaningful meals are critical to any attempts at renewal, and one doesn't work well without the other. Never trust a Christian fellowship where Christians regularly worship together but don't like to eat together, or where they eat together but neglect worship'.

be, the Communion rite must be baptized in and filled with the Spirit.

To avoid misunderstanding, it must be remembered that the Spirit is present to make Christ known, which means that the Spirit is *already* at work in the present by working in believers an anticipation of what is *not yet*. As the author of Hebrews says, while believers do not presently see 'everything in subjection' to the church as promised in Psalm 8, they do 'see Jesus ...' (Heb. 2.8-9). To be clear, transformation does take place here-and-now.[390] As Christ comes to the church through the Spirit in the Eucharist-event, the celebrants' eyes are opened to see the one who has gone before us into the Eschaton, a vision that alters the very structure of their being, both communally and personally. But this transformation is more than anything the awakening of desire for the beatific vision, a hunger for the glory of the Day of the Lord and eschatological marriage of heaven and earth. As Jenson puts it, 'Our liturgy is liturgy of the Spirit insofar as the sequence and rhythm of what we do is an eschatological tension'.[391] Without this 'eschatological tension', this sense of both the already-here-ness and the still-to-come-ness of the kingdom, the worship service is dead – or, worse, alive with something other than the Spirit's presence. Hence it is necessary that the Eucharist-event be celebrated in such a way[392] that celebrants are *moved* to praise, to petition, and to witness by the reality of God's promise of a future in which all things are put right and God is 'all in all' (1 Cor. 15.24-28). That means the Lord's Supper must be given and received εἴ τις κοινωνία πνεύματος (Phil.

---

[390] The kind of transformation the Spirit effects is illustrated in the testimony of an early British Pentecostal, William Bernard, who tells of how his 'Latter Rain experience' of the Spirit has transfigured his (Anglican) confession of the Nicene creed, which he reminds the readers, is 'recited in the beautiful communion liturgy each time the Lord's Supper is celebrated'. For years he had professed these convictions reverently, he says, 'but how differently they fell from my lips after the Indwelling Spirit put His great white light on Jesus and so revealed to my spirit the great, all-inspiring truth of which these words testify: the truth of God Incarnate in the flesh ...' He continues, 'The blessed Holy Spirit so burned this stupendous truth into my spirit that since that time this beloved creed as I utter it, is pronounced in the only way possible to me – with bated breath'. See *LRE* 21.6 (Mar 1929), p. 21.

[391] Robert W. Jenson, 'Liturgy of the Spirit', *The Lutheran Quarterly* 26 (May 1974), p. 190.

[392] Therefore, both *what* is done in the worship service and *how* it is done matter to the utmost. See Jenson, *Liturgy of the Spirit*, pp. 189-203.

2.1). For, when rightly celebrated, as the Holy Spirit is at work, then the church's celebration of the Lord's Supper provides a glimpse – 'through a glass, darkly' (1 Cor. 13.12) – of the glories of the End. By the Spirit's intimately effective presence, the simple acts of eating Christ's bread and drinking his cup become by faith and in hope an anticipatory share in the delights of the beatific vision, a foretaste of the eschatological banquet.

6

CONTRIBUTIONS & SUGGESTIONS FOR FURTHER RESEARCH

Contributions

This study has produced a number of contributions to academic Pentecostal scholarship, generally, and to the theology of the sacraments, more particularly. I will spell out these contributions in the order that they have emerged in the study.

First, Chapter 2 offers the first comprehensive survey of contemporary scholarly Pentecostal contributions to and engagements with sacramental theology and practice. This survey not only shows that there has been a recent upsurge of theological reflection on the sacraments among Pentecostals, but that in many ways this is a *recovery* of a lost vision.

Second, perhaps one of the more important contributions of this study is the inductive reading of the early Pentecostal periodical literature provided in Chapter 3, where the sacramentality of the first generation Pentecostal movement(s) is unearthed and carefully analyzed. Building on the work of Kimberly Alexander, I developed for that reading an interpretive strategy that allowed specifically Pentecostal categories and concerns to give direction and order to the reading. This strategy was used in order to allow the unique and many-faceted sacramentality so evident in the literature of the movement in its earliest days to reveal itself. Also, this interpretive model helped to excavate the unstated and inchoate convictions about the sacraments that undergirded first-generation Pentecostals' sacramental theology and praxis. It did so by attending not only to their overt statements but also to their *testimonies* of sacramental experiences and to the *implied* sacramentality embedded in their habits of speech and action. In the course of this reading, it was discovered that contra much of what has been reported in the secondary literature, early Pentecostals were *not* averse to sacramental language and they did not uniformly hold to a weakly memorialist view of the Lord's Supper. In fact, many signs of a robust sacramentality – especially as it relates to the Eucharist – were found. Therefore, in the light of these and other similar discoveries it seems clear that the story of early Pentecostalism needs to be rewritten to show that the sacraments, and especially the Communion rite, were central to the spirituality of the emerging movement.

Third, Chapter 4 first proposes an interpretive strategy for reading Scripture faithfully. This strategy is built upon and informed by an emerging Pentecostal hermeneutic, the distinguishing marks of which are identified, analyzed, and evaluated. A few improvements to this emerging methodology also are suggested. Then, the chapter puts this hermeneutical model into use, providing a sustained and intentionally Pentecostal reading of key New Testament Eucharistic texts. Informed by the interpretive strategy developed for and used in Chapter 3, this reading attends not only to those texts that explicitly refer to the Lord's Supper, but also to texts in which the sacramentality is merely implied or suggested. In this way, the foundation is laid for a full-bodied biblical theology of the Lord's Supper.

Fourth, drawing on the work of the previous sections, Chapter 5 provides a sustained, coherent, and robustly sacramental account of the Lord's Supper that arises from the distinct concerns of the Pentecostal theological and spiritual tradition while remaining in touch at every point with the wider Christian tradition as well. Consequently, this proposal is distinguished not only by being the most fully developed Pentecostal account of the Lord's Supper, but also by virtue of its conversance with the theology and experience of other Christian traditions.

Fifth, because it is both Pentecostal and catholic, this proposal opens up a number of possibilities for engagement in ecumenical conversation. This study shows that Pentecostals have positive contributions to make to the ecumenical process of discerning what the Supper means for and requires of the church, and it demonstrates that Pentecostals can deliver an account of the Eucharist that is not determined by either an outright rejection or an uncritical acceptance of the claims of the sacramental traditions.

Sixth, the results of this study suggest that the account of the Eucharist described in Chapter 5 squares with the biblical witness, the witness of early Pentecostals, and the testimony of the wider Christian tradition, and given that this is true it would appear not merely possible but even necessary for Pentecostals to revision the tradition in such a way that the sacrament of the Lord's Supper is central to the tradition's theology and praxis.

Seventh, this study offers one model for the Pentecostal theological constructive task. While deeply indebted to other Pentecostal theological models, this model is nonetheless unique in certain key respects. Like other Pentecostal theological works, it draws heavily on the witness of early Pentecostalism and on readings of Scripture, engaging extensively in dialogue with the Great Tradition. However, it goes beyond other works of its kind in that it self-consciously attempts to allow each of these factors both to determine and be determined by interaction with the other features, so that this study is biblical, Pentecostal, and catholic all-at-once. In this way, this study provides a paradigm for constructive Pentecostal theological work.

Implications and Suggestions for Further Study

In the light of the contributions of this study, the following present themselves as points of entry into areas for further research.

First, my reading of the early Pentecostal periodical literature reveals that while early Pentecostals as a whole held a rather 'high' view of the Eucharist they at the same time held a relatively 'low' view of water baptism, at least at the explicit level of discourse. Why was this so? What were the historical and theological causes that gave rise to these contrasting views? In fact, given that not only the Eucharist but also water baptism, footwashing, and the laying on of hands by anointing with oil were characteristic early Pentecostal practices, it would perhaps be rewarding to develop a Pentecostal theology of these practices/rites following the model used in this study.

Second, Kimberly Alexander's monograph on Pentecostal theologies of healing and Larry McQueen's work on the eschatological views of early Pentecostals have demonstrated that the basic soteriological convictions of Wesleyan-Holiness Pentecostals differed significantly from those of Finished Work Pentecostals, basic differences that gave rise to far-reaching effects in the thought and practice of these movements. However, my reading of early Pentecostal periodical literature has shown that no significant differences of sacramentality emerged to divide Wesleyan-Holiness from Finished Work Pentecostals, at least not in the early days of the movements. Further study is needed to determine why this was so and whether real differences eventually did reveal themselves at some point in the movements' histories.

Third, further research is needed to explicate early Pentecostals' understanding of the movement's relation to the *ecclesia catholica*. Some early Pentecostals understood the movement as the 'unfoldment' of a new chapter in the one story of the church while others understood it as a restoration of a lost identity. What historical factors gave rise to these differences? What were the long-term theological and practical outcomes of these different views? More specifically, what is the relationship of restorationism to sacramentality?

Fourth, Pentecostal scholarship has given comparatively little attention to the biblical witness to the sacrament of the Lord's Supper, focusing for the most part on readings of 1 Corinthians 11 and the narratives of institution. However, the hermeneutic laid out in Chapter 4 shows that many other scriptures – including Old Testament texts – can and should be allowed to inform a Pentecostal theology of the sacraments. How to encourage other scholars to read a variety of other texts relative to the Eucharist? What would a Pentecostal reading of the Eucharistic texts in the Gospel of Mark or reflection on meals in the divine presence in the Old Testament reveal?

Fifth, in this study, I have proposed certain ways in which Pentecostal theology works out in the life of the church in the hope of moving toward the development of a self-consciously Pentecostal praxis that is genuinely catholic without being a slavish reproduction of other Christians' patterns of worship. What liturgical reforms are in order in the light of the view of the Supper put forward in this study? More specifically, what role should early Pentecostal liturgical rubrics play in developing contemporary liturgies that make room for regular and frequent celebration of Communion as a central act of worship?

Sixth, it would be beneficial to bring the findings of this work into conversation with reflections on the sacramental thought and practice of Pentecostals in the majority world. For example, it would be instructive to know how Latin-American Pentecostals read the Eucharistic texts engaged in this study. Also, what would Pentecostals of Eastern Europe make of the view of the Lord's Supper proposed in this study?

BIBLIOGRAPHY

Early Pentecostal Periodicals

The Apostolic Faith (Azusa Street Mission, Los Angeles, CA).

The Bridegroom's Messenger (The Pentecostal Mission, Atlanta, GA).

The Christian Evangel (Assemblies of God, Plainfield, IN; Findley, OH).

The Church of God Book of Doctrines (Cleveland, TN; 1922).

The Church of God Evangel (Church of God, Cleveland, TN).

The Pentecost (J. Roswell Flower, Indianapolis, IN).

The Pentecostal Evangel (Assemblies of God, Springfield, MO).

The Pentecostal Holiness Advocate (The Pentecostal Holiness Church, Falcon, NC; Franklin Spring, GA).

Pentecostal Testimony (William H. Durham, Chicago, IL; Los Angeles, CA).

Weekly Evangel (Assemblies of God, St. Louis, MO; Springfield, MO).

Word and Witness (E.N. Bell, Malvern, AR; Findley, OH; St. Louis, MO).

Confidence (A.A. Boddy, Sunderland, England, UK).

Other Works Cited

Albrecht, D.E., 'Pentecostal Spirituality: Looking Through the Lens of Ritual', *Pneuma* 14.2 (1996), pp. 107-25.

—'Pentecostal Spirituality: Ecumenical Potential and Challenge', *Cyberjournal for Pentecostal-Charismatic Research* 2 (July 1997). [Internet] <http://www.pctii.org/cyberj/cyberj2/albrecht.html>. [Accessed March 2011.]

—*Rites in the Spirit: A Ritual Approach to Pentecostal/Charismatic Spirituality* (JPTSup 17; Sheffield: Sheffield Academic Press, 1999).

Alexander, K.E., *Pentecostal Healing: Models in Theology and Practice* (JPTSup 29; Blandford Forum: Deo Publishing, 2006).

Allison, Jr. D.C., 'The Living Water: John 4.10-14; 6.35c; 7.37-39', *SVTQ* 30.2 [1986], pp. 143-57.

Althouse, P., 'Ascension–Pentecost–Eschaton: A Theological Framework for Pentecostal Ecclesiology', in John Christopher Thomas (ed.), *Toward a Pentecostal Ecclesiology* (Cleveland: TN, 2010), pp. 225-47.

—*Spirit of the Last Days: Pentecostal Eschatology in Conversation with Jürgen Moltmann* (JPTSup 25; London: T&T Clark International, 2003).

Anderson, A., *An Introduction to Pentecostalism* (Cambridge: Cambridge University Press, 2004).

Anderson, P.N., *The Christology of the Fourth Gospel: Its Unity and Disunity in the Light of John* 6 (Tübingen: Mohr Siebeck, 1996).

Archer, K.J., *A Pentecostal Hermeneutic: Spirit, Scripture and Community* (JPTSup 28; Continuum, 2005; Cleveland, TN: CPT Press, 2009).

—'A Pentecostal Way of Doing Theology: Method and Manner', *IJST* 9.3 (July, 2007), pp. 301-14.

—Nourishment for our Journey: The Pentecostal *Via Salutis* and Sacramental Ordinances', *JPT* 13.1 (2004), pp. 88-95.

—'The Fivefold Gospel and the Mission of the Church: Ecclesiastical Implications and Opportunities', in John Christopher Thomas (ed.), *Toward a Pentecostal Ecclesiology* (Cleveland, TN: CPT Press, 2010), pp. 7-43.

Arrington, F.L., *Christian Doctrine: A Pentecostal Perspective Vol. 3* (Cleveland, TN: Pathway, 1994).

Athanasius, *On the Incarnation* (Crestwood, NY: SVS Press, 1996).

Augustine, D.C., 'Pentecost Communal Economics and the Household of God', *JPT* 19.2 (2010), pp. 219-42.

Ayers, A., 'Can the Behavior of Tongues Utterance Still Function as Ecclesial Boundary? The Significance of Art and Sacrament', *Pneuma* 22.2 (Fall 2000), pp. 271-301.

Bailey, K.E., 'The Structure of 1 Corinthians and Paul's Theological Method Also With Special Reference to 4.17', *Novum Testamentum* 25.2 (1983), pp. 152-81.

Baptism, Eucharist, and Ministry, Faith and Order Paper 111 (Geneva: World Council of Churches, 1982).

Bartholomew, C.G., Joel B. Green, and Anthony C. Thiselton (eds.) *Reading Luke: Interpretation, Reflection, Formation* (Grand Rapids: Zondervan, 2005).

Bartholomew, C.G., Mary Healy, Karl Moller, and Robin Parry (eds.) *Out of Egypt: Biblical Theology and Biblical Interpretation* (Grand Rapids: Zondervan, 2004).

Beacham, D., *Azusa East: The Life and Times of G.B. Cashwell* (Franklin Springs, GA: LifeSprings Resources, 2006).

Benedict XVI, *The Sacrament of Charity* (Washington, DC: USCCB, 2007).

Benz, E., *The Eastern Orthodox Church: Its Thought and Life* (Garden City, NY: Anchor Books, 1963).

Berge, P.S., 'John 6.1-71: The Bread Which Gives Life to the World', *Word & World* 5.3 (June 1985), pp. 311-20.

Bergsma, J.S., *The Jubilee from Leviticus to Qumran* (Leiden: Brill, 2007).

Best, T.F., *Baptism Today: Understanding, Practice, Ecumenical Implications* (Collegeville, MN: Liturgical Press, 2008).

Bicknell, R., 'In Memory of Christ's Sacrifice: Roots and Shoots of Elim's Eucharistic Expression', *JEPTA* 27 (1997), pp. 59-89.

—'The Ordinances: The Marginalised Aspects of Pentecostalism' in Keith Warrington (ed.), *Pentecostal Perspectives* (Carlisle: Paternoster, 1998), pp. 204-22.

Biddy, W.S., 'Re-envisioning the Pentecostal Understanding of the Eucharist: An Ecumenical Proposal', *Pneuma* 28.2 (Fall 2006), pp. 228-51.

Bingham, D.J., 'Eucharist and Incarnation: The Second Century and Luther' in Roch A. Kereszty (ed.), *Rediscovering the Eucharist: Ecumenical Conversations* (Mahwah, NJ: Paulist Press, 2003), pp. 116-41.

Bliese, R.H., 'Life on the Edge: A Small Church Redefines Its Mission', *Christian Century* 120.14 (July 12, 2003), pp. 24-27.

—'Speaking in Tongues and the Mission of God *Ad Gentes*', *JPT* 20.1 (2011), pp. 38-47.

Blomberg, C.L., 'Jesus, Sinners, and Table Fellowship', *Bulletin for Biblical Research*, 19.1 (2009), pp. 35-62.

Blumhofer, E.W., *Restoring the Faith: the Assemblies of God, Pentecostalism, and American Culture* (Champagne, IL: University of Illinois Press, 1993).

Böcher, O. 'Ass Johannes der Taufer kein Brot (Luk 7:33)', *New Testament Studies* 18.1 (Oct 1971), pp. 90-92.

Bonaventure, *Breviloquim* (Works of St Bonaventure Vol. IX; Saint Bonaventure, NY: Franciscan Institute Publications, 2005).

Bond, J., 'What is Distinctive about Pentecostal Theology', in M.S. Clark and H.I. Lederle (eds.) *What is Distinctive about Pentecostal Theology* (Pretoria: UNISA, 1989), pp. 133-42.

Bonhoeffer, D., *Christ the Center* (New York: Harper & Row, 1978).

—*Sanctorum Communio* (*Dietrich Bonhoeffer Works Vol. 1*; Minneapolis: Fortress Press, 1998).

Borchert, G.L., *John 1-11* (The New American Commentary; Grand Rapids: Broadman & Holman, 1996).

Borgen, O.E., *John Wesley on the Sacraments* (Grand Rapids: Francis Asbury Press, 1972).
Borgen, P., *Bread from Heaven: An Exegetical Study of the Concept of Manna in the Gospel of John* (Leiden: Brill, 1965).
—'Observations on the Midrashic Character of John 6', *Zeitschrift für die Neutestamentliche Wissenschaft* 54 (1963), pp. 232-40.
Bowen, C.E., *The Lord's Supper and Feet Washing* (Cleveland, TN: Church of God Publications, 1955).
Bradshaw, P.F., *Early Christian Worship: A Basic Introduction to Ideas and Practice* (2nd ed.; Collegeville, MN: Liturgical Press, 2010).
Brewer, B.C., 'Evangelical Anglicanism: John Wesley's Dialectical Theology of Baptism', *Evangelical Quarterly* 83.2 (Apr 2011), pp. 107-32.
Bromiley, G.W., *Historical Theology: An Introduction* (Grand Rapids: Eerdmans, 1978).
Brooks, N. *Charismatic Ministries in the New Testament* (Greenville, SC: Holmes Memorial Church, 1988).
—*Let There Be Life* (Franklin Springs, GA: Advocate Press, 1975).
—*Scriptural Holiness* (Franklin Springs, GA: Advocate Press, 1967).
Brown, R.E., *The Gospel According to John I-XII* (The Anchor Bible; Garden City, NY: Doubleday & Company, 1966).
—*The Gospel and Epistles of John: A Concise Commentary* (Collegeville, MN: Liturgical Press, 1988).
Bruce, F.F., *Paul: Apostle of the Heart Set Free* (Grand Rapids: Eerdmans, 1979).
Bruno, C.R., '"Jesus is Our Jubilee" … But How? The OT Background and Lukan Fulfillment of the Ethics of Jubilee', *JETS* 53.1 (Mar 2010), pp. 81-101.
Bulgakov, S. *The Comforter* (Grand Rapids: Eerdmans, 2004).
—*The Holy Grail and the Eucharist* (Hudson, NY: Lindisfarne, 1997).
Bultmann, R., *Theology of the New Testament* (Waco: Baylor University Press, 2007).
Burge, G., 'Revelation and Discipleship in St John's Gospel', in John Liermen (ed.), *Challenging Perspectives on the Gospel of John* (Tübingen: Mohr Siebeck, 2006), pp. 235-54.
Burgess, S.M., G.B. McGee, and P.H. Alexander (eds.), *Dictionary of Pentecostal and Charismatic Movements* (Grand Rapids: Zondervan, 1988).
Burgess, S.M., and E.M. van der Maas (eds.), *The New International Dictionary of Pentecostal and Charismatic Movements* (Grand Rapids: Zondervan, 2003).
Byrne, B.J., *The Hospitality of God: a Reading of Luke's Gospel* (Collegeville, MN: Liturgical Press, 2000).
Cabasilas, N. *The Life in Christ* (Crestwood, NY: SVS Press, 1998).
Cahalan, K.A., *Formed in the Image of Christ: The Sacramental-Moral Theology of Bernard Häring, C.Ss.R* (Collegeville, MN: Liturgical Press, 2004).
Campbell, J.E., *The Pentecostal Holiness Church* 1898-1948 (Franklin Springs, GA: Publishing House of Pentecostal Holiness Church, 1951).
Cantalamessa, R., *Come, Creator Spirit* (Collegeville, MN: Liturgical Press, 2003).
Carson, D.A., *The Gospel According to John* (TPNTC; Grand Rapids: Eerdmans, 1991).
—'Understanding Misunderstanding in the Fourth Gospel', *Tyndale Bulletin* 33 (1982), pp. 61-91.
Cartledge, M.J., *Charismatic Glossolalia: An Empirical-Theological Study* (Burlington, VT: Ashgate, 2002).
—'Pentecostal Theological Method and Intercultural Theology', *Transformation* 25.2-3 (2008), pp. 92-102.
—*Testimony in the Spirit: Rescripting Ordinary Pentecostal Theology* (Burlington, VT: Ashgate Publishing, 2010).
—*Testimony: Its Importance, Place and Potential* (Renewal 9; Cambridge: Grove Books, 2002).

—'The Early Pentecostal Theology of *Confidence* Magazine (1908-1926): A Version of the Five-Fold Gospel?', *JEPTA* 28.2 (2008), pp. 117-30.

Cartwright, M.G., 'Stanley Hauerwas's Essays in Theological Ethics: A Reader's Guide' in Berkman, J. and M.G. Cartwright (eds.), *The Hauerwas Reader* (Durham, NC: Duke University Press, 2001), pp. 623-71.

Castelo, D., 'Canonical Theism as Ecclesial and Ecumenical Response', *Pneuma* 33.3 (2011), pp. 370-89.

—'Tarrying on the Lord: Affections, Virtues, and Theological Ethics in Pentecostal Perspective', *JPT* 13.1 [Oct 2004], pp. 31-56.

—'The Improvisational Quality of Ecclesial Holiness', in John Christopher Thomas (ed.) *Toward a Pentecostal Ecclesiology: The Church and the Fivefold Gospel* (Cleveland, TN: CPT Press, 2010), pp. 87-104.

Ceresoli, J., 'Critical Mass: "We Had Church" in a Holy Catholic Way', *JPT* 17 (October 2000), pp. 7-11.

Chan, S., 'Jesus as Spirit-Baptizer: Its Significance for Pentecostal Ecclesiology', in John Christopher Thomas [ed.], *Toward a Pentecostal Ecclesiology: The Church and the Fivefold Gospel* (Cleveland, TN: CPT Press, 2010), pp. 139-56.

—*Liturgical Theology: The Church as Worshipping Community* (Downers Grove, Ill: IVP, 2006).

—*Pentecostal Theology and the Christian Spiritual Tradition* (JPTSup 21; Sheffield: Sheffield Academic Press, 2000).

—'The Church and the Development of Doctrine', *JPT* 13.1 (2004), pp. 57-77.

Chaplin, A.D. 'The Invisible and the Sublime: From Participation to Reconciliation', in James K.A. Smith and James H. Olthius [eds.] *Introducing Radical Orthodoxy: Mapping a Post-Secular Theology* (Grand Rapids: Baker Academic, 2005).

Chauvet, L-M., *The Sacraments: The Word of God at the Mercy of the Body* (Collegeville, MN: Liturgical Press, 1997).

—*Symbol and Sacrament: A Sacramental Reinterpretation of Christian Existence* (Collegeville, MN: Liturgical Press, 1995).

Chilcote, P.W., *Recapturing the Wesleys' Vision: An Introduction to the Faith of John and Charles Wesley* (Downers Grove, IL: IVP, 2004).

Childs, B., *The Book of Exodus: A Critical, Theological Commentary* (Louisville: WJKP, 1974).

Christensen, M.J. and J.A. Wittung (eds.), *Partakers of the Divine Nature: The History and Development of Deification in the Christian Traditions* (Grand Rapids: Baker Academic, 2007).

Clark, M.S. and H.I. Lederle (eds.), *What is Distinctive about Pentecostal Theology* (Pretoria: University of South Africa, 1989).

Collins, R.F., *First Corinthians* (Sacra Pagina; Collegeville, MN: Liturgical Press, 1999).

Cosgrove, C.H., 'The Place Where Jesus Is: Allusions to Baptism and the Eucharist in the Fourth Gospel', *New Testament Studies* 35 (1989), pp. 522-39.

Chrysostom, J., *Homilies on 1 Corinthians* 24.3, NPNF 1.12.

Coffey, D. 'The Holy Spirit as the Mutual Love of the Father and the Son', *Theological Studies* 51 (1990), pp. 193-229.

—'The "Incarnation" of the Holy Spirit in Christ', *Theological Studies* 45 (1984), pp. 466-80.

Conzelmann, H., *A Commentary on the First Epistle to the Corinthians* (Philadelphia: Fortress Press, 1975).

Corbin, M., 'Pain de la Vie: La Lecture de Jean VI par S Thomas d'Aquin', *Recherches de Science Religieuse* 65.1 (Jan-Mar 1977), pp. 107-38.

Coulter, D., '"Delivered by the Power of God": Toward a Pentecostal Understanding of Salvation', *IJST* 10.4 (October, 2008), pp. 447-67.

Cross, T.L., 'A Proposal to Break the Ice: What Can Pentecostal Theology Offer Evangelical Theology', *JPT* 10.2 (Apr 2002), pp. 44-73.

—'The Divine-Human Encounter: Towards a Pentecostal Theology of Experience', *Pneuma* 31.1 (2009), pp. 3-34.

—'The Rich Feast of Theology: Can Pentecostals Bring the Main Course or Only the Relish?' *JPT* 16 (Apr 2000), pp. 27-47.

Crossan, J.D., 'It is Written: A Structuralist Analysis of John 6', *Semeia* 26 (1983), pp. 3-21.

Cullmann, Oscar and F.J. Leenhardt, *Essays on the Lord's Supper* (Cambridge, UK: James Clarke & Co., 2004).

Culpepper, R.A., *A Study in the Fourth Gospel: A Study in Literary Design* (Minneapolis: Fortress Press, 1987).

Culpepper, R.A. (ed.), *Critical Readings of John 6* (Leiden: Brill, 1997).

Cummings, O.F., *Eucharistic Doctors: A Theological History* (Mahwah, NJ: Paulist Press, 2005).

Cunningham, D.S., 'A Response to Ephraim Radner's The End of the Church: A Pneumatology of Christian Division in the West', *Anglican Theological Review* 83.1 (Winter 2001), pp. 89-100.

Cyril of Jerusalem, 'Mystagogic Catechesis 4' in Edward Yarnold, *Cyril of Jerusalem* (Early Church Fathers, London: Routledge, 2000), pp. 179-81.

Daise, M.A., *Feasts in John: Jewish Festivals and Jesus' 'Hour' in the Fourth Gospel* (Tübingen: Mohr Siebeck, 2007).

Davis, E.F., 'Teaching the Bible Confessionally in the Church' in Richard B. Hays and Ellen F. Davis (eds.), *The Art of Reading Scripture* (Grand Rapids: Eerdmans, 2003).

Dauphinais, M., '"And They Shall Be Taught of God": Wisdom and the Eucharist in John 6' in Michael Dauphinais and Matthew Levering (eds.), *Reading John with St. Thomas Aquinas* (Washington, DC: Catholic University of America Press, 2005), pp. 312-17.

Dayton, D.W., *Theological Roots of Pentecostalism* (Peabody, MA: Hendrickson, 1987).

De Arteaga, W., *Forgotten Power: The Significance of the Lord's Supper in Revival* (Grand Rapids: Zondervan, 2002).

Del Colle, R., 'Pentecostal/Catholic Dialogue: Theological Suggestions for Consideration', *Pneuma* 25.1 (Spring 2003), pp. 93-96.

Dempster, M., 'The Church's Moral Witness: A Study in Glossolalia in Luke's Theology of Acts', *Paraclete* 23 [1989], pp. 1-7.

Dorrow, M., 'Worship is Mission: Seeing the Eucharist as the Drama of God's Mission to the World', *Missio Apostolica* 9.2 (Nov 2001), pp. 78-83.

Duffield, G.P. and N.M. Van Cleave, *Foundations of Pentecostal Theology* (Los Angeles: L.I.F.E. Bible College, 1983).

Dunn, J.D.G., 'John VI – A Eucharistic Discourse?', *New Testament Studies* 17 (1971), pp. 328-38.

Dusing, M., 'The New Testament Church', in Stanley Horton (ed.) *Systematic Theology* (rev. ed.; Springfield, MO: Logion Press, 1998), pp. 525-66.

Ellington, S.A., 'The Costly Loss of Testimony', *JPT* 16 (2000), pp. 48-59.

Emery, G., 'Holy Cene (Lord's Supper): Practice and Significance in the Pentecostal Tradition', *Ecumenism* 170 (Summer 2008), pp. 25-27.

Ervin, H.M., 'Hermeneutics: A Pentecostal Option', *Pneuma* 3.2 (1981), pp. 11–25.

Esler, P.F., *Community and Gospel in Luke-Acts: The Social and Political Motivations of Lucan Theology* (Cambridge: Cambridge University Press, 1987).

Evdokimov, P., *The Sacrament of Love* (Crestwood, NY: SVS Press, 1985).

Farelly, N., *The Disciples in the Fourth Gospel: A Narrative Analysis of Their Faith and Understanding* (Tübingen: Mohr Siebeck, 2010).

Farkasfalvy, D., 'The Eucharistic Provenance of New Testament Texts', in Roch Kereszty (ed.), *Rediscovering the Eucharist: Ecumenical Conversations* (Mahwah, NJ: Paulist Press, 2003).

Fee, G.D., *God's Empowering Presence: The Holy Spirit in the Letters of Paul* (Peabody, MA: Hendricksen, 1994).

—*Pauline Christology: An Exegetical-Theological Study* (Peabody, MA: Hendrickson, 2007).

Flett, J.G., *The Witness of God: The Trinity, Missio Dei, Karl Barth, and the Nature of Christian Community* (Grand Rapids: Eerdmans, 2010).

Florovsky, G., *Bible, Church, Tradition: An Eastern Orthodox View* (Belmont, MA: Nordland Publishers, 1972).

Focant, C. and André Wénin (eds.), *Analyse narrative et Bible* (Leuven: Leuven University Press, 2005).

Fotopoulos, J., *Food Offered to Idols in Roman Corinth: A Socio-Rhetorical Reconsideration* (Tübingen: Mohr Siebeck, 2003).

Fowl, S.E., 'John 6.25-35', *Interpretation* (July 2007), pp. 314-16.

Fowl, S.E. (ed.), *The Theological Interpretation of Scripture: Classic and Contemporary Readings* (Malden, MA: Blackwell Publishing, 1997).

Furnish, V.P., *The Theology of the First Letter to the Corinthians* (NTT; Cambridge: Cambridge University Press, 1999).

Gäckle, V., *Die Starken und die Schwachen in Korinth und in Rom: Zu Herkunft und Funktion der Antithese in 1 Kor 8.1-11.1 und in Rom 14.1-15* (Tübingen: Mohr Siebeck, 2004).

Garland, D.E., 'The Dispute Over Food Offered to Idols (1 Cor. 8.1-11.1)', *Perspectives in Religious Studies* 30.2 (Sum 2003), pp. 173-97.

Gelpi, D.L., *Committed Worship: A Sacramental Theology for Converting Christians Vol. 2* (Collegeville, MN: Liturgical Press, 1993).

Gibson, D., 'Eating Is Believing? On Midrash and the Mixing of Metaphors in John 6', *Themelios* 27.7 (Spring 2002), pp. 5-15.

Green, J.B., *The Theology of the Gospel of Luke* (Cambridge: Cambridge University Press, 1995).

Green, J.B., H.S. McKnight, and I.H. Marshall (eds.), *Dictionary of Jesus and the Gospels* (Downers Grove, IL: IVP, 1992).

Griffith, S.H., '"Spirit in the Bread; Fire in the Wine": The Eucharist as "Living Medicine" in the Thought of Ephraem the Syrian', *Modern Theology* 15.2 (Apr 1999), pp. 225-46.

Gupta, N.K. 'Which "Body" Is a Temple (1 Corinthians 6:19)? Paul Beyond the Individual/Communal Divine', *Catholic Biblical Quarterly* 72.3 (July 2010), pp. 518-36.

Guroian, V., 'Liturgy and the Lost Eschatological Vision of Christian Ethics', *Annual of the Society of Christian Ethics* 20 (2000), pp. 227-38.

Hamid-Kahni, S., *Revelation and Concealment of Christ: A Theological Inquiry into the Elusive Language of the Fourth Gospel* (Tübingen: Mohr Siebeck, 2000).

Hahn, S.W., 'Kingdom and Church in Luke-Acts: From Davidic Christology to Kingdom Ecclesiology', in Craig G. Bartholomew, Joel B. Green, and Anthony C. Thiselton (eds.) *Reading Luke: Interpretation, Reflection, Formation* (Grand Rapids: Zondervan, 2005), pp. 294-326.

Han, K.S., 'Theology of Prayer in the Gospel of Luke', *JETS* 43.4 (Dec 2000), pp. 675-93.

Hanna, E.B., 'Biblical Interpretation and Sacramental Practice: John Calvin's Interpretation of John 6.51-58', *Worship* 73.3 (May 1999), pp. 211-30.

Häring, B., 'Liturgical Piety and Christian Perfection', *Worship* 34.9 (Oct 1, 1960), pp. 523-35.

Harrington, H.K. and R. Patten, 'Pentecostal Hermeneutics and Postmodern Literary Theory', *Pneuma* 16.1 (Spring 1994), pp. 109-14.

Hauerwas, S., 'The Servant Community: Christian Social Ethics' in J. Berkman and M.G. Cartwright (eds.), *The Hauerwas Reader* (Durham, NC: Duke University Press, 2001), pp. 371-91.

Hays, R.B., *First Corinthians* (Interpretation; Louisville: Westminster John Knox Press, 1997).

—*The Conversion of the Imagination: Paul as Interpreter of Israel's Scripture* (Grand Rapids: Eerdmans, 2005).

Heise, J., *Bleiben: Menein in den Johanneischen Schriften* (Tübingen: Mohr Siebeck, 1967).

Hertig, P., 'The Jubilee Mission of Jesus in the Gospel of Luke: Reversals of Fortunes', *Missiology* 26.2 (Apr 2008), pp. 167-79.

Hocken, P., 'The Holy Spirit Makes the Church More Eschatological', in William K. Kay and Anne E. Dyer, *Pentecostal and Charismatic Studies: A Reader* (London: SCM Press, 2004), pp. 43-46.

Hollander, H.W., 'The Idea of Fellowship in 1 Corinthians 10.14–22', *New Testament Studies* 55.4 (Oct 2009), pp. 456-70.

Hollenweger,W.J., *The Pentecostals* (Peabody, MA: Hendrickson, 1988).

Horsley, R.A., '1 Corinthians: A Case Study of Paul's Assembly as an Alternative Society', in Richard A. Horsley [ed.], *Paul and Empire: Religion and Power in Roman Imperial Society* (Harrisburg, PA: Trinity Press International, 1997), p. 242-52.

Horton, S.M., *Into all Truth: A Survey of the Course and Content of Divine Revelation* (Springfield, MO: Gospel Publishing House, 1955).

Horton, S.M. (ed.), *Systematic Theology* (rev. ed.; Springfield, MO: Logion Press, 1995).

Hume, D.A., *The Early Christian Community: A Narrative Analysis of Acts 2.41-47 and 4.32-35* (Tübingen: Mohr Siebeck, 2011).

Hunter, H.D., 'Reflections by a Pentecostalist on Aspects of BEM', *Journal of Ecumenical Studies* 29.3-4 (Summer-Fall 1992), pp. 317-45.

Irenaues, *Against Heresies* in *The Ante-Nicene Fathers, Volume 1* (Grand Rapids: Eerdmans, 1973).

Jacobsen, D., *A Reader in Pentecostal Theology: Voices from the First Generation* (Bloomington, IN: Indiana University Press, 2006).

—*Thinking in the Spirit: Theologies of the Early Pentecostal Movement* (Bloomington: Indiana University Press, 2003).

Jasper, R.C.D. and G.J. Cuming, *Prayers of the Eucharist: Early and Reformed* (Collegeville, MN: Liturgical Press, 1990).

Jenson, R.W., 'A Second Thought About Inspiration', *Pro Ecclesia* 13.4 (Fall 2004), pp. 393-98.

—'A Lutheran Among Friendly Pentecostals', *JPT* 20.1 (2011), p. 50.

—*Canon and Creed* (Louisville: WJKP, 2010).

—'Liturgy of the Spirit', *The Lutheran Quarterly* 26 (May 1974), pp. 189-203.

—*On Thinking the Human: Resolutions of Difficult Notions* (Grand Rapids: Eerdmans, 2003).

— *Story and Promise: A Brief Theology of the Gospel about Jesus* (Philadelphia: Fortress Press, 1973).

—*Systematic Theology* (2 vols.; Oxford: OUP, 1997, 1999).

—'The Bible and the Trinity', *Pro Ecclesia* 11.3 (Summer 2002), pp. 329-39.

—*Visible Words* (Philadelphia: Fortress Press, 1978).

John of Damascus, *Exact Exposition of the Christian Faith* in NPNF, 2nd series, Vol. 9 (Grand Rapids: Eerdmans, 1983).

Johns, Cheryl Bridges, *Pentecostal Formation: A Pedagogy among the Oppressed* (JPTSup 2; Sheffield: Sheffield Academic Press, 1993).

Johnson, A., 'Our God Reigns: the Body of the Risen Lord in Luke 24', *Word & World* (Spring 2002), pp. 133-43.

Johnson, L.T., *The Acts of the Apostles* (Sacra Pagina; Collegeville, MN: Liturgical Press, 1992).

—*The Gospel of Luke* (Sacra Pagina; Collegeville, MN: Liturgical Press, 1991).

Jones, C., G. Wainwright, and E. Yarnold, SJ (eds.), *The Study of Spirituality* (New York: OUP, 1986).

Joncas, M., 'Tasting the Kingdom of God: The Meal Ministry of Jesus and Its Implications for Contemporary Worship and Life', *Worship* 74.4 (July 2000), pp. 329-65.

Jüngel, E., 'Texte zum Schwerpunktthema: Mission'. Internet <http://www.ekd.de/synode99/referate_juengel.html>. Accessed May 2011.

Just, Jr. A.A., 'Entering Holiness: Christology and Eucharist in Hebrews', *Concordia Theological Quarterly* 69.1 (Jan 2005), pp. 75-95.

Kärkkäinen, V-M., 'Authority, Revelation, and Interpretation in the Roman Catholic-Pentecostal Dialogue', *Pneuma* 21.1 (Spring 1999), pp. 89-114.

—'Spirit, Reconciliation and Healing in the Community: Missiological Insights from Pentecostals', *International Review of Mission* 94.372 (Jan 2005), pp. 43-50.

— 'The Pentecostal View', in Gordon T. Smith (ed.), *The Lord's Supper: Five Views* (Downers Grove, Ill: IVP, 2008), pp. 117-35.

Kärkkäinen, V-M. (ed.), *The Spirit in the World: Emerging Pentecostal Theologies in Global Context* (Grand Rapids: Eerdmans, 2009).

Keating, D.A., 'Aquinas on 1 and 2 Corinthians', in Thomas Gerard Weinandy, Daniel A. Keating, and John Yocum (eds.), *Aquinas on Scripture: An Introduction to His Biblical Commentaries* (London: T&T Clark, 2005), pp. 127-48.

Kelber, W.H., 'The Birth of a Beginning: John 1.1-18', in Mark W.G. Stibbe (ed.), *The Gospel of John as Literature: an Anthology of Twentieth-Century Perspectives* (Leiden: Brill, 1993), pp. 209-30.

Koester, C.R., 'John Six and the Lord's Supper', *Lutheran Quarterly* (Dec 1990), pp. 420-26.

—*Symbolism in the Fourth Gospel: Meaning, Mystery, Community* (2nd ed.; Minneapolis: Augsburg Fortress Press, 2003).

Köstenberger, A.J., *A Theology of John's Gospel and Letters: The Word, the Christ, the Son of God* (Grand Rapids: Zondervan, 2009).

—*The Missions of Jesus and the Disciples According to the Fourth Gospel* (Grand Rapids: Eerdmans, 1998).

Kurz, W.S., *Reading Luke-Acts: Dynamics of Biblical Narrative* (Louisville: John Knox Press, 1993).

Land, S.J., *Pentecostal Spirituality: A Passion for the Kingdom* (JPTSup 1; Sheffield: Sheffield Academic Press, 1993; Cleveland, TN: CPT Press, 2010).

Landrus, H.L., 'Hearing 3 John 2 in the Voices of History', *JPT* 11.1 (2002), pp. 70-88.

Laurence, J.D., 'The Eucharist as the Imitation of Christ', *Theological Studies* 47.2 (June 1986), pp. 286-96.

LaVerdiere, E., *Dining in the Kingdom of God: The Origins of the Eucharist in the Gospel of Luke* (Chicago: Liturgy Training Publications, 1994).

—*The Eucharist in the New Testament and the Early Church* (Collegeville, MN: Liturgical Press, 1996).

Lawler, M.G., 'Christian Rituals: An Essay in Sacramental Symbolisms', *Horizons* 7.1 (Spring 1980), pp. 7-35.

Lawyer, J.E., 'Eucharist and Martyrdom in the Letters of Ignatius of Antioch', *Anglican Theological Review* 73.3 (Summer 1991), pp. 280-97.

Lewis, A.E., *Between Cross and Resurrection: A Theology of Holy Saturday* (Grand Rapids: Eerdmans, 2003).

Lincoln, A.T., *The Gospel According to Saint John* (BNTC; London: Continuum, 2005).

Long, K.B., *The Eucharistic Theology of the American Holy Fairs* (Louisville: WJKP, 2011).

Lorenzen, T., *Resurrection, Discipleship, Justice: Affirming the Resurrection of Jesus Today* (Macon, GA: Smyth and Helwys, 2003).

Lutherans and Pentecostals in Dialogue (Strasbourg: Institute for Ecumenical Research, 2010).

Ma, W. and R.P. Menzies (eds.), *The Spirit and Spirituality: Essays in Honour of Russell P. Spittler* (JPTSup 24; London: T&T Clark, 2004).

Macchia, F.D., *Baptized in the Spirit: A Global Pentecostal Theology* (Grand Rapids: Zondervan, 2006).

—'Baptized in the Spirit: Toward a Global Theology of Spirit Baptism', in Veli-Matti Kärkkäinen (ed.), *The Spirit in the World: Emerging Pentecostal Theologies in Global Context* (Grand Rapids: Eerdmans, 2009), p. 10.

—'Is Footwashing the Neglected Sacrament? A Theological Response to John Christopher Thomas', *Pneuma* 19.2 (Fall 1997), pp. 239-49.

—'Eucharist: Pentecostal', in Paul F. Bradshaw (ed.), *The New Westminster Dictionary of Liturgy and Worship* (Louisville: WJKP, 2002), pp. 189-90.

—*Justified in the Spirit: Creation, Redemption, and the Triune God* (Pentecostal Manifestos; Grand Rapids: Eerdmans, 2010).

—'The Book of Revelation and the Hermeneutics of the Spirit: A Response to Robby Waddell', *JPT* 17 (2008), pp. 19-21.

—'The Church of the Latter Rain: The Church and Eschatology in Pentecostal Perspective', in John Christopher Thomas (ed.), *Toward a Pentecostal Ecclesiology* (Cleveland, TN: CPT Press, 2010), pp. 248-58.

Maddox, R.L., *Responsible Grace: John Wesley's Practical Theology* (Nashville: Abingdon, 1994).

Maloney, F.J., *The Gospel of John* (Sacra Pagina; Collegeville, MN: Liturgical Press, 1988).

Marrow, S.B., *Paul: His Letters and His Theology* (Mahwah, NJ: Paulist Press, 1986).

Marshall, B.D., 'The Disunity of the Church and the Credibility of the Gospel', *Theology Today* 50.1 (Apr 1993), pp. 78-89.

Martin, L.R., *The Unheard Voice of God: A Pentecostal Hearing of the Book of Judges* (JPTSup 32; Blandford Forum: Deo Publishing, 2008).

McCabe, H., 'Eucharistic Change', *Priests and People* 8.6 (June 1994), pp. 217-21.

—*God Matters* (London: Continuum, 1987).

McDonnell, K. and G.T. Montague, *Christian Initiation and Baptism in the Holy Spirit* (2nd ed.; Collegeville, MN: Liturgical Press, 1994).

McGrath, A.E., *Christianity's Dangerous Idea: The Protestant Revolution – A History from the Sixteenth Century to the Twenty-First* (New York: Harper Collins, 2007).

McGrath, J.F., *John's Apologetic Christology: Legitimation and Development in Johannine Christology* (SNTSMS 111; Cambridge: Cambridge University Press, 2004).

McIntyre, A.C., *After Virtue: A Study in Moral Theology* (2nd ed.; Notre Dame, IN: Notre Dame University Press, 1984).

McKay, J., 'When the Veil is Taken Away: The Impact of Prophetic Experience on Biblical Interpretation', *JPT* 5 (1994), pp. 17-40.

McKee, E.A., *John Calvin on the Diaconate and Liturgical Almsgiving* (Geneva: Librairie Droz, 1984).

McMichael, R.N., *Eucharist: A Guide for the Perplexed* (London: T&T Clark, 2010).

McQueen, L.R., *Joel and the Spirit: The Cry of a Prophetic Hermeneutic* (JPTSup 8; Sheffield: Sheffield Academic Press, 1995; Cleveland, TN: CPT Press, 2009).

Menken, M.J.J., 'John 6.51c-58: Eucharist or Christology?' in R. Alan Culpepper (ed.), *Critical Readings of John 6* (Leiden: Brill, 1997), pp. 183-204.

Menzies, W.W., 'Reflections on Suffering: A Pentecostal Perspective', in Ma and Menzies (eds.), *The Spirit and Spirituality*, pp. 141-49.

Menzies, W.W., and S.M. Horton, *Bible Doctrine: A Pentecostal Perspective* (Springfield, MO: Logion Press, 1993).

Miller, G.J.,'Huldrych Zwingli', in Carter Lindberg (ed.) *The Reformation Theologians: An Introduction to Theology in the Early Modern Period* (Malden, MA: Blackwell, 2002).

Mittelstadt, M.W., 'My Life as a Mennocostal: A Personal and Theological Narrative', *Theodidaktos* 3.2 (Sept 2008), pp. 10-17.

—*The Spirit and Suffering in Luke–Acts: Implications for a Pentecostal Pneumatology* (JPTSup 26; London: T&T Clark International, 2004).

Moltmann, J., *The Church in the Power of the Spirit* (Minneapolis: Fortress Press, 1993).

—*The Spirit of Life: A Universal Affirmation* (Minneapolis: Fortress Press, 1992).

Moore, R.D., 'A Pentecostal Approach to Scripture', *Seminary Viewpoint* 8.1 (1987), pp. 1-11.

—'Canon and Criticism in the Book of Deuteronomy', *JPT* 1 (Oct 1992), pp. 75-92.

Morales, R.J., 'A Liturgical Conversion of the Imagination: Worship and Ethics in 1 Corinthians', in Scott W. Hahn and David Scott (eds.), *Letter & Spirit Vol. 5* (Steubenville, OH: St Paul Center for Biblical Theology, 2009), pp. 103-24.

Neuhaus, R.J., 'Passion for the Presence: The Eucharist Today', *Currents in Theology and Mission* 5.1 (Feb 1978), pp. 4-15.

Neyrey, J.H., *The Gospel of John* (TNCBC; Cambridge: Cambridge University Press, 2007).

Nijenhuis, W., *Ecclesia Reformata: Studies on the Reformation* (Leiden: Brill, 1972).

O'Brien, P.T., 'Prayer in Luke-Acts', *Tyndale Bulletin* 24 (1973), pp. 111-27.

O'Conner, J.M., 'Eucharist and Community in First Corinthians', *Worship* 50.5 (Spring 1976), pp. 370-85.

Oden, T.C., *John Wesley's Scriptural Christianity: A Plain Exposition of His Teaching on Christian Doctrine* (Grand Rapids: Zondervan, 1994).

Olsen, R.E., *The Story of Christian Theology* (Downers Grove, IL: IVP, 1999).

Panikulam, G., *Koinonia in the New Testament: A Dynamic Expression of Christian Life* (Rome: Biblical Institute Press, 1979).

Pannenberg, W., *Systematic Theology Vol 3* (Grand Rapids: Eerdmans, 1998).

Peterson, D.G., *The Acts of the Apostles* (TPNTC; Grand Rapids: Eerdmans, 2009).

Phillips, G.A., '"This is a Hard Saying. Who Can Be Listener to It? Creating a Reader in John 6', *Semeia* 26 (1983), pp. 23-56.

Phillips, T.E., 'Reading Recent Readings of Issues of Wealth and Poverty in Luke and Acts', *Currents in Biblical Research* 1.2 (Apr 2003), pp. 231-69.

Pinnock, C.H., 'The Work of the Holy Spirit in Hermeneutics', *JPT* 2 (1993), pp. 3-23.

Poloma, M.M., 'The Symbolic Dilemma and the Future of Pentecostalism: Mysticism, Ritual, and Revival', in Eric Patterson and Edmund John Rybarcyck (eds.), *The Future of Pentecostalism in the United States* (Lanham, MD: Lexington Books, 2007), pp. 105-21.

Poon, W.C.K., 'Superabundant Table Fellowship in the Kingdom: The Feeding of the Five Thousand and the Meal Motif in Luke', *Expository Times* 114.7 (Apr 2003), pp. 224-30.

Power, W.L., 'Religious Experience and the Christian Experience of God', *International Journal for Philosophy of Religion* 31.2-3 (Apr-June 1992), pp. 177-86.

Powery, E.B. 'Ulrich Luz's *Matthew in History*: A Contribution to Pentecostal Hermeneutics?', *JPT* 14 (1999), pp. 3-17.

Pruitt, R.M., *Fundamentals of the Faith* (Cleveland, TN: White Wing Publishing House, 1995).

Radner, E., *Leviticus* (BTC; Grand Rapids: Brazos, 2008).

—'*The End of the Church: A Pneumatology of Christian Division in the West* (Grand Rapids: Eerdmans, 1998).

Rahner, K., *Spiritual Exercises* (New York: Herder and Herder, 1965).

Reno, R.R., 'Biblical Theology and Theological Exegesis', in Craig Bartholomew, Mary Healy, Karl Moller, and Robin Parry (eds.) *Out of Egypt: Biblical Theology and Biblical Interpretation* (Grand Rapids: Zondervan, 2004).

Reynolds, B.E., *The Apocalyptic Son of Man in the Gospel of John* (Tübingen: Mohr Siebeck, 2008).

Richard, E.J., 'Expressions of Double Meaning and Their Function in the Gospel of John', *New Testament Studies* 31.1 (Jan 1985), pp. 96-112.

Ridderbos, H.N., *Paul: An Outline of His Theology* (Grand Rapids: Eerdmans, 1975).

—*The Gospel According to John: A Theological Commentary* (Grand Rapids: Eerdmans, 1997).

Robeck, C.M., Jr, *The Azusa Street Mission and Revival: The Birth of the Global Pentecostal Movement* (Nashville: Thomas Nelson, 2007).

Robins, R.G., *Pentecostalism in America* (Santa Barbara, CA: ABCCLIO, 2010).

Roetzel, C.J. *The Letters of Paul: Conversations in Context* (Louisville: WJKP, 2009).

Rossing, B., 'Why Luke's Gospel? Daily Bread and "Recognition" of Christ in Food-Sharing', *Currents in Theology and Mission* (June 2010), pp. 225-29.

Rusch, F.A., 'The Signs and the Discourse – The Rich Theology of John 6', *Currents in Theology and Mission* 5.6 (Dec 1978), pp. 386-90.

Rusch, W.G. and J. Gros (eds.), *Deepening Communion: International Ecumenical Documents with Roman Catholic Participation* (Washington, DC: USCCB Publishing, 1998).

Samuel, V.C., 'The Mission Implications of Baptism, Eucharist, and Ministry', *International Review of Mission* 72.286 (Apr 1983), pp. 207-13.

Saxon, E., *The Eucharist in Romanesque France: Iconography and Theology* (Woodbridge, Suffolk, UK: Boydell Press, 2006).

Schmemann, A., *The Eucharist: Sacrament of the Kingdom* (New York: SVS Press, 1987).

Schnackenburg, R., *The Gospel According to St John Vol. 1* (New York: Seabury Press, 1990).

Shogren, G.S., 'How Did They Suppose "The Perfect" Would Come? 1 Corinthians 13.8-12 in Patristic Exegesis', *JPT* 15 (1999), pp. 99-121.

Simpson, C., 'Jonathan Paul and the German Pentecostal Movement – the First Seven Years, 1907-1914', *JEPTA* 28.2 (2008), pp. 169-82.

Skaggs, R.P., *The Pentecostal Commentary on 1 Peter, 2 Peter, and Jude* (London: T&T Clark, 2004).

Slay, J.L., *This We Believe* (Cleveland, TN: Pathway Press, 1963).

Smalley, S.S., *John: Evangelist and Interpreter* (New York: Thomas Nelson, 1984).

—'Spirit, Kingdom and Prayer in Luke-Acts', *Novum Testamentum* 15.1 (Jan 1973), pp. 59-71.

Smith, D.E., *From Symposium to Eucharist: The Banquet in the Early Christian World* (Minneapolis: Fortress Press, 2003).

—'Table Fellowship as a Literary Motif in the Gospel of Luke', *JBL* 106.4 (1987), pp. 613-38.

Smith, D.M., *The Theology of the Gospel of John* (NTT; Cambridge: Cambridge University Press, 1995).

Smith, J.E., 'Slogans in 1 Corinthians', *Bibliotheca Sacra* 167.665 (Jan-Mar 2010), pp. 68-88.

Smith, J.K.A., *Desiring the Kingdom: Worship, Worldview, and Cultural Formation* (Grand Rapids: Baker Academic, 2009).

—*Thinking in Tongues: Pentecostal Contributions to Christian Philosophy* (Grand Rapids: Eerdmans, 2010).

—*The Devil Reads Derrida* (Grand Rapids: Eerdmans, 2009).

—'What Hath Cambridge To Do With Azusa Street? Radical Orthodoxy and Pentecostal Theology in Conversation', *Pneuma* 25.1 (Spring 2003), pp. 97-114.

Spence, O.T., *The Quest for Christian Purity* (Richmond, VA: Whittet and Shepperson, 1964).

Spittler, R.P., 'Scripture and the Theological Enterprise: View from a Big Canoe', in Robert K. Johnston (ed.), *The Use of the Bible in Theology: Evangelical Options* (Eugene, OR: Wipf and Stock, 1997).

Steinmetz, D.C., 'The Superiority of Pre-Critical Exegesis', in Stephen E. Fowl (ed.), *The Theological Interpretation of Scripture: Classic and Contemporary Readings* (Malden, MA: Blackwell Publishing, 1997).

Stephenson, C.A., 'The Rule of Spirituality and the Rule of Doctrine: A Necessary Relationship in Theological Method', *JPT* 15 (Oct 2006), pp. 83-105.

Stibbe, M.W.G., *John's Gospel* (London: Routledge, 1994).

— *John as Storyteller: Narrative Criticism and the Fourth Gospel* (Cambridge, Cambridge University Press, 1992).

Stibbe, M.W.G. (ed.), *The Gospel of John as Literature: an Anthology of Twentieth-Century Perspectives* (Leiden: Brill, 1993).

Still III, E.C., 'The Meaning and Uses of EIDŌLOTHYTON in First Century Non-Pauline Literature and 1 Cor 8.1-11.1: Toward a Resolution of the Debate', *Trinity Journal* 23.2 (Fall 2002), pp. 225-34.

Story, J.L., 'All is Now Ready: An Exegesis of "The Great Banquet" (Luke 14.15-24) and "The Marriage Feast" (Matthew 22.1-14)', *American Theological Inquiry* 2.2 (July 2009), pp. 67-79.

Stronstad, R., 'Pentecostal Experience and Hermeneutics', *Paraclete* 26.1 (1992), pp. 14-30.

Stuhlman, B.D., *A Good and Joyful Thing: the Evolution of the Eucharistic Prayer* (New York: Church Publishing Inc., 2000).

Synan, H.V., 'Gaston Barnabas Cashwell', *NIDPCM*, pp. 457-58.

—*Old Time Power* (Franklin Springs, GA: LifeSprings, 1998).

—*The Holiness-Pentecostal Tradition: Charismatic Movements in the Twentieth Century* (Grand Rapids: Eerdmans, 1997).

Tan, S.G.H., 'Reassessing Believer's Baptism in Pentecostal Theology and Practice', *AJPS* 6.2 (2003), pp. 219-34.

Tan-Chow, M., *Pentecostal Theology for the Twenty-First Century: Engaging with Multi-Faith Singapore* (Aldershot, UK: Ashgate, 2007).

Tannehill, R.C., *The Narrative Unity of Luke-Acts: A Literary Interpretation* (2 Vols.; Minneapolis: Augsburg Fortress, 1990).

Thiselton, A.C., *The First Epistle to the Corinthians: A Commentary on the Greek Text* (New International Greek Testament Commentary; Grand Rapids: Eerdmans, 2000).

Thomas, J.C., *Footwashing in John 13 and the Johannine Community* (JSNTS 61; Sheffield: JSOT Press, 1991).

— 'Pentecostal Theology in the Twenty-First Century', *Pneuma* 20.1 (1998), pp. 3-19.

—*The Devil, Disease, and Deliverance: Origins of Illness in New Testament Thought* (JPTSup 13; Sheffield: Sheffield Academic Press, 1998).

—*The Spirit of the New Testament* (Blandford Forum: Deo Publishing, 2005).

—'Women, Pentecostals, and the Bible: An Experiment in Pentecostal Hermeneutics', *JPT* 5 (1994), pp. 41-56.

Thomas, J.C. and K.E. Alexander, '"And the Signs are Following": Mark 16.9-20 – A Journey into Pentecostal Hermeneutics', *JPT* 11.2 (2003), pp. 147-70.

Thompson, M.M., 'John, Gospel of', in Joel B. Green, Scot McKnight, and I. Howard Marshall (eds.), *Dictionary of Jesus and the Gospels* (Downers Grove, IL: IVP, 1992), pp. 373-74.

Tomlinson, A.J., *The Last Great Conflict* (Cleveland, TN: Walter E. Rodgers Press, 1913).

Tomlinson, M.A., *Basic Bible Beliefs* (Cleveland, TN: White Wing Publishing, 1961).

Torrance, T.F. *Atonement: The Person and Work of Christ* (Downers Grove, IL: IVP, 2009).

—*Theology in Reconstruction* (Grand Rapids: Eerdmans, 1965).

Trigg, J.D., *Baptism in the Theology of Martin Luther* (Leiden: Brill, 1994).

Turner, W.H., *The Finished Work of Calvary or The Second Blessing – Which?* (Franklin Springs, GA: Pentecostal Holiness Church Publishing, 1947).

Vander Hart, M.D., 'The Exodus as Sacrament: the Cloud, the Sea, and Moses Revisited', *Mid-America Journal of Theology* 12 (2001), pp. 9-46.

Vishnevskaya, E., 'Divinization as Perichoretic Embrace in Maximus the Confessor', in Michael J. Christensen and Jeffery A. Wittung (eds.), *Partakers of the Divine Nature: The History and Development of Deification in the Christian Traditions* (Grand Rapids: Baker Academic, 2007), pp. 132-45.

Voelz, J.W., 'The Discourse on the Bread of Life in John 6: Is It Eucharistic?', *Concordia Journal* 15.1 (Jan 1989), pp. 29-37.

von Balthasar, H.U. (ed.), *Origen, Spirit and Fire: A Thematic Anthology of His Writing* (Washington DC: Catholic University of America Press, 1984).

Vondey, W., *People of Bread: Rediscovering Ecclesiology* (Mahwah, NJ: Paulist Press, 2008).

—'Pentecostal Contributions to *The Nature and Mission of the Church*', in Wolfgang Vondey (ed.), *Pentecostalism and Christian Unity: Ecumenical Documents and Critical Assessments* (Eugene, OR: Pickwick, 2010), p. 259.

—'Pentecostal Ecclesiology and Eucharistic Hospitality: Toward a Systematic and Ecumenical Account of the Church', *Pneuma* 32 (2010), pp. 41-55.

—'Review of Kevin VanHoozer's *The Drama of Doctrine*', *Pneuma* 30 (2008), p. 365.

Vondey, W. and Chris W. Green, 'Between This and That: Reality and Sacramentality in the Pentecostal Worldview', *JPT* 19.2 (Fall 2010), pp. 243-64.

Wakefield, G., 'The Human Face of Pentecostalism: Why the British Pentecostal Moment Began in the Sunderland Parish of the Church of England Vicar Alexander Boddy', *JEPTA* 28.2 (2008), pp. 158-68.

—*Alexander Boddy: Pentecostal Anglican Pioneer* (Milton Keynes: Paternoster, 2007).

Wainwright, G., *Doxology: The Praise of God in Worship, Doctrine, and Life: A Systematic Theology* (New York: OUP, 1980).

—'Eucharist As/And Ethics', *Worship* 62.2 (Mar 1988), p. 131.

Ward, G. *Cities of God* (London: Routledge, 2000).

—*Christ and Culture* (Malden, MA: Blackwell, 2005).

Warrington, K., *Pentecostal Theology: A Theology of Encounter* (London: T&T Clark, 2008).

Wacker, G., *Heaven Below: Early Pentecostalism and American Culture* (Cambridge, MA: Harvard University Press, 2001).

Waddell, R.C., *The Spirit of the Book of Revelation* (JPTSup 30; Blandford Forum: Deo Publishing, 2006).

Wall, R. 'A Response to Thomas/Alexander, "And the Signs Are Following" (Mark 6.9-20)', *JPT* 11.2 (2003), pp. 176-77.

Webster, J.S., *Ingesting Jesus: Eating and Drinking in the Gospel of John* (Atlanta: SBL, 2003).

Welker, M., *What Happens in Holy Communion?* (Grand Rapids: Eerdmans, 2000).

Wenk, M., 'The Church as Sanctified Community', in John Christopher Thomas (ed.), *Toward a Pentecostal Ecclesiology* (Cleveland, TN: CPT Press, 2010), pp. 105-35.

Wheaton, G., *The Role of Feasts in John's Gospel* (PhD thesis; St Andrews, Scotland, 2009).

Williams, E.S., *Systematic Theology* (3 vols.; Springfield, MO: Gospel Publishing House, 1953).

Williams, J.R., *Renewal Theology* (3 vols.; Grand Rapids: Zondervan, 1988-96).

Williams, R., *On Christian Theology* (Oxford: Blackwell, 2000).

—'The Bible Today: "Reading" and "Hearing"'. [Internet], <http://www.archbishopof canterbury.org/1718>. [Accessed August 2009.]

—*Why Study the Past: The Quest for the Historical Church* (Grand Rapids: Eerdmans, 2005).

Williamson, L., *Preaching the Gospel of John: Proclaiming the Living Word* (Louisville: WJKP, 2004).

Willimon, W.H., *Acts* (Interpretation; Louisville: John Knox Press, 1988).

Witherington, B., *The Acts of the Apostles: A Socio-Rhetorical Commentary* (Grand Rapids: Eerdmans, 1998).

Work, T. *Ain't Too Proud to Beg: Exercises in Prayerful Theology* (Grand Rapids: Eerdmans, 2007).

—*Deuteronomy* (BTC; Grand Rapids: Brazos, 2009).

—*Living and Active: Scripture in the Economy of Salvation* (Grand Rapids: Eerdmans, 2002).

— 'Pentecostal and Charismatic Worship', in Geoffrey Wainwright and Karen Westerfield Tucker (eds.), *Oxford History of Christian Worship* (New York: OUP, 2006), pp. 574-80.

Wright, N.T., *Surprised by Hope: Rethinking Heaven, the Resurrection, and the Mission of the Church* (New York: Harper Collins, 2008).

—*The Last Word: Beyond the Bible Wars* (San Francisco: Harper Collins, 2005).

Yarnold, E., *Cyril of Jerusalem* (Early Church Fathers, London: Routledge, 2000).

Yeago, D.S., 'The Bread of Life: Patristic Christology and Evangelical Soteriology in Martin Luther's Sermons on John 6', *SVTQ* 39.3 (1995), pp. 257-79.

Yoder, J.H., *Body Politics: Five Practices of the Christian Community Before the Watching World* (Scottsdale, PA: Herald Press, 2001).

Yong, A., *Discerning the Spirits* (JPTSup 20; Sheffield: Sheffield Academic Press, 2000).

—*In the Days of Caesar: Pentecostalism and Political Theology* (Grand Rapids: Eerdmans, 2010).

—*Spirit-Word-Community: Theological Hermeneutics in Trinitarian Perspective* (Eugene, OR: Wipf & Stock, 2002).

—*The Spirit Poured Out on All Flesh: Pentecostalism and the Possibility of Global Theology* (Grand Rapids: Baker Academic, 2005).

—*Theology and Down Syndrome: Reimagining Disability in Late Modernity* (Waco, TX: Baylor University Press, 2007).

Zizioulas, J.D., *Lectures in Christian Dogmatics* (London: T&T Clark, 2008).

Zumstein, J., 'La réception de l'écriture en Jean 6', in Camille Focant and André Wénin (eds.), *Analyse narrative et Bible* (Leuven: Leuven University Press, 2005), pp. 147-66.

Index of Biblical References

Index of Names

Printed in Great Britain
by Amazon.co.uk, Ltd.,
Marston Gate.